Big Data and Machine Learning in Quantitative Investment

Founded in 1807, John Wiley & Sons is the oldest independent publishing company in the United States. With offices in North America, Europe, Australia, and Asia, Wiley is globally committed to developing and marketing print and electronic products and services for our customers' professional and personal knowledge and understanding.

The Wiley Finance series contains books written specifically for finance and investment professionals as well as sophisticated individual investors and their financial advisors. Book topics range from portfolio management to e-commerce, risk management, financial engineering, valuation and financial instrument analysis, as well as much more.

For a list of available titles, visit our website at www.WileyFinance.com.

Big Data and Machine Learning in Quantitative Investment

TONY GUIDA

WILEY

Library of Congress Cataloging-in-Publication Data is Available:

ISBN 9781119522195 (hardback) ISBN 9781119522218 (ePub)
ISBN 9781119522089 (ePDF)

Cover Design: Wiley
Cover Images: © Painterr/iStock /Getty Images;
© monsitj/ iStock /Getty Images

Set in 10/1 2pt, SabonLTStd by SPi Global, Chennai, India

10 9 8 7 6 5 4 3 2 1

Contents

CHAPTER 1

Do Algorithms Dream About Artificial Alphas?

Michael Kollo

1.1 INTRODUCTION

The core of most financial practice, whether drawn from equilibrium economics, behavioural psychology, or agency models, is traditionally formed through the marriage of elegant theory and a kind of 'dirty' empirical proof. As I learnt from my years on the PhD programme at the London School of Economics, elegant theory is the hallmark of a beautiful intellect, one that could discern the subtle tradeoffs in agent-based models, form complex equilibrium structures and point to the sometimes conflicting paradoxes at the heart of conventional truths. Yet 'dirty' empirical work is often scoffed at with suspicion, but reluctantly acknowledged as necessary to give substance and real-world application. I recall many conversations in the windy courtyards and narrow passageways, with brilliant PhD students wrangling over questions of 'but how can I find a test for my hypothesis?'.

Many pseudo-mathematical frameworks have come and gone in quantitative finance, usually borrowed from nearby sciences: thermodynamics from physics, Eto's Lemma, information theory, network theory, assorted parts from number theory, and occasionally from less high-tech but reluctantly acknowledged social sciences like psychology. They have come, and they have gone, absorbed (not defeated) by the markets.

Machine learning, and extreme pattern recognition, offer a strong focus on large-scale empirical data, transformed and analyzed at such scale as never seen before for details of patterns that lay undetectable to previous inspection. Interestingly, machine learning offers very little in conceptual framework. In some circles, it boasts that the absence of a conceptual framework is its strength and removes the human bias that would otherwise limit a model. Whether you feel it is a good tool or not, you have to respect the notion that process speed is only getting faster and more powerful. We may call it neural networks or something else tomorrow, and we will eventually reach a point where most if not all permutations of patterns can be discovered and examined in close to real time, at which point the focus will be almost exclusively on defining the objective function rather than the structure of the framework.

The rest of this chapter is a set of observations and examples of how machine learning could help us learn more about financial markets, and is doing so. It is drawn not only from my experience, but from many conversations with academics, practitioners, computer scientists, and from volumes of books, articles, podcasts and the vast sea of intellect that is now engaged in these topics.

It is an incredible time to be intellectually curious and quantitatively minded, and we at best can be effective conduits for the future generations to think about these problems in a considered and scientific manner, even as they wield these monolithic technological tools.

1.2   REPLICATION OR REINVENTION

The quantification of the world is again a fascination of humanity. Quantification here is the idea that we can break down patterns that we observe as humans into component parts and replicate them over much larger observations, and in a much faster way. The foundations of quantitative finance found their roots in investment principles, or observations, made by generations and generations of astute investors, who recognized these ideas without the help of large-scale data.

The early ideas of factor investing and quantitative finance were replications of these insights; they did not themselves invent investment principles. The ideas of value investing (component valuation of assets and companies) are concepts that have been studied and understood for many generations. Quantitative finance took these ideas, broke them down, took the observable and scalable elements and spread them across a large number of (comparable) companies.

The cost to achieving scale is still the complexity in and nuance about how to apply a specific investment insight to a specific company, but these nuances were assumed to diversify away in a larger-scale portfolio, and were and are still largely overlooked.[1] The relationship between investment insights and future returns were replicated as linear relationships between exposure and returns, with little attention to non-linear dynamics or complexities, but instead, focusing on diversification and large-scale application which were regarded as better outcomes for modern portfolios.

There was, however, a subtle recognition of co-movement and correlation that emerged from the early factor work, and it is now at the core of modern risk management techniques. The idea is that stocks that have common characteristics (let's call it a quantified investment insight) have also correlation and co-dependence potentially on macro-style factors.

This small observation, in my opinion, is actually a reinvention of the investment world which up until then, and in many circles still, thought about stocks in isolation, valuing and appraising them as if they were standalone private equity investments. It was a reinvention because it moved the object of focus from an individual stock to

---

[1]Consider the nuances in the way that you would value a bank or a healthcare company, and contrast this to the idea that everything could be compared under the broad umbrella of a single empirical measure of book to price.

a common 'thread' or factor that linked many stocks that individually had no direct business relationship, but still had a similar characteristic that could mean that they would be bought and sold together. The 'factor' link became the objective of the investment process, and its identification and improvement became the objective of many investment processes – now (in the later 2010s) it is seeing another renaissance of interest. Importantly, we began to see the world as a series of factors, some transient, some long-standing, some short- and some long-term forecasting, some providing risk and to be removed, and some providing risky returns.

Factors represented the invisible (but detectable) threads that wove the tapestry of global financial markets. While we (quantitative researchers) searched to discover and understand these threads, much of the world focused on the visible world of companies, products and periodic earnings. We painted the world as a network, where connections and nodes were the most important, while others painted it as a series of investment ideas and events.

The reinvention was in a shift in the object of interest, from individual stocks to a series of network relationships, and their ebb and flow through time. It was subtle, as it was severe, and is probably still not fully understood.[2] Good factor timing models are rare, and there is an active debate about how to think about timing at all. Contextual factor models are even more rare and pose especially interesting areas for empirical and theoretical work.

1.3 REINVENTION WITH MACHINE LEARNING

Reinvention with machine learning poses a similar opportunity for us to reinvent the way we think about the financial markets, I think in both the identification of the investment object and the way we think of the financial networks.

Allow me a simple analogy as a thought exercise. In handwriting or facial recognition, we as humans look for certain patterns to help us understand the world. On a conscious, perceptive level, we look to see patterns in the face of a person, in their nose, their eyes and their mouth. In this example, the objects of perception are those units, and we appraise their similarity to others that we know. Our pattern recognition then functions on a fairly low dimension in terms of components. We have broken down the problem into a finite set of grouped information (in this case, the features of the face), and we appraise those categories. In modern machine learning techniques, the face or a handwritten number is broken down into much smaller and therefore more numerous components. In the case of a handwritten number, for example, the pixels of the picture are converted to numeric representations, and the patterns in the pixels are sought using a deep learning algorithm.

We have incredible tools to take large-scale data and to look for patterns in the sub-atomic level of our sample. In the case of human faces or numbers, and many other

---

[2] We are just now again beginning to prod the limits of our understanding of factors by considering how to define them better, how to time them, all the meanwhile expanding considerable effort trying to explain them to non-technical investors.

things, we can find these patterns through complex patterns that are no longer intuitive or understandable by us (consciously); they do not identify a nose, or an eye, but look for patterns in deep folds of the information.[3] Sometimes the tools can be much more efficient and find patterns better, quicker than us, without our intuition being able to keep up.

Taking this analogy to finance, much of asset management concerns itself with financial (fundamental) data, like income statements, balance sheets, and earnings. These items effectively characterize a company, in the same way the major patterns of a face may characterize a person. If we take these items, we may have a few hundred, and use them in a large-scale algorithm like machine learning, we may find that we are already constraining ourselves heavily before we have begun.

The 'magic' of neural networks comes in their ability to recognize patterns in atomic (e.g. pixel-level) information, and by feeding them higher constructs, we may already be constraining their ability to find new patterns, that is, patterns beyond those already identified by us in linear frameworks. Reinvention lies in our ability to find new constructs and more 'atomic' representations of investments to allow these algorithms to better find patterns. This may mean moving away from the reported quarterly or annual financial accounts, perhaps using higher-frequency indicators of sales and revenue (relying on alternate data sources), as a way to find higher frequency and, potentially, more connected patterns with which to forecast price movements.

Reinvention through machine learning may also mean turning our attention to modelling financial markets as a complex (or just expansive) network, where the dimensionality of the problem is potentially explosively high and prohibitive for our minds to work with. To estimate a single dimension of a network is to effectively estimate a covariance matrix of $n \times n$. Once we make this system endogenous, many of the links within the 2D matrix become a function of other links, in which case the model is recursive, and iterative. And this is only in two dimensions. Modelling the financial markets like a neural network has been attempted with limited application, and more recently the idea of supply chains is gaining popularity as a way of detecting the fine strands between companies. Alternate data may well open up new explicitly observable links between companies, in terms of their business dealings, that can form the basis of a network, but it's more likely that prices will move too fast, and too much, to be simply determined by average supply contracts.

1.4   A MATTER OF TRUST

The reality is that patterns that escape our human attention will be either too subtle, or too numerous, or too fast in the data. Our inability to identify with them in an intuitive way, or to construct stories around them, will naturally cause us to mistrust them. Some patterns in the data will be not useful for investment (e.g. noise, illiquid,

---

[3] Early experiments are mixed, and adversarial systems have shown some of these early patterns to be extremely fragile. But as technology grows, and our use of it too, these patterns are likely to become increasingly robust, but will retain their complexity.

and/or uninvestable), so these will quickly end up on the 'cutting room floor'.[4] But many others will be robust, and useful, but entirely unintuitive, and perhaps obfuscated to us. Our natural reaction will be to question ourselves, and if we are to use them, ensure that they are part of a very large cohort of signals, so as to diversify questions about a particular signal in isolation.

So long as our clients are humans as well, we will face communication challenges, especially during times of weak performance. When performance is strong, opaque investment processes are less questioned, and complexity can even be considered a positive, differentiating characteristic. However, on most occasions, an opaque investment process that underperforms is quickly mistrusted. In many examples of modern investment history, the 'quants' struggled to explain their models in poor performance periods and were quickly abandoned by investors. The same merits of intellectual superiority bestowed upon them rapidly became weaknesses and points of ridicule.

Storytelling, the art of wrapping complexity in comfortable and familiar anecdotes and analogies, feels like a necessary cost of using technical models. However, the same can be a large barrier to innovation in finance. Investment beliefs, and our capability to generate comfortable anecdotal stories, are often there to reconfirm commonly held intuitive investment truths, which in turn are supported by 'sensible' patterns in data.

If innovation means moving to 'machine patterns' in finance, with greater complexity and dynamic characteristics, it will come from a leap of faith where we relinquish our authorship of investment insights, and/or from some kind of obfuscation such as bundling, where scrutiny of an individual signal is not possible. Either way, there is a certain additional business risk involved in moving outside the accepted realm of stories, even if the investment signals themselves add value.

If we are to innovate signals, we may very well need to innovate storytelling as well. Data visualization is one promising area in this field, but we may find ourselves embracing virtual and augmented reality devices quicker than the rest of finance if we are to showcase the visual brilliance of a market network or a full factor structure.

1.5 ECONOMIC EXISTENTIALISM: A GRAND DESIGN OR AN ACCIDENT?

If I told you that I built a model to forecast economic sector returns, but that the model itself was largely unintuitive and highly contextualized, would this concern you? What if I told you that a core component was the recent number of articles in newspapers covering the products of that industry, but that this component wasn't guaranteed to 'make' the model in my next estimation. Most researchers I have encountered have a conceptual framework for how they choose between potential models. Normally, there is a thought exercise involved to relate a given finding back to the macro-picture and ask: 'Is this really how the world works? Does it make sense?' Without this, the results are easily picked apart for their empirical fragility and in-sample biases. There is a subtle leap that we take there, and it is to assume that there is a central 'order' or design to

---

[4]There is an entire book that could be written on the importance of noise versus signal, but I would suggest we suspend our natural scepticism and allow for the possibility that unusual patterns do exist and could be important.

the economic system. That economic forces are efficiently pricing and trading off risks and returns, usually from the collective actions of a group of informed and rational (if not pseudo-rational) agents. Even if we don't think that agents are informed, or fully rational, their collective actions can bring about ordered systems.

Our thinking in economics is very much grounded in the idea that there is a 'grand design' in play, a grand system, that we are detecting and estimating, and occasionally exploiting. I am not referring to the idea that there are temporary 'mini-equilibria' that are constantly changing or evolving, but to the notion that there are any equilibria at all.

Darwinian notions of random mutations, evolution, and learning challenge the very core of this world view. Dennett[5] elegantly expresses this world view as a series of accidents, with little reference to a macro-level order or a larger purpose. The notion of 'competence without comprehension' is developed as a framework to describe how intelligent systems can come out of a series of adaptive responses, without a larger order or a 'design' behind them. In his book, Harari[6] describes the evolution of humans as moving from foraging for food to organized farms. In doing so, their numbers increase, and they are now unable to go back to foraging. The path dependence is an important part of the evolution and constrains the evolution in terms of its future direction. For example, it is unable to 'evolve' foraging practices because it doesn't do that any more and now it is evolving farming.

Machine learning, and models like random forests, give little indication of a bigger picture, or a conceptual framework, but are most easily interpreted as a series of (random) evolutions in the data that has led us to the current 'truth' that we observe. The idea of a set of economic forces working in unison to give rise to a state of the economy is instead replaced by a series of random mutations and evolutionary pathways. For finance quantitative models, the implication is that there is strong path dependency.

This is challenging, and in some cases outright disturbing, for an economically trained thinker. The idea that a model can produce a series of correlations with little explanation other than 'just because' is concerning, especially if the path directions (mutations) are random (to the researcher) – it can seem as though we have mapped out the path of a water droplet rolling down glass, but with little idea of what guided that path itself. As the famous investor George Soros[7] described his investment philosophy and market: a series of inputs and outputs, like an 'alchemy' experiment, a series of trails and failures.

1.6   WHAT IS THIS SYSTEM ANYWAY?

Reinvention requires a re-examination of the root cause of returns and, potentially, abnormal returns. In nature, in games, and in feature identification, we generally know the rules (if any) of an engagement, and we know the game, and we know the challenges

---

[5] 'From Bacteria to Bach and Back: The Evolution of Minds' by Daniel C. Dennett, 2018, Penguin.
[6] 'Homo Deus: A Brief History of Tomorrow' by Yuval Noah Harari, 2015, Vintage.
[7] The Alchemy of Finance by George Soros, 2003.

of identification of features. One central element in financial markets, that is yet to be addressed, is their dynamic nature. As elements are identified, correlations estimated, returns calculated, the system can be moving and changing very quickly.

Most (common) quantitative finance models focus more on cross-sectional identification and less on time-series forecasting. Of the time-series models, they tend to be continuous in nature, or have state dependency with usually a kind of switching model embedded. Neither approach has a deeper understanding, ex ante, of the reasons why the market dynamics may change, and forecasting (in my experience) of either model tends to rely on serial correlation of states and the occasional market extreme environment to 'jolt' the system.[8] In this sense, the true complexity of the financial markets is likely grossly understated. Can we expect more from a machine learning algorithm that can dig into the subtle complexities and relationships of the markets? Potentially, yes. However, the lack of clean data, and the likelihood of information segmentations in the cross-section, suggest some kind of supervised learning models, where the ex-ante structures set up by the researcher are as likely to be the root of success or failure as the parameters estimated by the model itself.

One hope is that structures of relationships suggested by machine learning models can inspire and inform a new generation of theorists and agent-based simulation models, that in turn could give rise to more refined ex-ante structures for understanding the dynamic complexities of markets. It is less likely that we can learn about latent dynamic attributes of markets without some kind of ex ante model, whose latent characteristics we may never be able to observe, but potentially may infer.

One thought exercise to demonstrate this idea is a simple 2D matrix, of 5×5 elements (or as many as it takes to make this point). Each second, there is a grain of sand that drops from above this plane and lands on a single square. Over time, the number of grains of sand builds up in each square. There is a rule whereby if the tower of sand on one square is much greater than on another, it will collapse onto its neighbour, conferring the sand over. Eventually, some of the sand will fall over one of the four edges of the plane. The system itself is complex, it builds up 'pressure' in various areas, and occasionally releases the pressure as a head of sand falls from one square to another, and finally over the edge. Now picture a single researcher, standing well below the plane of squares, having no visibility of what happens on the plane itself. They can only observe the number of sand particles that fall over the edge, and which edge. From their point of view, they know only that if no sand has fallen for a while, they should be more worried, but they have no sense as to the system that gives rise to the occasional avalanche. Machine learning models, based on prices, suffer from a similar limitation. There is only so much they can infer, and there is a continuum of complex systems that could give rise to a given configuration of market characteristics. Choosing a unique or 'true' model, especially when faced with natural obfuscations of the complexities, is a near impossible task for a researcher.

---

[8] Consider, for example, a classic state switching model, where the returns to a factor/signal persist until there is an extreme valuation or return observed, perhaps a bubble, where the state of the future returns turns out to be negative. Most forecasting models for momentum will have some similar structures behind them, where the unconditional returns are assumed to persist and are positive, until an extreme event or condition is observed.

1.7   DYNAMIC FORECASTING AND NEW METHODOLOGIES

We return now to the more direct problems of quantitative asset management. Asset pricing (equities) broadly begins with one of two premises that are usually reliant on your chosen horizon:

1. Markets are composed of financial assets, and prices are fair valuations of the future benefit (cash flows usually) of owning those assets. Forecasting takes place of future cash-flows/fundamentals/earnings. The data field is composed of firms, that are bundles of future cash-flows, and whose prices reflect the relative (or absolute) valuation of these cash-flows.
2. Markets are composed of financial assets that are traded by agents with imperfect information based on a range of considerations. Returns are therefore simply a 'trading game'; to forecast prices is to forecast future demand and supply of other agents. This may or may not (usually not) involve understanding fundamental information. In fact, for higher-frequency strategies, little to no information is necessary about the underlying asset, only about its expected price at some future date. Typically using higher frequency micro-structures like volume, bid-ask spreads, and calendar (timing) effects, these models seek to forecast future demand/supply imbalances and benefit over a period of anywhere from nano-seconds to usually days. There's not much prior modelling, as the tradeoff, almost by design, is too high frequency always to be reacting to economic information, which means that it is likely to be driven by trading patterns and to rebalance frequencies that run parallel to normal economic information.

1.8   FUNDAMENTAL FACTORS, FORECASTING AND MACHINE LEARNING

In the case of a fundamental investment process, the 'language' of asset pricing is one filled with reference to the business conditions of firms, their financial statements, earnings, assets, and generally business prospects. The majority of the mutual fund industry operates with this viewpoint, analyzing firms in isolation, relative to industry peers, relative to global peers, and relative to the market as a whole, based on their prospective business success. The vast majority of the finance literature that seeks to price systematic risk beyond that of CAPM, so multi-factor risk premia, and new factor research, usually presents some undiversifiable business risk as the case of potential returns. The process for these models is fairly simple: extract fundamental characteristics based on a combination of financial statements, analysis, and modelling, and apply to either relative (cross-sectional) or total (time-series) returns.

For cross-sectional return analysis, the characteristics (take a very common measure like earnings/price) are defined in the broad cross-section, are transformed into a z-score, $Z \sim N(0,1)$, or a percentile rank (1–100), and then related through a function f^* to some future returns, r_{t+n}, where 'n' is typically 1–12 months forward returns. The function f^* finds its home in the Arbitrage Pricing Theory (APT) literature, and so is derived through either sorting or linear regressions, but can also be a simple linear correlation with future returns (otherwise known as an information coefficient, IC), a simple heuristic bucket-sorting exercise, a linear regression, a step-wise linear regression (for multiple Z

characteristics, and where the marginal use is of interest), or it can be quite complex, and as the 'Z' signal is implanted into an existing mean-variance optimized portfolios with multitude of characteristics.

Importantly, the forecast of 'Z' is typically defined so as to have broad-sectional appeal (e.g. all stocks should be measurable in the cross-section). Once handed over to a well-diversified application (e.g. with many stocks), any errors around the linear fit will (hopefully) be diversified away. However, not much time is typically spent defining different f^* functional forms. Outside of the usual quadratic forms (typically used to handle 'size') or the occasional interaction (e.g. *Quality*Size*), there isn't really a good way to think about how to use information in 'Z'. It is an area that largely has been neglected in favour of better stock-specific measurements, but still the same standardization, and the same f^*.

So our objective is to improve f^*. Typically, we have a set of several hundred fundamental 'Z' to draw from, each a continuous variable in the cross-section, and at best around 3000 stocks in the cross-section. We can transform the Z into indicator variables for decile membership for example, but typically, we want to use the extreme deciles as indicators, not the middle of the distribution. Armed with fundamental variables 'Z' and some indicators Z^I based on 'Z', we start to explore different non-linear methodologies. We start to get excited now, as the potential new uber-solving model lies somewhere before us.

The first problem we run into is the question: 'What do I want to forecast?' Random forests, neural networks, are typically looking for binary outcomes as predictors. Returns are continuous, and most fundamental outcomes are equally so (A percentage by which a company has beat/miss estimates, for example). Before we choose our object, we should consider what kind of system we are looking to identify.

1. I want to forecast a company's choice to do something, e.g. firms that 'choose' to replace CEOs, to buy or sell assets, to acquire competitors. I then hope to benefit from returns associated from these actions. But how do firms make these choices? Do they make them in isolation from economic factors, is there really unconditional choice, or are these firms already conditioned by some kind of latent economic event? For example, firms rarely cancel dividends in isolation. Typically, the choice to cancel is already heavily influenced by very poor market conditions. So our model may well be identifying firms that are under financial duress, more than those that actually 'choose' to cancel dividends. Think hard as to what is a 'choice' and what is a 'state', where certain choices are foregone conclusions.

2. I want to forecast wrongdoing by the firm and then make money by shorting/ avoiding those firms. Intentional or not, firms that misreport their financials but then are ultimately discovered (we hope!), and therefore we have a sample set. This is especially interesting for emerging economies, where financial controls, e.g. for state-owned enterprises, could have conflicting interests with simply open disclosure. This feels like an exciting area of forensic accounting, where 'clues' are picked up and matched by the algorithm in patterns that are impossible to follow through human intuition alone. I think we have to revisit here the original assumption: is this unintentional, and therefore we are modelling inherent uncertainty/complexity within the organization, or is it intentional, in which case it is a 'choice' of sorts.

The choice of independent variables should inform both ideally, but the 'choice' idea would require a lot more information on ulterior motives.

3. I just want to forecast returns. Straight for the jugular, we can say: Can we use fundamental characteristics to forecast stock returns? We can define relative returns (top decile, top quintile?) over some future period 'n' within some peer group and denote this as '1' and everything else as '0'. It is attractive to think that if we can line up our (small) army of fundamental data, re-estimate our model (neural net or something else) with some look-back window, we should be able to do crack this problem with brute force. It is, however, likely to result in an extremely dynamic model, with extreme variations in importance between factors, and probably not clear 'local maxima' for which model is the best. Alternately, we can define our dependent variable based on a total return target, for example anything +20% over the future period 'n' (clearly, the two choices are related), and aim to identify an 'extreme movers' model. But why do firms experience unusually large price jumps? Any of the above models (acquisition, beating forecasts, big surprises, etc.) could be candidates, or if not, we are effectively forecasting cross-sectional volatility. In 2008, for example, achieving a positive return of +20% may have been near impossible, whereas in the latter part of 2009, if you were a bank, it was expected. Cross-sectional volatility and market direction are necessarily 'states' to enable (or disqualify) the probability of a +x% move in stock prices. Therefore, total return target models are unlikely to perform well across different market cycles (cross-sectional volatility regimes), where the unconditional probability of achieving a +20% varies significantly. Embedding these is effectively transforming the +20% to a standard deviation move in the cross-section, when you are now back in the relative-return game.

4. If you were particularly keen on letting methodology drive your model decisions, you would have to reconcile yourself to the idea that prices are continuous and that fundamental accounting data (as least reported) is discrete and usually highly managed. If your forecast period is anywhere below the reporting frequency of accounting information, e.g. monthly, you are essentially relying on the diverging movements between historically stated financial accounts and prices today to drive information change, and therefore, to a large extent, turnover. This is less of a concern when you are dealing with large, 'grouped' analytics like bucketing or regression analysis. It can be a much bigger concern if you are using very fine instruments, like neural nets, that will pick up subtle deviations and assign meaningful relationships to them.

5. Using conditional models like dynamic nested logits (e.g. random forests) will probably highlight those average groups that are marginally more likely to outperform the market than some others, but their characterization (in terms of what determines the nodes) will be extremely dynamic. Conditional factor models (contextual models) exist today; in fact, most factor models are determined within geographic contexts (see any of the commercially available risk models, for example) and in some case within size. This effectively means that return forecasting is conditional based on which part of the market you are in. This is difficult to justify from an economic principle standpoint because it would necessitate some amount of segmentation in either information generation or strong clientele effects. For example, one set of clients (for US small cap) thinks about top-line growth as a way of driving

returns, while another set of clients (Japan large cap) looks for something totally different. If the world was that segmented, it would be difficult (but not impossible) to argue for asset pricing being compensation for some kind of global (undiversifiable) risk. In any case, conditional asset pricing models, whatever the empirical methodology, should work to justify why they think that prices are so dynamically driven by such different fundamentals over the relatively short period between financial statements.

In summary, the marriage of large-scale but sensitive instruments like machine learning methodologies to forecasting cross-sectional returns using fundamental information must be done with great care and attention. Much of the quantitative work in this area has relied on brute force (approximations) to sensitivities like beta. Researchers will find little emphasis on error-correction methodologies in the mainstream calculations of APT regressions, or of ICs, which rely on picking up broad, average relationships between signals (Z) and future returns. Occasionally (usually during high cross-sectional volatility periods) there will be a presentation at a conference around non-linear factor returns, to which the audience will knowingly nod in acknowledgement but essentially fail to adjust for. The lure of the linear function f^* is altogether too great and too ingrained to be easily overcome.

In the past, we have done experiments to ascertain how much additional value non-linear estimators could add to simulation backtests. For slower-moving signals (monthly rebalance, 6–12-month horizons), it is hard to conclusively beat a linear model that isn't over-fitted (or at least can be defended easily). Similarly, factor timing is an alluring area for non-linear modelling. However, factor returns are themselves calculated with a great amount of noise and inherent assumptions around calculation. These assumptions make the timing itself very subjective. A well-constructed (which usually means well-backtested) factor will have a smooth return series, except for a few potentially catastrophic bumps in history. Using a time-series neural network to try to forecast when those events will happen will, even more than a linear framework, leverage exceptionally strongly on a few tell-tale signs that are usually non-repeatable. Ironically, factors were built to work well as buy-and-hold additions to a portfolio. This means that it is especially difficult to improve on a buy-and-hold return by using a continuous timing mechanism, even one that is fitted. Missing one or two of the extreme return events through history, then accounting for trading costs, will usually see the steady-as-she-goes linear factor win, frustrating the methodologically eager researcher. Ultimately, we would be better served to generate a less well-constructed factor that had some time-series characteristics and aim to time that.

At this point, it feels as though we have come to a difficult passage. For fundamental researchers, the unit of interest is usually some kind of accounting-based metric (earnings, revenue, etc.), so using machine learning in this world seems analogous to making a Ferrari drive in London peak-hour traffic. In other words: it looks attractive, but probably feels like agony. What else can we do?

1.9 CONCLUSION: LOOKING FOR NAILS

It is for scientifically minded researchers to fall in love with a new methodology and spend their time looking for problems to deploy it on. Like wielding your favourite hammer, wandering around the house looking for nails, machine learning can seem like an exciting branch of methodology with no obviously unique application. We are increasingly seeing traditional models re-estimated using machine learning techniques, and in some cases, these models could give rise to new insights. More often than not, if the models are constrained, because they have been built and designed for linear estimation, we will need to reinvent the original problem and redesign the experiment in order to have a hope of glimpsing something brand new from the data.

A useful guiding principle when evaluating models, designing new models, or just kicking around ideas in front of a whiteboard is to ask yourself, or a colleague: 'What have we learnt about the world here?' Ultimately, the purpose of empirical or anecdotal investigation is to learn more about the fantastically intricate, amazing, and inspiring way in which the world functions around us, from elegant mathematics, to messy complex systems, and the messiest of all: data. A researcher who has the conviction that they represent some kind of 'truth' about the world through their models, no matter what the methodology and complexity, is more likely to be believed, remembered, and, ultimately, rewarded. We should not aggrandize or fall in love with individual models, but always seek to better our understanding of the world, and that of our clients.

Strong pattern recognition methodologies, like machine learning, have enormous capability to add to humanity's understanding of complex systems, including financial markets, but also of many social systems. I am reminded often that those who use and wield these models should be careful with inference, humility, and trust. The world falls in and out of love with quantification, and usually falls out of love because it has been promised too much, too soon. Machine learning and artificial intelligence (AI) are almost certain to fail us at some point, but this should not deter us; rather, it should encourage us to seek better and more interesting models to learn more about the world.

CHAPTER 2

Taming Big Data

Rado Lipuš and Daryl Smith

2.1 INTRODUCTION: ALTERNATIVE DATA – AN OVERVIEW

Around 20 years ago alternative data and machine learning techniques were being used by a select group of innovative hedge funds and asset managers. In recent years, however, both the number of fund managers using alternative data and the supply of new commercially available data sources have dramatically increased.

We have identified over 600 alternative datasets which have become commercially available in the past few years. Currently, around 40 new and thoroughly vetted alternative datasets are added to the total number of alternative datasets on the Neudata platform per month. We expect the total number of datasets to increase steadily over the next few years as (i) more data exhaust firms monetize their existing data, and (ii) new and existing start-ups enter the space with fresh and additional alternative data offerings.

2.1.1 Definition: Why 'alternative'? Opposition with conventional

For the uninitiated, the term 'alternative data' refers to novel data sources which can be used for investment management analysis and decision-making purposes in quantitative and discretionary investment strategies. Essentially, alternative data refers to data which was, in the main, created in the past seven years and which until very recently has not been available to the investment world. In some cases, the original purpose for creating alternative data was to provide an analysis tool for use by non-investment firms – entities across a wide range of industries. In many other cases alternative data is a by-product of economic activity, often referred to as 'exhaust data'. Alternative data is mainly used by both the buy side and the sell side, as well as to some degree by private equity, venture capital, and corporate non-investment clients.

2.1.2 Alternative is not always big and big is not always alternative

The terms 'big data' and 'alternative data' are often used interchangeably and many use both in the context of unstructured data and in some cases to refer to large volumes of data.

The term 'alternative data' was initially used by data brokers and consultants in the US and it found widespread acceptance around five years ago. The meaning of alternative data is much more widely understood by the asset management industry in the US than in other regions: in Europe, for example, the term has become more widely recognized only as recently as 2017.

The large number of conferences and events hosted in 2016 and 2017 by the sell side, traditional data vendors, and other categories of conference organizer has certainly helped to proliferate the awareness of alternative data. In addition, many surveys and reports on alternative data and artificial intelligence by sell-side banks, data providers and consultants in the past year have helped to educate both the buy side and the wider industry.

What exactly do we mean by alternative data sources, how many sources are available, and which ones are most applicable?

2.2   DRIVERS OF ADOPTION

2.2.1   Diffusion of innovations: Where are we now?

The financial industry is still in the early adoption stages with regards to alternative data (Figure 2.1). This is evidenced by the number of buy side firms actively seeking and researching alternative data sources. However, the adoption of alternative data is at the cusp of transitioning into an early majority phase as we observe a larger number of asset managers, hedge funds, pension funds, and sovereign wealth funds setting up alternative data research capabilities.

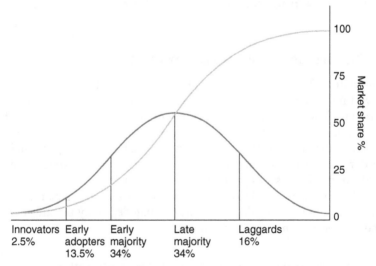

FIGURE 2.1   The law of diffusion of innovation.
Source: Rogers, 1962.

The majority of innovators and early adopters are based in the US, with a small percentage of European and an even lower number of Asian funds. Most of the innovators and early adopters have systematic and quantitative investment strategies, and, to a significant degree, consumer-focused discretionary funds.

In 2017 we saw a proliferation of interest from funds using fundamental strategies. However, despite the increased interest from these more traditional managers in using alternative data, the uptake for quantitative strategies is at a notably more rapid pace. We suspect one of the main reasons for this is operational know-how. Put simply, it is more challenging for firms driven by fundamental strategies to integrate and research alternative datasets given that the required technical and data infrastructure needed is often not adequate, and that research teams frequently have significant skill set gaps. As a result, the task of evaluating, processing, ensuring legal compliance, and procuring a large number of datasets requires an overhaul of existing processes and can represent a significant organizational challenge.

For large, established traditional asset managers, one significant obstacle is the slow internal process of providing the research team with test data. This procedure often requires (i) due diligence on the new data provider, (ii) signing legal agreements for (in most cases free) test data, and (iii) approval by compliance teams. The framework for these internal processes at an asset manager, and hence the time required to organize a large number of new datasets for research teams, varies significantly. It can take from a few days/weeks at an innovative hedge fund to several months at a less data-focused and less efficiently organized asset manager.

The adoption of alternative data within the investment community has been driven by the advancements of financial technology and has improved technological capabilities for analyzing different datasets. Many investors, hedge funds, and asset managers alike view these developments as a complementary tool alongside conventional investment methodologies, offering an advantage over investment managers that have not deployed such capabilities.

Today, despite many investment professionals claiming that alternative data is something of a new investment frontier, arguably, this frontier is already fairly well established, given that the presence of industry practitioners is now fairly common. As noted by EY's 2017 global hedge fund and investor survey,[1] when participants were asked 'What proportion of the hedge funds in which you invest use non-traditional or next-generation data and "big data" analytics/artificial intelligence to support their investment process?', the average answer was 24%. Perhaps most interestingly, when asking the same participants what they expected that proportion to be in three years, the answer increased to 38%.

Indeed, according to Opimas Analysis,[2] global spending by investment managers on alternative data is forecast to grow at a CAGR of 21% for the next four years and is expected to exceed $7 billion by 2020 (Figure 2.2).

---

[1]http://www.ey.com/Publication/vwLUAssets/EY-2017-global-hedge-fund-and-investor-survey-press-release/$File/EY-2017-global-hedge-fund-and-investor-survey-press-release.pdf
[2]http://www.opimas.com/research/267/detail

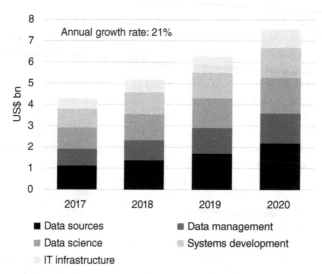

FIGURE 2.2   Spending on alternative data.
Source: Opimas Analysis.
Source: https://www.ft.com/content/0e29ec10-f925-11e7-9b32-d7d59aace167

2.3   ALTERNATIVE DATA TYPES, FORMATS AND UNIVERSE

The classification of alternative data sources is challenging for several reasons. First, the information provided by the data providers describing their offering can often be inconsistent and incomplete, and not sufficiently relevant for investment management purposes. Second, the nature of alternative data can be complex and multi-faceted, and

FIGURE 2.3   Alternative dataset types.
Source: Neudata.

sources cannot easily be classified or described as a single type. Traditional sources such as tick or price data, fundamental or reference data are less complex and easier to define.

We categorize each data source into 20 different types and for most alternative data examples, multiple categories apply. For instance, an environmental, social, and governance (ESG) dataset could have components of 'Crowd sourced', 'Web scraped', 'News', and 'Social media' (Figure 2.3). To complicate things further, a dataset could also be a derived product and be made available in different formats:

1. Raw, accounting for 28% of our feed type.
2. Structured or aggregated, 35%.
3. Signal (derived metric), 22%.
4. Report, 15%.

2.3.1 Alternative data categorization and definitions

TABLE 2.1   Data categorization types

Dataset category	Definition
Crowd sourced	Data has been gathered from a large group of contributors, typically using social media or smartphone apps
Economic	Data gathered is relevant to the economy of a particular region. Examples include trade flow, inflation, employment, or consumer spending data
ESG	Data is collected to help investors identify environmental, social, and governance risks across different companies
Event	Any dataset that can inform users of a price-sensitive event for equities. Examples include takeover notification, catalyst calendar or trading alert offerings
Financial products	Any dataset related to financial products. Examples include options pricing, implied volatility, ETF, or structured products data
Fund flows	Any datasets related to institutional or retail investment activity
Fundamental	Data is derived from proprietary analysis techniques and relates to company fundamentals
Internet of things	Data is derived from interconnected physical devices, such as Wi-Fi infrastructures and devices with embedded internet connectivity
Location	Dataset is typically derived from mobile phone location data
News	Data is derived from news sources including publicly available news websites, news video channels or company-specific announcement vendors
Price	Pricing data sourced either on or off exchange
Surveys and Polls	Underlying data has been gathered using surveys, questionnaires or focus groups
Satellite and aerial	Underlying data has been gathered using satellites, drones or other aerial devices
Search	Dataset contains, or is derived from, internet search data
Sentiment	Output data is derived from methods such as natural language processing (NLP), text analysis, audio analysis, or video analysis
Social media	Underlying data has been gathered using social media sources

(Continued)

TABLE 2.1   (*Continued*)

Dataset category	Definition
Transactional	Dataset is derived from sources such as receipts, bank statements, credit card, or other data transactions
Weather	Data is derived from sources that collect weather-related data, such as ground stations and satellites
Web scraping	Data is derived from an automated process that collects specific data from websites on a regular basis
Web and app tracking	Data is derived from either (i) an automated process that archives existing websites and apps and tracks specific changes to each website over time or (ii) monitoring website visitor behaviour

Source: Neudata.

2.3.2   How many alternative datasets are there?

We estimate that there are over 1000 alternative data sources used by the buy side today. The majority of these – 21% (Figure 2.4) – fall into the category of web- and apps-related data, 8% macro-economic data, which consists of several subcategories such as employment, gross domestic product (GDP), inflation, production, economic indicators, and many others (Figure 2.4).

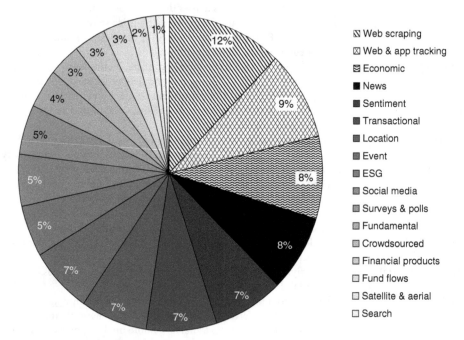

FIGURE 2.4   Breakdown of alternative data sources used by the buy side.
Source: Neudata.

The first six data categories make up 50% of all data sources. It is important to note that a dataset can be classified in multiple categories. One dataset could consist of multiple sources and be applicable for different use cases.

However, the way of using these data sources in investment management is not uniform and does not mirror the supply-side of the data sources.

2.4 HOW TO KNOW WHAT ALTERNATIVE DATA IS USEFUL (AND WHAT ISN'T)

The ultimate question for many fund managers is which data source to select for research or to backtest. One of the key questions is, which dataset is easily actionable? How much data cleaning, mapping, and preparation work has to be carried out to prepare and to integrate a dataset within a research database?

One way we attempt to answer these questions is by scoring each dataset on the eight factors in Table 2.2. Understandably, each fund manager will have a different opinion on which are the most important of the factors in Table 2.2. Many will have particular 'hard stops'. For example, one may want to backtest a dataset only if it has at least five years of history, costs less than $50 000 per year, is updated at least daily, and is relevant to at least 1000 publicly listed equities.

Of course, the above factors are only an initial overview in order for institutional investors to ascertain exactly how one dataset varies from the next. Beyond this, there are numerous qualitative factors that need to be taken into account in order to gauge whether a dataset is worth investigating further. This is carried out through a thorough investigation process, which attempts to answer between 80 and 100 questions which reflect the queries we most frequently receive from the investment community. Examples include:

1. What are the underlying sources of the data?
2. Exactly how is the data collected and subsequently delivered?
3. Was the data as complete three years ago as it is today?

TABLE 2.2 Key criteria for assessing alternative data usefulness

Factor	Description
Data history length	The earliest point from which historical point in time data is available
Data frequency	The frequency with which data can be delivered
Universe coverage	How many investable companies the dataset relates to
Market obscurity	Neudata's assessment of how well-known this dataset is to institutional investors
Crowding factor	Neudata's estimate of how many hedge funds and asset management clients are using this dataset
Uniqueness	Neudata's assessment of how unique this specific dataset is
Data quality	A function of Neudata's assessment of completeness, structure, accuracy and timeliness of data
Annual price	Annual subscription price charged by the data provider

Source: Neudata.

4. How has the panel size changed over time and what are the biases?
5. How timely is the data delivery?
6. Is the data 'point-in-time'?
7. Is the data mapped to identifiers or tickers, and if so, how?
8. How is this dataset differentiated from similar offerings?
9. What institutional investors have so far been interested in the offering, if any?
10. What is the geographical coverage and how might this expand?
11. What is the specific list of investable companies related to this dataset?

We find answers to these questions by holding multiple meetings with the data provider, reviewing sample data (which is often shared with interested clients), and reviewing independent relevant sources (e.g. academic papers). In carrying out these steps, not only is a comprehensive and unique dataset profile created, but suggested use cases can be provided which can be applied to the backtesting process.

2.5   HOW MUCH DOES ALTERNATIVE DATA COST?

One of the most challenging questions for both the data providers and purchasers of alternative data is how to determine the price of a dataset.

For many new data provider entrants to the financial services industry it can be very difficult to work out a price, for two reasons. The first is that in many cases new providers' understanding and knowledge of peer or comparable data subscription pricings is non-existent or very limited. Second, data providers do not know how their data will be used by the buy side and how much value or alpha a dataset provides to an asset manager. To an asset manager, the value-add of a dataset will be dependent on many factors, such as investment strategy, time horizon, universe size, and many other factors that will be unique to a fund manager strategy. The marginal alpha of a new alternative dataset could be too small if the new data source is highly correlated with datasets already used by an asset manager.

For asset managers starting to research alternative data, the challenge is in budgeting for data subscriptions. Annual data subscription prices will vary widely depending on the data formats (as described in Section 2.3), data quality, and other data provider-specific factors. The price of alternative datasets ranges from free to $2.5 million annual subscription fees. About 70% of all datasets are priced in the range of $1–150 000 per year. There are also several free alternative datasets. However, for some free data sources there might be the indirect cost of data retrieval, cleaning, normalizing, mapping to identifiers, and other preparations to make these data sources useful for research and production at a fund manager (Figure 2.5).

2.6   CASE STUDIES

Five examples are shown below which have been sourced by Neudata's data scouting team in the past year. Only summarized extracts from full reports are given, and provider names have been obfuscated.

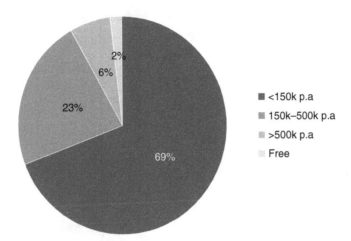

FIGURE 2.5   Breakdown of dataset's annual price.
Source: Neudata.

2.6.1   US medical records

Provider: an early-stage data provider capable of delivering healthcare brand sales data within three days of prescription.

2.6.1.1   Summary   The group provides insights into the healthcare sector derived from medical records. For the past seven years the firm has partnered with medical transcription companies across the US and uses natural language processing (NLP) techniques to process data.

The dataset offers around 20 million medical transcription records covering all 50 states, with 1.25 million new records added every month (250 000 every month in 2016), 7000 physicians covering every specialty, and 7 million patients. Data becomes available as quickly as 72 hours after the patient leaves the doctor's office and can be accessed in either unstructured or structured format (CSV file).

2.6.1.2   Key Takeaways   The group claims to be the only company commercializing this data. To date the offering has been used for (i) tracking a medication immediately following launch, (ii) investigating the reasons behind the underutilization of particular brands, and (iii) spotting adverse events involving a company product and label expansion before FDA approval.

2.6.1.3   Status   The company has worked with two discretionary hedge funds in the past six months and is now looking to strike an exclusive deal (Figure 2.6).

2.6.2   Indian power generation data

Provider: an established data provider yet to launch a daily data delivery pertaining to the Indian power sector.

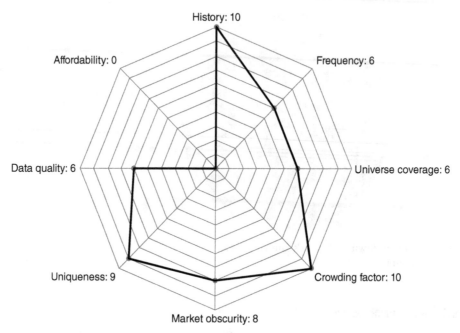

FIGURE 2.6   Neudata's rating for medical record dataset.
Source: Neudata.

2.6.2.1   Summary   This data provider's core business involves supplying data analytics and research services to a client base of hedge funds, brokers, and commercial banks. One such offering (yet to be launched) will provide daily updates on the Indian power sector. Specifically, this includes quantity (energy met in million units) and quality (peak shortage in megawatts) data on electricity provision, by region and state. The dataset will also include a split of electricity generation across both state and source (i.e. coal, solar, wind, and hydro energy). In total, around 10 000 data points will be updated on a daily basis.

2.6.2.2   Key Takeaways   We believe this is a unique offering given the granularity of data and delivery frequency. Comprehensive granularity, such as power generation at the plant level, can be provided from 2014. Less detailed datasets can be provided from as early as 2012. Once launched, the dataset can be delivered through an API feed.

2.6.2.3   Status   No clients to date are using this dataset and the group is actively seeking out institutions that would find such a dataset useful. On finding interested parties, we understand it would take around four weeks to set up an API feed (Figure 2.7).

2.6.3   US earnings performance forecasts

Provider: the data services division of an investment bank, which provides earnings performance forecasts for 360 US companies, predominantly within the retail sector.

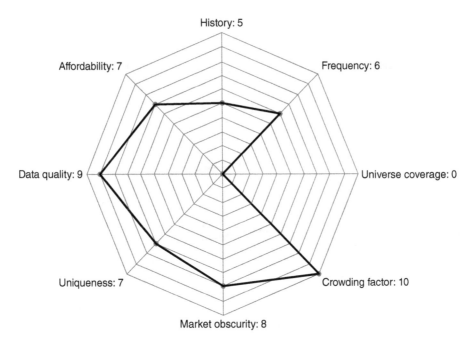

FIGURE 2.7 Neudata's rating for Indian power generation dataset.
Source: Neudata.

2.6.3.1 Summary Launched in September 2016, this offering combines (i) online user search data, (ii) geolocation data from a panel of 65 million devices, and (iii) point-of-sale transaction data. The output is a quarterly signal designed to give clients an idea of how well a given company has performed relative to previous quarters. The earnings signals are delivered between 3 and 10 days after a given company's fiscal quarter end via FTP or the group's website. Historical data for the entire universe is available from late 2012.

2.6.3.2 Key Takeaways Prospective users should be aware that (i) rather than an absolute earnings figure, only relative earnings measures are provided for each company on an arbitrary scale compared with previous periods, (ii) out-of-sample data for the recently expanded universe is only four months old, (iii) until recently this offering covered only around 60 US stocks; in August 2017, the universe was widened to 360 stocks and expanded beyond the retail sector to include cinema, restaurant, and hotel chains. Since this time the group has informed us that client interest has picked up significantly.

2.6.3.3 Status Around eight clients are using this dataset, of which half are quant funds. Despite the increased interest in recent months, we understand that the group is keen to limit access (Figure 2.8).

2.6.4 China manufacturing data

Provider: a data provider using advanced satellite imagery analysis in order to assist users in tracking economic activity in China.

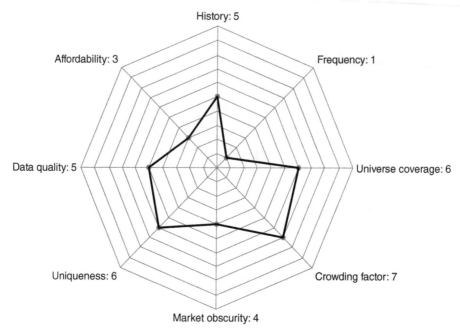

FIGURE 2.8 Neudata's rating for US earnings performance forecast.
Source: Neudata.

2.6.4.1 Summary This offering is a manufacturing index, which is calculated based on images of around 6000 industrial sites across mainland China, covering 500 000 km². Datapoints that are used to construct the index are delivered to clients via CSV file three times per week with a two-week delay. History is available from 2004.

2.6.4.2 Key Takeaways The group claims that this product is both the fastest and the most reliable gauge of Chinese industrial activity. Specifically, the group claims this index is more accurate than the Chinese Purchasing Managers Index (PMI), which has often been questioned by observers for a lack of accuracy and reliability.

2.6.4.3 Status The group began selling the underlying data to the quantitative division of a large multinational bank in early 2017. Other quants more recently have become interested, and to date the group has four clients receiving the same underlying data. Due to client demand, the group is undergoing a mapping process of specific industrial sites to underlying companies using CUSIPs, which is expected to be completed by early 2018 (Figure 2.9).

2.6.5 Short position data

Provider: this company collects, consolidates and analyzes ownership data for publicly traded securities held by over 600 investment managers globally.

2.6.5.1 Summary The group collects disclosures from regulators in over 30 countries which detail long and short positions for around 3200 equities. These disclosures are

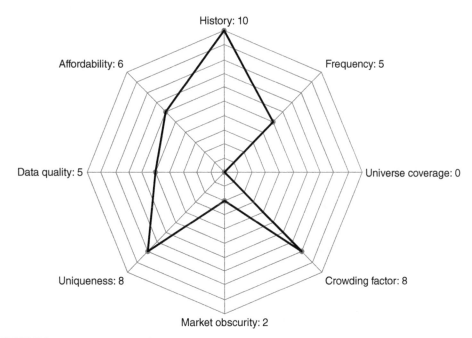

FIGURE 2.9 Neudata's rating for China manufacturing dataset.
Source: Neudata.

consolidated by an investment manager and allow clients to perform their own analytics on the aggregated output. For example, clients can discover how many other managers have entered the same short position on a given stock over a particular time period and how large their position is. Updates are provided on a daily basis and historical data is available from 2012.

2.6.5.2 Key Takeaways Ownership data is presented in a simple, standardized format that is easy to analyze. Conversely, data presented by regulators often isn't standardized and at times can be misleading. For example, many asset managers disclose short positions under different names, which may be an attempt to understate their position. The data collection methodology behind this offering, however, is able to recognize this activity and aggregate disclosures accordingly, presenting a global, accurate, manager-level holding for a given security.

2.6.5.3 Status The group expanded in 2017, in terms of both coverage (in 2H17 Nordic and additional Asian countries, including Taiwan, Singapore, and South Korea were added) and asset management clients (from none in 1H17 to 12 in 2H17) (Figure 2.10).

2.6.6 The collapse of carillion – a use case example for alt data

Which alternative data providers could have identified the collapse of Carillion, the British construction services company that entered liquidation in January 2018?

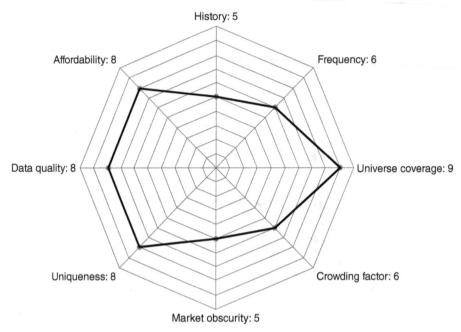

FIGURE 2.10   Neudata's rating for short positions dataset.
Source: Neudata.

Below we describe five very different alternative data offerings and the read-across between the output from their data and Carillion.

2.6.6.1   One Procurement Data Provider Identified Carillion's Growing Debt Burden   As has been highly publicized, one of Carillion's biggest issues in 2017 was that of increasing debt. By the end of the year, average net debt reached £925 million, +58% year over year, as depicted in Figure 2.11.

What we find most interesting, however, is the fact that between Carillion's initial profit warning in July 2017 and liquidation in January 2018, the group (and its subsidiaries) won 10 public sector awards worth a total value of £1.3 billion – further adding to the group's debt burden and potentially revealing a failure by the government to appreciate just how much financial difficulty Carillion was in.

One data provider would have not only spotted these contract awards (and as such the ever-growing debt burden) but also provided additional analytics. This provider's database covers public procurement notices going back over five years and provides details on more than 62 000 suppliers. Updated daily, it contains tender notices worth over £2 trillion and contract award notices worth £799 billion. By searching for specific names like Carillion, users can obtain indicators such as:

1. Volume and value of contracts expiring in the future.
2. Ratio of contracts won to contracts expiring over any period.
3. Trends in market share, average contract size, revenue concentration, and customer churn.

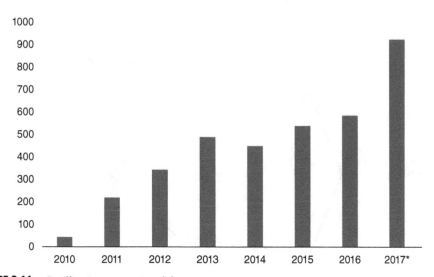

FIGURE 2.11 Carillion's average net debt.
Source: Carillion. *Estimated by Carillion as of November 2017.

2.6.6.2 This Trade Aggregator Provides Detailed Short Position Analytics Carillion's failure has also put under the spotlight hedge funds that made bearish bets (e.g. Marshall Wace and CapeView Capital), and that started taking short positions on the group as early as 2013. Before the group's 39% share price fall on 10 July 2017, Carillion was one of the most shorted stocks on the FTSE 250. Despite this significant short interest being relatively well known, it was still difficult and time consuming to ascertain from public disclosures exactly (i) who had what stake, (ii) for how long, and (iii) what each short holder's profit and loss (P&L) was at any point in time.

In our view this is where one particular data vendor would have proved extremely useful. The group collects, consolidates and analyzes ownership data for publicly traded securities held by over 600 investment managers globally. Moreover, this company consolidates these disclosures by investment manager and allows clients to perform their own analytics on the aggregated output. In the case of Carillion, users would have known how long, for example, Marshall Wace had been in their position, how that had changed over time and the current P&L of all open trades. Data is updated daily and historical data is provided from 2012 (Figure 2.12).

2.6.6.3 Another Provider Could Have Helped Identify a History of Late Invoice Payments The Carillion case also highlighted the issue of late payments after it was revealed the group paid subcontractors with a 120-day delay. As highlighted in the FT article 'Carillion failure adds to subcontractors' case against late payment', the UK government passed regulations in 2017 which mean big companies are required to report their payment terms twice a year (most of which will do so for the first time in April 2018). However, a more granular analysis, with more frequent updates, can be found from observing company invoice data, such as that offered by another provider.

While the group was not able to confirm to us it had invoice data specific to Carillion, we believe the group, along with other discounted invoicers, is worth a mention as a useful source to help identify the initial stages of companies in financial difficulty on which companies are undergoing (Figure 2.13).

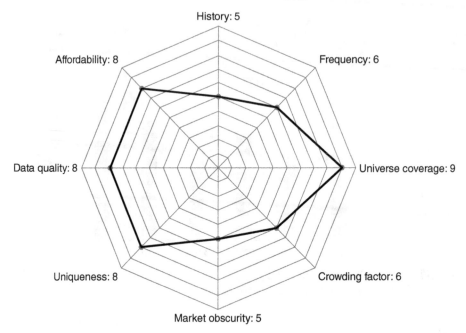

FIGURE 2.12 Neudata's rating for short positions dataset.
Source: Neudata.

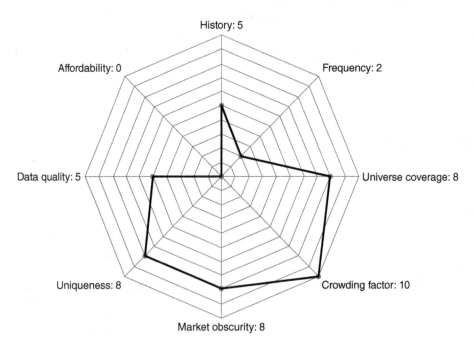

FIGURE 2.13 Neudata's rating for invoice dataset.
Source: Neudata.

2.6.6.4 This Salary Benchmarking Data Provider Flagged Up that the Ratio of Executive Pay to Average Pay Was Higher vs that of Peers
After the collapse, the Institute of Directors, the main lobby group representing UK bosses, called the pay packets awarded to Carillion's directors 'highly inappropriate', noting that 'effective governance was lacking at Carillion' and adding that one must now 'consider if the board and shareholders have exercised appropriate oversight prior to collapse'.

Indeed, the relaxation of clawback conditions for executive bonuses at Carillion in 2016 does, with hindsight, seem to be rather inappropriate.

We asked the CEO of a particular salary benchmarking data provider whether any red flags could have been found by simply studying Carillion's remuneration data.

According to this provider's records, although the average employee salary at Carillion was roughly in line with its competitors, the ratio of executive pay was higher than average when compared with executive pay in the same sector (Figure 2.14 and 2.15).

On further discussions with this data provider, it became clear that its fund manager clients would have been able to ascertain that the ratio of executive to average pay was on an upward trend from 2015 onwards. Moreover, referring to the CEO's pay hike in 2014, signs of questionable executive remuneration appear to have been noticed several years ago:

> Having seen Enron, Valeant and other debacles of management, when the company needs two pages to disclose a pay rise for their CEO, things are not adding up.

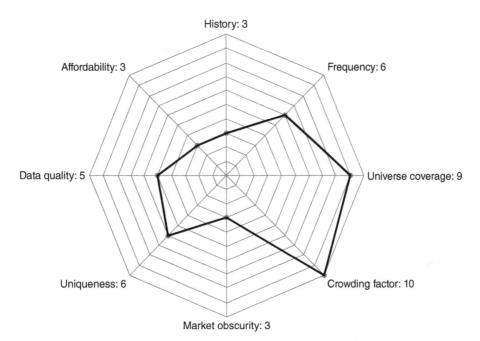

FIGURE 2.14 Neudata's rating for salary benchmarking dataset.
Source: Neudata.

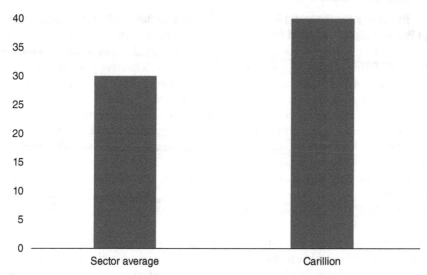

FIGURE 2.15 Ratio of CEO total compensation vs employee average, 2017.
Source: Neudata.

2.6.6.5 This Corporate Governance Data Provider Noted Unexplained Executive Departures

When asked about its view on Carillion, a corporate governance data provider noted that one of the biggest red flags for them was the fact that several executives left the company without any explanation.

For example, in September 2017 Carillion finance director Zafar Khan stepped down after less than one year in the position, with no explanation for his abrupt exit. Carillion also embarked on a series of management reshuffles which saw the exit of Shaun Carter from his position as strategy director – again with no explanation in the announcement.

'These unexplained exits raise potential governance flags in our opinion,' stated the data provider's CEO.

... as well as an undiversified board composition.

In addition, the same provider highlighted that one could challenge the mix of the board composition as well as question whether board members had the appropriate skills/expertise to manage the company or had a robust risk management and corporate governance practice in place (Figure 2.16).

2.7 THE BIGGEST ALTERNATIVE DATA TRENDS

In this section we briefly introduce some of biggest trend that we are seeing in the alternative data space.

2.7.1 Is alternative data for equities only?

One of the surprising findings on analyzing alt data is that it is applicable to all asset classes and not just to listed equities, as is most commonly assumed. Twenty

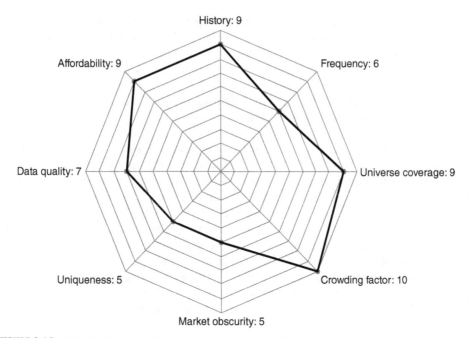

FIGURE 2.16 Neudata's rating for corporate governance dataset.
Source: Neudata.

per cent of all alt datasets are applicable for non-listed equities or privately held firms.

Data on privately held firms and their brands and products is being used for comparison analysis by discretionary managers and also by private equity firms (Figure 2.4).

2.7.2 Supply-side: Dataset launches

In 2017 we saw a large increase in location, web, and app tracking sources. Forty per cent of all new commercially available sources in 2017 were from these three data categories.

The other data group worth mentioning is transactional datasets, particularly covering non-US regions (Figure 2.5).

2.7.3 Most common queries

With regard to demand, the top categories enquired about were ESG, Transactional, Sentiment, and Economic data in the majority of months in 2017.

2.8 CONCLUSION

The alternative data landscape is very fragmented, with new data providers and existing providers launching new datasets at an accelerating rate. The largest percentage of datasets is applicable to US markets. However, providers of non-US data are catching up with offerings of alternative datasets. We believe alternative data applicable to public equities represents nearly 50% of all data, and the availability of data for non-listed equities, fixed income, foreign exchange, and commodities is wider than the buy-side community realizes.

Use cases for alternative data are well guarded, and evidence of alpha and the usefulness of a dataset is generally difficult to come by.

The adoption of alternative data is still in an early phase. However, systematic and quant strategies have been most aggressively exploring alternative data sources with significant data budgets and research teams. In 2017 we observed a significant increase in alternative data research projects and efforts by fundamental or discretionary strategies. Overall, compared with usage of traditional data sources by the buy side, the usage of alternative sources is still minuscule. In addition to the limited use of alternative data by the buy side, it is important to point out that alternative data in most cases is used as part of a multi-factor approach. The same dataset could be used for different time horizons, plus, the use-case and approach vary widely.

There are clear advantages and opportunities for early adopters. Furthermore, there is strong evidence that certain datasets will replace, or substitute, existing widely used sources and will become the new mainstream data sources of the future.

REFERENCE

Rogers, E. (1962). Diffusion of innovations. https://en.wikipedia.org/wiki/Diffusion_of _innovations

State of Machine Learning Applications in Investment Management

Ekaterina Sirotyuk

3.1   INTRODUCTION

Excited by applications of artificial intelligence (AI) used daily via smartphone apps, home products like Alexa and Google Home, as well as matching algorithms used in services of Uber and Facebook,[1] industry professionals outside of financial services and academia wonder why not more, if not the overwhelming majority, of the investment management industry is run on algorithmic principles used by the above-mentioned tech companies. Quite often I have had conversations with professionals and clients who speculated that if AlphaGo can learn to beat the human so fast, then in a matter of years, it is predominantly the AlphaGos of the world that will be managing institutional and retail investor money. However, aside of questions of trading costs, data collection and processing and execution infrastructure, financial markets represent a much more complex eco system of players with continuous feedback loops that continually rewrite the rule book.

3.2   DATA, DATA, DATA EVERYWHERE

In this context, a common assumption has been that access to proprietary data or big data would a priori create a long-lasting competitive advantage for an investment strategy. For example, at conference presentations it has been discussed that corporate treasury and finance departments of global businesses with access to customer data (the likes of Ikea) hired quants to make sense out of company global information feed and to create proprietary trading signals. Possessing information on customers' purchasing behaviour and e-commerce/website analytics/'check-in status' on social media as a base alone has proven to be not enough to generate superior signals. For better trading results, signals with macro information (interest rates, currencies), technical data

---

[1]Face and voice recognition, aggregating and analyzing data feed in real time.

(trading patterns) and fundamental sources (company earnings information) have to be incorporated. The number of traditional and alternative mandate searches for external asset managers by global corporate pension plans and financial arms of companies like Apple quasi confirm the point that data access is not a sufficient condition for an investment strategy success.

These results are not surprising. Financial data is different to the data on which 99.9% of AI has been taking place. Also, wider access to big data for financial professionals has opened fairly recently. Increasingly, data scientists have been transforming emerging datasets for financial trading purposes. What makes processing and utilizing of big data different from financial data? For a start, let's compare data behind the image (one can pick an image from a publicly available library of CIFAR (n.d.) or take a photograph) and daily share price data of Apple stock since inception (TechEmergence 2018). What becomes obvious is that the (CIFAR) image datasets are static and complete – relationships between their elements are fixed for all time (or any photograph for that matter). In the CIFAR case, the image has 100% labelling. In contrast, upon calculation (TechEmergence 2018), Apple's daily share price has $>\sim 10k$ data points – one per day of trading since it listed on 12 December 1980. Even if one took minute-to-minute resolution (TechEmergence 2018), the number of data points would be similar to a single low-resolution photograph and would have fundamentally different relationships between data points than there are in pixels of normal photos. Financial data series of a stock are not a big data. Data scientists can create an Apple big data analysis problem when projecting from various data sources such as price of raw materials of electronics, exchange rates or sentiment towards Apple on Twitter. Yet, one has to realize that there will be many combinations of variables in the big data which can coincidentally correlate with Apple's price. Therefore, successful application of AI methods in finance would depend on data scientists' work of transforming data about Apple into features. An integral part of the value chain features engineering is the process of transforming raw data into features that better represent the underlying problem to predictive models, resulting in improved model accuracy on unseen data. Doing well in artificial intelligence ultimately goes back to representation questions, where the scientist has to turn inputs into things the algorithm can understand. That demands a lot of work in defining datasets, cleaning a dataset and training as well as economic intuition.

While mentioned less often, AI generally has been used for years at some asset management firms (initially high-frequency trading firms) (Kearns and Nevmyvaka 2013), mostly in execution (to decrease overall trading costs) rather than in investment signal generation and portfolio management. Increases in processing power speed as well as decreases in costs of data processing and storage have changed the economics for financial firms to apply artificial intelligence techniques in broader parts of the investment management process. Yet, differences remain which relate to modelling the financial market state that prompted a cautious approach to incorporating AI in finance vs other industries (NVIDIA Deep Learning Blog n.d.):

(a) Unlike in some other settings with static relationships (as in the case of a photo), the rules of the game change over time and hence the question is how to forget strategies that worked in the past but may apply no longer.
(b) The state of the market is only partially observable – as a result, even fairly similar market configurations can lead to opposite developments.

(c) Signal objective is not as simple as a cats and dogs classification problem and one cannot immediately verify validity of the signal.

Further parts of this chapter will walk readers through the spectrum of AI applications in finance, elaborate on the interconnectedness of industries and AI enablers, and open the debate on scenarios of future industry developments. We will conclude with advice for practitioners, students and young professionals.

3.3 SPECTRUM OF ARTIFICIAL INTELLIGENCE APPLICATIONS

3.3.1 AI applications classification

To better understand potential developments in investing through AI and utilization of big data (Sirotyuk and Bennett 2017), AI specialists at Credit Suisse classified the industry in Figure 3.1. When the reader moves up the y-axis, data complexity increases in line with the four Vs of big data (velocity, variety, volume, veracity). Lower columns imply utilization of standard price data (contracts price feed), fundamental metrics (P/E, P/B, Div Yield) and sentiment data. Higher columns use more complex data (incorporation of unstructured data such as text and speech) and include data collected or processed in proprietary ways (for example, market impact, counterparts bid-ask on short time frames). The top level on the y-axis represents big data like tracking of marine flows and parking lots occupancy through satellite images.

On the x-axis, the authors gradually introduce more advanced data processing techniques that are better equipped to interpret and react to these complex datasets – from traditional tools (like analytical statistics) to AI-based research systems (e.g. natural language processing, NLP) to fully autonomous AI trading systems.

A common denominator – McDonald's stock trading – is introduced as an example to illustrate how algorithm design and trading would evolve in each of the boxes. The McDonald's case is followed by an example of investment management industry application.

Increasing alpha from AI applications in the short to medium term is projected to happen in the medium column of the table, represented by 'advanced trading', 'competitive data scientists' and 'master data scientists'.

3.3.1.1 Advanced Trading What is classified as 'advanced trading' tends to use sophisticated analytical techniques to process existing data and enable faster reaction times. Those traders are able to process large datasets or text and to extract valuable information. A good example is where you have different footnotes in company statements (balance sheets or income statements) and the AI system is able to pick it up systematically (Allison 2017).

3.3.1.2 Competitive Data Scientists Competitive data scientists represent portfolios which utilize public and proprietary, structured and unstructured datasets – for example, a portfolio manager who would try to use NLP techniques to analyze whether media is positive or negative on a group of stocks in a region or country (Allison 2017).

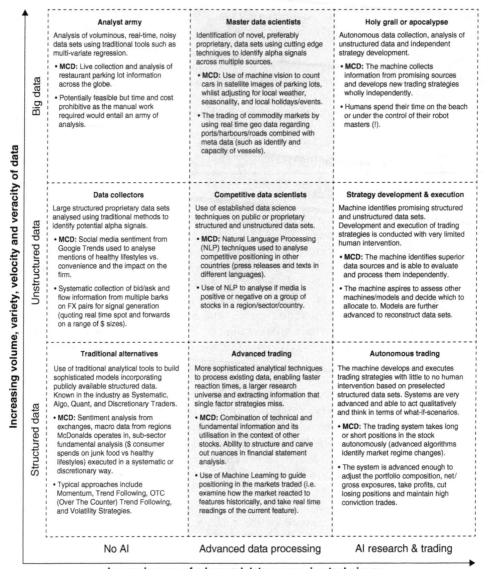

FIGURE 3.1 AI in finance classification
Source: Sirotyuk and Bennett (2017).

3.3.1.3 Master Data Scientists Master data scientists are the ones who probably already use things like very advanced satellite images to understand the position of vessels on the sea or in harbours, in order to understand the flows in the market.

As systems get access to more data, have been trained and tested, the evolution moves further to the right (Allison 2017). Looking into the future we should expect to see the investment industry going from structured data and limited AI to incorporating some elements of less structured data and more advanced data processing techniques. The way participants do it will obviously depend on their skill set, as well as the availability of certain data or developing their own proprietary datasets and/or economics of big data incorporation.

3.3.2 Financial analyst or competitive data scientist?

To demonstrate how an AI system puts itself in the role of a financial analyst (aka 'competitive data scientist', as per Figure 3.1), one can look at cases where graphic processing units (GPUs) and translators facilitate implementation of deep learning (family of machine learning methods based on learning data representations) (NVIDIA Deep Learning Blog n.d.). For many years it would be the job of financial analysts to screen news articles routinely, listen to company conference calls, get in touch with investor relations departments, draw conclusions from qualitative discussions and pass recommendations to traders. This process is time consuming and quite manual. It also requires specialization as analysts are divided by sector and/or geography and are required to possess either local language knowledge or 'home' industry understanding via prior working credentials. Now imagine that, using GPUs and the deep neural network library, the 'virtual analyst' – The Machine – could feed news from public and proprietary databases into a deep learning system (NVIDIA Deep Learning Blog n.d.). After the training the machine can dissect an article every three milliseconds (in comparison, a financial analyst skims an article in 2–3 minutes); this way the machine churns through hundreds of thousands of articles per day. The process works in the following way. The AI system identifies hundreds of keywords within articles. Then, 'an unsupervised learning algorithm gives each keyword a number value that the rest of the system's models can then interpret and work with. The outcome of the deep learning system consists of:

(a) linking articles to appropriate stocks and companies;
(b) discerning a sentiment score ranging from positive to neutral to negative for each article; and
(c) accessing the likelihood of the news to impact the market. The system is also aware of 'fake news' as reputable sources are weighted higher to boost reliability of the outcome' (NVIDIA Deep Learning Blog n.d.).

3.3.3 Investment process change: An 'Autonomous Trading' case

The introduction of AI processing influences investment team organization and subsequently investment process flow. Take the case of an equities portfolio manager (fundamental stock picker), who has final authority for the stocks in the portfolio. He used to rely on inputs from the research team, execution traders and his own understanding of the market he trades. Analysts tend to have multiple years of experience in niche industries, possessing large networks of industry contacts and having spoken with key C-level executives multiple times. Analysts' tasks have gravitated towards building and maintaining sophisticated models, talking to senior management, records, set-up of key dates and notifications alerts, among others. Essentially, there has been an iterative decision-making process in place, such as:

- Step 1: analyst research, then
- Step 2: provide input to the portfolio manager, then

- Step 3: portfolio manager constructs the portfolio, e.g. weights on stock inclusion/exclusion, then
- Step 4: portfolio manager implements the portfolio, focusing e.g. on trade sizing and trade structuring, then
- Step 5: go back to Step 1.

Now imagine that we can give the process of stock selection and portfolio construction to a machine and we ask the machine to make a joint decision on research and portfolio construction. Joint decision making gives plenty more data to work with and moves into the big data/AI problem domain. If the machine then also starts to trade securities to implement the portfolio, we move to 'autonomous trading' as per Figure 3.1. This problem design results in the example of a deep learning framework, as illustrated in Figure 3.2.

3.3.4 Artificial intelligence and strategies development

Asset managers with big libraries of models and histories of trading are well positioned to take advantage of automated capital allocation policies. It happened quite often in investor conversations that when an allocator discussed the multi-strategy offering with the systematic firm, they heard the sales pitch saying that the allocation between styles or clusters of models was 1/3, 1/3, 1/3, or whichever N was relevant in the portfolio context. Often naïve styles or clusters of models allocation strategy were explained by diversification benefits and limited ability to do model timing. Firms are increasingly

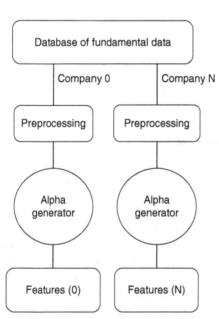

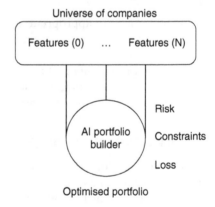

No supervision on what signal to extract

FIGURE 3.2   Deep Learning Framework Example
Source: NVIDIA Deep Learning Blog (n.d.).

testing deployment of neural networks on the library of models to see whether some timing is actually possible. Therefore, asset management firms with stronger infrastructure and models registry could potentially come up with automated capital allocation strategies.

Faster information gathering will only support further evolution of the investment management industry on the AI–big data track. Looking at well-known leading indicators, investment managers historically have taken into account purchasing managers' indexes (PMIs), employment, dry bulk index for decision making, among others. The arrival of so-called nowcasting techniques would potentially allow a view on gross domestic product (GDP) and other benchmarks earlier (before the release) (Björnfot 2017). The basic principle behind nowcasting is that signals about the direction of change in GDP can be extracted from a large and heterogeneous set of information sources (for example, industrial orders and energy consumption) before GDP itself is published. Not only GDP but also manufacturing activity can be measured differently. Thus, SpaceKnow, a US company, has launched a dedicated China Satellite Manufacturing index, which uses 2.2 billion satellite observations of over $500\,000\,km^2$ and 6000 industrial facilities across China (Kensho Indices n.d.).

3.4 INTERCONNECTEDNESS OF INDUSTRIES AND ENABLERS OF ARTIFICIAL INTELLIGENCE

3.4.1 Investments in development of AI

Advancements in AI usage in financial markets have been enabled by the broader penetration of AI in service industries as well as the interconnectedness of industries development.

The concept of AI, or neural nets, in particular isn't new; however, vast computational power finally enables sophisticated processing of enormous databases – image, video, audio and text files – that create enough feed for the AI to operate on (Parloff 2016). Venture capital investing in AI start-ups has also increased. According to CB insights (CB Insights n.d.), in 2017, the top 100 AI start-ups raised $11.7 billion, with a total of 367 deals. For comparison, the total funding for start-ups using AI as a core part of their products was $5 billion five years ago. Since 2012, deals and money committed to the sector have been on a rise.

The numbers cited above exclude tech giants' internal investments in their own AI capabilities. At the company level, Google had two deep learning projects under way in 2012 (Parloff 2016), whereas presently the company is pursuing more than 1000, in all its major product sectors, including search, Android, Gmail, translation, maps, YouTube and self-driving cars. For a discretionary thematic investor, looking for local insights into foreign markets, the obvious route is to read the online press or forums in foreign languages (with the help of local analysts) or to listen to C-suite comments for a differentiated take on investments, as we discussed earlier. Naively, one could use Google Translate for translation services plus 1–2 key analysts instead of local analysts. Nowadays Google Translate (Parloff 2016) is able to transform spoken sentences in one language into spoken sentences in another for 32 (!) pairs of languages while offering text translations for 103 tongues. At the moment, the quality of such language transformation could be questioned but the direction is there.

3.4.2 Hardware and software development

NVIDIA made a hardware revolution in 2000s with the introduction of GPUs, the chips that were first designed to give gamers a rich experience of visual 3D,[2] which were flexible enough for other workloads. For the tasks they are suited for, GPUs are many times more efficient than traditional central processing units (CPUs) used previously. Competitors have been catching up as well. For example, Intel bought a deep learning start-up, Nervana Systems, in August 2016, and chipmaker Movidius and vision specialist Mobileye in March 2017. Those acquisitions enabled the company to create a family of chips designed especially for artificial intelligence. This development will certainly support the big data providers industry. Furthermore, in 2016 Google announced that it was utilizing a tensor processing unit (TPU) (Google Cloud 2017) inside its data centres (the unit is designed for a high volume of comparably low-precision calculations and used in particular in conjunction with Google's open source library TensorFlow). Essentially it meant that Google services such as Google Search, Street View, Google Photos, Google Translate were all using TPUs to accelerate their neural network computations behind the scenes. Google is now rolling out the second generation of these chips in its cloud offerings, thus creating far wider ability.

In addition to hardware development, software development and in particular open source frameworks have helped big data providers (Financial Stability Board 2017). The concept of open source has been around for many years in the software industry. Essentially, it means that the source code of a particular technology or a solution is open for everyone to add to and improve (Shujath 2017). It has been shown that this approach speeds product innovation and improves product quality through a community of developers working together to address bugs. It enables the development of new features to original product. Vendors including Microsoft, Google and Amazon have open sourced their AI solutions (Shujath 2017).

3.4.3 Regulation

While less frequently outlined, market regulation in the United States and some other countries allowed publicly traded firms to use social media for public announcements, which contributed to events datasets creation (Financial Stability Board 2017). So far, geospatial data aggregators have been able to aggregate and resell their aggregated analytics. What came with computational power and decreased costs was precision and timeliness – until recently, the challenge with satellite imagery was that the data was simply not frequent enough to react to crop stress in a timely manner. Daily imagery is becoming a game changer (Anon n.d.-a). Big data providers have boomed over the past few years; however, one has to be mindful of the young nature of these companies – they have been in existence only a few years. Cases in point are Terra Bella (formerly Skybox), which offers analytics into the number of cars in a retailer's parking lot or the size of stockpiles of natural resources in ports, and Orbital Insights, another satellite imagery provider (Anon n.d.-b).

---

[2] https://gputechconf2017.smarteventscloud.com/connect/search.ww#loadSearchsearchPhrase=
&searchType=session&tc=0&sortBy=dayTime&i(38737) = 107 050&i(40701) = 109 207&p=.

3.4.4 Internet of things

When it comes to specific industries, for example agriculture or energy, big data collection has been enabled by wireless sensors and other monitoring devices deployment (Financial Stability Board 2017; Anon n.d.-b). New technologies commonly bundled under the Internet of Things (IoT) umbrella are deeply in many industries, as those technologies allow us to know (i) precisely and in real time which problem arises in the field, and (ii) rapid and effective intervention and therefore a prompt solution to the problem. IoT solutions were again enabled by tech companies such as Microsoft and Amazon as well as by ever cheaper chips. Increased interest and applicability of IoT in agriculture can be demonstrated by the number of start-ups operating in the field (e.g. Farmobile Device, OnFarm, CropX, FarmX, Farmlogs; robotics/material handling – Harvest AI, DroneSeed; dairy – Farmeron, Anemon, eCow; mapping – HoneyComb, AgDrone; end-to-end – The Yield). As digitalization advances,[3] and as more commodity markets approach hyper-liquidity, the sources of competitive advantage in understanding the state of crops, for example, are changing. Information is becoming more vast in scale and scope and, simultaneously, more widely available. If one looks at historical charts of certain agricultural markets, one can see that over the past few years, the price range has been particularly tight. Although there are many forces at work, smooth data collection enables better planning by big firms and thus smooths the curve, which in the end suggests that going forward, alpha plays are likely to be restricted to the short term in general.

3.4.5 Drones

Speaking about commodity markets, one can't ignore the influence of the drones industry as it contributes to making movements over large distances such as fields observed and quantifiable (Goldman Sachs Equity Research 2016). As Goldman Sachs showed in its Drones Industry Report, the industry has made a huge leap from military to consumer use in recent years, and unmanned vehicles are expected to see their next leg of growth from commercial to civil and government applications. On the government side, NASA announced plans to build up the unmanned airspace management system (UAS) over the next five years, and test flights are already taking place. This constitutes an important requirement for broader commercial and consumer use of drones.[4] NASA estimates that the commercial drone aircraft fleet in the US will increase from 42 000 to 420 000 units between 2016 and 2021 (for the US). On the corporate side, companies like Northrop Grumman are developing a range of affordable unmanned vehicles; however, there are constraints on the power usage/altitude/flight cost.[5] Independent research is actively progressing in the area, where scientists are trying to address the cost and life span of autonomous aircraft. Most recently, Massachusetts Institute of Technology (MIT) researchers have come up with a much less expensive UAS design that

---

[3]https://www.bcg.com/publications/2017/commodity-trading-risk-management-energy-
environment-capturing-commodity-trading-billion-prize.aspx
[4]https://oig.nasa.gov/audits/reports/FY17/IG-17-025.pdf
[5]http://uk.businessinsider.com/nasa-drones-could-provide-better-weather-data-2017-2?r=US&
IR=T

can hover for longer durations – researchers designed, built and tested a UAS resembling a thin glider with a 24 ft wingspan.[6] The vehicle is reported to carry 10–20 pounds of communications equipment while flying at an altitude of 15 000 ft with weight under 150 pounds, where the vehicle is powered by a 5 horse power gasoline engine and can keep itself aloft for more than five days. Such vehicles could be used not only for disaster relief but also for other purposes, such as environment monitoring (i.e. watch on wildfires, outflow of a river).

Drones matter due to efficiency, cost reduction and safety. For example, regarding the clean energy industry, drones can decrease the time, risk and labour involved in wind turbine inspection, which currently involves workers being hoisted off the ground to rappel down turbines and inspect their blades (Goldman Sachs Equity Research 2016).

Furthermore, what started as consumer drones (in some cases, toys even) are getting ever more powerful – refer to manufacturers such as DJI.

3.4.6   Digital transformation in steps – case study

In order to demonstrate the commodities digitalization process and iterations between established and start-up companies and their implications for market structure, we can move from the 'macro' view of the market to the 'micro' view. Let's take the corn market for this illustrative study – a market where there are individual farmers, established local companies and international players. Big players are likely to have installed analytics capabilities already. Hence, the question becomes, what might be the impact of small farmers around the world getting access to real-time data management to wield their influence collectively? For the value chain process, we should also consider storage places and elevator providers as well as expeditors who work with logistics.

Looking at the seeding/harvesting cycle, at the start of the season all players look at soil, weather conditions and inventories from the year before (surplus or deficit) and start projecting seeding and harvesting goals. During the season all participants check again on weather, diseases, draught/precipitation and other metrics, and adjust forecasts. Harvesting start tends to be the busiest period because it is when all market participants look at progress, conditions around harvesting, weather, crop quality and volumes. Final data on the harvest appears in a month's time, after harvest ends. Afterwards, focus shifts to the consumption side – micro and macro factors, consumer shifts and patterns. Re-evaluation of inventories starts as well as next season planning.

Government agencies and trade associations collect information on commodity markets and share it with farmers. As land is regulated all over the world as well as food security, government reporting will remain an important part. Historically, small farmers collected information about their business manually and passed on this information to government agencies. Satellites and drones improve the process of monitoring of businesses and information transfer on to government agencies (hence, making the process faster, which potentially leads to faster price discovery). Improvements in meteorology (take IBM Watson) create conditions to improve farm management. Currently, tractors going into the fields are driven by a human. In the future, as tractors become

---

[6]http://www.uasmagazine.com/articles/1710/mit-engineers-unveil-drone-that-can-fly-for-5-days

smart agents (without human guidance), the machines would monitor land on their own. Drones connected to tractors can set the parameters and alert if the field is uneven or there are damaged crops – à la Google cars but in commodities. The hurdle so far has been in the price of such integrated technologies; however, as price declines, adoption is likely to rise. During the season agronomists study fields, take representative samples and decide which additional measures the land needs. If representation sampling was much cheaper to get, that would potentially lead to a bigger harvest as farmers would be able to react to field conditions. With limited information on far away regions in Eastern Europe and China, where farming is done the old way, some participants tend to underestimate the effect of new technologies and benefits of scale they could bring to smaller farm businesses and the effect on markets. We could further speculate that with data collection done in real time and more transparent commodity prices, volatility would decrease even further, yet very short-term volatility can increase as well. Implications for portfolio management are plentiful – from the requirement to capture very short-term frames in analysis to trading on shorter time frames.

3.5 SCENARIOS FOR INDUSTRY DEVELOPMENTS

3.5.1 Lessons from autonomous driving technology

Having outlined the plausible cases of AI applications in financial markets, let's look at some scenarios of investment industry developments and cases from industries where AI usage has advanced further. For a start, autonomous driving technologies present a good comparative base due to research and development lasting over decades – Carnegie Mellon University recently celebrated its 30-year anniversary of faculty engagement with self-driving technology (Carnegie Mellon University n.d.). Applying the self-driving car technology process to financial markets, one can see how the rigid domain rules can limit opportunities rather than expand them. The concept of 'shadow risk' in machine learning has been introduced by the specialists from Artemis Capital Management (Cole 2017). They describe the process of the programmer using artificial intelligence to develop a self-driving car. It can be done by 'training' the AI algorithm by driving the car thousands of miles through the desert. AI learns the route fast and can drive at a high speed of 120 miles per hour with precision and safety. Now imagine you take the car for a cross-country trip in the United States, with highways, forest curves, mountain passes, hills, congested towns. As results show, when the car reaches hilly and twisted roads, the car can't handle the route safely any more – it goes off the cliff or undertakes unforeseen manoeuvres. The key assumption behind the thought experiment is that the driving algorithm has never seen a hilly road or a mountain pass. Limitations of AI-based learning in this case become obvious. Of course, as a step further, the algorithm will be trained in other surroundings and eventually will learn what a mountain pass, hilly road or severe traffic jam looks like (Soper 2017; Isidore 2015). Enthusiasts of the autonomous vehicle technologies would point to a number of cross-country test drives completed in the US fairly recently, but most often they neglect the fact that 99% of the ride was autonomous, which leaves 1% discretion. One percentage of discretion for the 2000–4000-mile trip is a big number for decision making: taking discretionary decisions for 20–40 miles of your road trip, probably key ones.

Let's take Google's experience with self-driving cars. In the early days, 2009 to be precise, the Google car couldn't get through a four-way stop because its sensors kept waiting for other (human) drivers to stop completely and to let it go (Richtell and Dougherty 2015). The human drivers kept inching forward, looking for the advantage, and paralyzed Google's algorithm. Researchers in the field of autonomous vehicles say that one of the biggest challenges facing automated cars is blending them into a world in which humans don't behave by the book. Creating a rule book for self-driving vehicles also shows that generally it results in more cautious behaviour on the part of the cars (at least, as demonstrated by the Google example). Researchers point to a part of the driving process when a self-driving car leaves a safe distance between itself and a car ahead. There tends to be enough space for a car in an adjoining lane to squeeze into. In another test by Google (Richtell and Dougherty 2015), the driverless car performed a few evasive manoeuvres that simultaneously displayed how the car stayed on the cautious side. In one manoeuvre, the car turned sharply in a residential neighbourhood to avoid a car that was poorly parked. In another manoeuvre, the Google car approached a red light in moderate traffic. The laser system mounted on top of the driverless car sensed that a vehicle coming in the other direction was approaching the red light at higher-than-safe speeds. In this case, the Google car moved to the right side in case it had to avoid a collision. However, it is nothing uncommon with cars approaching a red light this way – the other car wasn't approaching a red light cautiously enough but the driver did stop well in time.

Drawing parallels to financial markets, it is obvious that markets are much more complicated than the desert surroundings used for the test drive and furthermore that the rules change. So far, discretionary traders have co-existed with quant investing approaches. However, let's assume that more and more machines will be trading against the machines and not against human traders. Then, as Artemis specialists suggest, self-reflexivity risk becomes exacerbated (Cole 2017). In economics, reflexivity refers to the self-reinforcing effect of market sentiment. For example, rising prices attract buyers whose actions drive prices higher until the process becomes unsustainable and the bubble pops. This is the case of a positive feedback loop. Yet, there is also a scenario for a negative feedback loop, when the process can lead to a catastrophic collapse in prices.

The common saying that 90% of the world data has been generated over the last two years poses the question of generated data quart and how actionable it can be. What if an AI trading system training dataset goes back only 10 years, and even less? Post the financial crisis of 2008, as investment processionals know, investing in a stock market from the long side has been one of the best trades. Most likely the AI system trading US stocks would have stayed long and hasn't had much experience in volatility regime shifts. In that case, this AI trading system, which has been implicitly short volatility and has significant long exposure in stocks, will eventually come across the signal to start selling, resulting in downward pressure on prices. What if a number of AI trading systems had similar short training set-up? Some sceptics would point to the precedents of 'flash crashes', their potential chain effect on the markets and the possibility of systematic investors exacerbating the moves (BIS Markets Committee Working Group 2017; Condliffe 2016; Bullock 2017). Taking a more recent example, which was covered extensively in the news, on 7 October 2016 the British pound fell by 6% in a matter of minutes, touching $1.18, which was a 31-year low, before recovering to

$1.24. Some experts attributed such a sudden sell-off to the algorithm picking up comments by François Hollande addressed to Theresa May: 'If Theresa May wants hard Brexit, they will get hard Brexit.' As more and more algorithms trade on the news feed and even on what is trending on social media, a negative Brexit headline could have led to a significant sell signal by an algorithm (Bullock 2017). Yet, the official report by the Bank for International Settlements (Condliffe 2016) concluded that the sell-off could not be attributed to algorithmic trading alone but to a confluence of factors which catalyzed the move, including time of day and mechanistic amplifiers such as options, related to hedging flows as contributing factors.

3.5.2 New technologies – new threats

Many tests of autonomous vehicle technology still sort out hypothetical risks like hacking/cybersecurity crime and real-world challenges (e.g. what happens when an autonomous car breaks down on the highway). These operational questions are extremely relevant for financial market participants as well. In fact, in numerous interviews with ICE, Eurex NYSE heads, cyber security is mentioned as one of the key risks to financial stability (Accenture on Cybersecurity 2017). Cybersecurity experts confirm that they have seen a number of cases targeted at gaining access to automated trading models.

The transition from small data to big data also opens a variety of concerns about privacy, ownership and use of data (Sykuta 2016), not only from the perspective of buying data as a financial player and trading but also from the perspective of underlying market organization. If the underlying market organization changes in favour of some providers having substantially superior information, it will have effects on price dynamics. Again, looking at agriculture, precision farming practices have existed for a while and utilized technologies such as GPS guided equipment and variable rate planting and spraying equipment, on-board field monitors and grid oil sampling. While volume, velocity and variety of data have been available for years, the ability to aggregate, analyze and discern important information tools has been in the early stages of development. As incumbents such as Monsanto and agricultural technology providers enter the market, there is more focus on aggregating individual farmers' data and concerns over data ownership become more apparent. Who owns data? Who is entitled to the value of data? How will data be shared? I would argue that at some point we will see government agencies having a much more thorough look at those practices. In the case of commodity markets, we can take a closer look at players like DuPont and Monsanto, which have interest in selling their own agronomic products in addition to the data services. How will it evolve for product recommendations based on the knowledge of local farm operations? Would continued development of automated agricultural equipment, driven by big data analytics, fundamentally change the organization and management of production agriculture? Would it mean more tailored-to-needs production? Does it mean commodities volatilities would decrease further? These are all open questions with huge ramifications for financial markets and for society at large.

3.5.3 Place for discretionary management

Even if there are more and more automated processes and more and more machines will be trading more against machines, the case for discretionary high-conviction investing

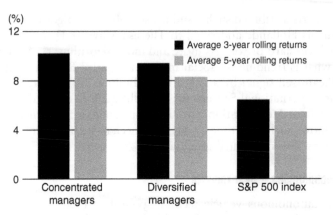

FIGURE 3.3 Equity performance and concentration in portfolio
Source: Lazard Asset Management (2015).

remains plausible (Lazard Asset Management 2015). By design, concentrated strategies facilitate investing in the highest-conviction ideas and therefore limit overlap with the index – leading to high active share, which in turn gets linked to potential outperformance. Both theoretical and empirical evidence supports the notion that concentrated portfolios are well positioned to generate alpha. In its paper, Lazard Asset Management summarizes empirical results of diversified stock portfolios (of mutual funds) vs concentrated portfolios. The authors conducted the study in which they were able to confirm the outperformance of more concentrated institutional mandates by examining separate account data in e-vestment. They grouped actively managed strategies in the US large cap universe into concentrated strategies (which they defined as those with 30 holdings or less) and diversified strategies (which they defined as those greater than 30 holdings). Then they measured the average three-year and five-year rolling returns of the concentrated and diversified manager groups, as well as the S&P 500 Index over the last 15 years. They found that concentrated managers outperformed diversified managers and the respective index (after costs). Finally, marrying proprietary data sources with human intuition suggests having a substantial competitive advantage (Figure 3.3).

3.6 FOR THE FUTURE

3.6.1 Changing economic relationships

Taking finance lectures at universities most often implies studying the well-known mix of formulas and papers (Black Scholes option pricing, Fama–French factors, corporate finance signalling theories, etc.). While some concepts remain relevant today in construction of financial products, for example risk premia, some other concepts have undergone a significant change. Thus, the relationship between inflation and unemployment seems to change partially due to technology and partially due to unorthodox economic policies. Over the years, post-financial crisis central banks and economists focused on growth and its link to inflation, yet, after the period of significant quantitative easing, the core inflation rate in the US, Europe and Japan is below 2%. This empirical observation suggests that central banks can no longer rely on traditional models for managing inflation rates such as the Phillips curve (a measure developed in 1958 for outlining the inverse relationship between unemployment and inflation).

The technology infrastructure of financial firms enables much faster processing, making old investment models to decay faster and to switch out of trading relationships which don't hold (i.e. inflation/unemployment). While appreciating the financial history, it is imperative to keep an eye open for new paradigms. Most likely general university courses still lag financial industry developments; however, the industry needs talent with a fresh look at the business problems. AI libraries of technology giants such as Google, NVIDIA, Microsoft and Amazon offer a good education base for understanding the key concepts.

3.6.2   Future education focus

It is clear that discretionary portfolio management will be greatly enhanced by big data and usage of AI as described in Figure 3.1. Quant investing will undergo a similar transformation (Figure 3.4). Looking at the evolution of quant investing, in late 1980s CTA started to gain traction and the models behind generated buy and sell signals which were usually not more complicated than prices crossing moving averages or exiting a channel. Yet, these models sometimes covered more than 100 markets over different time frames, suggesting a big differentiation in execution practices and contract allocation strategies. Early CTAs tended to take into account only price data. Classical medium-term CTAs have a holding horizon of 80–120 days, so can be classified as long-term investors. Further along, short-term CTAs appeared. As computer speed progressed, the industry saw the appearance of statistical arbitrage strategies, which used sophisticated mathematical models to identify potential profit opportunities from a pricing inefficiency that existed

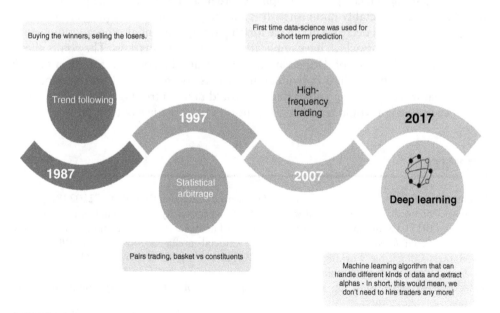

FIGURE 3.4   Evolution of Quant Investing
Source: Qlum, www.qplum.co/

between two or more securities. Further advancements in technology led to the appearance of high-frequency trading – a type of algorithmic trading characterized by high speeds and high turnover rates. High-frequency traders move in and out of short-term positions at high volumes and high speeds, aiming to capture sometimes a fraction of a cent in profit on every trade. Paradigms influenced each other and with further advancements in technology, a new paradigm becomes applicable – artificial intelligence.

When one looks at the historical performance of trend-following programs, the early days of trading were characterized by significant volatility of underlying instruments. When more and more industry professionals kept on trading, those markets' volatility decreased. Furthermore, quantitative easing by central banks post financial crisis essentially 'killed' volatility in key FX forwards and interest rates futures markets as well as equity index futures, which resulted in muted performance of trend-following programs. It was the alternative markets, such as over-the-counter (OTC) derivatives, that kept on delivering returns in the post-quantitative easing era. A decrease in the overall level of volatility also reduced the opportunity set for statistical arbitrage and high-frequency firms. Total volumes of trading went down, prompting some players to opt for consolidation (high-frequency trader Virtu Financial–KCG Holdings), to close all together (Teza Technologies) or to team up on resources pooling (such as the Go West venture, where top traders including DRW, IMC, Jump Trading and XR Trading have opted to pool resources to build an ultrafast wireless and cable route between the financial centres of Chicago and Tokyo rather than each paying for its own network).

3.7 CONCLUSION

Every new paradigm has a period of alpha where first-mover advantage prevails. Over time this alpha predictably diminishes. It is not only the number of players that leads to crowdedness and a decrease in the pie for all participants but also broader monetary and fiscal developments which have implications for financial markets. The points above and the accelerating pace of data creation demonstrate the potential for AI in finance and warrant a deep dive into individual algorithms. With more AI being adopted in finance, features engineering and extraction would take centre stage as the differences in the process design would result in differences in performance outcomes.

REFERENCES

Accenture on Cybersecurity. (2017). https://www.accenture.com/t20170418T210238Z__w__/us-en/_acnmedia/PDF-49/Accenture-InsideOps-Cybersecurity-Asset-Management.pdf
Allison, I. (2017). Credit Suisse charts the evolution of artificial intelligence and investing. www.ibtimes.co.uk/credit-suisse-charts-evolution-artificial-intelligence-investing-1649014
BIS Markets Committee Working Group. (2017). The sterling 'flash event of 7 October 2016'. https://www.bis.org/publ/mktc09.htm
Planet (n.d.-a) Planet start up description. https://www.planet.com/markets/monitoring-for-precision-agriculture
Citi Business Advisory Services (n.d.-b) Big data & investment management: the potential to quantify the traditionally qualitative factors, Citi Business Advisory Services. https://

www.cmegroup.com/education/files/big-data-investment-management-the-potential-to-quantify-traditionally-qualitative-factors.pdf

Björnfot, F. (2017). GDP growth rate nowcasting and forecasting. https://www.diva-portal.org/smash/get/diva2:1084527/FULLTEXT01.pdf

Bullock, N. (2017). High-frequency traders adjust to overcapacity and leaner times. https://www.ft.com/content/ca98bd2c-80c6-11e7-94e2-c5b903247afd.

Carnegie Mellon University. (2014). From 0-70 in 30. https://www.cmu.edu/homepage/environment/2014/fall/from-0-70-in-30.shtml

CB Insights. AI 100: the artificial intelligence startups redefining industries. https://www.cbinsights.com/research/artificial-intelligence-top-startups

CIFAR (n.d.) 10 Image Library. https://www.kaggle.com/c/cifar-10

Cole, C. (2017). Artemis Capital Management, volatility and the alchemy of risk, p. 7. http://www.artemiscm.com/welcome

Condliffe, J. (2016). Algorithms probably caused a flash crash of the British pound. https://www.technologyreview.com/s/602586/algorithms-probably-caused-a-flash-crash-of-the-british-pound/

Financial Stability Board. (2017). Artificial Intelligence and machine learning in financial services. http://www.fsb.org/2017/11/artificial-intelligence-and-machine-learning-in-financial-service/

Goldman Sachs Equity Research. (2016). Drones: flying into the mainstream. Internal Goldman Sachs publication.

Google Cloud (2017). An in-depth look at Google's First Tensor Processing Unit (TPU). https://cloud.google.com/blog/big-data/2017/05/an-in-depth-look-at-googles-first-tensor-processing-unit-tpu

Isidore, C. (2015). Driverless car finishes 3,400 mile cross-country trip. http://money.cnn.com/2015/04/03/autos/delphi-driverless-car-cross-country-trip/index.html

Kearns, M. and Nevmyvaka Y. (2013). Machine learning for market microstructure and high frequency trading. https://www.cis.upenn.edu/~mkearns/papers/KearnsNevmyvakaHFTRiskBooks.pdf

Kensho Indices. https://indices.kensho.com

Lazard Asset Management. (2015). Less is more – a case for concentrated portfolios. https://www.startupvalley.news/uk/jonathan-masci-quantenstein

NVIDIA Deep Learning Blog. https://blogs.nvidia.com/blog/2017/08/30/qualitative-financial-analysis

Parloff, R. (2016). Why Deep Learning is suddenly changing your life. http://fortune.com/ai-artificial-intelligence-deep-machine-learning

Richtell, M. and Dougherty, C. (2015). Google's driverless cars run into problem: cars with drivers. https://www.nytimes.com/2015/09/02/technology/personaltech/google-says-its-not-the-driverless-cars-fault-its-other-drivers.html

Shujath, J. (2017). Why open source should drive AI development in Life Sciences. https://blogs.opentext.com/why-open-source-should-drive-ai-development-in-life-sciences

Sirotyuk, E. and Bennett, R. (2017). *The Rise of Machines, Technology Enabled Investing, IS&P Liquid Alternatives*. Credit Suisse, internal publication.

Soper, T. (2017). Self-driving car arrives in Seattle after 2,500-mile autonomous cross-country trip. https://www.geekwire.com/2017/self-driving-car-arrives-washington-2500-mile-autonomous-cross-country-trip

Sykuta, M.E. (2016). Big data in agriculture: property rights, privacy, and competition in Ag data services. *International Food and Agribusiness Management Review* A (Special Issue).

TechEmergence. (2018). Overfit for purpose - why crowdsourced AI may not work for hedge funds. www.techemergence.com/overfit-purpose-crowdsourced-ai-may-not-work-hedge-funds/

Implementing Alternative Data in an Investment Process

Vinesh Jha

4.1 INTRODUCTION

In August 2007 there was a wakeup call in systematic investing when many quants across the Street suffered their worst losses – before or since – over a three-day period that has been called the 'Quant Quake'. The event wasn't widely reported outside of the quant world, but it was a worldview-changing week for portfolio managers who traded through it. In a sense, the search for alternative data sources started during those days.

In this chapter, we look at this foundational event and how it motivated the search for alternative datasets, the degree to which alternative data has in fact been adopted and explanations for why adoption has been gradual, and some prescriptions for fund managers to adopt alternative data more widely. We then examine some important issues with alternative data, including data quality and quantity; we examine how alternative data can realistically help a traditional quantitative or fundamental process; and we look at techniques for finding alpha in alternative datasets. Finally, we provide four examples of alternative data along with backtest results.

4.2 THE QUAKE: MOTIVATING THE SEARCH FOR ALTERNATIVE DATA

After poor but not hugely unusual performance in July 2007, many quantitative strategies experienced dramatic losses – 12 standard deviation events or more by some accounts – over the three consecutive days of 7, 8 and 9 August. In the normally highly risk-controlled world of market-neutral quant investing, such a string of returns was unheard of. Typically secretive quants even reached out to their competitors to get a handle on what was going on, though no clear answers were immediately forthcoming.

Many quants believed that the dislocations must be temporary since they were deviations from what the models considered fair value. During the chaos, however, each manager had to decide whether to cut capital to stem the bleeding – thereby locking in losses – or to hang on and risk having to close shop if the expected snapback didn't arrive on time. And the decision was sometimes not in their hands, in cases where they didn't have access to steady sources of capital. Hedge funds with monthly liquidity couldn't be compelled by their investors to liquidate, but managers of separated managed accounts (SMAs) and proprietary trading desks didn't necessarily have that luxury.

On 10 August, the strategies rebounded strongly, as shown in a postmortem paper published soon after the event (Khandani and Lo 2008). By the end of the week, those quants that had held on to their positions were nearly back where they had started; their monthly return streams wouldn't even register anything unusual. Unfortunately, many hadn't, or couldn't, hold on; they cut capital or reduced leverage – in some cases to this day. Some large funds shut down soon afterwards.

4.2.1 What happened?

Gradually a consensus emerged about what had happened. Most likely, a multi-strategy fund which traded both classic quant signals and some less liquid strategies suffered some large losses in those less liquid books, and they liquidated their quant equity books quickly to cover the margin calls. The positions they liquidated turned out to be very similar to the positions held by many other quant-driven portfolios across the world, and the liquidation put downward pressure on those particular stocks, thereby negatively affecting other managers, some of whom in turn liquidated, causing a domino effect. Meanwhile, the broader investment world didn't notice – these strategies were mostly market neutral and there were no large directional moves in the market at the time.

With hindsight, we can look back at some factors which we knew to have been crowded and some others which were not and see quite clearly the difference in performance during the Quake. In Table 4.1, we look at three simple crowded factors: earnings yield, 12-month price momentum and 5-day price reversal. Most of the datasets we now use to reduce the crowdedness of our portfolios weren't around in 2007, but for a few of these less-crowded alphas we can go back that far in a backtest. Here, we use components of some ExtractAlpha models, namely the Tactical Model (TM1)'s Seasonality component, which measures the historical tendency of a stock to perform well at that time of year (Heston and Sadka 2008); the Cross-Asset Model (CAM1)'s Volume component, which compares put to call volume and option to stock volume (Fodor et al. 2011; Pan and Poteshman 2006); and CAM1's Skew component, which measures the implied volatility of out-of-the-money puts (Xing et al. 2010). The academic research documenting these anomalies was mostly published between 2008 and 2012, and the ideas weren't very widely known at the time; arguably, these anomalies are still relatively uncrowded compared with their 'smart beta' counterparts.

Table 4.1 shows the average annualized return of dollar-neutral, equally-weighted portfolios of liquid US equities built from these single factors and rebalanced daily. For the seven-year period up to and through the Quant Quake, the less crowded factors didn't perform spectacularly, on average, whereas the crowded factors did quite well – their average annualized return for the period was around 10% before costs, about half that of the crowded factors. But their drawdowns during the Quake were minimal compared with those of the crowded factors. Therefore, we can view some of these factors as diversifiers or hedges against crowding. And to the extent that one does want to unwind positions, there should be more liquidity in a less-crowded portfolio.

TABLE 4.1 Average annualized return of dollar-neutral, equally-weighted portfolios of liquid US equities

	More crowded factors				Less crowded factors			
	Earnings yield (%)	Momentum (%)	Simple reversal (%)	Average (%)	TM1 seasonality (%)	CAM1 volume (%)	CAM1 Skew (%)	Average (%)
2001–2007								
Avg. Ann return	11.00	14.76	35.09	20.28	8.64	3.60	17.10	9.78
Daily factor return in August 2007								
7 Aug. 2007	−1.06	−0.11	−0.34	−0.50	−0.06	0.33	−0.85	−0.19
8 Aug. 2007	−2.76	−4.19	0.23	−2.24	−0.21	−0.04	0.21	−0.01
9 Aug. 2007	−1.66	−3.36	−3.41	−2.81	−0.29	−1.27	−0.23	−0.60
10 Aug. 2007	3.91	4.09	12.45	6.82	0.71	−0.01	1.70	0.80

The inferior performance of the factors which we now know to have been crowded was a shocking revelation to some managers at the time who viewed their methodology as unique or at least uncommon. It turned out that they were all trading very similar strategies. Most equity market-neutral quants traded within a similar universe, controlling risk-similar risk models and for the most part betting on the same alphas built on the same data sources.

4.2.2 The next quake?

Quant returns were generally good in the ensuing years, but many groups took years to rehabilitate their reputations and assets under management (AUMs). By early 2016, the Quant Quake seemed distant enough and returns had been good enough for long enough that complacency may have set in. Quant returns remained fairly strong until the more recent quant drawdowns in the 18 months up to mid-2017, by which time at least one sizeable quant fund had closed and several well-known multi-manager firms had shut their quant books. Meanwhile, many alternative alphas have predicted returns well. The recent underperformance may have been due to recent crowding in common quant factors, in part as a consequence of the proliferation of quant funds, their decent performance relative to discretionary managers over the prior decade, and the rise of smart beta products. One clear prescription seems to be for managers to diversify their alpha sources.

With so much data available today – most of which was unavailable in 2007 – there is a clear move towards alternative data adoption by top-tier investment managers, but many managers' portfolios are still dominated by classic, likely crowded factors. The most forward-thinking quantitative fund managers have very actively pursued alternative data, based on extensive conversations with systematic portfolio managers.

However, most quant managers still rely on the same factors they always have, though they may trade them with more attention to risk, crowding and liquidity. There are several possible explanations for our current point on the adoption curve. Chief among them is that figuring out which datasets are useful is difficult and turning them into alphas is difficult.

To put it another way, as of the time of writing, alternative data hasn't 'crossed the chasm'. Moore (1991) details the life cycle of a product from the perspective of innovative technology vendors – noting that the toughest part of the adoption cycle is moving from visionary 'early adopters' to the more pragmatic 'early mainstream' adopters, who are more risk averse in their adoption of new technologies (Figure 4.1).

The concept is well known among tech start-ups but hasn't been widely thought about in the institutional investment landscape – yet it applies equally well. It is clear to alternative data participants that we are currently at the early stage of adoption but perhaps at the tail end of the early stage – at the edge of the chasm. A Greenwich Associates survey (McPartland 2017) notes that 80% of buy-side respondents would like to adopt alternative data as part of their process. In our experience, relatively few have made significant progress, though the ranks continue to grow. The early adopters tend to be those quantitative fund management companies that are already especially data-savvy and that command the resources to experiment with new datasets.

News stories about alternative data can, unfortunately, be misleading and hype-filled. Only a tiny proportion of the returns of funds run by multi-trillion-dollar AUM managers are likely driven by advanced machine learning techniques (Willmer 2017). Very few truly AI-based funds exist, not enough to know whether such techniques lead to outperformance (Eurekahedge 2017). It's unclear how much scalable alpha is there, really, in counting cars in Walmart's parking lots using satellite images, to take one commonly cited example (Hope 2016).

So, the adoption has fallen a bit short of the hype, even though data and quantitative techniques are far more prevalent currently than at the time of the Quant Quake. Some fund managers have expressed concern about crowdedness in alternative datasets, but at least according to reasonable estimates of adoption as of the current date, these concerns are so far unfounded.

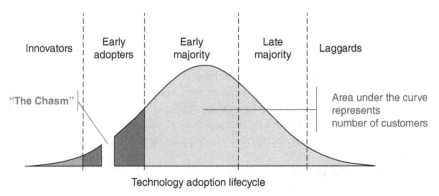

FIGURE 4.1 Technology Adoption Lifecycle
Source: Wikimedia Commons. Author: Craig Chelius https://commons.wikimedia.org/wiki/File: Technology-Adoption-Lifecycle.png

Perhaps the holdouts who have not embraced alternative data are hoping that value, momentum and mean reversion aren't very crowded, or that their take on these factors is sufficiently differentiated – which would be a bold bet in the absence of better information about one's competitors. It's also true that there were many more quants and quant funds in the market in 2017 than there were in 2007, across more geographies and styles, and so some institutional memory has faded.

It is possible that a behavioural explanation is at work: herding. As with allocators who invest primarily in the largest funds despite large funds' underperformance relative to emerging funds, or sell-side research analysts who move their forecasts with the crowd to avoid a bold, but potentially wrong, call, perhaps fund managers prefer to have their bets proven wrong at the same time as their competitors' bets. In all of the aforementioned cases, stakeholders cannot fault the herding actor for a decision which many of their peers have also already made. This may seem to some managers to be a better outcome than adopting an alternative data strategy that is innovative but has a short track record and is potentially harder to explain to an allocator or to internal bureaucracy, particularly if it doesn't go well.

Whatever the rationale, it seems clear that another Quant Quake may be *more* likely in 2017 than in 2007. The particular mechanism might be different, but a crowdedness-driven liquidation event seems very possible in these competitive markets.

4.3 TAKING ADVANTAGE OF THE ALTERNATIVE DATA EXPLOSION

We have observed in many conversations with fund managers that they have generally become better at reaching out to data providers and working through the evaluation process in terms of vendor management. Increasingly, many larger funds have data sourcing teams. Many of these groups are not yet efficient at evaluating the datasets in the sense of finding alpha in them.

Some possible prescriptions for improving this efficiency could include:

1. Allocating increased *research resources specifically to new datasets*, setting a clear time horizon for evaluating each (say, 4–6 weeks), and then making a definitive decision about the presence or absence of added value from a dataset. This requires maintaining a pipeline of new datasets and holding to a schedule and a process.
2. Building a *turnkey backtesting environment* which can efficiently evaluate new alphas and determine their potential added value to the existing process. There will always be creativity involved in testing datasets, but the more mundane data processing, evaluation and reporting aspects can be automated to expedite the process in (1).
3. Assigning an *experienced quantitative analyst* to be responsible for evaluating new datasets – someone who has seen a lot of alpha factors before and can think about how the current one might be similar or different. Alternative data evaluation should be viewed as a core competency of any systematic fund.
4. Increasing outreach to *innovative data suppliers* rather than what's available from the big data providers, whose products are harder to consider truly alternative.
5. Giving priority to *datasets which are relatively easy to test*, in order to expedite one's exposure to alternative alpha. More complex, raw or unstructured datasets

can indeed get one to more diversification and more unique implementations, but at the cost of sitting on one's existing factors for longer – so it may be best to start with some low hanging fruit if one is new to alternative data

6. *Gaining more comfort with the limited history length* that we often see with alternative datasets. With many new datasets, one is 'making a call' subject to a short history. One can't necessarily judge these datasets by the same criteria of 20-year backtests as we can with more traditional factors, both because the older data simply isn't there and because the world 20 years ago has little bearing on the crowded quant space of today. But the alternative, *not* evaluating these datasets, can be considered riskier. Below, we address some techniques which can be used to account for limited history.

The process of turning alternative data into a trading strategy is not straight forward. Furthermore, it competes for attention and time with the core activities of a portfolio manager, including day-to-day portfolio management, capital raising and an ever-increasing compliance burden. But with careful planning, alternative data strategies can be built on top of an existing framework which is used to evaluate traditional datasets such as pricing or fundamentals. This is particularly true for quantitative fund managers.

4.4   SELECTING A DATA SOURCE FOR EVALUATION

Here we examine some issues with selecting data for evaluation within the context of a quant equity process.

First, one must collect the data, or source it from data providers. Most funds will not expend significant capital on direct data collection unless they have large resources at their disposal. Even working with data vendors requires dedicated resources, given the explosion in the number of providers today.

It's unclear to most managers which providers' datasets have investment value at first glance. Most data providers do not have the capability to rigorously backtest their own data or signals in a way which is consistent with the methodologies of top practitioners. Many vendor backtests ignore transaction costs; backtest using an unrealistic universe where illiquid assets drive the returns; compare an equally weighted portfolio against a capitalization weighted benchmark; use only current index constituents or currently live stocks; are not point in time; or do not consider the holdings' risk exposures. And, of course, vendors' backtests rarely show poor performance, so they are often viewed skeptically. As a result, vendor evaluation is typically an in-house process.

At a minimum, a dataset should have sufficient history and breadth; it should be possible to transform the data into something approximating point in time; and it should be tagged, or taggable, to securities. Traditional quant backtesting techniques tend to be less effective for datasets with coverage narrower than a few hundred assets, and with lengths of history shorter than three years, particularly if the datasets are to be used to predict quarterly fundamentals.

Once a vendor is chosen for evaluation, one needs to carefully examine their datasets. Because many of them were collected by vendors with limited experience in the capital markets, they may not be designed for easy consumption or backtesting.

For example, the records may not be tagged to security identifiers, or they may be tagged only to a non-unique identifier such as a ticker. The history may be relatively short, particularly if the dataset is based on mobile or social media activity, and the older years of the history may not be representative of the current state of technology usage. They may exhibit survivorship bias, especially if the data was backfilled, and vendor datasets are only rarely truly point in time. The time stamps provided may not be accurate and may need to be verified.

These datasets have not been as thoroughly combed over as those provided by the large data vendors such as Bloomberg, FactSet and Thomson Reuters. Because of this, data errors and gaps are more likely.

Typically, there is not much academic research on such datasets, so one must develop one's own hypotheses on why these datasets may be predictive or useful rather than leveraging published or working papers. In some cases, sell-side research groups have looked at the better-known data providers' datasets.

The dataset may be in 'signal' form, in other words processed to the point where it can be easily incorporated into a multifactor quantitative process. Signals are generally easier to test, and to interpret, but their use effectively entails research outsourcing by the portfolio manager to the vendor. As such, evaluating the pedigree of the vendor and the rigour with which the model was built is paramount. More often, the data is provided in a relatively raw form, which allows for more flexibility but significantly increases the amount of time required to evaluate the data's efficacy. Many larger quant funds will prefer raw data, whereas more resource-constrained quants, or non-quantitative managers, will be happy with a signal product, though there are exceptions to both statements.

A majority of alternative datasets simply do not contain investment value, or their value is naturally limited. The datasets often sound intuitively appealing, but may lack breadth; for example, many vendors have recently emerged that use satellite imagery to count the number of cars in the parking lots of big box retailers, especially in the United States, or to gauge the contents of oil containers. However, the total number of assets for which this information may be relevant is naturally limited.

As another example, datasets which capture sentiment from online activity, perhaps the earliest form of what we now consider alternative data, have exploded, with many dozens of providers, the majority of which mine Twitter for sentiment. Beyond the obvious observation that Twitter contains significant noise, some empirical studies of microblog sentiment have shown that the predictive power in such signals does not last beyond a few days and therefore is difficult to incorporate into a scalable investment strategy (Granholm and Gustafsson 2017).

Finally, one should aim to formulate at least a general hypothesis for *why* one might find value in a dataset, whether that value comes from predicting stock prices, volatility, fundamentals or something else.

4.5 TECHNIQUES FOR EVALUATION

For quantitative managers, the evaluation process of an alternative dataset may look very similar to what is used in evaluating non-alternative data such as fundamentals. One can formulate hypotheses for why something in the data should predict returns – or earnings, or something else which investors care about – and then draw up a set of formulations which will allow for in-sample testing of those hypotheses. This is especially true if the data is structured and has a lengthy history. The formulations can then be tested for their predictive power within backtests or event studies, subject to risk exposures and transaction costs; optimized, or chosen simply, in an in-sample context to generate an as strong as possible univariate prediction; checked against existing (often non-alternative) predictors for uniqueness and contribution to a broader strategy; and then, assuming the results are intuitive, robust and unique, validated out of sample.

Nothing in the preceding paragraph differs from what most quantitative equity portfolio managers do when evaluating a traditional dataset. Although machine learning and artificial intelligence are often mentioned in conjunction with alternative data, it is very often unnecessary to bring in these techniques when the data is somewhat structured, and doing so may result in less intuitive results than one might desire – especially in the hands of researchers who are not as well versed in such techniques.

But in some cases, alternative datasets have characteristics which make parts of that process more difficult. For example, unstructured data, or data with a more limited history, may require newer approaches to processing data and to creating formulations. The most common example is sentiment analysis, the details of which are beyond the scope of this chapter, but it deals with using natural language processing or other machine learning techniques to condense human-generated text or speech information into measures of optimism or pessimism which are then relatively easy to roll up to the asset level.

Some alternative datasets may be poorly tagged with robust security identifiers such as CUSIP, SEDOL and ISIN. Many data vendors begin their tagging with tickers, but tickers can change and can be reused. And some more raw datasets are tagged simply by company or entity name. For these, a robust technique for company name matching needs to be built that properly considers abbreviations, misspellings and so on. Once built, these tools can be applied to multiple datasets.

Many alternative datasets are not provided with clear timestamps indicating when the data would have been available historically, thereby making backtesting difficult. Often the only solution is to watch the vendor collect data for some amount of time and to assess the typical lag between the date provided and the date on which the data was available, assume this lag was the same back in history and apply it to older data.

As mentioned, anyone working with alternative datasets will eventually come across an otherwise appealing dataset which has less historical data availability than one would prefer. A short history has several implications:

1. The history may not encompass multiple different macroeconomic environments such as both high- and low-volatility times.
2. With less data, backtest results are naturally noisier and cannot be subdivided (say, by sector) with the same robustness as one could do with longer histories.
3. Traditional in-sample and out-of-sample techniques, such as using the first 10 years for in-sample and the remaining 5 years for out-of-sample, may not apply.

There isn't much of a solution to the first problem, but the second and third can be addressed to some degree.

Short backtests are noisy because stock prices are noisy. This is especially true for predictions of lengths of a day or more, and those are the lengths of the greatest interest to large institutional investors. A very intuitive approach to addressing this problem – and the related problem of too-narrow cross-sectional coverage, as with sector-specific datasets – is to build a forecast not of stock prices or returns but of something more fundamental, such as earnings or revenues, or of simple derivatives of those values, such as earnings surprises or revenue growth. Because asset volatility – which can be driven by sentiment and exogenous shocks – exceeds earnings volatility in the long run, fundamental predictions tend to be more stable than asset price predictions. Therefore, one can potentially build a robust prediction of fundamental values with a relatively short history.

Fundamental predictions are not new in the academic literature. For example, a well-known paper (Sloan 1996) showed that accruals-driven earnings are less persistent than cash flow-driven earnings, and that the differential persistence is subsequently reflected in share prices. Studies from the late 1990s and early 2000s also showed that individual analysts have different abilities to make earnings forecasts and that these differences can be translated into trading strategies (Mozes and Jha 2001). This work on earnings forecasting has more recently been extended to an alternative dataset of crowdsourced earnings estimates collected by Estimize (Drogen and Jha 2013).

Of course, making a fundamental prediction useful in a portfolio management context assumes that an accurate prediction of fundamentals leads to portfolios which outperform, in other words that the market cares about fundamentals. Although evidence shows that over the long haul that is true, there are not-infrequent market conditions in which asset prices are primarily driven by other effects. We have seen this several times in the last few years, including the 'risk-on' rally after the global financial crisis and during 2016 when stock prices were buffeted by changing expectations around macro events such as Brexit and the US presidential elections. Identifying these environments as they occur can help to make a fundamental prediction more robust.

Asset volatility itself tends to be fairly stable, so one relatively unsung application of alternative datasets with a limited history is to improve volatility forecasts. Later in this chapter we explore one such example.

In-sample and out-of-sample methodologies might have to change to account for the shorter history and evolving quant landscape. For example, one can alternate between in- and out-of-sample months, thereby allowing the backtest to include more recent in-sample dates, measure how well the factor has performed in current market conditions, and ensure a similar split between in- and out-of-sample periods for any length of historical data. Such an approach must be handled very carefully to avoid any leakage from the in-sample into the out-of-sample and to avoid seasonal biases.

As another consideration, many alphas derived from alternative data, especially those based on sentiment, are relatively short horizon compared with their crowded peers; the alpha horizons are often in the one-day to two-month range. For large AUM asset managers who cannot move capital too nimbly, using these faster new alphas in unconventional ways such as determining better entry and exit points for longer-term trades (Jha 2016) – or trading them separately in faster trading books – can allow them to move the needle with these datasets. We have observed a convergence to the mid-horizon as quants that run lower-Sharpe books look to enhance their returns and simultaneously higher-frequency quants look for additional capacity, making the need for differentiated mid-horizon alphas even greater.

When evaluating alternative data which is event-based – for example, a crowdsourced collection of forecasts from the web, or a dataset of company events which is separate from the usual earnings surprises, mergers and so on – event studies can be an enormously helpful technique. A typical event study involves tracking an asset's return in a window before and after the event. These studies can demonstrate whether an event is preceded by or is followed by large returns, of course, but they can also tell you the horizon over which those returns are realized, which will give the researcher a sense of whether the event can be used in the context of short-horizon or longer-horizon alpha generation and how quickly one must act in response to a new event. One can also partition the events into different types along many dimensions: events for large versus small-cap stocks, or at different times in the earnings cycle, or those generated by different types of forecasters, for example. Finally, instead of using raw asset returns, one can residualize the returns, that is, control for exposures to common risk factors, thereby allowing the researcher to determine whether any outperformance they see following an event is the result of an inherent bet within the event dataset, for example a small-cap or momentum bias.

The above possible adjustments can account for some of the idiosyncrasies of alternative data, but the fundamentals of basic quantitative research are still relevant: one should build point-in-time databases of intuitive factors and test them rigorously in a carefully designed in-sample period while considering risk and transaction costs.

4.6 ALTERNATIVE DATA FOR FUNDAMENTAL MANAGERS

Although quantitative funds, and especially systematic hedge funds, have been the earliest adopters of alternative data, discretionary and fundamental managers have begun to embrace alternative data as well. This move towards 'quantamental' investing mirrors some other trends in the market, including increased flows into quant strategies and away from equity long/short strategies and a greater acceptance of mechanical 'smart beta' or risk-premium investing styles.

Quantamental takes many forms, including a growth in the usage of traditional quantitative techniques such as backtesting, risk management and portfolio attribution in the context of a fundamental analysis-driven portfolio. Here we will focus primarily on alternative data adoption among discretionary analysts and portfolio managers.

The increase in quantamental means that funds which previously had limited experience in data science will need to understand some of the fundamentals of quantitative research. The challenge is reconciling these broad data-driven approaches with an investing philosophy which has always emphasized depth rather than breadth. Grinold (1989) captured this distinction in 'The fundamental law of active management':

$$IR = IC * \sqrt{N}$$

Here, a manager's information ratio (IR), a measure of his or her risk-adjusted active return, is shown to be a function of two things:

- The information coefficient (IC), which is the correlation between the manager's predictions and subsequent realized returns; a measure of *skill*.
- The number of independent bets (N); a measure of *breadth*.

Simplistically, discretionary managers focus on IC and quant managers focus on breadth; a quant strategy is replicable across many assets, but rarely provides high conviction on any particular trade, whereas a fundamental analyst theoretically can provide a high, but unscalable, IC through in-depth research.

Therefore, one use for alternative data among fundamental managers is to gather even deeper insights about a company, without necessarily increasing the number of total bets. It is generally left to the individual analyst to determine whether a new piece of data ought to be helpful for providing such insights. Because the data does not need to be produced broadly or very efficiently across many stocks or for automated ingestion, it is often delivered in the form of reports, which may contain sector-specific information. This is probably the simplest way for a fundamental analyst to use alternative data and can only loosely be considered quantamental.

A little further up the data-adoption curve, some fundamental teams are ingesting data through user interfaces (UIs) designed to provide visualization, screening and alerts regarding alternative datasets. For example, a fundamental portfolio manager may input their watchlist into such a tool and look for stocks where recent trends in consumer or social media behaviour suggest upcoming problems which would inform position sizing, or an analyst may wish to screen for trade ideas driven by these datasets. These UI tools can fit well into a fundamental portfolio manager's or analyst's workflow, which historically has been dominated by Bloomberg terminals and Excel models.

Finally, some fundamental teams have recently brought in teams to both manage vendor relationships and provide data science tools in-house. These tools can include visualization similar to what's described above, but they can also include the development of quantitative models which leverage new datasets to create rankings and scores on stocks. Some asset managers have had quantitative teams fulfilling this role using traditional data for many years, but it is relatively newer in the equity long/short hedge fund space.

One challenge in both cases is getting the portfolio managers and analysts to pay attention to the in-house products generated by the data science team. The fundamental users may not fully buy into a quantitative approach and may not want a quant process dictating their decisions to a significant degree. Therefore, a manager might prefer to design a quant approach in collaboration with the fundamental teams, taking into account their desires, feedback and workflow, with continual coordination between the data science team and the fundamental teams.

Another issue is that fundamental teams are often not well versed in the subtle issues of sample sizes, backtesting, robustness and so on. Because of their reliance on *IC* and not *N*, fundamental portfolio managers and analysts seek high-conviction information, but empirical evidence in capital markets rarely provides such a level of conviction. Quantitative bets can be wrong a large proportion of the time yet still make money on average, but a single wrong bet can sour a fundamental analyst on quant techniques. Here, there is little substitute for continued education in quant techniques to increase familiarity.

On a practical level, new quantamental teams will realistically also have to modify the tools they use. Historically, discretionary managers' workflows have relied upon some blend of written reports, Excel models and Bloomberg terminals. A traditional quant process does not use any of these tools; instead it relies on data feeds. New quantitative and alternative data sources will have to be delivered to fundamental teams using the aforementioned workflow tools such as visualization, screening and email alerts, which will enable greater adoption, and the quantamental teams will need to shift some of their attention away from the typical tools in order to best leverage new datasets.

4.7 SOME EXAMPLES

Here we work through four examples of using alternative data to generate a signal which can be used in a portfolio management process. Although in some cases the details of the signal generation are somewhat proprietary, we hope to provide enough information on these techniques to motivate the study of other datasets.

4.7.1 Example 1: Blogger sentiment

We begin with the analysis of a financial blogs dataset provided by TipRanks. TipRanks collects online advice from a variety of sources, including news articles and several financial blog sites. Its proprietary Natural Language Processing algorithm, which was trained using manual classification of a training set of articles, is employed to generate sentiment for each article. In particular, the algorithm categorizes articles as Bullish vs Bearish (or Buy vs Sell). Articles which cannot be classified with a high degree of confidence are sent back to a human reader in order to be classified and to better train the algorithm in the future.

News articles include bullish or bearish comments by sell-side analysts, which are often redundant with analysts' Buy and Sell recommendations that are already captured in widely used structured datasets as provided by data vendors such as Thomson Reuters and FactSet. Therefore, here we focus on the less well-known data source of financial blogs. The content of financial blogs such as Seeking Alpha and the Motley Fool differs from microblogs such as Twitter in that they typically involve long-form writing and contain significant analysis of a company's business and prospects; as such, they are more like sell-side research reports than either microblog posts or news articles.

We begin our research by looking at event studies in order to understand stock price behaviour before and after the publication of a blog article which has been categorized as a Buy or a Sell. We can partition our data in a variety of ways, but the most important finding in-sample seems to be that certain blog sites contain articles which are predictive whereas others do not. This is likely due to the varying editorial standards of the various sites. Of the sites which prove to have predictive value, we see event studies like the one in Figure 4.2 around the publication dates.

Note that here we are plotting the average cumulative *residual* returns, that is, returns controlled for industry and risk factor, as a function of trading days before and after the article publication date. One can see from the chart that there is a large effect on the day of publication, which could be a combination of the article's effect on

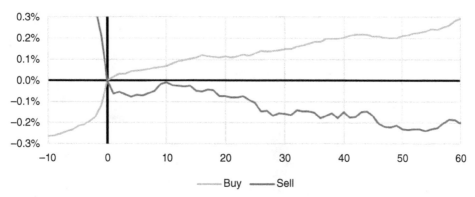

FIGURE 4.2   Cumulative residual returns to blogger recommendations.

the market and the fact that article publication may coincide with significant company events. We also see a large runup effect, in that Buy articles are typically preceded by a price increase and Sell articles are typically preceded by a price drop.

We also see a continued drift in the expected direction for several weeks after the article publication, consistent with the articles' authors either continuing to move the market and/or their ability to predict future price movements.

We can then wrap these Buy and Sell signals into a simple stock-scoring algorithm which has scored more than 2000 US equities each day since late 2010. The approach taken by the TRESS algorithm, built as a collaboration between TipRanks and Extract-Alpha, was straightforward and involved taking a sum of the recent article-level Buy or Sell (+1 or −1) signals for a given stock, weighted by the number of days since that article's publication. This way, the highest-scoring stocks are those with the most recent Buy recommendations and the lowest-scoring stocks are those with the most recent Sell recommendations. In order to have comparable scores between stocks with many recommendations (typically larger or more popular stocks) and those with few, we scale by the frequency of blog articles for that stock.

Financial blogs are typically aimed at an audience of individual investors and traders who have concentrated long portfolios and so usually are looking for Buy ideas rather than Sell ideas. As a result, about 85% of blogger recommendations end up categorized as Buys. This means that once we aggregate to the stock level, we end up with relatively few stocks with net Sell sentiment across a majority of bloggers.

That being said, we see that when most bloggers are bearish, the stocks tend to significantly underperform, as shown Figure 4.3 which plots the average annualized returns of those stocks with low scores (TRESS values of 1–10) versus those with high scores (TRESS values of 91–100), so the Sell or short signals are rare, but powerful.

The difference in performance between low-TRESS scores and high-TRESS scores has been consistent across time, including the in-sample period (ending in mid-2013), the go-live date (in late 2014) and the ensuing three years of live data (Figure 4.4). This suggests that financial blog sentiment is a consistent predictor of returns. There are many ways to slice this performance to demonstrate its robustness, but a simple long/short portfolio, rebalanced each day and consisting of a long book of stocks scored 91–100 and a short book of stocks scored 1–10, is a handy visual tool.

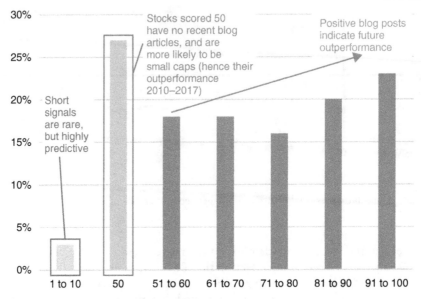

FIGURE 4.3   Annualized return by TRESS bin.

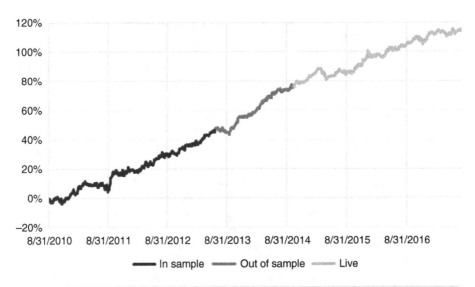

	Avg.ann.ret. (%)	Sharpe
In sample	16.9	1.79
Out of sample	22.2	3.17
Live	13.6	1.68

FIGURE 4.4   TRESS gross dollar-neutral cumulative returns.

In this case, we have plotted the returns before considering transaction costs, but subject to minimum requirements of market capitalization (US$100 million), average daily dollar trading volume (US$1 m), and nominal price (US$4). The daily turnover of each side of the portfolio is approximately 6% each way, so these results should survive reasonable transaction cost assumptions.

4.7.2 Example 2: Online consumer demand

The above example looks at the predictive power in an alternative source of senti-ment from intermediaries – in this case bloggers – who may have insights about a company's fundamentals. Some alternative datasets look more directly at proxies for a company's fundamentals, such as panel transactional data – we show one example in item 3 below. In between these two extremes, we can examine data which gives us insights into consumer preferences. Web-based demand data can help provide these insights.

As an increasing share of time is spent online, consumers don't just buy products online, they also research those products prior to making purchasing decisions. This is true of retail consumers as well as business-to-business (B2B) buyers. Therefore, demand for a company's products can be proxied by the amount of attention which is paid to the company's web presence. Although attention can be a negative sign (as in the case of a scandal), literature has shown that on average more attention is a good thing for a company's prospects.

This type of attention data has been used for some time in the digital marketing space but is relatively new to stock selection models. Here we examine a dataset col-lected by alpha-DNA, who are experts in digital demand data. The alpha-DNA dataset includes attention measures across three categories:

- Web search: are consumers searching for a company's brands and products online via search engines?
- Website: are consumers visiting a company's various websites?
- Social media: are consumers expressing their attention by Liking, Following, etc. a company's various social media pages on multiple platforms?

In order to map the relevant terms and properties up to the company level, alpha-DNA maintains a Digital Bureau, which is an evolving, point-in-time database of each company's brand and product names, websites and social media handles (Figure 4.5). A significant amount of the upfront work required for this analysis is in producing this Digital Bureau.

alpha-DNA has developed a proprietary scoring system to rank approximately 2000 companies on their overall performance strength across digital platforms (site, search, social) and consumer effectiveness (penetration, engagement, popularity). The ranking is done each day and historical data starts in 2012. A 'poll of polls' approach is used to combine many different digital dimensions sourced from multiple datasets to create weighted performance scores.

Using this poll of polls, digital strength measures for each company are built rela-tive to its peers. alpha-DNA's Digital Revenue Signal (DRS), built in collaboration with ExtractAlpha, measures this digital strength as a function of its ability to predict revenue

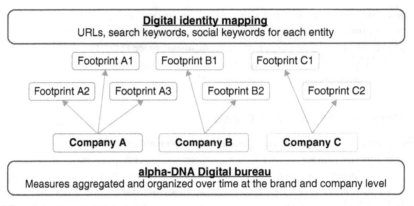

FIGURE 4.5   alpha-DNA's Digital Bureau.

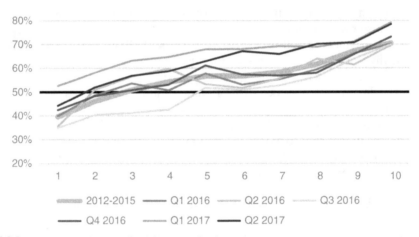

FIGURE 4.6   Percentage revenue beat by DRS decile.

surprises; when consumer demand increases, companies are more likely to beat their sell-side consensus revenue targets and when consumer demand slows, companies are more likely to miss. As such, high-scoring DRS stocks tend to exhibit positive revenue surprises as well as positive revenue growth. In Figure 4.6 we plot the percentage of stocks which beat their revenue targets by decile of the DRS, subject to the same universe constraints used above for TRESS (and further excluding financials stocks for which alpha-DNA did not collect data at the time of writing), shown for the combined in- and out-of-sample period 2012–2015, and for each subsequent quarter since DRS has been live.

It seems clear that one can use the digital demand data embedded in DRS to predict revenue surprises with regularity. As one might expect, that prediction also leads to profitable portfolios built with the DRS. In Figure 4.7 we plot the cumulative return of a portfolio based on DRS, using the same technique used above for TRESS.

The returns annualize to 11.4% with a Sharpe ratio of 1.64. A further look reveals that the results are consistent across capitalization ranges and most other reasonable

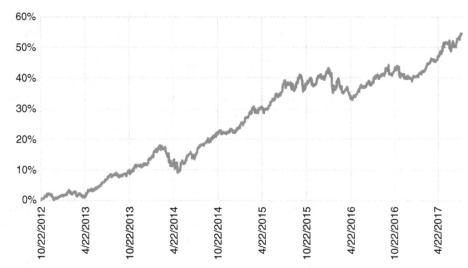

FIGURE 4.7 DRS gross dollar-neutral cumulative returns.

cross-sectional slices of the universe, and easily survive transaction costs and various rebalancing rules, given the daily turnover which is similar to TRESS at 6% per day per side, each way. Thus, it seems that an accurate revenue surprise prediction, in this case based on a combination of online alternative datasets, yields a potentially profitable investment strategy.

4.7.3 Example 3: Transactional data

One of the early examples of alternative data used in the United States was credit card transaction data. These datasets are used to get an early view into an industry's revenues ahead of corporate earnings announcements. With the recent increase in consumer activity in China has come the realization that transactional data in the world's most populous economy can be informative for the revenues of companies with significant customer bases in China, wherever those companies are headquartered and listed.

Sandalwood Advisors is the first alternative data platform focused on the Chinese consumer market. The company has collected several unique high-value datasets which capture both online and offline mainland Chinese retail transactions. In this study, we focus on one of its datasets, from the largest business-to-consumer (B2C) e-commerce site in China, Tmall.com, which as of 2016 had a 57% market share. Chinese and international consumer goods producers use Tmall to gain access to the Chinese consumer market. A wide variety of products is available for sale on Tmall, including clothing, footwear, home appliances and electronics. Foreign companies must meet strict requirements – in particular, a minimum amount of annual revenue – before being able to list their products on Tmall.

In this study, we examine company-level metrics in the Tmall data, which is collected monthly with a lag of five business days. The underlying data includes total sales value in RMB and number of units sold each month. We are able to map the Tmall data to 250 liquid securities which trade in five markets: China, Hong Kong, Japan, Korea and the United States. The length of the Tmall historical data is somewhat limited, spanning March 2016 to June 2017.

We examine a very simple alpha, the change in month-over-month sales. This measure allows us to score any stock in the Tmall dataset, but it is subject to some noise due to companies increasing or decreasing their sales efforts on the platform, jumps due to promotional activity, the effects of currency fluctuations on stocks which may have differing international exposures, and seasonal effects which might affect sales for each stock differently.

An alternative formulation would be to look at the monthly change in market share. For each category, we can calculate a particular brand's market share compared with that of all other companies, whether or not we are able to map those companies to liquid public equities (for example, private companies). We can then aggregate the market share up to the company level, weighted by the contribution of that category to the company's overall revenues from Tmall. This may be a cleaner measure than change in monthly sales, but there are a few shortcomings. The revenue split for the company may not reflect its revenue split on Tmall and, perhaps most importantly, we do not have category-level data yet mapped for all companies, thus our sample size is too low for this metric, so we leave market share analysis for future research.

Following our earlier remarks on looking at the short-history datasets to predict fundamentals, we first observe that stocks with month-over-month Tmall revenue growth less than −10% have lower actual reported quarterly growth rates (1.8%) than those with Tmall revenue growth greater than 10% (6.1%). This analysis provides reassurance that the Tmall dataset is representative of company revenues.

We then follow our earlier approach of building long-short portfolios from monthly sales growth, which essentially results in a monthly turnover strategy (although we do rebalance daily). We look at each region independently: the United States, China and Developed Asia – which in this case means Hong Kong, Japan and Korea. We use local currency returns for each market. Because the data is fairly sparse within each region compared with the earlier model examples, we cut the data into terciles (thirds) rather than deciles and simply go long the top third of stocks in a region and short the bottom third. The result is portfolios which are still fairly concentrated in each region.

In Figure 4.8 we show cumulative returns within each region and then a simple global portfolio which is equally weighted across the three regions and which shows the diversification benefits to risk-adjusted returns when doing so.

The before-cost nature of these results is noteworthy, given that transaction costs – which are low in the US and Japan and have come down substantially for Chinese A-shares – are still relatively high in Hong Kong and Korea due to a stamp duty and a securities transaction tax, respectively. Furthermore, we have assumed a long-short portfolio here, and stock borrow may be limited or expensive in the Chinese equity markets in particular. But we do see that the top-ranked stocks outperform the universe, suggesting a use case on the long side alone.

Nonetheless these results are very promising given the fairly simple nature of the metric we have constructed. Although both the history length and the cross-sectional coverage are somewhat limited with these datasets, the clear intuition behind them and the fact that Chinese online purchases are increasingly important to global retail-focused names and yet rarely examined by investors means that they are worth thoughtful consideration.

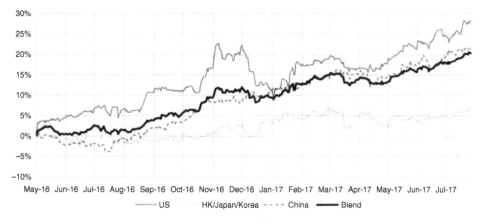

	USA	HK/Japan/Korea	China	Blend
Ann. return (%)	23.4	5.4	18.0	16.3
Sharpe	1.98	0.55	2.18	2.58

FIGURE 4.8 Cumulative gross local currency-neutral returns.

4.7.4 Example 4: ESG

Despite the growth in environmental, social and governance (ESG) investing, most techniques to capture ESG use simple measures such as divesting of energy companies or focusing on board diversity. ESG investors are typically not data driven or systematic, despite the broad availability of data about companies' sustainability and responsible behaviour.

Some recent research has begun to uncover relationships between a few ESG datasets and returns, but this evidence is still quite mixed. A potentially intriguing alternative direction is the use of ESG factors for risk management. Here we follow the example of Dunn et al. (2017) and measure risk using a novel dataset specific to the financial services sector.

The US Consumer Financial Protection Bureau (CFPB) was established after the global financial crisis to increase oversight of financial service providers such as credit card and mortgage issuers. The CFPB maintains a consumer complaint database, updated daily, which logs complaints by consumers relating to retail financial services and creates a platform for financial service providers to respond to the complaints. The complaints data is freely available from the CFPB, but it requires some work to make it usable in a quant context. As with many government data sources, the data formats have changed over time and the data is not tagged to a security identifier. Therefore, we employ a proprietary fuzzy name-matching algorithm which considers misspellings, abbreviations such as 'Inc.' and 'Corp.', changes in company names over time and the relative uniqueness of words in the company name to map the CFPB-provided company names to a master company name dataset and from there to common security identifiers such as CUSIP.

We then have a database which contains, for approximately 100 publicly traded financial service companies, 48 000 complaints per year, with data starting in 2011.

The dataset is quite rich, containing the date the complaint was received, the particular product it pertains to (e.g. debit cards, student loans), whether the company responded to the complaint in a timely manner and whether that response was disputed. The text of the complaint is also included.

Our hypothesis is that companies with relatively more complaints face greater business risk, either because they have alienated their customers or because they are more likely to be subject to punitive regulatory actions. To the extent that news about these existential risks eventually becomes known to investors, they should impact stock volatility as well.

For simplicity's sake, here we simply count the number of complaints associated with each security over a given timeframe. Of course, larger issuers of financial products typically receive more complaints, so we simply take the number of complaints issued within the prior year – lagging by one quarter to ensure historical data availability – and scale by market capitalization. We then flip the sign, so that high-scoring stocks are those with relatively few complaints.

We first run a quick test to see whether our complaints count predicts returns, using the same methodology as before (Table 4.2). Here we use portfolios built using quintiles rather than deciles because of the sparser cross-sectional coverage of the CFPB data relative to the previous datasets. The data prior to 2014 is too sparse to allow us to create robust quintile portfolios within our liquid universe, so we build portfolios between early 2014 and mid-2017.

We can see there is some evidence that companies with fewer complaints do out-perform, and a strategy based on this data would not be heavily affected by transaction costs given the slow-moving nature of our formulation, but the results are not consistent over time and are largely driven by calendar year 2016. Such non-robust results are common when evaluating a dataset with both limited cross-sectional coverage and limited history, as slight changes in the evaluation parameters (such as the number of fractiles, universe selection and trading parameters) can result in large changes in outcomes due to the low sample size. Although the return effects are worth further investigation, we now turn to measuring whether the complaints data can tell us something about risk, where we might expect somewhat more robust results.

We examine the general risk characteristics of our measure by looking at the average exposure to common risk factors (which are scaled to be mean 0 and standard deviation 1) by quintile (Table 4.3).

We can see that the firms with the most complaints tend to be more volatile and more highly levered and that they have lower dividend yields. So we will need to

TABLE 4.2 Do complaints count predicts returns?

Group	Companies	Number of days/occurrences	Ann. ret. (%)	Ann. Sharpe
Overall	71	903	6.20	0.5
2014	60	248	−3.30	−0.29
2015	72	252	2.00	0.15
2016	76	252	28.10	2.31
2017	79	151	−7.60	−0.53

TABLE 4.3 The average exposure to common risk factors by quintile

	Yield	Volatility	Momentum	Size	Value	Growth	Leverage
Few complaints	(0.09)	(0.55)	—	0.53	0.19	(0.05)	0.11
2	(0.05)	(0.40)	0.02	0.67	0.38	(0.10)	0.18
3	0.04	(0.33)	(0.13)	0.75	0.48	(0.17)	0.43
4	(0.10)	(0.27)	(0.03)	1.77	0.59	(0.03)	0.24
Many complaints	(0.27)	(0.15)	0.03	0.64	0.28	0.04	0.47

determine whether the complaints explain risk over and above what we would know by looking at these standard risk factors.

We start by examining stock price volatility by quintile of complaints, as measured over the course of the month following our complaints calculation. We measure volatility in two ways:

- Standard deviation of daily stock returns.
- Standard deviation of *residualized* daily stock returns, where each day's return is regressed cross-sectionally against industry and common risk factors, leaving only the idiosyncratic return.

The residual return volatility should tell us the degree to which the complaints data tells us about future risk which isn't explained by common risk factors, including the stock's own historical volatility. For both of these measures, we then percentile them each month to account for the fact that volatility in the market as a whole changes over time.

We can see in Figure 4.9 that stocks with fewer complaints relative to their market cap exhibit lower future volatility even after controlling for known risk factors. The effect is more consistent than what we saw earlier with return-based measures.

Finally, we can also use a regression approach to explain the cross-section of return volatility using our basic risk factors and then by adding in our complaints factor. Here, a higher value means more complaints, so we expect to see a positive coefficient on the Complaints variable if companies which experience more complaints are riskier (Table 4.4).

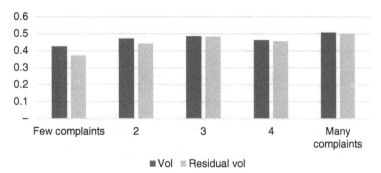

FIGURE 4.9 Percentile of volatility, by complaint frequency.

TABLE 4.4 Regression approach to explain the cross-section of return volatility

	Baseline			With complaints		
	Parameter estimate	t Value	Pr > |t|	Parameter estimate	t Value	Pr > |t|
Intercept	0.020	101.81	<0.0001	0.019	92.24	<0.0001
Volatility	0.008	34.38	<0.0001	0.007	28.91	<0.0001
Size	(0.000)	(5.23)	<0.0001	(0.000)	(5.15)	<0.0001
Value	0.001	4.00	<0.0001	0.001	5.40	<0.0001
Growth	(0.000)	(0.03)	0.98	0.000	0.10	0.92
Leverage	(0.000)	(0.33)	0.74	(0.000)	(1.70)	0.09
Momentum	(0.000)	(2.70)	0.01	(0.000)	(0.75)	0.45
Yield	(0.000)	(1.69)	0.09	(0.000)	(1.90)	0.06
Complaints				0.003	8.86	<0.0001
Adj R Squared	0.350			0.363		

We can see that although the aforementioned correlation between historical volatility (the best predictor of future volatility) and complaints manifests in a lower coefficient on historical volatility in the second regression. But the complaints factor is very strongly significant in the second regression, with a T value of 8.86, and the regression exhibits a higher adjusted R squared than the baseline regression. In other words, complaints provide unique, incremental explanatory power for future risk over and above a traditional fundamental risk model.

We can repeat the exercise by year and we see that the Complaints factor is significant at the 3% or better level every year, with an improvement in the adjusted R squared across all years (Table 4.5).

An ESG-enhanced risk model could be used in several ways. The new factor could be used as a constraint in an optimization process in order to mitigate ESG risk at the portfolio level; portfolio and stock-level ESG risks can be monitored; and one can measure returns residualized to ESG factors for use in, for example, mean reversion stock selection models. These exploratory results show that unconventional ESG datasets can help managers build smarter models for measuring and mitigating risk.

TABLE 4.5 Complaints factor: significant at the 3% or better level every year

	Baseline	With complaints		
Year	Adj R sq.	Adj R sq.	t value	Pr > |t|
2014	0.294	0.317	5.00	<0.0001
2015	0.397	0.400	2.22	0.03
2016	0.386	0.409	6.06	<0.0001
2017	0.349	0.364	3.47	0.00

4.8 CONCLUSIONS

In the years following the Quant Quake, data-driven investment has grown rapidly. Forward-thinking investors in the quantitative and discretionary segments have begun to use alternative datasets in their decision-making processes, though there is significant room for additional adoption by the mainstream. Asset managers are grappling with the best approaches to alternative data adoption and with finding the right datasets to help their alpha, fundamental and volatility forecasts. We find empirical evidence that alternative datasets can help with all of these things if they are carefully vetted and rigorously tested. It is likely that as more data about the physical and online worlds is collected, researchers will find ever more value in processing these emerging datasets to unlock value.

REFERENCES

Drogen, L.A. and Jha, V. (2013). *Generating abnormal returns using crowdsourced earnings estimates*. Estimize white paper.

Dunn, J., Fitzgibbons, S., and Pomorski, L. (2017). *Assessing risk through environmental, social and governance exposures*. AQR Capital Management.

Eurekahedge. (2017). Artificial intelligence: the new frontier for hedge funds. eurekahedge.com

Fodor, A., Krieger, K., and Doran, J. (2011). Do option open-interest changes foreshadow future equity returns? *Financial Markets and Portfolio Management*, 25 (3): 265.

Granholm, J. and Gustafsson, P. (2017). *The quest for the abnormal return: a study of trading strategies based on Twitter sentiment*. Umea School of Business and Economics.

Grinold, R.C. (1989). The fundamental law of active management. *The Journal of Portfolio Management* 15 (3): 30–37.

Heston, S.L. and Sadka, R. (2008). Seasonality in the cross-section of stock returns. *Journal of Financial Economics*, 87 (2): 418–445.

Hope, B. (2016). Tiny satellites: the latest innovation hedge funds are using to get a leg up. *Wall Street Journal*.

Jha, V. (2016). Timing equity quant positions with short-horizon alphas. *Journal of Trading* 11 (3): 53–59.

Khandani, A.E. and Lo, A.W. (2008). What happened to the quants in August 2007?: Evidence from factors and transactions data. NBER Working Paper No. 14465.

McPartland, K. (2017). Alternative data for alpha. Greenwich Associates report, Q1.

Moore, G.A. (1991). *Crossing the Chasm: Marketing and Selling High-Tech Products to Mainstream Customers*. HarperBusiness Essentials.

Mozes, H. and Jha, V. (2001). *Creating and profiting from more accurate earnings estimates with StarMine Professional*. StarMine White Paper.

Pan, J. and Poteshman, A. (2006). The information in option volume for future stock prices. *Review of Financial Studies*, 19 (3): 871–908.

Sloan, R. (1996). Do stock prices fully reflect information in accruals and cash flows about future earnings? *The Accounting Review* 71 (3): 289–315.

Willmer, S. (2017). *BlackRock's Robot Stock-Pickers Post Record Losses*. Bloomberg.

Xing, Y., Zhang, X., and Zhao, R. (2010). What does individual option volatility smirk tell us about future equity returns? *Journal of Financial and Quantitative Analysis*, 45 (3): 641–662.

CHAPTER 5

Using Alternative and Big Data to Trade Macro Assets

Saeed Amen and Iain Clark

5.1 INTRODUCTION

In recent years, there has been a rapid increase in the amount of data being generated from a wide variety of sources, both by individuals and by companies. Traditionally, the most important datasets for traders have consisted of data describing price moves. For macro traders, economic data has also been a key part of the trading process. However, by augmenting their existing processes with these new alternative datasets, traders can gain greater insights into the market. In this chapter, we delve into the topic of alternative data and big data. We split our discussion into three parts.

In the first section, we seek to define general concepts around big data and alternative data. We explain why data is being generated at a rapidly increasing rate and the concept of 'exhaust data'. We discuss various approaches to developing models to describe the market, comparing traditional approaches to machine learning. We elaborate on the various forms of machine learning and how they might be applied in a financial setting.

In the next section, we focus more on general applications for alternative data in macro trading. We note how it can be used to improve economic forecasts, for example, or in the construction of nowcasts. Real-life examples of big data and alternative datasets such as those derived from newswires and social media are also listed.

In the final section, we go into more detail, presenting several case studies using alternative datasets or unusual techniques to understand macro markets. We show how there is a strong relationship between sentiment derived from Federal Reserve communications and moves in the US Treasury yields. We discuss using machine readable news to inform price action in the foreign exchange (FX) market and how news volume relates to implied volatility. We also examine an index representing investor anxiety based upon web traffic to the financial website Investopedia. We show how it can be used to create an active trading rule on the S&P 500 to outperform long-only and VIX-based filters. Finally, in a case study, we use a more conventional dataset (FX volatility data) but analyzed in a novel way to try to understand the risks in price action around scheduled events, using the example of GBP/USD around Brexit.

5.2 UNDERSTANDING GENERAL CONCEPTS WITHIN BIG DATA AND ALTERNATIVE DATA

5.2.1 What is big data?

The term big data has perhaps become overused in recent years. There are certain characteristics of what constitutes big data, which are collectively known as the 4Vs: volume, variety, velocity and veracity.

5.2.1.1 Volume One of the most well-known characteristics of what constitutes big data is the sheer volume. Big data can range from many gigabytes to terabytes or even petabytes. One of the challenges of using big data is simply trying to store it.

5.2.1.2 Variety Big data can come in many varieties. Whilst data traditionally used by traders is generally in a time series format containing numerical values and is structured, this is not always the case with big data. Take, for example, web content. A large amount of the web consists of text and other media, not purely numerical data.

5.2.1.3 Velocity Another defining characteristic of big data is the frequency with which it is generated. Unlike more typical datasets, it can be generated at high frequencies and at irregular time intervals. One example of high-velocity data in finance is tick data for traded assets.

5.2.1.4 Veracity The veracity of big data is often more uncertain. Often big data can emanate from unverified individuals or organizations. One of the most obvious examples is Twitter, where accounts may try to actively spread disinformation. However, even with financial big data, whose source may be regulated exchanges, data can often still require cleaning to remove invalid observations.

5.2.2 Structured and unstructured data

Structured data, as the name might suggests, is a dataset which is relatively organized. Typically, it might have enough structure to be stored as a database table. The dataset will often be relatively clean. If a structured dataset is primarily text data, it will also have metadata to describe it. For example, it might be accompanied by sentiment scores and usually tags outlining the general topic of the text and timestamps representing when it was collected.

By contrast, unstructured data is much less organized. Typically, it could consist of text scraped from web pages or other sources. Web scraped data will often be in its raw form, including all its HTML tags or formatting, which will need to be removed at a later stage. It will have minimal metadata to describe it. It is often a time-consuming step to transform unstructured data into a more usable structured dataset. In practice, most big data starts in an unstructured form and requires work to turn it into structured data.

5.2.3 Should you use unstructured or structured datasets?

It is easier and quicker to use structured datasets. Rather than spending a lot of time cleaning the unstructured data and creating metadata, a vendor has already done this for you. However, in some instances, you might still prefer to use unstructured datasets, for reasons other than cost, particularly if there are no associated structured datasets available from data vendors. Furthermore, there might be instances where the unstructured dataset is proprietary and a ready-made structured dataset is not available. It can also be the case that you might wish to structure data in a different way. Once a dataset is structured into a specific format, it can reduce the types of analysis you are able to perform on it, for example. In order to do that, you need to have access to the actual raw data. Whilst large quant funds are often keen on having access to raw data and have the capabilities to number crunch it, many other investors are likely to prefer using smaller structured datasets.

In Figure 5.1, we give an example of a structured dataset, the Hedonometer Index, created by the University of Vermont, which was developed to give an idea of users' happiness on Twitter. It takes around 10% of the tweets and classifies each according to happiness, using a bag of words-style technique. A dictionary contains a large number of words, which are scored for their relative happiness, by people, using the Amazon Mechanical Turk service. Words such as 'joy' score highly, whilst words such as 'destruction' score lowly in the dictionary (see Figure 5.2).

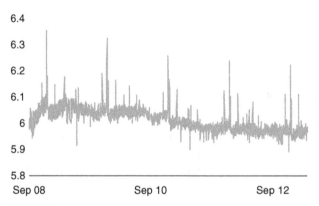

FIGURE 5.1 Structured dataset – Hedonometer Index.

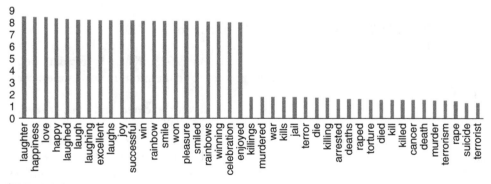

FIGURE 5.2 Scoring of words.

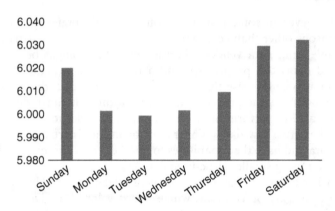

FIGURE 5.3   Days of the week – Hedonometer Index.

In Figure 5.3, we take an average score for each day of the week. Perhaps unsurprisingly, we see that people are least happy on Monday and their happiness rises throughout the week. We have shown this example to illustrate how despite the fact that unstructured big data (in this case extracted from Twitter) can be compromised of very large datasets, once structured, it is easier to make inferences about the data.

5.2.4   Is big data also alternative data?

Let us first consider what alternative data is in the context of financial markets. It is simplest to consider those datasets which are not commonly used in finance. Admittedly, in the years ahead, the datasets which we currently consider as 'alternative' are likely to become more mainstream and newer datasets may appear in alternative data space. Importantly, alternative data need not always consist of big data. An alternative dataset could actually be relatively small in the order of megabytes as opposed to gigabytes/terabytes or petabytes, which we tend to associate with big data. Indeed, it may be possible to even store the whole raw alternative dataset in an Excel spreadsheet, which is certainly not the case with big data.

5.2.4.1   Where Is All This Data Coming From?   According to IDC (2017), in 2016 around 16.3 ZB of data were being generated globally, which equates to around 1.5 GB per person per day. IDC forecast this to rise to 163 ZB in 2025. Where is this data being generated? In its report it breaks down the sources for data into three categories: core, edge and endpoint.

The core relates to datacentres including those on the cloud and enterprise networks. The edge is comprised of servers outside of their datacentres. The endpoint encompasses everything at the edge of a network, which includes PCs as well as other devices such as phones, connected cars, sensors and so on. Many of these data sources in the edge are, of course, new devices. Many devices at the endpoint are IoT devices (Internet of Things). The report estimates that the majority of data is actually created in the endpoint, with the rest split between the core and edge areas. A large amount of this data is in unstructured form.

The pace of storage technology has not kept up with how fast we are generating data. As a result, large amounts of data are not stored. In many cases, we can avoid storing data in multiple places. Take, for example, the streaming of music or video content – typically it is consumed by users and not stored locally, given it can be streamed again from copies on the cloud at any point. There might be other instances where data is not stored in any place at all and is simply lost once it has been consumed.

5.2.4.2 Monetizing Datasets and the Exhaust We have discussed on a broad basis the areas where data is generated. In this section, we give examples of how datasets can be monetized by selling to traders. We also discuss the idea of 'exhaust data', which can be the source of alternative datasets which are used by traders.

Data usually has a primary usage. Consider a financial exchange. As part of its everyday business, it generates a large amount of market data, which is generated by market participants using the exchange. This can be both from quotes posted and actual executions between market participants. Clearly, this market data is important for the exchange to function.

Whilst trading fees can make up a large part of the income for an exchange, they can generate additional income by selling their data feeds. If market participants want a very granular feed with market-depth data, they will pay more than those simply wanting to receive daily closing quotes. Exchanges can also store all the data generated and sell the history for quants to use in their backtesting of models.

What about an example outside of finance? Let's return to our media content example. If we consider video data, such as movies or TV, it is primarily generated for consumers to watch as entertainment. The same is true of music content. These might seem like obvious statements. However, we might be able to use this dataset for other purposes. For example, they might be able to do speech recognition on movies to generate subtitles and then perhaps natural language processing to identify the sentiment of a movie, to help classify it.

A media streaming company is also likely to collect secondary data, which is a by-product of users listening to music or watching TV. What songs and video are they streaming, at what time and from what location? There are countless data points we could collect. Once all the datasets are properly aligned, which in itself can be a time-consuming process, the media streaming company can answer many questions to help personalize the experience for each user. Recommendations about what to watch will obviously vary considerably between users. However, there are other uses of this so-called 'exhaust data' which is generated by companies as part of their everyday business. In practice, it can often be the case that data is collected before its full utility is understood. This can be the case in multiple domains, not purely in finance.

In our earlier financial example, we noted that exchanges monetize their datasets by selling them to financial market participants, which seems like a very direct use case. Corporates can also monetize their datasets by selling them to traders to help them make better trading decisions. However, before doing so they need to be aware of the legal issues associated with doing this.

5.2.5 Legal questions around distributing alternative datasets

5.2.5.1 Personal Data In our example about a media streaming company, we noted that one of the uses of 'exhaust data' was to help personalize the experience of individual users. However, if a company wishes to distribute such data to traders, it needs to consider several legal questions, in particular its adherence to various data protection terms. Do the legal terms of its agreement with users allow this, and what is the format in which the data can be distributed? For example, very often the company will need to anonymize the dataset. Sometimes simply blanking out personal details might not be sufficient. Consider a social network. Even if a user's real name is not available, it is possible to infer a lot of details about an individual by who they are connected to. It might also be possible to combine this with linguistic analysis to identify individuals.

In practice, traders do not need or require the identity of individuals from data to use in their trading strategies. Companies can also aggregate the raw data into a more structured form before distributing.

5.2.5.2   Alternative Datasets and Non-Public Information   Alternative datasets are 'alternative' because they are not in as common use as traditional datasets are within finance such as price data. We might conjecture that if certain alternative datasets have some specific tradable value, if fewer market are participants using them there could be more of an edge. This is particularly the case when there might be limited capacity on a strategy. One example from a macro viewpoint could be a dataset which helps us better predict economic data releases and enables us to trade around these actual data releases. For liquidity reasons, such trading strategies have a relatively small capacity.

If a company is distributing data exclusively about itself to a single client, which no one else can buy, is there a risk that it is giving out 'material, non-public information'? This obviously depends on the nature of the dataset. One way to alleviate this can be if the data is aggregated in some form and in such a way that any sensitive information cannot be reverse engineered from it. Fortado et al. (2017) note that certain funds prefer not to deal with exclusive datasets for this reason.

We could argue that if a third party is collecting information about a specific company, a process which others could potentially replicate, this is much less of a risk, particularly if the source is public information available on the web. Traders of macro assets typically are more interested in broader-based macro modelling as opposed to data on specific companies. There is, of course, still potential for 'material non-public information' in macro markets, such as through leaks in economic data releases or decisions by central banks.

5.2.6   How much is an alternative dataset worth?

The marketplace for data is not new. Data about financial markets has been sold and distributed for centuries in many forms, even if the way it is distributed has changed from paper, such as in newspapers, to electronic methods, over the various public and private networks. In many cases, there might be multiple vendors distributing similar price datasets, which can aid price discovery.

However, by definition, as we have mentioned, alternative datasets are much less commoditized than most price datasets. Even the most 'common' alternative datasets such as machine-readable news, which are distributed by multiple vendors, are still far less common than price datasets. Furthermore, even here there is variation between the machine-readable news datasets in how they are structured and also the raw data sources which are used.

For some alternative datasets, there could potentially be only a single vendor who sells that specific data. As discussed earlier, it is also possible for funds to be exclusive users of a specific alternative dataset, which would likely raise the price of the dataset.

The question for any trader, whether macro or otherwise, is how much is an alternative dataset worth? Equally, for sellers of such datasets, what price point should they pitch? It is difficult for both parties. A trader for obvious reasons is not obliged to say precisely how they use a dataset to a vendor. However, without such information it is difficult for a vendor to know how valuable a dataset is to a trader (and hence how much they should charge).

Clearly, traders need to consider how useful the dataset is to understand how much they are willing to pay for it. Just because a dataset is considered 'alternative' does not necessarily mean that it is worth millions of dollars. The amount of history in a dataset can help determine its price. Without any history, it becomes very difficult to do any historical backtesting on an alternative dataset to understand how useful it is. Unfortunately, given that alternative datasets are often newer (and in some cases collected using totally new techniques), their history can be much smaller than more traditional datasets. More generally, as with any dataset, the quality of the data is very important. If the dataset is messy and has many missing values, it could reduce its utility.

When considering the value of an alternative dataset, we also need to be able to quantify how much it might improve our strategy. If the effect of the alternative dataset is marginal on a backtest, then it might not be worth buying, particularly if we cannot offset the initial cost of purchasing it.

There is also the question of economies of scale when using data. A larger fund may find it easier to absorb the costs of data. Whilst a dataset cost is often related to the number of users, the additional cost might be proportionally less than the amount of capital a larger firm can run on a strategy related to that dataset.

We need to ask whether the dataset will be used only for very specific and very low-capacity strategies, or whether it can be used in multiple trading strategies. A larger fund is likely not as interested in data which is only useful in lower-capacity strategies, compared with a small-scale trading operation. In effect, here it is advantageous to be a smaller trader. More broadly, the value of data is unlikely to be the same for different traders. From my experience, I have found very different feedback on the use of exactly the same alternative datasets from multiple funds. There can be many reasons for this, in terms of asset classes traded and also the varying approaches used in actually contrasting a trading strategy.

The costs of an alternative dataset should not be measured purely in financial terms of buying a licence to use it, there is also the cost of evaluating the dataset and developing strategies around it. A dataset is worthless without the resources to consume it. Hence, we need to consider whether this alternative dataset is worth investigating versus other priorities. Very often, large quant hedge funds are regularly approached by data vendors with new datasets. It is difficult to evaluate every single dataset offered in a full fashion, even for very large funds.

5.3   TRADITIONAL MODEL BUILDING APPROACHES AND MACHINE LEARNING

Traditionally, when developing a trading strategy or indeed any sort of forecast, we try to find a hypothesis first. We can then validate (or indeed invalidate) our hypothesis using statistical analysis. The rationale is that this exercise can help to reduce the like-lihood of data mining. We are essentially pruning our search space to (hopefully) only the areas which we think are relevant.

5.3.1   What is machine learning?

The idea of machine learning techniques is that we don't need to know the form of the relationship between variables beforehand. This contrasts to linear regression, for example, where we are already assuming a certain type of relationship between vari-ables (or features, to use machine learning terminology). Instead, our machine learning algorithm can help us model the function, even if it is highly nonlinear. This will enable us to find relationships between variables we have not already thought of, particularly if we use techniques from machine learning.

5.3.2   Difference between traditional machine learning and deep learning

With traditional machine learning, we define a set of features and then allow the algorithm to find the appropriate function. However, in some instances, it is very difficult to hand craft features which are likely to be relevant. Take the case where we are trying to identify an object in an image. Easy-to-define features, such as taking the average brightness or colour of all the pixels in an image, are unlikely to give us any useful information for gauging what object is in an image. Deep learning techniques instead try to extract the features without having to define them. Deep learning techniques have become very successful for certain areas such as image classification. For deep learning to be effective, it requires the availability of large amounts of training data.

5.3.2.1   Supervised, Unsupervised and Reinforcement Learning   Machine learning relies on training to identify patterns. This usually requires a training set. In supervised learning, we provide a training set which has been labelled in pairs. It can be time consuming to manually label data and this can limit the size of the training set we use. With unsupervised learning, we have unlabelled training data and the algorithm is designed to infer patterns from the training data without 'hints'. As a result, it can be easier to use much larger datasets, given that we do not have the constraints associated with labelling data. Deep learning often uses unsupervised learning. Reinforcement learning is a different approach. Here, we create a simple set of rules that our algorithm can follow, which is designed to maximize a reward function. This has been used successfully in the field of games. In this situation, the reward function could be defined as winning a game against an opponent. Reinforcement learning lets a computer teach itself the best approach to solve a problem. In the example of games, it may end up playing in a way very different from that of a human player. DeepMind has used

reinforcement learning extensively in the field of games. DeepMind's AlphaZero learnt how to play chess using reinforcement learning and managed to beat the world's best chess playing computer, Stockfish 8 (Gibbs 2017).

5.3.2.2 Should We Use Machine Learning to Develop Trading Strategies? It could be argued that with very large datasets, we might try to let the data 'talk' using machine learning techniques. The difficulty, however, is that we might end up finding patterns in what is essentially noise. Furthermore, the nature of financial problems is not stable. Financial time series are non-stationary. Markets experience changing regimes. The market in 2008 was very different to the market in 2016, for example. This contrasts to other situations in areas where machine learning has been successful, where the problems do not change over time, such as image classification or playing games.

In practice, identifying and constructing the important factors (or features, to use the terminology from machine learning) is still a key part of developing trading strategies. However, we believe that techniques from machine learning are still useful for trading, it is just that we must apply a cautious approach when using machine learning in developing trading strategies.

There is also the case that if we are running a black box trading model, we might simply have to turn off the model when it starts losing money if we cannot understand what it is doing. There are ways we can try to alleviate the problem of model interpretability. One way is to create a simpler linear model to proxy a machine learning trading rule, which might make it easier to understand how changing inputs affect our trade.

To avoid the issues around non-stationary financial time series, we can instead apply machine learning in our trading problem, not purely focusing on forecasting the time series of the asset itself. After all, creating a trading strategy is not purely about defining the signal; we also need to pre-process and clean the dataset before constructing any actual trading rule. In our discussion about the effectiveness of machine learning in trading, we would draw the distinction between the various areas. Domains such as high-frequency trading have very large datasets and as such could be more amenable to machine learning techniques (Dixon et al. 2017). Machine learning, in particular deep learning, has also been used to improve the performance of longer-term equity factor models (Alberg and Lipton 2017).

Pre-processing can also involve classifying parts of the dataset, applying techniques such as sentiment analysis or topic identification of text. In these instances, we would suggest that machine learning could be a useful technique.

5.4 BIG DATA AND ALTERNATIVE DATA: BROAD-BASED USAGE IN MACRO-BASED TRADING

5.4.1 How do we use big data and alternative data in a macro context?

What are the general approaches we can use to make sense of big data and alternative data more broadly for macro traders? Here, we give a few ideas of where to start.

5.4.1.1 Improve Nowcasts/Economic Forecasts There are many different unusual datasets we might wish to use to improve our forecasts for the monthly change in nonfarm payrolls. If we have a sufficiently good forecast of this number we can trade around this number on an intraday basis. We might also seek to get a real-time estimate that can be generated throughout the month to aid our trading strategy. Obviously, this approach can be replicated for other economic releases, aside from nonfarm payrolls. We might also seek to use alternative datasets to improve longer-run economic forecasts or there can be alternative datasets which directly give us a forecast, which may be useful for broader-based investing. We can also trade on a short-term basis, around economic data releases, if we can generate reasonable forecasts.

5.4.1.2 Market Positioning and Sentiment for Assets A key part of trading is to understand what the rest of the market is thinking and in particular how they are positioned. If the market is very heavily long, it can sometimes increase the chances of a short squeeze, for example. There is potential to use alternative datasets to help model these factors. We could use alpha capture data, which we discuss later, to gauge market positioning, and also combine this with proprietary flow indicators from market makers.

5.4.1.3 Improving Volatility Estimates It is possible to show that there is a reasonable relationship between market volatility and the volume of news, whether it is derived from more traditional sources such as newswires or newer sources such as social media. Hence, we can use enhance volatility forecasts through the use of volume data related to news and social media.

5.4.2 Real-life examples of big data and alternative datasets

In this section, we build upon the generalized cases described earlier. We list a few examples of big data and alternative data, which could be relevant for traders. Later, we describe structured datasets suitable for financial applications, which can be considered as alternative data. These datasets are often available both for human traders and in machine-readable form. Typically, this machine-readable data can be distributed in via APIs for real-time ingestion by computers or on a lower-frequency basis (for example end of day) in flat files, which is more suitable for longer-term investors.

5.4.2.1 Big Data
5.4.2.1.1 High-Frequency Market Data Market data is disseminated from exchanges, trading platforms and market makers. As well as top of book data, which gives quotes for smaller trade sizes and also executed trade data, more granular data, such as market depth, can be available. Traders can use the market depth data to calculate metrics such as market imbalance and its skew, which can be used to shed insights into high-frequency price action.

5.4.2.1.2 Web Content On a broad basis, content from the web is unstructured. If we scrape data from the web, it will often be in an unstructured form. It is then necessary to clean the dataset and also classify it, creating additional metadata to describe it. Web content can be made up of many different forms, including text, video and audio. We can also have exhaust data derived from web content, such as page views.

5.4.2.1.3 Social Media Many forms of social media are available for machine-readable parsing, such as Twitter, which is available via Twitter's Gnip feed. The format of this text, however, can be particularly difficult for a computer to understand. Not only is the text typically much shorter than that from a news article, it can be difficult to understand the veracity of the text. Interpreting the sentiment of such text can be tricky, given the use of abbreviations and sarcasm. There are also issues of understanding the context of tweets. One way to help understand context is to combine with other similar sources such as machine-readable news.

Breaking news can sometimes be on Twitter before it is reported on newswires and before an impact is felt on markets. Hence, it has become an important source of news in its own right. One particular example was seen during the earlier days of President Trump's office, when he would often tweet about companies. Indeed, apps have been created specifically to flag when such tweets were sent by him (Turner 2017). As a result of Twitter's importance in breaking news, some newswires, such as Bloomberg News (BN), also directly report important tweets in their feed.

5.4.2.1.4 Mobile Phone Data Tracking data associated with mobile phones is available from various vendors. On an aggregate level this data can be used to map flows of people. We could use this to model the foot flow through shops, for example, to help estimate retail sales data. We can also use such data to understand employment levels if we consider the overall foot flow in and out of rail stations during the rush hour, or the volume of cars on the roads during these periods.

5.4.2.2 More Specific Datasets

5.4.2.2.1 Newswires News articles generated by newswires are primarily output for human readership. BN articles are typically designed to be used for consumption by Bloomberg Terminal users. However, Bloomberg also provides this news in a machine-readable form, with considerable amounts of additional metadata, including topic classification. Other newswires such as Thomson Reuters and Dow Jones (via RavenPack) offer machine-readable news. News datasets can be used to assess market sentiment, both in terms of broader economic sentiment and around specific assets.

5.4.2.2.2 Alpha Capture One of the most well-known alpha capture datasets is aggregated by TIM Group, an independent trade ideas network. Essentially this involves collecting together broker trade recommendations in a systematic manner. Many hedge funds also use alpha capture-based strategies in their portfolios, in particular for single stocks. They are also used to a lesser extent in macro asset classes. Alpha capture datasets can be followed by investors in a systematic manner. They can also be used to give indications of market positioning. For example, if many brokers are recommending the purchase of a specific bond, this suggests that positioning is quite heavily long in that asset.

5.4.2.2.3 Forecasts and Nowcasts Forecasts have long been available for market participants. Historically, the sources of these forecasts have usually been the research teams of sell-side brokers, which are then aggregated by data vendors such as Bloomberg.

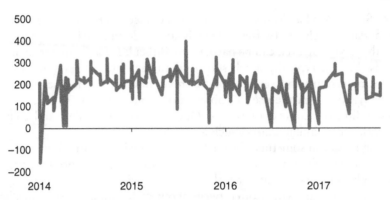

FIGURE 5.4 Bloomberg nonfarm payrolls chart.

However, many forecasts now available have been crowdsourced from both the sell side and individual investors.

Bloomberg publishes a forecast based on estimates provided by individuals on Twitter (see Figure 5.4) for the monthly change in US nonfarm payrolls, which is one of the most important economic data releases in a month. Later, in a case study, we present a forecast for payrolls based on several variables, including one derived from tweets.

Estimize crowdsources forecasts for equity earnings numbers and economic releases. Alpha capture datasets involve collecting together trade recommendations from sell-side brokers into an easily navigable dataset.

There are many vendors providing satellite photography, such as Orbital Insights. This can be used by commodity traders to estimate current oil storage levels in silos or crop yields, for example.

5.4.2.2.4 Web Content Whilst it is possible to directly scrape content from the web, there are several datasets of specific web content which can be downloaded in easier-to-use formats. One of the most well known of these is the Wikipedia corpus. The entire dataset is available for downloading and analysis. Furthermore, readership statistics are available, which can shed insights into what are hot topics. Another way to view the popularity of topics is through Google Trends. This gives statistics on the relative volume for specific search terms over time.

5.4.2.2.5 Social Media We noted that broadly, social media can present challenges, in particular because of the length of messages. There are many financial data vendors that offer their own structured datasets derived from Twitter, tagging messages for their topics and sometimes with sentiment. These vendors include Dataminr, Knowsis, Bloomberg and Thomson Reuters, amongst many others.

There are also social media networks specifically for financial applications, such as StockTwits, which has around 1.5 million active users (Roof 2016), which is also available in machine-readable form.

5.5 CASE STUDIES: DIGGING DEEPER INTO MACRO TRADING WITH BIG DATA AND ALTERNATIVE DATA

We have given many broad-based examples on various datasets and a quick summary of how they could be used by macro traders. In this section, we dig deeper into the subject, giving brief case studies on each of them.

5.5.1 Federal reserve: Cuemacro federal reserve sentiment index for FX and bonds

From an intuitive perspective, it seems reasonable to expect that Federal Reserve communications impact macros. In particular, we note significant volatility around Federal Open Market Committee (FOMC) meetings. However, it is more difficult to quantify the impact on markets. Cuemacro's Federal Reserve sentiment index attempts to quantify the communications in a systematic manner.

The raw input data consists of text extracted from Federal Reserve communications, which is of a relatively small size. It is then structured into a tabular data format. This includes speeches, statements and minutes released by the Federal Reserve. Metadata is then derived from this text, such as sentiment scores, which are generated using natural language processing.

These sentiment scores are aggregated into a time series to represent an index which tracks the overall sentiment of the Federal Reserve over time. The idea isn't so much to create an index, which is traded at high frequency – for example, only around FOMC announcements – instead it is designed to give a representative view of Fed sentiment over recent weeks.

This time series can then be more easily used by traders particularly to understand moves in FX or bond markets. In Figure 5.5, we plot 1M changes in US Treasury

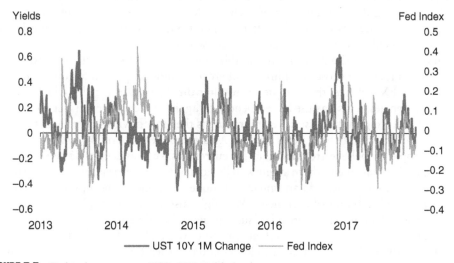

FIGURE 5.5 Fed index vs recent USD 10Y yield changes.

10Y yields against the sentiment index. We note that stylistically there is a strong relationship between both the time series. Furthermore, if we regress them against each other, the T statistic is around 2, which suggests this relationship is significant. We note that there are of course some divergences in the index, which is intuitive, given the Fed is not always the key driver of the US Treasury curve. One such example can be seen in November 2017, when yields moved higher following the election of Donald Trump rather than any specific changes in Fed policy.

5.5.2   Machine-readable news: Bloomberg news to understand price action in FX

The various newswires produce a large amount of news daily. The notion that news is an important facet of what moves markets is not new. After all, human traders follow news as part of their decision-making process, attempting to extract the signal from the noise within news. However, it is extremely difficult for a human to read all this news on a daily basis; in practice, a human will be able to read only a small snapshot. Hence, it seems reasonable to ask whether this news reading process can be automated in some way, to help shed insight on markets.

In our case study, which is based upon results from Amen (2018), we examine articles from the BN newswire from 2009 to 2017. Whilst BN is typically consumed by users of the Bloomberg Terminal, it is also available in a machine-readable form, making it amenable as an input into systematic trading strategies.

The focus of our case study is on understanding whether this news dataset can be used to trade developed market FX crosses. In particular, the idea is to develop a daily trading rule rather than a high-frequency trading rule, which makes trading decisions after a single news article.

The dataset is already structured, which helps make the analysis somewhat easier. However, we still need to do a small amount of cleaning of the body text of each news article, removing the start and end of each article, which have the names and contact details of the journalists writing the article. In addition, we reduce the size of the dataset by removing fields which we are not going to use later.

In order to make the dataset more usable, we need to prune which news articles to examine and focus on those we think are likely to be most impactful for our asset class (in our case, FX). Hence, the next step is to filter the dataset for articles which refer to specific currencies. This has the added benefit of again reducing the dataset size.

Whilst filtering for the assets we are trading is the most obvious approach, there are equally valid ways of filtering news articles. An alternative way could have been to filter for news topic we believe are important for currencies, such as economic news for each country. In these instances, there might well be no mention of currencies in these articles. However, economic news has an impact on monetary policy expectations, which is a key part of the behaviour of currencies. We might also choose to read news relating to other factors which impact currencies, such as geopolitical news.

Natural language processing is then applied to these filtered articles to create sentiment scores for each filtered news article. As noted earlier, the objective of our analysis is to assess sentiment for a large number of news articles rather than attempting to do high-frequency trades immediately after each article. Hence, these sentiment scores are then aggregated into daily normalized scores for each currency. Using individual

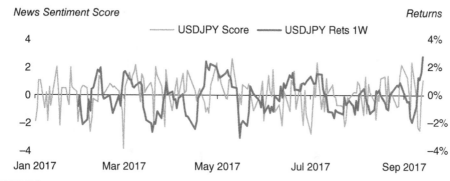

FIGURE 5.6 USD/JPY Bloomberg score.

currency scores, we can then generate daily scores for currency pairs. For example, the score for USD/JPY is simply USD score – JPY score (see Figure 5.6).

Our trading rule is based upon the short-term momentum. It is based on the premise that in the short term, 'good' news about an asset is likely to impact an asset in a positive fashion. Hence, we buy a currency pair if its news score is positive. Conversely, we sell a currency pair if it has a negative score. Potentially, there can be other approaches for deriving signals from news. In particular, we could have attempted to apply much longer-term windows for assessing news and then used mean reversion-based trading rules. The rationale is that over very long periods, if news is persistently 'good', the market will adjust expectations to it. We might expect a similar effect with continually poor news.

In Figure 5.7, we show the historical returns for a basket of developed market currencies against USD. Both transaction costs and carry are included. We plot the returns versus a generic trend-following model in FX. We have chosen trend, given it is typically one of the strategies that is used by traders to trade FX. Amen (2013) discusses how trend- and carry-based strategies can be used to explain a large amount of FX fund returns. Hence, generic trend and carry strategies can be considered as proxies for beta in FX.

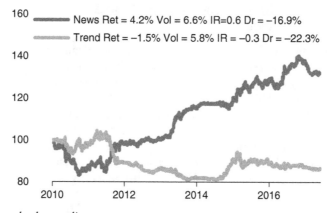

FIGURE 5.7 News basket trading returns.

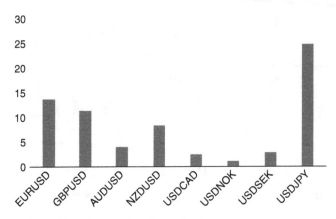

FIGURE 5.8 Regressing news volume vs implied volatility.

We find that our news-based strategy outperforms trend on a risk adjusted basis over this period. Furthermore, there is little correlation between the two strategies. This suggests a news-basis strategy can be used to diversify the returns of a typical FX fund manager.

Whilst it is possible to extract a directional signal from gauging the sentiment of machine-readable news, the volume of news can also be useful in itself for other reasons. In Figure 5.8, we plot the T statistics of the linear regressions between implied volatilities in various crosses alongside news volume related to those currencies. We see that there is very often a statistically significant positive correlation between implied volatility and news volume. This suggests that we can use news volume as an input to model implied volatility.

There are many further results in Amen (2018). The paper also discusses how news before European Central Bank (ECB) and FOMC meetings can be used to estimate the behaviour of FX volatility around these data points. The volume of news linked to FOMC and ECB statements have a strong impact on short-term FX volatility.

5.5.3 Web traffic data: Using investopedia's anxiety index to understand market sentiment

Investopedia is a financial education website. Can we glean anything from the topics users search for on Investopedia? The principle behind its Anxiety Index is to track search terms made by users, which results in Investopedia page views. It focuses on those search terms related to investor anxiety, such as 'short selling'. In total there are 12 different URLs referenced in the final index, which typically have high page view counts (Kenton 2017). In Figure 5.9, we plot the Investopedia Anxiety Index (IAI) against VIX, which is often referred to as the 'Wall Street Fear Gauge'. We note that when VIX rises, indicating options are becoming more expensive, we see a rise in investor anxiety as indicated by IAI. Conversely, falls in VIX are also generally accompanied by declines in investor anxiety. These observations seem intuitive, namely that option prices are related to investor anxiety.

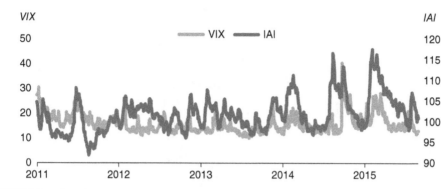

FIGURE 5.9 Plot of VIX versus IAI.

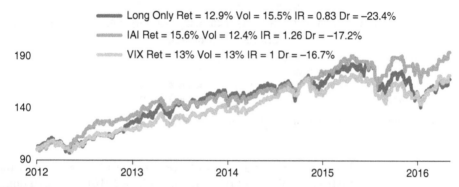

FIGURE 5.10 Trading S&P 500 using IAI based rule vs VIX and long only.

Amen (2016) discusses how IAI can be used to create an active trading rule on the S&P 500. In Figure 5.10, we present the returns from this paper for an active trading rule for S&P 500 futures based upon IAI and compare it to one using VIX, and also long only the S&P 500. Essentially, when IAI is high, we are flat S&P 500 and long otherwise. We apply a similar rule for VIX. We find that risk adjusted returns in our sample are highest for the IAI filtered strategy, improving upon those from the VIX filtered strategy. The lowest risk adjusted returns are from a long-only strategy.

5.5.4   Volatility data: Forecasting FX spot behaviour around scheduled events with a focus on BREXIT

As a dataset, volatility data is not especially unusual; after all, FX options have been trading for several decades. However, perhaps less common is the use of volatility data to inform the behaviour of spot around scheduled data events. In particular, we can infer from the volatility surface before an event the implied distribution of spot. Clark and Amen (2017) discuss how the GBP/USD volatility surface could be used to infer distributions of spot over the subsequent Brexit vote on 23 June 2016.

They originally estimated, based on their visual observation of implied probability densities available up to 13 June 2016, extracted from GBP/USD implied volatility

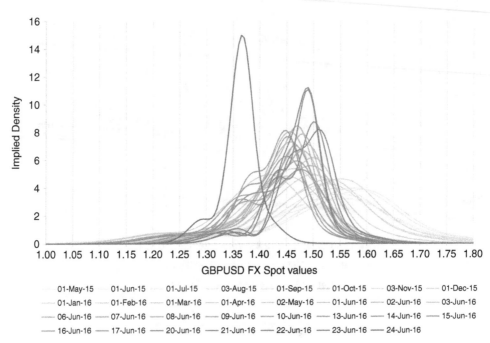

FIGURE 5.11 Implied distribution of GBP/USD around Brexit.

surface, that the market expected that a vote to leave could result in a move in the GBP/USD exchange rate from 1.4390 (spot reference on 10 June 2016) down to a range in 1.10–1.30, i.e. a 10–25% decline – very probably with highly volatile price action. In Figure 5.11, we present the implied probability distributions of GBP/USD on a number of dates preceding the Brexit vote.

They also constructed a mixture model related to two scenarios for the GBP/USD exchange rate after the referendum vote, one scenario for 'remain' and one for 'leave'. Calibrating this model to four months of market data, from 24 February to 22 June 2016, we find that a 'leave' vote was associated with a predicted devaluation of the British pound to approximately 1.37 USD per GBP, a 4.5% devaluation, and quite consistent with the observed post-referendum exchange rate move down from 1.4877 to 1.3622.

5.6 CONCLUSION

We have discussed the general characteristics of big data, namely the 4Vs. In addition, we have talked about the differences between structured and unstructured data, and how most of the data generated is in an unstructured form.

We noted how the data being generated is growing rapidly and is forecast to increase further. Large amounts of data are collected by companies as part of their everyday business, so-called 'exhaust data'. These datasets can be monetized by selling to traders.

Machine learning can be used to find patterns in large datasets. We wrote about the various forms of machine learning and also where they could be used within the trading process. We then spent time discussing the various types of big data and alternative data, which could be relevant for financial market participants.

Lastly, we dug into more detail, presenting several case studies for macro-based traders using alternative datasets, including the use of machine-readable news and web traffic data, as well as a novel technique on FX options data to infer the subsequent distribution of price action in spot.

REFERENCES

Alberg, J. and Lipton, Z.C. (2017). *Improving Factor-Based Quantitative Investing by Forecasting Company Fundamentals*. Retrieved from arxiv.org: https://arxiv.org/abs/1711.04837

Amen, S. (2013). *Beta'em Up: What is Market Beta in FX?* Retrieved from SSRN: https://papers.ssrn.com/sol3/papers.cfm?abstract_id=2439854

Amen, S. (2016). *Trading Anxiety – Using Investopedia's Proprietary Dataset to Trade Risk*. London: Cuemacro.

Amen, S. (2018). *Robo-News Reader*. London: Cuemacro.

Clark, I. and Amen, S. (2017). Implied Distributions from GBPUSD Risk-Reversals and Implication for Brexit Scenarios. Retrieved from MDPI: http://www.mdpi.com/2227-9091/5/3/35/pdf

Dixon, M.F., Polson, N.G. and Sokolov, V.O. (2017). Deep Learning for Spatio-Temporal Modeling: Dynamic Traffic Flows and High Frequency Trading. Retrieved from arxiv.org: https://arxiv.org/abs/1705.09851

Fortado, L., Wigglesworth, R. and Scannell, K. (2017). Hedge funds see a gold rush in data mining. Retrieved from FT: https://www.ft.com/content/d86ad460-8802-11e7-bf50-e1c239b45787

Gibbs, S. (2017). AlphaZero AI beats champion chess program after teaching itself in four hours. Retrieved from Guardian: https://www.theguardian.com/technology/2017/dec/07/alphazero-google-deepmind-ai-beats-champion-program-teaching-itself-to-play-four-hours

IDC. (2017). Data Age 2025. Retrieved from Seagate: https://www.seagate.com/files/www-content/our-story/trends/files/Seagate-WP-DataAge2025-March-2017.pdf

Kenton, W. (2017). The Investopedia Anxiety Index. Retrieved from Investopedia: https://www.investopedia.com/anxiety-index-explained

Roof, K. (2016). StockTwits raises funding, gets new CEO. Retrieved from Techcrunch: https://techcrunch.com/2016/07/06/stocktwits-raises-funding-gets-new-ceo

Turner, K. (2017). This app will notify you if Trump tweets about a company you're invested in. Retrieved from Washington Post: https://www.washingtonpost.com/news/the-switch/wp/2017/01/07/this-app-will-notify-you-if-trump-tweets-about-a-company-youre-invested-in/?utm_term=.2c6d2a89d135

Big Is Beautiful: How Email Receipt Data Can Help Predict Company Sales

Giuliano De Rossi, Jakub Kolodziej and Gurvinder Brar

6.1 INTRODUCTION

This chapter describes our experience working on a big data project. In this chapter our goal is twofold: 1. To assess the potential of electronic receipt data as a source of information, particularly to predict company sales in real time. 2. To document the challenges of dealing with such a large dataset and the solutions we adopted.

The dataset we employ in the analysis consists of a vast table that details the purchases made by a large sample of US consumers on the online platforms of a number of companies, including Amazon, Expedia and Domino's Pizza.

Consumer data organized in large panels is not a new phenomenon in economics and finance. For example, the University of Michigan's Panel Study of Income Dynamics (PSID) has followed 18 000 individuals (and their descendants) since 1968 by collecting responses to questionnaires at regular time intervals. The Quandl database, however, is very different from a 'longitudinal panel' in two respects.

First, the data is not collected with a view to building a representative sample. The individuals that opt in to the data sharing agreement with Quandl typically do so when they register to use the email productivity tools they have obtained from Quandl's partners. As a result, we know very little about the demographics, income and other characteristics of the sample. This may well introduce a bias if the sample is used to draw inferences about the overall population.

Second, the size of our sample and level of detail captured are completely different. Whereas the largest longitudinal panel can rely on around 25 000 individuals and biennial updates, our big data sample currently has more than 3 million active users that are sampled at weekly frequency. Longitudinal panels typically ask high-level questions about the amount spent by each family on food, leisure and other categories of expenditure. With big data it is possible to obtain the full detail on a product-by-product basis of the goods and services purchased by each user. Because the data is based on actual

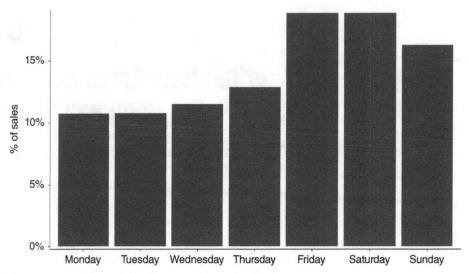

FIGURE 6.1   Domino's Pizza sales peak at weekends...
Source: Macquarie Research, Quandl, September 2017.

transactions, it is free from the potential inaccuracies and distortions typically observed in self-reported data. It is worth pointing out, however, that the history is very limited, i.e. unlike the cross-sectional dimension, the length of the time series is currently modest.

One of the main goals of our statistical analysis will be to mitigate the potential bias while exploiting the sheer size of the sample.

Examples of the type of analytics that can be produced from the Quandl database are given in Figures 6.1–6.5. Figure 6.1 displays the breakdown by day of the week of Domino's Pizza orders available from our sample. The weekend is clearly the most popular time for pizza lovers. Figure 6.2 focuses on the time of the day when orders are placed, showing a distinct peak at lunchtime (between 12 p.m. and 2 p.m.) and a noticeable reduction in booking activity at night. The picture also shows that we are able to break down sales by pizza size, suggesting that the medium size dominates consistently. Figure 6.3 plots the frequency of the top 30 ingredients we identified from the orders placed in our sample. To our surprise, we found that the most requested ingredient by far (after cheese and tomato) is pepperoni. Bacon also turns out to be unexpectedly popular in the data.

The time pattern is completely different for an e-commerce firm like Amazon. Figure 6.4 shows that the number of Amazon orders placed by users in our sample declines steadily from Monday until Saturday. If we plot the intraday pattern for each day of the week (Figure 6.5) we can see that Sunday is consistently the quietest day of the week for Amazon e-commerce until about 10 a.m. Later in the day, Sunday orders grow faster than orders placed on weekdays and continue to grow even in the

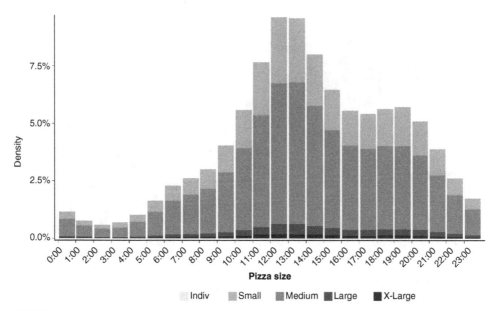

FIGURE 6.2   ...and at lunchtime.
Source: Macquarie Research, Quandl, September 2017.

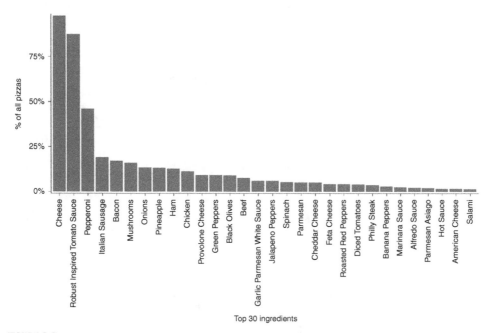

FIGURE 6.3   Most popular pizza toppings: the pepperoni effect.
Source: Macquarie Research, Quandl, September 2017.

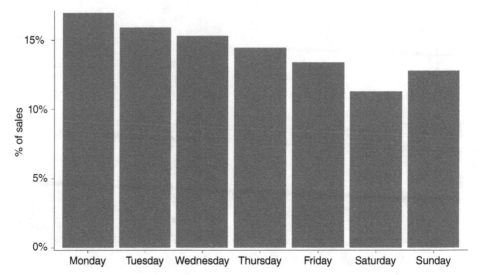

FIGURE 6.4   Amazon customers prefer Mondays...
Source: Macquarie Research, Quandl, September 2017.

afternoon when other days display a decline. By 10 p.m. Sunday ranks as the third busiest day of the week.

These examples illustrate some of the important features of the Quandl database. The granularity of the information, down to the level of individual products, is remarkable. In addition, the fact that orders are collected with timestamps ensures that data trends can be captured at higher frequencies than was previously possible and in real time. It is also worth mentioning that although we do not pursue this idea here, it is

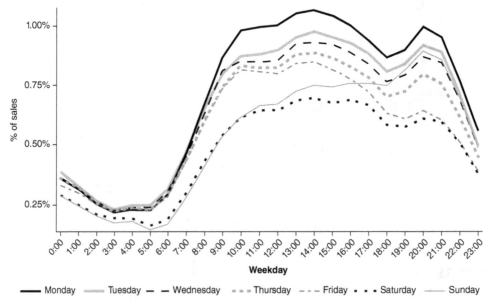

FIGURE 6.5   ...and take it easy at the weekend.

possible to use the data to infer data patterns across different companies. An example would be to check whether customers tend to substitute Domino's products with those of its competitors or tend to spread their spending on restaurants in roughly constant proportions across alternative providers. It would also be possible to cluster sample participants based on their purchases (e.g. big spenders versus small spenders) and analyze any difference in data patterns between the clusters, which may identify early adopters.

6.2   QUANDL'S EMAIL RECEIPTS DATABASE

6.2.1   Processing electronic receipts

We start by describing the structure of the Quandl dataset which will be analyzed in the report. The dataset relies on a large sample of US consumers who agreed to share information on their online purchases with Quandl's partners. Typically, they opt in to this data sharing agreement when installing an email productivity enhancement application.

Our data provider is thus able to scan on a weekly basis the inboxes of all active sample participants in order to identify any electronic receipts they may have received from a number of participating online merchants (e.g. Amazon, Walmart, H&M). Figure 6.6 illustrates the process: the electronic receipt (shown on the left-hand side) is scanned and transformed into a series of records, one for each individual product purchased. In our example, three distinct products were purchased but the total number of items is equal to four because the order included two units of the line tracking sensor. In the database, this is represented by three rows as shown on the right-hand side of Figure 6.6. The data is delivered on Tuesdays with an eight-day lag (i.e. it covers the period until the previous Monday).

Needless to say, each user is anonymized in the sense that we only observe a permanent id and all information on names, email addresses and payment methods is discarded. The user id can be used to query a separate table which contains additional information such as zip code, dates when the user entered and exited the sample, the

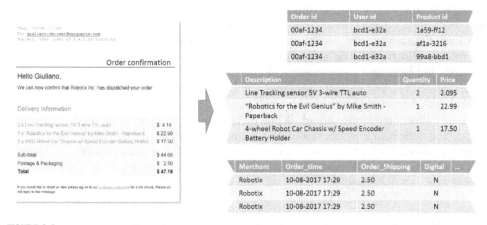

FIGURE 6.6   How an email receipt is turned into purchase records.
Source: Macquarie Research, Quandl, September 2017. For illustrative purposes only.
The actual Quandl data table comprises 50 fields, most of which are not shown in the figure.

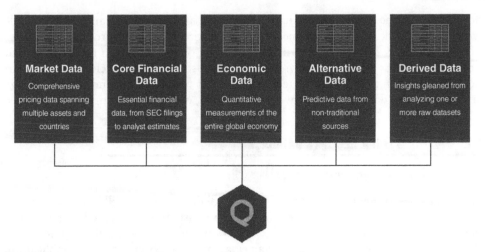

FIGURE 6.7   The structure of Quandl's data offering.
Source: Quandl, September 2017.

date of his or her last purchase and so on. It is worth emphasizing that the user id is unique and permanent and therefore it is possible to reconstruct the purchase history of each individual user across different platforms (e.g. items ordered on Amazon, Tiffany and Walmart) and over time.

The table in Figure 6.6 displays a small subset of the fields that are actually provided by Quandl. These include permanent identifiers for the order, the product and the user each record refers to. We are also given a description of each product, quantity, price and many potentially useful additional fields such as tax, delivery cost, discounts and so on. Some of the fields refer to a specific product (e.g. price, description) while others like shipping costs and timestamp refer to the order as a whole.

The e-commerce receipts database we used for our analysis is one of the *alternative data* products offered by Quandl (Figure 6.7). The product range covers, in addition to consumer data, data sourced from IoT devices, agricultural data from sensors in crop and fields, data on logistics and construction activity.

Each time a new user joins the sample, Quandl's partners scan their inbox looking for receipts that are still available in saved emails. For example, if a user joins in September 2017 but her email account retains Expedia receipts going back to September 2007, then those 10 years of Expedia bookings will be immediately added to the database. As a result, the database does contain a small number of transactions that occurred before the data collection exercise began. While there is no obvious reason to believe that this backfilling approach introduces a bias, it is true that backfilled observations would not have been available had we used the data in real time. As we detail below, for this reason we decide to concentrate on the transactions that were recorded while the user was actually part of the sample.

6.2.2   The sample

Figure 6.8 displays the total number of users that were active in the sample over time, i.e. those whose inbox was accessible to the tools deployed by Quandl's partners. As

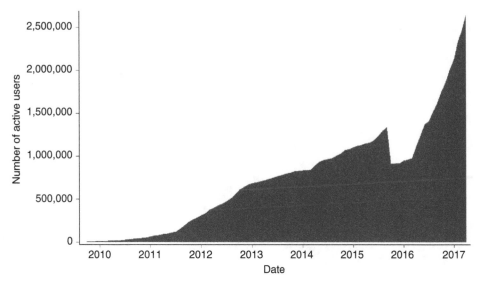

FIGURE 6.8   Sample size over time.
Source: Macquarie Research, Quandl, September 2017.

mentioned above, new users join the sample when individuals opt in to the data sharing agreement while some of the existing users drop off when their inboxes are no longer accessible. The data shows a sharp drop in the sample size at the end of 2015 when one of Quandl's partners withdrew. For the remainder of the sample period, size has grown consistently, with a notable acceleration in mid-2016. The total number of unique users that make up the database is close to 4.7 million.

For our analysis we have access to data on the receipts issued by three companies: Amazon, Domino's Pizza and Expedia. Moreover, the dataset available to us ends in April 2017.

We mentioned that all users in our sample are located in the US. Figure 6.9 is a graphical illustration of their distribution (using the delivery postcode if available, otherwise the billing postcode) on the US territory as of April 2017. Darker colours correspond to zip code areas with larger numbers of users. The map shows a strong concentration around large urban areas around cities like Los Angeles, San Francisco, Houston, and New York.

In order to put these figures in context, we display in Figure 6.10 the number of users as a percentage of the population of each US state (excluding Alaska and Hawaii) as of April 2017. Overall, the database tracked roughly 2.5 million users while the US population was approximately 325 million (a 0.77% ratio). Most states display a coverage ratio around that value, which indicates that our coverage is not concentrated on a few geographic areas. The extremes are Delaware (highest coverage) and New Mexico (lowest coverage).

By inspecting a number of Amazon transactions we were able to conclude that the majority of the *users* appear to be individuals or families. In a few cases, however, a *user* seemed to place orders on behalf of a much larger group. In one case we processed a purchase of 500 microcontrollers (with as many cases and electric adaptors) at the same time, which suggested that the order was placed on behalf of a school.

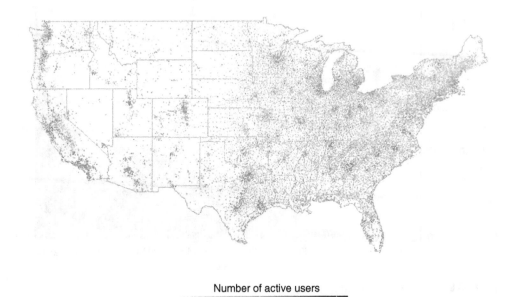

Number of active users

1   100   10,000

FIGURE 6.9 Geographic distribution as of April 2017.
Source: Macquarie Research, Quandl, September 2017.

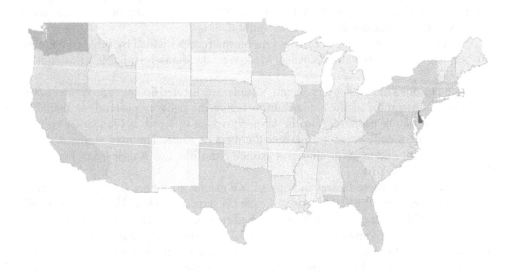

Users as % of population

0.50%   0.75%   1.00%   1.25%

FIGURE 6.10 Coverage of US population on a state-by-state basis as of April 2017.
Source: Macquarie Research, Quandl, September 2017.

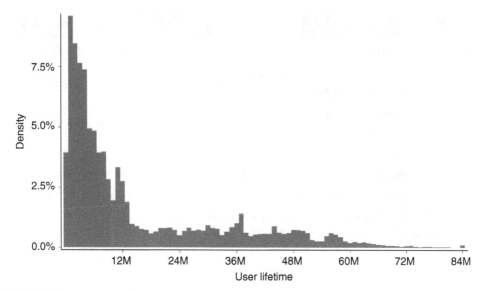

FIGURE 6.11   How long does a user typically spend in our sample?
Source: Macquarie Research, Quandl, September 2017.

How frequently do individual users enter and exit the sample? Figure 6.11 is the histogram of the time spent in the sample by each of the 4.7 m unique users. We included the ones that are currently active (e.g. a user who joined on 1 January 2017 shows up as having a duration of three months as of 1 April regardless of whether he left the sample after 1 April zor not). The figure shows that the majority of users spend less than 12 months in the sample. This is not surprising given that the last 18 months have seen a surge in the number of participants. There seems to be a peak at exactly 12 months, which may be related to the length of a trial period or initial subscription to the applications provided by Quandl's partners. A significant proportion of users who joined the sample three years ago or earlier remain active while very few have been available for more than five years.

In an attempt to gauge the quality of the data, we queried the database to identify the largest transactions that occurred on the Amazon e-commerce platform over the sample period (Figure 6.12). Most of the items were sold by a third party rather than directly by Amazon. Of the six items in the table, three seem genuine data points: a rare poster for a movie that was never released, a luxury watch and a rare coin. The remaining products do seem suspicious. Nevertheless, the fact that very few of the items overall purport to have prices above US$100 000 suggests that data errors caused by poor parsing of the email receipts are unlikely to be an issue.

Another simple check consists of aggregating the data and checking the total purchases made by Quandl's sample participants against the patterns we expect to see in retail e-commerce. It is well known that Amazon sales display a strong seasonal pattern. By using accounting data, we can detect a peak in Q4 followed by a trough in Q2 (Figure 6.13). With our big data sample we can aggregate the purchases made on Amazon at a much higher frequency. In Figure 6.14 we compute average *weekly* sales for each of the 52 weeks of the year and rescale them so that the average value

Description	Category	Price, USD
1907 Saint Gaudens Twenty Dollar PR69 PCGS	Rare coin	4,194,800.00
Office of the Holy Spirit: A most necessary study for all churches by Ulrich Rische Beeson	Book	4,000,003.99
FREAKS 1932 TOD BROWNING 27 x 41 ONE SHEET CLASSIC HORROR EXTREMELY RARE!!	Movie poster	850,000.00
A Really Expensive Rock	?	500,004.99
Samsung SmartCam HD Pro 1080p Full-HD Wi-Fi Camera	Wi-fi camera	360,006.24
Audemars Piguet Jules Grande Complication	Watch	275,504.49

FIGURE 6.12   Six of the most expensive purchases made on Amazon.com.
Source: Macquarie Research, Quandl, September 2017.

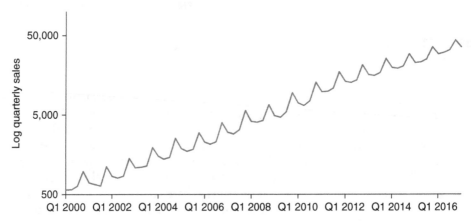

FIGURE 6.13   Seasonal pattern in fundamental data: Amazon's quarterly sales.
Source: Macquarie Research, Factset, September 2017. The chart is plotted on a log scale.

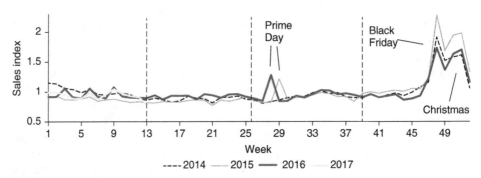

FIGURE 6.14   Seasonal patterns in big data: Amazon's weekly sales. The sales index is computed by normalizing the weekly average amount spent on Amazon.com by each user so that the annual average is equal to one.
Source: Macquarie Research, Quandl, September 2017.

of the sales index is equal to one. The data clearly shows significant peaks that correspond to Amazon's *prime days* and Black Friday, which is traditionally considered the beginning of the Christmas shopping period. The peaks that characterize sales growth in Q4 (Figure 6.13) are concentrated on the weeks between Black Friday and the end of December.

We mentioned in the introduction that deriving financial forecasts from big data is not always straightforward. A good example is the case of Expedia, one of the companies covered by Quandl's email receipts database. As the notes to Expedia's income statement explain, the company does not recognize the total value of the services booked by users of its platform as revenue. Instead, revenues are driven by the booking fees charged by Expedia which cannot be directly inferred from the receipts that are sent to its customers.

Even if the fees were calculated by applying a fixed percentage on the cost of the booking, we would not be able to derive an estimate of total sales from our data. Each of the business lines is likely to charge a different fee and the breakdown of sales by business segment changes significantly over time, as Expedia's receipt data clearly shows (Figure 6.15). For example, flights tend to command a lower margin compared with lodging.

Thus it is crucial to incorporate deep fundamental insights in the analysis in order to fully exploit the potential of big data. In this case, we would have to start from an estimate of the typical fee charged by the company for each business line (flights, lodging, car rental). We would then be able to forecast, using our big data sample, the

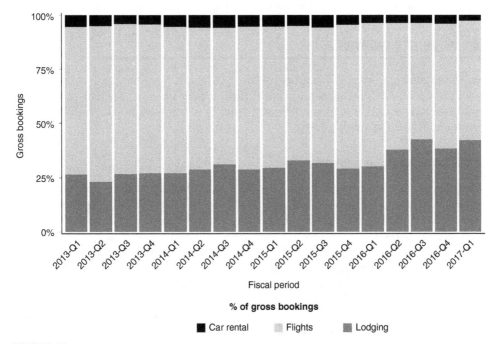

FIGURE 6.15 Expedia's big data bookings split has changed significantly over the last three years.
Source: Macquarie Research, Quandl, September 2017.

total booked on a segment-by-segment basis and aggregate up to obtain an estimate of headline sales.

6.3 THE CHALLENGES OF WORKING WITH BIG DATA

The data we use in the analysis, which covers only three listed companies, occupies over 80 GB when stored in flat files. It includes 144.1 million purchases (rows) of 4.7 million unique users. As a consequence, the sheer size of our dataset (even though we have access to only three of the names covered by the Quandl database) makes it difficult to run even the simplest queries with standard database tools. Faced with this technological challenge, we experimented with alternative solutions to crunch the data in a reasonable timeframe.

Amazon Redshift turned out to be our preferred solution as it is optimized to do analytical processing using a simple syntax (only a few modifications of our standard SQL queries were necessary) and it offers, in our setup, a considerable speedup versus MySQL (around 10 times). Redshift stores database table information in a compressed form by column rather than by row and this reduces the number of disk Input/Output requests and the amount of data load from disk, particularly when dealing with a large number of columns as in our case.

Loading less data into memory enables Redshift to perform more in-memory processing when executing queries. In addition, the Redshift query engine is optimized to run queries on multiple computing nodes in parallel and, to boost speed further, the fully optimized code is sent to computing nodes in the compiled format.

6.4 PREDICTING COMPANY SALES

One of the most important indicators followed by equity investors and analysts is the growth in a company's revenues. As a consequence, sales surprises are known to trigger stock price moves, and analyst-momentum signals (i.e. revisions to sales forecasts) have been found to predict stock returns.

6.4.1 Summary of our approach

The purpose of this section is to convey the rationale behind our forecasting method. The setup is illustrated in Figure 6.16: our task is to predict sales for quarter t based on the guidance issued by management and the information available in our email receipts dataset.

As Figure 6.16 shows, the actual revenue figure for fiscal quarter t is available after the end of quarter t, typically well into quarter $t+1$. An advantage of working with the receipts dataset is that we can generate a prediction immediately after the end of the quarter because all the sample information is updated weekly. In other words, all the information about purchases made during quarter t by the users that make up our sample becomes available a few days after the end of the quarter.

In addition, we can exploit the frequent updates to generate real-time predictions *during* quarter t as new data on weekly purchases becomes available. We explain our methodology in more detail at the end of this section.

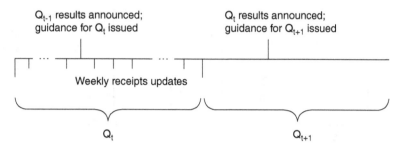

FIGURE 6.16   A timeline for quarterly sales forecasts.
Source: Macquarie Research, September 2017.

We exploit two sources of information: management guidance and email receipts. The former consists of a range of values (predicted revenues) which can be transformed into a range of growth rates on the latest reported quarter.[1] We can start by measuring the increase in purchases for a group of users who were part of the sample over both quarters. This rate of growth can then be compared with the range implied by guidance in order to predict whether sales will come in at the lower or upper side of the range indicated by management. If the in-sample growth rate falls outside the guidance range, then we can simply assume that sales will be either at the bottom or at the top of the range.

For example, during the third quarter of 2016 Amazon's guidance on sales was between US\$31 billion and US\$33.5 billion. This corresponds to a growth rate between 2% and 10.2% on the second quarter, when revenues totalled US\$30.4 billion. If the sample of users monitored by Quandl spent 3.6% more in Q3 than in Q2, then we would take 3.6% as our estimate, close to the bottom of the range. If, however, the growth rate in our sample were 12.5% (outside the guidance range), then we would take this result to indicate that sales are likely to be at the top of the range indicated by management. Hence we would use 10.2% as our estimate.

The rest of this section shows that this simple approach can be justified in a formal statistical framework. In particular, we argue that a natural way to combine the two sources of information is to adopt a Bayesian approach and treat the guidance as *prior information*. We then process the data in order to characterize the *posterior distribution* of sales growth (Figure 6.17), i.e. the distribution of the growth rate given the data.

As Figure 6.17 suggests, the prior distribution merely exploits the range implicit in the guidance, e.g. a growth rate between 2% and 10.2%. The mode of the posterior is the hypothetical in-sample growth rate of 3.6% used in our example above.

6.4.2   A Bayesian approach

The goal is to estimate the change in sales between period 1 and period 2 based on two samples. Formally, we assume that two sets of observations are available: $\{y_{11}, \ldots, y_{1n}\}$

---

[1]The framework described in this section mimics the process whereby companies like Amazon provide guidance on their quarterly revenues. It can be adapted to other cases, e.g. guidance provided as a single expected value (instead of a range) or at irregularly spaced intervals.

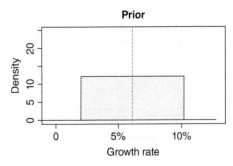
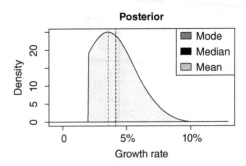

FIGURE 6.17 Bayesian estimation of quarterly revenue growth: An example. The chart plots the densities of the quantity denoted $\varphi_1 - 1$ in the model. The prior distribution reflects management guidance while the posterior incorporates the information available from the email receipts database.
Source: Macquarie Research, September 2017.

and $\{y_{21}, \ldots, y_{2n}\}$. Let us for the moment leave aside two complications that will be dealt with later in this section:

1. Our sample may introduce some selection bias because the 'Quandl population' is different from the overall population.
2. The population grows over time.

We assume that each sample is drawn from a large population at two points in time. The individuals in the population remain the same: some will spend zero but no new users join and no user drops out. We also assume that, given the parameters of the distribution at each point in time, the amounts spent in the two periods are independent, i.e. the shape of the distribution summarizes all the relevant information about growth in consumption.

Each sample is assumed to be drawn from a negative exponential distribution with parameter λ_i:

$$p(y \mid \lambda_i) = \lambda_i e^{-\lambda_i y} \tag{6.1}$$

The exponential distribution (Figure 6.18) is a simple device to model a positive random variable with a heavily skewed distribution. In practice, a sample of consumer purchases will be characterized by a long right tail which reflects a small number of users spending very large amounts during the period.[2]

Given the parameters λ_1 and λ_2, the two samples are assumed to be drawn independently. This is equivalent to assuming that the change in mean parameter summarizes all the information about the changes in the population between period 1 and period 2.

The mean of each population is $1/\lambda_i$, a property of the exponential distribution.

---

[2]The exponential distribution is typically used to model waiting times. However, it has also been applied to problems that require a highly skewed distribution, like modelling rainfall records (Madi and Raqab, 2007). In economics, it has often been applied to modelling income and wealth distributions, e.g. in Drăgulescu and Yakovenko (2001).

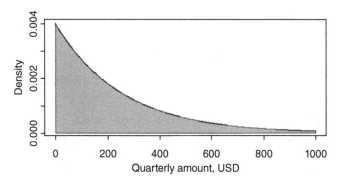

FIGURE 6.18 Negative exponential distribution.
Source: Macquarie Research, September 2017.

6.4.2.1 Prior Distribution The main quantity of interest is the ratio of means $\frac{\lambda_1}{\lambda_2}$, which captures the growth in the mean amount purchased from period 1 to period 2. We define $\phi_1 = \lambda_1/\lambda_2$ and impose a uniform prior as follows:[3]

$$\phi_1 \sim U(\underline{\mu}, \overline{\mu}) \tag{6.2}$$

where $\underline{\mu}$ and $\overline{\mu}$ are the bounds of the guidance range, expressed as (one plus) the growth rates on a quarter-on-quarter basis. We stress that the prior is uninformative in the sense that we do not impose any other structure on the model within the range of values indicated by management. This was illustrated in Figure 6.17.

The derivation, available from the authors upon request, starts by making a common choice for the prior distribution of the parameter λ, the Gamma distribution. This is our assumption for λ_1: $\lambda_1 \sim Gamma(\alpha, \beta)$. We then impose a prior on the mean of the population in period 2 so as to take into account the range of growth rates implied by the guidance on the stock:

$$\lambda_2^{-1} \mid \lambda_1 \sim U\left(\frac{\underline{\mu}}{\lambda_1}, \frac{\overline{\mu}}{\lambda_1}\right)$$

where the quantity $\underline{\mu}/\lambda_1$ can be viewed as the mean of period 1 multiplied by a growth rate equal to the lower bound of guidance range.

As an alternative, we also considered a Gaussian prior and the improper prior of Datta and Ghosh (1996) for ϕ_1. Details can be obtained from the authors upon request.

6.4.2.2 Posterior Distribution This section characterizes the distribution of the parameter of interest, i.e. the growth rate in average spending, given the evidence in our receipts dataset. In deriving the posterior distribution we use our assumptions on the priors (Eq. (6.2)) (Gamma and uniform) and the likelihood (Eq. (6.1)) (exponential) to work out the distribution of the parameter ϕ_1 given the data.

---

[3]We shall refer to this quantity as growth even though the usual measure of growth rate is, obviously, $\phi_1 - 1$.

It can be shown that

$$p(\phi_1 \mid data) \propto \begin{cases} \left(\frac{\phi_1}{s}\right)^{\alpha+n}\left(1+\frac{\phi_1}{s}\right)^{-(\alpha+2n)} & \text{if } \underline{\mu} \leq \phi_1 \leq \overline{\mu} \\ 0 & \text{otherwise} \end{cases}$$

where $s = \sum_i y_{2i}/(\beta + \sum_i y_{1i})$. The posterior distribution has, within the interval $\underline{\mu} \leq \phi_1 \leq \overline{\mu}$, a well-known expression that belongs to the family of Pearson distributions and can be rewritten as a transformation of the F distribution.[4] Hence its mode can be calculated explicitly while its mean and median can be computed with very little effort by integrating the pdf numerically. The posterior is illustrated on the right-hand side of Figure 6.17.

In practice, we can use the mode of the posterior distribution as an estimate of the growth in sales. We start by building estimators for the mean expenditure in each period:

$$\hat{\lambda}_1 = \frac{\alpha + n}{\beta + \sum_i y_{1i}}, \quad \hat{\lambda}_2 = \frac{n}{\sum_i y_{2i}}$$

It is worth noting that $\hat{\lambda}_1$ is just the mean of the posterior distribution of λ_1 while $\hat{\lambda}_2$ is the inverse of the sample average in period 2. Then the maximum *a posteriori* (MAP) estimator of the growth rate is given by

$$\widehat{\phi}_{1MAP} = \begin{cases} \underline{\mu} & \text{if } \hat{\lambda}_1/\hat{\lambda}_2 < \underline{\mu} \\ \hat{\lambda}_1/\hat{\lambda}_2 & \text{if } \underline{\mu} \leq \hat{\lambda}_1/\hat{\lambda}_2 \leq \overline{\mu} \\ \overline{\mu} & \text{if } \hat{\lambda}_1/\hat{\lambda}_2 > \overline{\mu} \end{cases} \tag{6.3}$$

Hence we can estimate the rate of growth by taking the ratio of the parameter estimates in the two periods. If the estimate falls outside the range implicit in the guidance, then we take either the lower or the upper bound as our estimate. It is worth noting that the effect of the prior distribution of λ_1 on the estimate tends to disappear as the sample size increases, i.e. the parameters α and β become irrelevant.

6.4.2.3 Is our Sample Representative?

In this section we introduce a simple adjustment that deals with the potential distortions due to sampling error. The population that is relevant for the Quandl dataset may be different in nature from the broader population of global customers and potential customers. Moreover, as detailed in the next section for the Amazon case study, the e-commerce part of the business may not allow us to draw conclusions on the sales growth of the whole business.

Quarterly seasonal effects are likely to be a problem because the different parts of the business may have very different patterns. E-commerce, in particular, may display more pronounced peaks in December and during the periods of seasonal sales, which would lead us to overestimate the impact of those effects. Also, we most likely capture a

---

[4]More details can be found in Johnson et al. (1995).

subset of the customers which tends to be younger and use e-commerce platforms more extensively than the rest of the population.

A simple and pragmatic approach is to regard the growth rate measured from our sample as a signal that is related to the actual variable of interest, i.e. the growth rate over the whole population. Formally we could write this as

$$g_t = f(\phi_t) + \varepsilon_t$$

where g_t is the growth rate in sales quarter-on-quarter. We can then use the data to fit a suitable function f, for example by using a nonparametric approach like kernel regression. In our case, however, due to the extremely short length of our historical sample, we prefer to focus on a linear model that takes seasonality into account:

$$g_t = \beta' f_t \, \phi_t + \varepsilon_t$$

where β is a 4×1 vector of quarterly slopes and f_t a 4×1 vector that selects the correct slope according to the quarter indicated by the time index t, i.e. $f_t = (f_{1t}, f_{2t}, f_{3t}, f_{4t})'$ and

$$f_{qt} = \begin{cases} 1 & \text{if } t = 4k + q \text{ for some } k \in \mathbb{N} \\ 0 & \text{otherwise} \end{cases}$$

The product $\beta' f_t$ is a scaling factor that changes over time because of the seasonal effects. The coefficient vector β can be estimated from the data by regression. In the empirical analysis we also consider a simple variant where all components of β are equal.

Once the model has been estimated, it is possible to generate a bias-corrected version of the big data forecast $\widehat{\phi}_{1\,MAP}$:

$$\widetilde{\phi}_{1tMAP} = \widehat{\beta}' f_t \, \widehat{\phi}_{1tMAP} \tag{6.4}$$

However, it seems important to allow for time variation of the seasonal components themselves. For example, if the relative importance of the different businesses of a company changes, then we can expect the optimal scaling coefficient to change as well. A simple way to deal with this potential issue is to treat the vector of slopes β as a (slowly) time-varying coefficient. A popular model[5] that can be used in this context is a state space model that treats the coefficient vector as a random walk:

$$g_t = \beta_t' f_t \, \phi_t + \varepsilon_t$$

$$\beta_t = \beta_{t-1} + \eta_t$$

where ε_t and η_t are disturbances with zero mean and $Var(\varepsilon_t) = \sigma_\varepsilon^2$, $Var(\eta_t) = \sigma_\eta^2 I$. The model can be initialised with the prior $\beta_0 \sim N(1, \kappa I)$ and estimated via the Kalman filter

---

[5] Time-varying coefficient models of this kind have a long history in finance. Adrian and Franzoni (2009) is an example.

and smoother (KFS). The parameters $\sigma_\varepsilon^2, \sigma_\eta^2$ and κ can be calibrated on the data. We do not pursue this idea further due to the limited duration of our sample.

Another potential source of bias is represented by population growth. Our sample does include any users who are active (i.e. have opted into the Quandl database and are reachable) but choose not to make any purchases on the e-commerce platform. This should capture one aspect of the growth in users at the general population level, i.e. new customers that start using the platform. However, changes in the size and demographic composition of the US population driven by births, deaths and migration are also likely to affect the growth in e-commerce sales. For example, a strong inflow of migrants might increase sales. Similarly, a younger population may be more inclined to shop online.

In our analysis we keep the population constant deliberately when computing growth rates so that our results do not depend spuriously on the growth in app users that opt in to share their data with Quandl. Given that most of the revenues accrue in developed countries with low population growth,[6] this effect seems negligible and we decide to ignore it. An alternative approach would be to model user growth explicitly and add it to the predicted growth in sales obtained from the sample.

6.5 REAL-TIME PREDICTIONS

6.5.1 Our structural time series model

This section deals with the problem of generating forecasts of the quarterly sales numbers in real time, i.e. updating the current forecast as a new weekly update becomes available during the quarter. To avoid unnecessarily complicating the notation, we somewhat artificially divide each quarter into 13 periods which will be referred to as 'weeks'. In practice, we allow for a longer or a shorter 13th 'week' when the quarter does not contain exactly 91 days. In leap years we always assume that week 9 of the first quarter has eight days. The full description of our naming convention is given in Figure 6.19.

Taking Amazon as an example, Figure 6.20 shows that the purchases captured in our dataset display strong seasonality patterns within each quarter. We plotted an index of weekly sales that is normalized to have unit average over each quarter (unlike in Figure 6.14, where we imposed unit average for the whole calendar year). It is therefore necessary to model seasonality in order to generate useful forecasts based on weekly data. For example, if we simply looked at the cumulative sales for the first half of Q4 we might end up underestimating growth because most of the purchases are typically made in December.

To keep notation simple, we will distinguish between quarterly sales Y_t and weekly sales observed during quarter t, $Y_{t,n}$, where n identifies a specific week and therefore $1 \leq n \leq 13$. By construction $\sum_{n=1}^{13} Y_{t,n} = Y_t$.

Our weekly time series model can be written as

$$Y_{t,n} = Y_t(I_{t,n} + \Lambda_n M_{t,n}) + u_{t,n}, \quad n = 1, \ldots, 13$$

---

[6]As we argued above, more than half of the sales are booked in the US, where the population grows at a rate of less than 0.25% per quarter.

Week	Q1			Q2			Q3			Q4		
	From	To	n	From	To	n	From	To	n	From	To	n
1	01 Jan	07 Jan	7	01 Apr	07 Apr	7	01 Jul	07 Jul	7	01 Oct	07 Oct	7
2	08 Jan	14 Jan	7	08 Apr	14 Apr	7	08 Jul	14 Jul	7	08 Oct	14 Oct	7
3	15 Jan	21 Jan	7	15 Apr	21 Apr	7	15 Jul	21 Jul	7	15 Oct	21 Oct	7
4	22 Jan	28 Jan	7	22 Apr	28 Apr	7	22 Jul	28 Jul	7	22 Oct	28 Oct	7
5	29 Jan	04 Feb	7	29 Apr	05 May	7	29 Jul	04 Aug	7	29 Oct	04 Nov	7
6	05 Feb	11 Feb	7	06 May	12 May	7	05 Aug	11 Aug	7	05 Nov	11 Nov	7
7	12 Feb	18 Feb	7	13 May	19 May	7	12 Aug	18 Aug	7	12 Nov	18 Nov	7
8	19 Feb	25 Feb	7	20 May	26 May	7	19 Aug	25 Aug	7	19 Nov	25 Nov	7
9	26 Feb	04 Mar	7/8	27 May	02 Jun	7	26 Aug	01 Sep	7	26 Nov	02 Dec	7
10	05 Mar	11 Mar	7	03 Jun	09 Jun	7	02 Sep	08 Sep	7	03 Dec	09 Dec	7
11	12 Mar	18 Mar	7	10 Jun	16 Jun	7	09 Sep	15 Sep	7	10 Dec	16 Dec	7
12	19 Mar	25 Mar	7	17 Jun	23 Jun	7	16 Sep	22 Sep	7	17 Dec	23 Dec	7
13	26 Mar	31 Mar	6	24 Jun	30 Jun	7	23 Sep	30 Sep	8	24 Dec	31 Dec	8

FIGURE 6.19   Dividing each quarter into 13 weeks.
Source: Macquarie Research, September 2017.

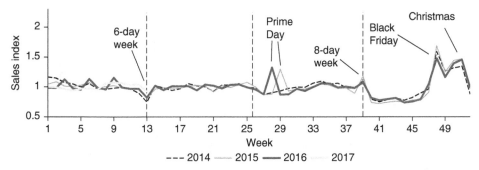

FIGURE 6.20   Seasonal patterns in big data: Amazon's weekly sales. The sales index is computed by normalizing the weekly average amount spent on Amazon.com by each user so that the quarterly average is equal to one. The quantity plotted is $Y_{t,n}/Y_t$ (multiplied by 13, the number of weeks in a quarter) in the notation used in the text.
Source: Macquarie Research, Quandl, September 2017.

where $I_{t,n}$ is an irregular component that captures, e.g. the effect of Amazon's *prime days* on sales, Λ_n is the seasonal component and $M_{t,n}$ is a multiplier that captures the effect of weeks with irregular duration (e.g. during the six-day week at the end of Q1 $M_{t,n} = 6/7$). The term u_t is an error with mean zero. The coefficients change according to the quarter we are modelling (i.e. the first week of Q1 is different from the first week of Q4) but we only use the subscript t to keep the notation simple.

It is important to note that the seasonal component Λ_n is assumed to be constant across different years, while both the date of *prime day* and the multiplier M change over time (the latter because of leap years). To close the model we impose the restriction

$$\sum_{t=1}^{13} (I_{t,n} + \Lambda_n M_{t,n}) = 1$$

so that

$$E\left(\sum_{t=1}^{13} Y_{t,n}\right) = E(Y_t)$$

and $E(Y)$ can be viewed as the expected total quarterly sales.

6.5.2 Estimation and prediction

Because of the multiplicative nature of the model, we can estimate the parameters directly from the series of normalized sales illustrated in Figure 6.20, i.e. we can work with the ratio $Y_{t,n}/Y_t$. The effect of *prime day*, I_t, can be estimated by averaging the

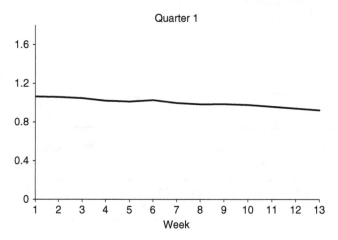

FIGURE 6.21   Estimated seasonal component, Q1.
Source: Macquarie Research, Quandl, September 2017.

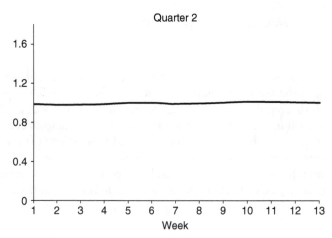

FIGURE 6.22   Estimated seasonal component, Q2.
Source: Macquarie Research, Quandl, September 2017.

difference between normalized sales in a *prime day* week and normalized sales for the same week when no prime day takes place.

The multiplier M_t is known given the number of days in a year.

In order to estimate the seasonal component Λ_n we fit a cubic spline to the ratio $Y_{t,n}/Y_t$ (after subtracting the irregular component) using the KFS.[7] The estimates for Amazon are plotted in Figures 6.21–6.24. It is clear from the picture that seasonal effects are much more pronounced in the last quarter.

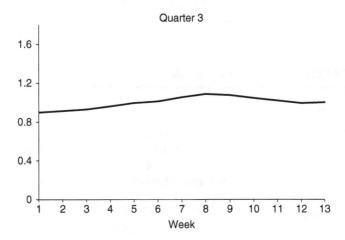

FIGURE 6.23 Estimated seasonal component, Q3.
Source: Macquarie Research, Quandl, September 2017.

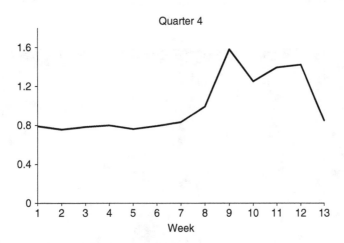

FIGURE 6.24 Estimated seasonal component, Q4.
Source: Macquarie Research, Quandl, September 2017.

---

[7]More details can be found in Wahba (1978).

Assuming that we have observed the weekly purchases of a sample of customers for $s < 13$ weeks in the new quarter, we can then predict the total for the whole quarter as

$$\hat{Y}_{t|s} = \sum_{n=1}^{s} Y_{t,n} \left(\sum_{n=1}^{s} (I_{t,n} + \hat{\Lambda}_n M_{t,n}) \right)^{-1}$$

The quarter-on-quarter growth rate can then be predicted using the methodology introduced in the previous section.

6.6   A CASE STUDY: http://amazon.com SALES

6.6.1   Background

In this section we apply the methodology discussed above to the problem of predicting the quarterly revenues of Amazon. In the Quandl database, Amazon is by far the company with the largest number of observations. In addition, it is a good example of a company with a complex structure that requires a combination of quantitative and fundamental insights.

Amazon reports a quarterly split of sales by business segments, which has changed over time. In Figure 6.25 we plot the relative importance of two broad categories: e-commerce and other sales (which includes Amazon Web Services, AWS). Because of the nature of our dataset, by concentrating on email receipts, we will only be able to investigate the trends in US e-commerce sales. Figure 6.25 suggests that revenue from e-commerce represent a large portion of the total, albeit a shrinking one due to the fast

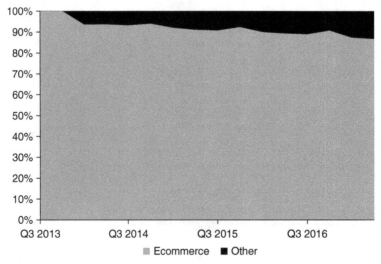

FIGURE 6.25   Sales breakdown per type, Amazon.
Source: Bloomberg, September 2017.

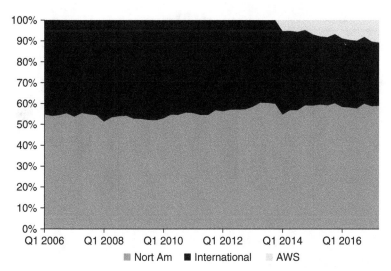

FIGURE 6.26   Sales breakdown per region, Amazon.
Source: Bloomberg, September 2017.

growth of AWS.[8] Similarly, we can see from Figure 6.26 that sales to North American customers (the closest we can get to US sales) represent more than half of the total.

We are not, however, in a position to conclude that focusing on US e-commerce will yield unbiased predictions. First, as we argued in the previous section, our sample may still be characterized by significant selection bias as we have no way to ascertain whether the Quandl sample is representative of the US population.

Second, even though both the proportion of sales that are not booked through the e-commerce platform and the proportion of sales that happen outside the US are small, these segments may have very different growth rates and ultimately cause our prediction to be biased.

To address this potential issue we decompose sales growth (quarter-on-quarter) into regional contributions plus AWS (Figures 6.27–6.30). In each figure the total height of the bar represents the growth rate of Amazon's revenues for the corresponding quarter. The individual components are obtained by multiplying the relative weight of each segment by its quarterly growth rate.

The results suggest that the contribution of AWS to headline sales growth is still marginal, particularly in Q1 and Q4. However, it is becoming increasingly important for predictions in Q2 and Q3. North America and the rest of the world both contribute significantly to the overall growth rate but in most cases the former accounts for a larger share.

The conclusion is that focusing on the US is unlikely to result in a strong bias but ignoring the AWS segment (which has recently grown at much faster rates than e-commerce) seems increasingly dangerous. The decomposition by business segment (omitted here in order to save space) yields similar results.

---

[8] E-commerce sales after 2016 are defined as the sum of the following segments: 'Retail products', 'Retail third-party seller services' and 'Retail subscription services'.

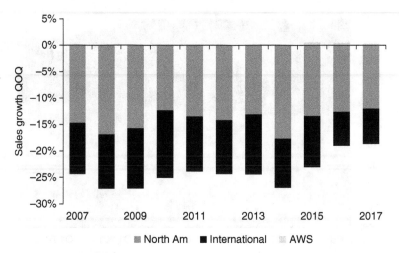

FIGURE 6.27 Contributions to sales growth in Q1.
Source: Macquarie Research, Bloomberg, September 2017.

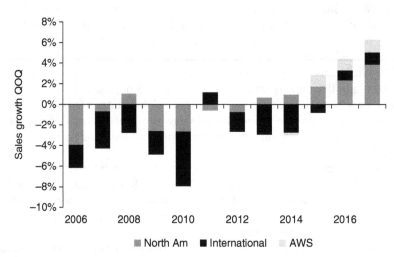

FIGURE 6.28 Contributions to sales growth in Q2.
Source: Macquarie Research, Bloomberg, September 2017.

6.6.2 Results

We now turn to the problem of forecasting the headline sales number. Before doing so, however, we examine the differences between growth in total sales and growth in e-commerce revenues through a scatterplot (Figure 6.31). Points above the solid black line represent quarters in which e-commerce grew more rapidly than the total. As expected, this tends to happen in Q4 (when growth rates quarter on quarter

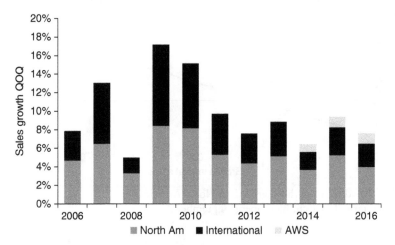

FIGURE 6.29 Contributions to sales growth in Q3.
Source: Macquarie Research, Bloomberg, September 2017.

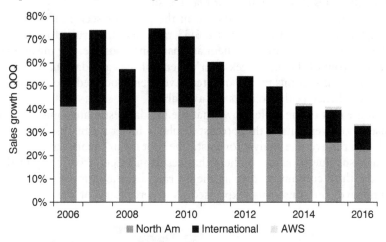

FIGURE 6.30 Contributions to sales growth in Q4.
Source: Macquarie Research, Bloomberg, September 2017.

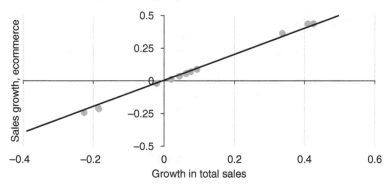

FIGURE 6.31 e-commerce vs. headline growth.
Source: Macquarie Research, Bloomberg, September 2017.

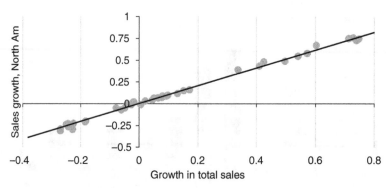

FIGURE 6.32 Headline growth vs. growth in North America.
Source: Macquarie Research, Bloomberg, September 2017.

exceed 30%) because of the Christmas peak. Figure 6.32 shows that focusing on US sales is unlikely to result in a significant bias per se.

We implement the estimator discussed in the previous section in order to predict Amazon's quarterly sales growth. Figure 6.33 presents our results for alternative versions of the forecast and compares them against consensus, i.e. the mean analyst estimate obtained from I/B/E/S one week after the end of the calendar quarter. By that time all the customer transactions for the quarter have been processed and added by Quandl to the database, hence both forecasts are available.

The middle part of the table shows that the big data estimate compares favourably to consensus: both versions of the forecast display a lower mean absolute error (MAE) compared with the average analyst forecast. The root mean square error (RMSE) would favour consensus due to a few outliers that result in large errors early in the sample period. In the third column we display the hit rate, i.e. the number of times when our forecast improves on consensus, expressed as a percentage of the total sample size.

Predictor	MAE	RMSE	Hit rate
Consensus (1)	1.76%	2.11%	
Receipts and guidance (2)			
No bias correction	1.64%	2.34%	66.7%
Bias correction	1.51%	2.40%	66.7%
Combination (1) - (2)			
No bias correction	1.21%	1.47%	75.0%
Bias correction	1.32%	2.15%	75.0%

FIGURE 6.33 Combining big data and consensus delivers superior forecasts of total sales growth. The estimator without bias correction is $\hat{\phi}_{1MAP}$ in the text, defined in Eq. (6.3). The version with bias correction corresponds to the estimator $\tilde{\phi}_{1MAP}$ defined in Eq. (6.4). The combination is the simple average of consensus and our MAP estimator.
Source: Macquarie Research, September 2017.

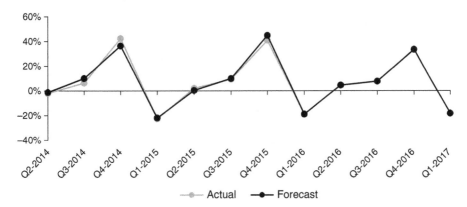

FIGURE 6.34 Improving forecasting ability as the sample size increases. The plot refers to the version of the big data estimate that uses receipts data and guidance, with bias correction. *Source:* Macquarie Research, September 2017.

We achieve an improvement two-thirds of the time. While the number of observations in the time series is admittedly limited, our analysis seems to suggest that the big data estimate is at least as accurate as consensus.

Bias correction improves the estimate further (in terms of MAE), again suggesting that the Quandl sample is not free from selection bias. Nevertheless, our results suggest that the bias can be modelled accurately by using the simple solution detailed in the previous section, Eq. (6.4). As longer time series become available, one might need to use adaptive estimates as suggested earlier if the seasonal pattern that characterizes our sample bias changes over time.

At the bottom of Figure 6.33 we present the results of combining analyst estimates and big data. Here the two forecasts are combined simply by taking the average of the two values. This results in an improvement in accuracy as measured both by the MAE and by the hit rate, which reaches 75%. While in terms of RMSE the evidence is not as conclusive (the bias corrected version has a slightly higher error compared with consensus), overall the results highlight the improvement in forecasting ability that can be obtained by combining big data and fundamental insight from the analysts.

Figure 6.34 gives a graphical impression of the distance between forecast and actual value for the big data forecast (no analyst input is used in the chart). The prediction appears to follow closely the actual growth in sales and the estimation error seems to decrease as the number of time series observations increases. Again, this result can be attributed to the fact that, as the expanding window used in the estimation increases, the bias correction mechanism becomes more and more accurate.

6.6.3 Putting it all together

It is also useful to compare our big data estimate against consensus over time (Figures 6.35 and 6.36). In Figure 6.35 we plot the prediction errors of both estimators. Relatively large errors that occur early in the sample period (2014 Q4 in particular) cause the higher RMSE displayed by our forecast. Interestingly, consensus displays a

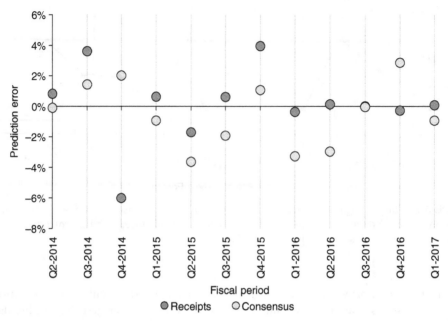

FIGURE 6.35   Big data can be used to predict sales...
Source: Macquarie Research, September 2017.

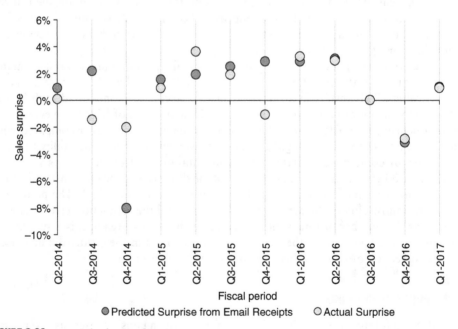

FIGURE 6.36   ...and sales surprises.
Source: Macquarie Research, September 2017.

seasonal pattern: analysts have tended to underestimate Q1 sales and overestimate in Q4. No such pattern can be found in the big data prediction.

Figure 6.36 represents the same information in a slightly different way by plotting the predicted and actual sales surprises. The actual figure is calculated as the difference between the reported figure (which would not have been accessible at the time when the forecast is formed) and consensus. The predicted surprise is the difference between our big data estimate and consensus, i.e. the surprise that would occur if our estimator turned out to be 100% accurate. The pattern of strong negative surprises in Q4 is apparent from the figure. With only two exceptions (Q3 2014 and Q4 2015), we would have been able to predict correctly the sign of the surprise in every single quarter.

A surprising result in Figure 6.33 is that the forecast combination that uses bias correction (last row of the table) underperforms the one without it. This is at odds with the evidence that the big data estimator, when used on its own, benefits from bias correction. Why does the conclusion change when our estimator is combined with consensus? It turns out that if we rely on Quandl data without trying to correct the bias, we tend to be less bullish than consensus in Q4 and more bullish Q1–Q3. As Figure 6.37 clearly shows, growth rates in our sample tend to be lower than the reported numbers for Q4 and higher for the rest of the year, particularly in Q1. This is exactly the opposite of the pattern of errors displayed by consensus (Figure 6.35). Hence, in contrast to the old saying that 'two wrongs don't make a right', when we combine the two estimates, the errors offset each other, which results in an improvement in MAE

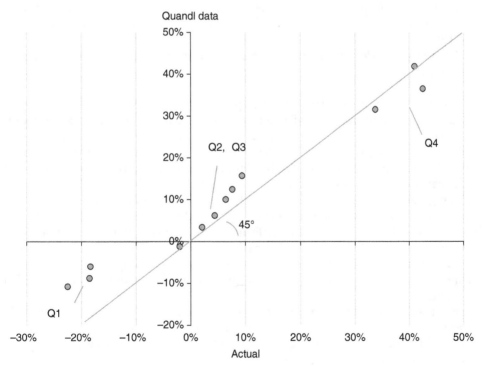

FIGURE 6.37 In-sample vs. actual sales growth.
Source: Macquarie Research, Quandl, FactSet, I/B/E/S, September 2017.

Model	Inputs	MAE	RMSE	Hit rate
Improper prior	Receipts data	5.14%	6.52%	33.3%
Exponential	Receipts, guidance	1.64%	2.34%	66.7%
Gaussian	Receipts, guidance	1.64%	2.34%	66.7%
Guidance midpoint	Guidance	2.73%	3.23%	16.7%
Quarterly mean g	Historical growth rate	7.86%	12.94%	25.0%

FIGURE 6.38   The results are robust. The data covers the period 2014Q2–2017Q1.
Source: Macquarie Research, Quandl, Fact Set, I/B/E/S, September 2017.

and particularly RMSE. However, we do not interpret our result as suggesting that one should use the raw estimator $\widehat{\phi}_{1MAP}$ when combining big data with analyst forecasts. A better understanding of the drivers of the bias would be needed in order to draw a strong conclusion.

The top half of Figure 6.38 assesses to what extent the performance of our big data estimator is driven by each of the two inputs, i.e. guidance and receipts data. We start by checking the sensitivity of the results to our choice of prior distribution. This is done in two ways:

1. By deriving a forecast that relies solely on the Quandl data. This is equivalent to an improper prior on the rate of growth like the one advocated by Datta and Ghosh (1996).
2. By using a model based on normal priors instead of our Gamma–exponential model.[9]

Our baseline model is referred to as *Exponential* in the table.

Ignoring the information available from management guidance results in a significant deterioration of the quality of the estimator, e.g. the MAE rises from 1.64% to 5.14%. The hit rate is just 33.3%. Nevertheless, guidance per se is not sufficient to match the predictive accuracy of our big data estimator. In Figure 6.38 we display the performance metrics for the guidance midpoint (i.e. the point in the middle of the guidance range) as an estimate of future quarterly growth. The resulting MAE (2.73%) and RMSE (3.23%) are clearly higher than any of the predictors in Figure 6.33. The hit rate is below 20%. To conclude, both ingredients in our approach (guidance and big data) play an important role in delivering remarkably accurate sales estimates. Our results suggest that guidance is important in reducing the range of likely outcomes while the Quandl dataset provides valuable information on the likelihood of growth rates within the range.

Figure 6.38 also contains the results for a naive forecast, the historical mean growth. Given the strong seasonal effects, we compute historical seasonal averages for each quarter (Q1–Q4) from expanding windows. Its performance is clearly much worse compared with the other methods considered so far.

---

[9]Details can be obtained from the authors upon request.

6.6.4 Real-time predictions

In this section we implement the methodology discussed in the previous section in order to simulate the real-time estimation of sales growth as weekly updates to the Quandl database become available.

We extrapolate, given the first $t < 13$ weeks of data, the growth rate for the whole quarter and then apply the estimation procedure discussed above that corrects potential biases and incorporates the information available from management guidance.

The available database is far too short for a systematic analysis. Instead, we focus on the last four quarters of our sample period (Q2 2016–Q1 2017) and present the results of an out-of-sample analysis. The only parameters that are estimated using the full sample are the seasonal components that affect weekly sales (depicted in Figures 6.21–6.24), which are estimated using data from 2014 until 2016 and used to extrapolate weekly sales trends. We acknowledge that this potentially generates a slight look-ahead bias. However, the bias does not affect the out-of-sample analysis for Q1 2017. In addition, any look-ahead bias will be relevant only for the early part of each quarter because as more weeks of data become available, the effect of our extrapolation process on the result becomes less important. Once the calendar quarter is over, the estimate no longer changes and our estimates of the weekly seasonal effects are no longer needed.

Figures 6.39–6.42 display the results as time series plots. The grey line represents the consensus estimate while the black line shows the evolution of our real-time big data prediction. In addition, we represent graphically the range of growth rates implied by management guidance as a grey shaded area which starts from the date when guidance is issued. Finally, the red dot in each picture represents the actual reported value.

In all four cases the big data estimate turns out to be more accurate than consensus when Amazon reports its results. Here we assess how long it takes for the information in the Quandl database to result in a sufficiently accurate estimate.

It is interesting to note that consensus tends to move relatively sharply when guidance is issued (Figure 6.39 is a clear example) and then remains within the range

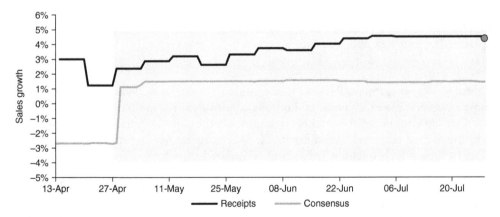

FIGURE 6.39 Real-time prediction of sales growth in 2016 Q2. The shaded area identifies the range of sales growth values implied by management guidance. The dot represents the actual growth rate reported by Amazon. The dotted line is the estimate obtained from receipts data ignoring the guidance.
Source: Macquarie Research, Quandl, Factset, I/B/E/S, September 2017.

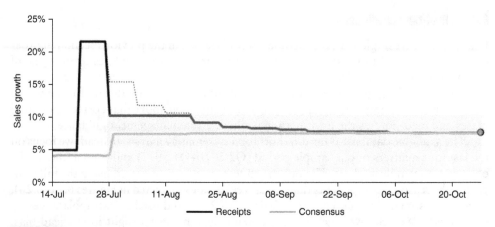

FIGURE 6.40　Real-time prediction of sales growth in 2016 Q3.
Source: Macquarie Research, Quandl, Factset, I/B/E/S, September 2017.

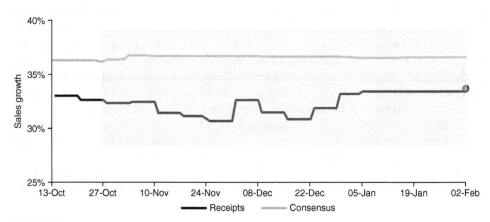

FIGURE 6.41　Real-time prediction of sales growth in 2016 Q4.
Source: Macquarie Research, Quandl, Factset, I/B/E/S, September 2017.

indicated by management. Relative to the guidance range, the consensus value tends to move very little after that point and remains typically in the top half.

Our big data estimate remains constant once the calendar quarter is over (e.g. on 30 June, with a one-week lag in Figure 6.39) because no new information is available after that point. Throughout the period considered in this analysis, only in one case does the Quandl sample produce a growth rate that exceeds the guidance bounds (Figure 6.42). The dotted line in the figure represents the raw estimate. In Q3 2016 (Figure 6.40) the estimate starts above the upper bound (and is shrunk towards the middle), but as more weeks of data become available, it decreases until it enters the guidance range.

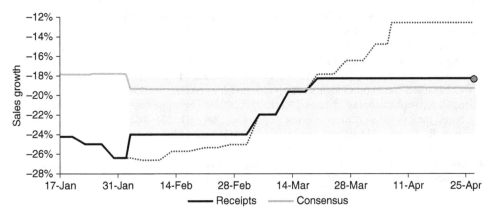

FIGURE 6.42   Real-time prediction of sales growth in 2017 Q1.
Source: Macquarie Research, Quandl, Factset, I/B/E/S, September 2017.

Our big data prediction is typically more volatile than consensus, particularly early in the quarter and even more markedly before guidance is issued. Nevertheless, it is worth highlighting that the two predictions – analyst forecast and big data forecast – rarely cross (only once in Figure 6.42), suggesting that the direction of the sales surprise can be predicted even early in the quarter.

REFERENCES

Adrian, T. and Franzoni, F. (2009). Learning about Beta: time-varying factor loadings, expected returns and the conditional CAPM. *J. Empir. Financ.* 16: 537–556.

Ben-Rephael, A., Da, Z., and Israelsen, R.D. (2017). It depends on where you search: institutional investor attention and underreaction to news. *Rev. Financ. Stud.,* 30: 3009–3047.

Brar, G., De Rossi, G., and Kalamkar, N. (2016). Predicting stock returns using text mining tools. In: *Handbook of Sentiment Analysis in Finance* (ed. G. Mitra and X. Yu). London: OptiRisk.

Das, S.R. and Chen, M.Y. (2007). Yahoo! For Amazon: sentiment extraction from small talk on the web. *Manag. Sci.,* 53: 1375–1388.

Datta, G.S. and Ghosh, M. (1996). On the invariance of non-informative priors. *Ann. Stat.,* 24: 141–159.

Donaldson, D. and Storeygard, A. (2016). The view from above: applications of satellite data in economics. *J. Econ. Perspect.,* 30: 171–198.

Drăgulescu, A. and Yakovenko, V.M. (2001). Exponential and power-law probability distributions of wealth and income in the United Kingdom and the United States. *Phys. A.,* 299: 213–221.

Gholampour, V. and van Wincoop, E. (2017). What can we Learn from Euro-Dollar Tweets? NBER Working Paper No. 23293.

Green, T.C., Huang, R., Wen, Q. and Zhou, D. (2017). Wisdom of the Employee Crowd: Employer Reviews and Stock Returns, Working paper. Available at SSRN: https://ssrn.com/abstract=3002707.

Johnson, N.L., Kotz, S., and Balakrishnan, N. (1995). *Continuous Univariate Distributions*, vol. 2. New York: Wiley.

Madi, M.T. and Raqab, M.Z. (2007). Bayesian prediction of rainfall records using the generalized exponential distribution. *Environmetrics*, 18: 541–549.

Perlin, M.S., Caldeira, J.F., Santos, A.A.P., and Pontuschka, M. (2017). Can we predict the financial markets based on Google's search queries? *J. Forecast.*, 36: 454–467.

Rajgopal, S., Venkatachalam, M., and Kotha, S. (2003). The value relevance of network advantages: the case of e–commerce firms. *J. Account. Res.*, 41: 135–162.

Trueman, B., Wong, M.H.F., and Zhang, X.J. (2001). Back to basics: forecasting the revenues of internet firms. *Rev. Acc. Stud.*, 6: 305–329.

Wahba, G. (1978). Improper priors, spline smoothing and the problem of guarding against model errors in regression. *J. R. Stat. Soc. Ser. B* 40: 364–372.

CHAPTER **7**

Ensemble Learning Applied to Quant Equity: Gradient Boosting in a Multifactor Framework

Tony Guida and Guillaume Coqueret

7.1 INTRODUCTION

It is a both intuitive and well-documented fact that firms' performance on the stock market is driven by some of their core characteristics. In their seminal article, Fama and French (1992) show that firms with higher book-to-market ratios significantly outperform those with low book-to-market ratios. They also report that small firms tend to yield returns that are higher than those of large firms.[1] Later, Jegadeesh and Titman (1993, 2001) constructed abnormally profitable (momentum) portfolios by buying outperforming stocks and shorting underperforming ones.

Findings such as these have led to the construction of so-called factor indices in which the investor buys the above-average performing stocks and sells the below-average ones. The literature on these *anomalies* is incredibly vast and has its own meta-studies (see e.g. Subrahmanyam 2010; Green et al. 2013; Harvey et al. 2016).[2]

It can be debated whether these discrepancies in performance originate from truly pervasive (and priced) factors that structure the cross-section of stock returns (a stream of literature that was launched by Fama and French 1993) or from the firms' characteristics directly, as put forward by Daniel and Titman (1997).

In any case, there seems to be a large consensus that investors should be able to benefit from the introduction of firms' characteristics in their asset allocation process.

---

[1]This is usually referred to as the size premium. This stream of literature was initiated by Banz (1981) and is reviewed in Van Dijk (2011).
[2]In addition, McLean and Pontiff (2016) shed some light on this topic through the lens of predictability.

This seemingly obvious advice is all the more pertinent since smart-beta indices are reshaping the asset management industry (Kahn and Lemmon 2016). Beyond simple portfolio construction processes,[3] more sophisticated methods have emerged, for instance in Brandt et al. (2009) and Ammann et al. (2016).

The rise of artificial intelligence (AI) and more specifically machine learning (ML) in unrelated fields (computer vision, translation, etc.) has had an impact on how quantitative managers can process all of the data they have at hand. Recent contributions encompass techniques such as Bayesian inference (Bodnar et al. 2017), flag pattern recognition (Arévalo et al. 2017), clustering (Nair et al. 2017), random forests, boosted trees and neural networks (Ballings et al. 2015; Patel et al. 2015; Krauss et al. 2017) or even recurrent neural networks (Fischer and Krauss 2018).

The limitation of most of these articles is that the predictors are usually limited to price data or possibly technical data. This is suboptimal because as the asset pricing literature has demonstrated, there are many other candidates for explanatory variables. In this chapter we propose to benefit from the advantages of ML in general and boosted trees in particular, e.g. non-linearity, regularization and good generalization results, scaling up well with lots of data. The present contribution is closest in spirit to the work of Ballings et al. (2015). The main difference between the two lies in the sophistication of the labelling process: Ballings et al. (2015) look simply at price direction, while we take a more structured approach.

This chapter is organized as follows. In Section 7.2, we give a mildly technical introduction to boosted trees. Section 7.3 is dedicated to data and protocol and will introduce the construction of the dataset with the feature and labels engineering, the protocol that we will use in the subsequent section and the calibration of the ML applying rigorous protocol established by the computer science community.

7.2   A PRIMER ON BOOSTED TREES

This section is dedicated to a self-contained and reasonably technical introduction to decision tress and boosted trees. For more details, we refer to Chapters 9 and 10 of Friedman et al. (2009).

We consider a database that is split in two: the explanatory variables, gathered in the matrix x, and the variable we aim to forecast, which, for simplicity here, we assume to be a vector, y. Let T be the number of occurrences in the data and K be the number of explanatory variables: the matrix $x = x_{t,k}$ has dimensions $(T \times K)$. Henceforth, we note x_t for the K-valued vector containing all fields of occurrence t.

The purpose of the tree is to partition the data (i.e. the collection of (x,y)) in clusters in which the elements y_t are as similar as possible. If y is a numerical variable, this means reducing the variance inside the cluster and if it is a categorical variable, then it amounts to reducing the 'impurity' of the cluster (we seek a strongly dominant class).

To ease the presentation, we deal with regression trees first. At the root of the tree, the optimal split s for variable j is such that the two clusters formed according to this

---

[3]For a more detailed view of the intertwining between factor investing and asset management, we refer to the monographs of Ilmanen (2011) and Ang (2014).

variable have the smallest total variance in y:

$$V_j^s = \sum_{t=1}^{T} \mathbf{1}_{\{x_{t,k}>s\}} (y_t - \mu_j^+)^2 + \sum_{t=1}^{T} \mathbf{1}_{\{x_{t,k}\leq s\}} (y_t - \mu_j^-)^2,$$

where μ_j^+ and μ_j^- are the intra-cluster averages:

$$\mu_j^+ = \frac{\sum_{t=1}^{T} \mathbf{1}_{\{x_{t,k}>s\}} y_t}{\sum_{t=1}^{T} \mathbf{1}_{\{x_{t,k}>s\}}}, \qquad \mu_j^- = \frac{\sum_{t=1}^{T} \mathbf{1}_{\{x_{t,k}\leq s\}} y_t}{\sum_{t=1}^{T} \mathbf{1}_{\{x_{t,k}\leq s\}}}.$$

The notation $\mathbf{1}_{\{.\}}$ denotes the indicator operator: $\mathbf{1}_{\{x\}}$ is equal to one if x is true and to zero if not. For all explanatory variables j, the algorithm minimizes V_j^s across all plausible values s and retains the one for which the total variance is the smallest. The first split is then performed and the procedure is repeated on the two resulting clusters.

Note that in the definition of V_j^s, the terms $(y_t - \mu_j^\pm)^2$ are simply scaled variances because we build a regression tree. The analogy with linear regression is straightforward: the classical OLS estimator also seeks to minimize the variance between the actual data and the predicted values. In the case of classification trees, the computation of the variance is replaced by a metric that captures the impurity of the cluster. One popular of such measures is the cross-entropy. If $\pi_k^{s\pm}$ are the $K^\pm$ proportions of the classes of y in the two clusters resulting from the sort s, cross-entropy is a common measure of impurity: $-\sum_{k=1}^{k^\pm} \pi_k^{s\pm} \log(\pi_k^{s\pm})$. Minimizing the cross-entropy usually leads to the emergence of one dominant class (at least, that is its purpose).

The tree progressively grows when nodes are split in two and the fit naturally increases with the number of leaves. Obviously, a tree with hundreds of leaves is likely to overfit the data. The criterion for fixing the number of nodes is usually a linear combination: goodness of fit minus a penalizing term consisting of a multiple of the number of leaves.

Once one tree is built, the idea behind boosting is to combine it with one or many other trees to increase the goodness-of-fit (this is a particular case of ensemble learning). An intuitive solution is to train several classifiers and to combine their predictions into one output signal. In his seminal contribution, Schapire (1990) proposes to fit three trees and to then use a majority vote for a binary classification. Refinements of this idea led to the development of the family of AdaBoost classifiers (Freund and Schapire 1997). We refer to Friedman et al. (2000) for a review on this topic. In the latter papers, the authors show that the AdaBoost principle admits a simple additive representation.

To graphically illustrate these ideas, we plot two simple trees in Figure 7.1. We are interested only in the determinant feature, i.e. y. The values of the latter are coded through colours and the purpose of the tree is to build clusters with similar colours. Both trees end up with a 'hot' cluster (left/leaf1/first tree), but they differ on where to locate the second instance y_2. Now, if we were to predict the colour of a new occurrence with features like those of y_2, our prediction would mix the outcomes of the two corresponding clusters.

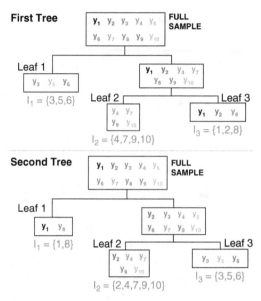

FIGURE 7.1 Two symbolic trees. Variations in the dependent variable (y) are represented with colours. The black rectangles and segments show the structure of the tree. The I_j in grey are the instance sets of the leaves.

We now specify the additive method in more depth. Let us start with one fitted tree and let's add another tree 'on top of it' that reduces the errors of the first tree (e.g. by fitting the new tree to the residuals). Let us call T_1 the first tree.

The second tree T_2 is built in the following manner: $T_2(x_t) = T_1(x_t) + \gamma_2 f_2(x_t)$ where γ_2 and f_2 are chosen so that T_2 minimizes the loss function (total variance or weighted sum of cross-entropy for instance). The procedure can be iterated any number of times, of course:

$$T_m(x_t) = T_{m-1}(x_t) + \gamma_m f_m(x_t).$$

The true challenge is obviously to find the optimal γ_m and f_m. Recent approaches[4] tackle this problem using gradient-based techniques. Below, we describe the algorithm behind XGBoost (Chen and Guestrin 2016). For each occurrence, the method boils down to the computation of the weighted sum of prediction stemming from the different trees.

We start with some notation. We write $\hat{y}^m$ as the prediction of the mth iteration of the process. L is the loss function, e.g. weighted variance for a regression tree or weighted cross-entropy for multi-class classification. The objective we seek to minimize is the following:

$$\Lambda^m = \sum_{t=1}^{T} L(y_t, \hat{y}_t^m + f^m(x_t)) + \Omega(f^m),$$

---

[4]For instance, XGBoost and LightGBM; both are based on the seminal idea from Friedman (2001).

where f^m is the function (here, the tree) we are seeking. $\Omega(f^m)$ is a regularization term that penalizes the complexity of the tree. We abstractly write q for the structure of the f^m (nodes/splits). In addition, we set, without loss of generality, the number of leaves to J and their weights (in the final weighted sum) to w_j. Assuming an L^2 form for $\Omega(f^m)$ and using a second order Taylor expansion of L with respect to $\widehat{y}_t^m$, the objective simplifies to the approximate form

$$\widetilde{\Lambda}^m = \sum_{t=1}^{T} \left[g_i f^m(x_t) + \frac{1}{2} h_i f^m(x_t)^2 \right] + \frac{\lambda}{2} \sum_{j=1}^{J} w_j^2,$$

where g_i and h_i correspond to the first two derivatives in the Taylor expansion. If we define the instance set of leaf number j: $I_j = \{i \mid q(x_t) = j\}$, then

$$\widetilde{\Lambda}^m = \sum_{j=1}^{J} \left[w_j \sum_{k \in I_j} g_k + \frac{w_j^2}{2} \left(\sum_{k \in I_j} h_k + \lambda \right) \right],$$

and the minimizing weights are, for each given leaf:

$$w_j^* = -\frac{\sum\limits_{k \in I_j} g_k}{\sum\limits_{k \in I_j} h_k + \lambda}.$$

The question is then to find a proper tree structure and this is usually performed via some greedy algorithm. Note that in the weights above, the gradient sits at the numerator, which seems intuitive given the negative sign: as is customary, the algorithm goes in the opposite direction. Finally, refinements can be incorporated to further enhance the algorithm. One such possibility is shrinkage. The idea behind it is that full-scale learning can lead the optimization in the good direction, but *too far*.[5] Hence, newly added trees can be slightly diluted by a factor η, which leaves more room for future trees:

$$T_m(x_t) = T_{m-1}(x_t) + \eta \, \gamma_m f_m(x_t).$$

Another possibility is subsampling and we refer to the original contributions for more details on this topic.

7.3   DATA AND PROTOCOL

This section describes the data used and the empirical protocol for our ML model. We focus on US stocks in order to avoid dealing with different currencies and countries as we might find in European or global stocks. We also selected the universe of US stocks for its higher coverage of financial metrics and its relative efficiency.

Henceforth, we use interchangeably the term 'feature' or dependent variable to express a stock characteristic. In this section, we will explain the features transformation

---

[5]We invite the interested reader to visit the Kaggle blog for a deep dive into hyper-parameters tuning. http://blog.kaggle.com/2017/01/23/a-kaggle-master-explains-gradient-boosting

that has been performed to linearize each characteristic and to express them in the same unit (even if XGBoost and tree regression are designed to cope with non-normalized variables).

7.3.1   Data

We collect monthly returns and monthly stocks' characteristics for the top 3000 US stocks according to their market capitalization, free-float adjusted. The full dataset goes from December 1999 until December 2017. The universe of stocks consists of all common equities using Quandl premium equity packages. The dataset is point in time and therefore does not suffer from survivorship bias. Prices are monthly discrete total return, taking into account stocks splits and dividend adjustments. Prices are expressed in dollars as all the other amounts.

This dataset represents approximately 620 000 instances, an instance consisting of the combination of a stock and a date. The variable y we want to predict is the probability of one-year forward sector-neutral outperformance. The explanatory variables in our model encompass a large set of 200 features based on traditional, financial, price and volume-based metrics.

In order to avoid a look-ahead bias we will use a 24-months rolling windows for training the model. Therefore, prediction will be possible only at $t + 12$ months, and we offset the prediction date by the forward time period used for training. We will repeat the training every month, hence updating every month the probability for each stock to outperform after 12 months. Each rolling analysis period will be split according to 80% training data and 20% of testing data, keeping the testing data in the most recent part of the rolling window to avoid 'testing in the past'. The testing part is used to adjust the hyper-parameters because it is paramount to avoid overfitting in order to produce outperformance out-of-sample.

7.3.2   Features and labels engineering

A substantial portion of research in ML-based financial applications fails because of a lack of economic framing and unrealistic or ill-defined goals, such as finding the 'best stocks'. Instead, our purpose is more reasonable, as we seek to predict extreme behaviour and single out the goods stocks from the worst ones within each sector and express this as a probability in order to rank the full cross-section of stocks.

We 'engineer' both labels (future returns) and features so as to put a structure that will provide the algorithm with a more causal representation of the equity markets. Again, we shift away from the traditional approach that seeks to infer future performance from past prices or short-term returns. We set fundamental, risk, volume and momentum-based signals as our features. Each feature and label is expressed in z-scores and then translated into percentiles to ease the comparison in the results analysis part.

Following the old quant saying 'garbage in, garbage out', we try as much as possible to impose some structure to features.

In the same fashion, we impose some structure in the labels by sequentially:

1. Resorting to one-year (1Y) performance, which is enough for having a certain degree of causality between the nature of the features in the datasets and the tenor of the labels.

2. Normalizing according to the sector of each stock. An alternative would be to use dummy sector variables in the features, but the purpose is much clearer by putting the right structure on the labels.

3. Getting rid of the outliers in the labels: stocks outside the (5th; 95th) percentile of their sector-neutral performance are excluded for the training. Our goal here is to imply as much causality for the features with the labels. For instance, we are getting rid of stocks that have been acquired in an M&A, or stocks that have been in fraud accounting scandals, because we want the labels to be truly linked to the features.

4. Processing only the remaining top and bottom quintiles of the filtered stocks. We want to approximate a function for the top and bottom parts of the cross-section. By doing so, we hope to have a clear hierarchical representation of sector under/outperforming stocks.

We define Y_1^i as the probability of a stock i to outperform its sector S over a one-year-ahead period. Accordingly, $Y_0^i = 1 - Y_1^i$ will be the probability of a stock i to underperform its sector after one year. Y_1^i serves as the primary input of our classification task. The label we process in the algorithm is the following:

$$y^i = \begin{cases} 1 \ if \ Y_0^i \geq 0.5 \\ 0 \ if \ Y_0^i < 0.5 \end{cases}.$$

Hence, this variable tracks whether or not the corresponding stock is likely to outperform. In the next subsection, we focus on the explanatory variables that we rely on to predict y^i.

7.3.3 Variables/Features used

In our model, we aim to predict, each month, the probability of a stock outperforming its sector using extreme gradient boosted trees. Since we want to sequentially create weak learners (individual trees) and use the residuals (badly classified labels) for the next round, we will use all features in our dataset. In the case of ML prediction using trees, highly correlated variables will not perturb the models. A large number of highly correlated variables will give the algorithm more degrees of freedom to determine the added value of each single variable.

In order to assess the potential level of correlation between the features datasets we computed a hierarchical clustering for the rank correlation of the features. As depicted in Figure 7.2, we can identify different groups of metrics that represent family of signals. For instance, the left rectangle in Figure 7.2 shows the metrics based on valuation ratios, from simple earnings yield and book-to-price metrics to more rules-based composite metrics, imposing more conditionality depending on the nature of the company.

The centre rectangle represents the cluster for risk signals based on prices, such as different tenor for price volatilities signals, or correlation acceleration in volatility. In total, the 200 features can be clustered into six families of metrics and we list them in Table 7.1.

In this chapter, we keep all features in the dataset. Said differently, we do not resort to important feature discovery in the first phase, but rather leave the tree-boosted model

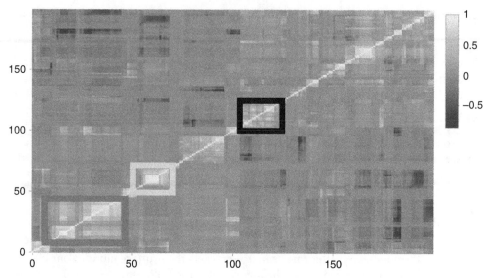

FIGURE 7.2 Hierarchical clustering for rank-correlation between variable. Rank-correlation is computed for the entire dataset and clustered afterwards using Euclidian distance. The hierarchical heatmap graph is colour-coded as follows: the more (less) saturated, the more (less) correlated.

TABLE 7.1 Summary and examples of features per family type

Valuation	Prof/Qual	MoM/technical	Risk	Estimates	Volume/ liquidity
Earnings yield	ROE	12-1 monthly returns	5-year bear volume	EPS revision	Market cap
Book yield	FCF/assets	6 months RSI	3-year correlation	EY FY1	Volume
Sales yield	Gross profit/ capital employed	12–1 m returns/ volume	Specific risk residual from PCA	EPS growth FY1	Liquidity at risk

According to hierarchical cluster, six main families of features based on metrics' types. We provide some examples for each family.

to determine which features matter through the regularization parameter in the training part. Moreover, we are using a very short period of time for each step of the training (two years), hence keeping a high number of characteristics is a good way of having more degrees of freedom when adapting to changing market conditions, e.g. sector and style rotation, risk on-risk off periods, etc.

7.4 BUILDING THE MODEL

In the previous section we presented and explained the objective of the method, the dataset and variables and how they were structured. We now dig into the details of the general parameters and hyper-parameters used in the XGBoost[6] model. In this section, we introduce the ML model, as well as its hyper-parameters that we found of interest using our data. Additionally, we will cover how to tune them in order to give a more practical 'how to' to the reader.

XGBoost is an open source model available in different languages (C++, R, Python, Julia, Scala) that has been extremely popular in the computer science community thanks to its flexibility in hyper-parameter tuning and to its fast code execution.

We covered the mathematical aspects of tree boosting in Section 7.2, therefore we will restrict the scope of this section to the practical side of things. Our goal in this exercise is to predict the probability of sector-neutral outperformance for a stock and we rely on a classification approach (we recall that our label y^i can take only one or zero as values).

In order to obtain a probability of sector-neutral outperformance, we resort to logistics-based classification: the score of the occurrence will be processed through the sigmoid function,[7] which will result in a figure between zero and one.

The objective function will be the usual logistic loss function complemented with a regularization term which we use to control the model complexity. Controlling for model complexity is a first order point for boosted trees as they tend to overfit the data and could exhibit poor generalization behaviour out of sample.

7.4.1 Hyper-parameters

There are many different hyper-parameters in tree boosting; covering them all is outside the scope of the chapter (they often depend on the method of tree aggregation and on the implementation). We will confine our introduction to the parameters that we have tested or used along this exercise. The list is as follows:

- The learning rate, η: it is the step size shrinkage used to prevent overfitting. After each boosting step, we can directly get the weights of new features and η actually shrinks the feature weights to make the boosting process more conservative.
- The minimum split loss, γ: it is the minimum loss reduction required to make a further partition on a leaf node of the tree. The larger the algorithm, the more conservative it will be (trees will be smaller).
- The maximum depth: it is the longest path (in terms of node) from the root to a leaf of the tree. Increasing this value will make the model more complex and more likely to be overfitting.
- The scale of positive weights controls the balance of positive and negative weights: it is useful for unbalanced classes. A typical value to consider: sum(negative cases)/sum(positive cases).
- Regression λ: it is the L^2 regularization term on weights (mentioned in the technical section) and increasing this value will make the model more conservative.

---

[6]XGBoost (eXtreme Gradient Boosting) is an open source package, often referred to as the third generation of tree boosting model. The interest reader could find documentation, codes and example on the official website: http://xgboost.readthedocs.io/en/latest

[7]The sigmoid function is defined by $S(x) = (1 + e^{-x})^{-1}$.

7.4.2 Cross-validation

In Figure 7.3 we perform cross-validation on three different parameters.[8] In order to give the reader a step-by-step approach, we computed a chart keeping the training and the test prediction error for each pair of parameters tested on the aggregation of 1000 trees. The evaluation metric used for this cross-validation exercise is the simple mean error, defined by the probability threshold of 0.5, giving the binary classification error rate.

From left to right we are increasing the depth of the trees, making them more complex following the sequence of (3,5,7). From top to bottom we are increasing the

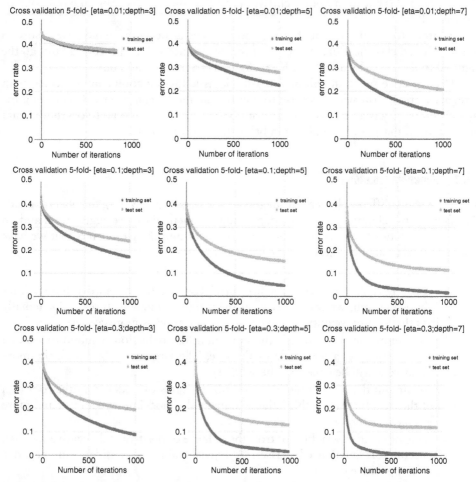

FIGURE 7.3 Fivefold cross-validation for tree boosted models. We maintain all default parameters except number of rounds, depth of the trees and learning rate.

---

[8]For more details on cross-validation, refer to Chapter 7 of Friedman et al. (2009).

learning rate from 0.01 to 0.1 to finally 0.3. A higher learning rate means that the model will learn faster and potentially overfit and will not generalize well when predicting on unseen instances.

The bias/variance tradeoff is at the core of the ML algorithms and echoes the core principle of the penalized objective function in XGBoost: minimizing loss and controlling complexity. A higher error rate associated with a simpler model is more likely to generalize well out of sample. As an example, the model tested with a low shrinkage (eta = 0.01) and very shallow trees (depth = 3) does learn extremely slowly, even after 1000 iterations. This model, which is the one on the top left part of Figure 7.3, clearly underfits the data: it is not learning fast enough. On the contrary, the model in the bottom right part of Figure 7.3 (depth = 7; eta = 0.3) is learning fast (reaching 20% error rate after 100 rounds in the test set) and is plateauing afterwards. In this example the model is more likely to overfit: this model reaches almost 99% accuracy in the training set.

Generally speaking, one can see that increasing the depth of the trees helps in decreasing the error for a lower level of shrinkage. One can note that for an eta of 0.3, the difference in test error between a depth level of 5 or 7 is very marginal, which suggests some bias in those two models (they managed to reach 99% of accuracy in the training set after 1000 rounds).

We performed a grid search in order to confirm our conclusions drawn from Figure 7.3. The parameters selected for our predictive boosted tree model are:

- 1000 rounds with an early stop at 100 in order to prevent overfitting
- η set at 0.1 to ensure a reasonable learning pace
- γ set to 0: in our test γ seemed to be of inferior importance compared with the other parameters
- depth of 5: we need to have some (but not too much) complexity to benefit from the full set of 200 features
- L^2 regularization parameter fixed at 1, which is the default value in the XGBoost model.

7.4.3 Assessing the quality of the model

In the process of assessing the quality of the model, many different evaluation metrics are available. In the cross-validation part, we deliberately disclosed only the mean error for the training and test datasets. In this sub-section, we want to introduce the concept of confusion matrix and all the related metrics in order to precisely assess a ML model's quality.

Each part of Figure 7.4 can be explicated as:

- **Fp**: false positive. Stock predicted to outperform and that did not outperform out of sample.
- **Fn**: false negative. Stock predicted to underperform that outperform out of sample.
- **Tp**: true positive. Stock predicted to outperform which outperform out of sample.
- **Tn**: true negative. Stock predicted to underperform which underperform out of sample.

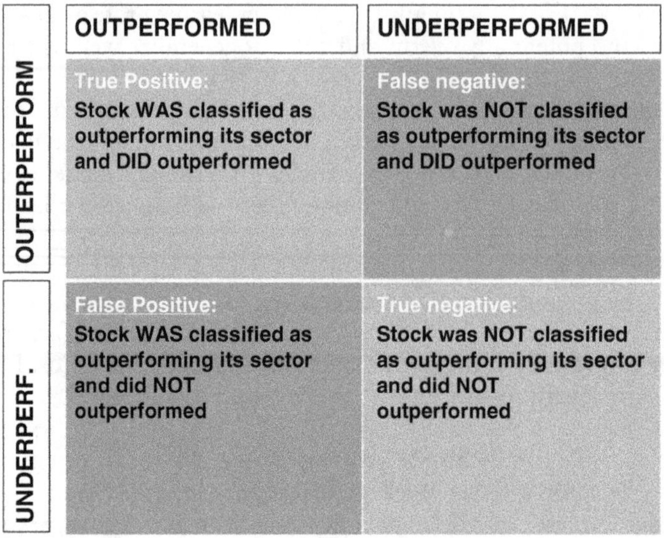

	OUTPERFORMED	UNDERPERFORMED
OUTERPERFORM	**True Positive:** Stock WAS classified as outperforming its sector and DID outperformed	**False negative:** Stock was NOT classified as outperforming its sector and DID outperformed
UNDERPERF.	**False Positive:** Stock WAS classified as outperforming its sector and did NOT outperformed	**True negative:** Stock was NOT classified as outperforming its sector and did NOT outperformed

FIGURE 7.4 Confusion matrix illustration. We explain the confusion matrix in our exercise which is a supervised classification model to predict sector-neutral outperforming stocks. On the y-axis the real labels, on the x-axis the predicted labels.

From those four cases, we can derive several classical metrics that assess the quality of the model.

Precision: $\mathbf{Tp/(Tp + Fp)}$

Precision could be defined as a rate of successful prediction for sector-neutral outperforming stocks.

Recall: $\mathbf{Tp/(Tp + Fn)}$

Recall could be defined as a true rate, since we include the instances that have been wrongly classified in negative.

Accuracy: $\mathbf{(Tp + Tn)/(Tp + Tn + Fp + Fn)}$

This is the accuracy level used in the cross-validation part.

Those measures can help detecting imbalances in classes, that could lead to a 'lazy' classifier problem, where the global accuracy results are good but one class is underrepresented and showing a lower level of accuracy. In our exercise, we will be less interested in having a great accuracy in finding true negative than true positive.

In our selected model, the outcome for the different evaluation metrics are as follows:

- Accuracy: 0.80
- Precision: 0.797
- Recall: 0.795.

At early stages, we decided to train on the tails of the cross-sectional distribution, hence there is very little imbalance in the class: recall, precision and accuracy are therefore very close.

7.4.4   Variable importance

One common criticism against ML is the so-called 'black-box'[9] nature of the prediction, as if it was impossible to understand or trace which feature or combination of features is responsible for the forecast. Ensemble learning using trees does have a very nice feature that rules out this criticism: variable importance.

In Figure 7.5, we display the average variable importance of our model that we trained and used for prediction every month from December 2002 until December 2017.[10] Each month, we keep the variable importance from the trained model. There are a lot a different metrics for variable importance. A popular metric in trees ensemble is the Gini impurity index used for selecting split points.

In our exercise, we use the gain metric, which is equal to the relative contribution (in terms of accuracy) to the model from the corresponding features. To compute the gain metric, one has to take the contribution for each feature for each tree averaged for each month. One can summarize the gain metric as a prediction usefulness indicator. All gain measures across features sum to 1.

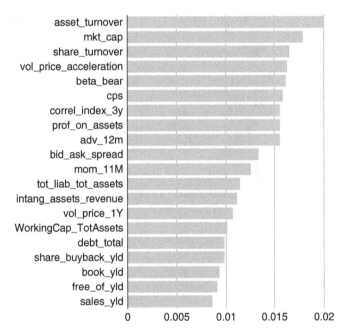

FIGURE 7.5   Top 20 most important variables. We show the most important variables in our model. We averaged the monthly results for the gain measure after training.

---

[9]Criticism that is not always justified for more complex models, e.g. neural nets, which can be 'white boxed' with 20 lines of Python.

[10]In order to clarify the protocol: we make predictions every month, e.g. for the last prediction of end of November 2017, we used the features matrix as of November 2017 and used the model that has been trained using a 24-months dataset that started in November 2014 until November 2016.

First, we can see that on average there is not a feature that is dominating and explaining the majority of the prediction's importance. Then, looking at the type of features, one can note:

- We have features coming from the six different metrics families gathered in Table 7.1.
- Within the top 20 features, price-risk metrics seem to have a better ranking as a group than valuation, liquidity metrics, etc.
- We find some common, well-known and over-researched characteristics mentioned in the asset pricing literature (book yield for value, market cap for size, profitability on assets for quality, price volatility for low volatility anomaly and 12-1 month momentum).

7.5   RESULTS AND DISCUSSION

We now proceed to a use case. Our use case will test our ML-based signals as a base for constructing equally-weighted portfolios. We process our probability of sector outperformance just like any other signal. We normalize it, express it in a percentile and assess the performance of monthly rebalanced decile portfolios.[11] As a benchmark, we construct two signals and follow the same protocol mentioned above. Those two signals are:

1. A simple multifactor signal blending using commonly accepted composites metrics to reflect the definition of 'factor investing'.
2. A linear combination of the top 20 metrics picked according to the top 20 most important features from our boosting tree model.

In this section we provide a statistical evaluation of the signal implemented as a naïve strategy. We will use as benchmarks an equally-weighted (EW) portfolio made of commonly accepted stock characteristics, which are:

1. Value: earnings yield, book yield, EV/EBITDA.
2. Quality: return on equity, debt/equity.
3. Momentum: 12-1 total return performance.
4. Low volatility: three-year and one-year price volatility.
5. Size: market cap.

The second benchmark will be an equal-weight portfolio, using the signal made of a linear combination of the top 20 most important features.

7.5.1   Time series analysis for equally-weighted decile portfolios

Our purpose in this backtest is to assess the added value of using an ML signal in a multi-factor framework compared to existing methodology. In order to compare the different

---

[11]Such portfolio sorting procedures are commonplace since the seminal work of Fama and French (1992).

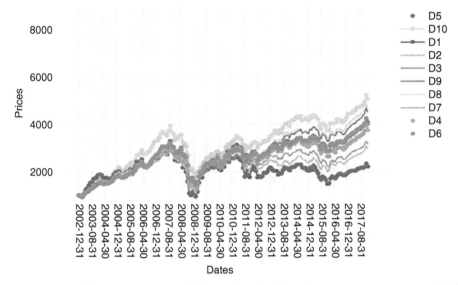

FIGURE 7.6 Wealth curve for decile portfolios based on multifactor signal.

signals, we create equal-weight decile portfolios according to the ranked z-score of each signal. We then analyze the computed time series of those signals using monthly returns. We finally focus on the top decile (D10, the most tilted) to give more analytical results.

Figures 7.6–7.8 are wealth curves expressed in dollars for the two benchmarks (multifactor signal and linear combination of the top 20 features) and the ML model using boosted trees classification.

One can note that the three models show a cumulated monotonic performance pattern across the deciles, i.e. the performance of the first decile is lower than that of the second, which is lower than that of the third, etc.

The scale of the three graphs is deliberately the same, making the visual comparison much easier. One can see that the dispersion of performance between deciles is much clearer with the ML model, which has been trained to classify sector-neutral outperforming and underperforming stocks. The portfolios using the linear combination of the top 20 features is also exhibiting a better cumulated performance monotonic pattern.

7.5.2 Further evidence of economic gains

In order to further simplify the comparison between our model and the two benchmarks, we plot the annualized return per decile per model in one plot. In Figure 7.9, one can see that the spread between the average returns of decile 1 and decile 10 is higher for the ML model (9.8%) compared with the linear combination of the top 20 features (6%) and the simple multifactor portfolio (5.1%).

The ML model benefits here from its tail training where we focused on the top and bottom quintiles according to the one-year-forward performance to train the model. Accordingly, and as expected, the ML model yields the worst performance for the lowest decile (D1) and the highest one for the tenth decile (D10).

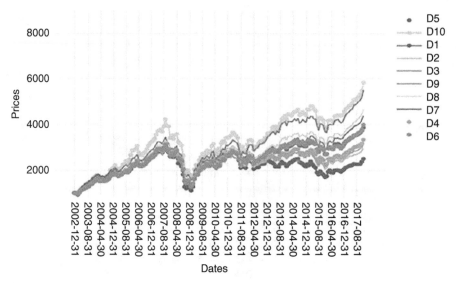

FIGURE 7.7   Wealth curve for decile portfolios based on linear combination of the top 20 features from the ML model.

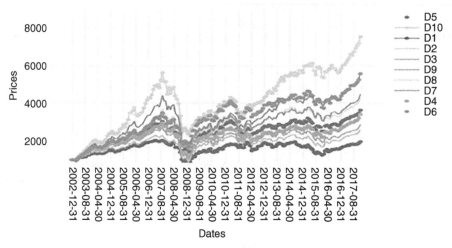

FIGURE 7.8   Wealth curve for decile portfolios based on the machine learning model.

So far, we have focused our analysis on pure performance and Table 7.2 sheds some light on alternative and complementary metrics of interest. This assesses the robustness of the ML model more deeply.

Analyzing risks measures shows that the multifactor portfolio has the lowest volatility (14.7%) compared with the linear combination (19%) and the ML approach (17.6%). This result is not surprising: the multifactor portfolio has 1/5 of the final blended signal that is coming from a low volatility exposure. On top of that, it is well

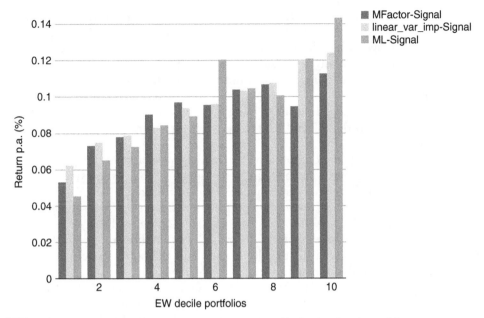

FIGURE 7.9 Annualized performance comparison for each decile of each model.

TABLE 7.2 Analytics

	MFactor	lin_var_imp	ML
Observations	180	180	180
Median monthly return (%)	1.2	1.5	1.9
Annualized return (%)	11.2	12.4	14.3
Annualized volatility (%)	14.7	19.0	17.6
Avg Rank IC (12 M)	0.05	0.06	0.11
Avg Rank IC (12 M forward vol)	−0.46	0.02	−0.05
Return/risk	0.76	0.65	0.81
t-stats	2.87	2.39	2.95
Average annual turnover (two ways) (%)	155	203	189

We are comparing the analytics for the top decile (decile 10) portfolio for each model – the two benchmarks on the left and the machine learning model on the right.

known that certain simple quality associated metrics such as debt to equity overlap with a low volatility profile.

Regarding the risk-adjusted performance, the ML model generates a Sharpe ratio of 0.81 compared with 0.76 for the multifactor and 0.65 for the linear combination of top 20 features.

Looking at average rank information coefficient (IC) reveals that the ML signal is better to predict the forward 12-months performance. ML signal shows an average IC of 11% compared with 5% for the multifactor and 6% for the linear combination of top 20 variables.

Most interestingly, the average IC numbers for predicting the forward realized volatility show a result of −46% for the multifactor signal. This number should be interpreted as follows: a high level of multifactor signal implies a negative correlation with volatility. Said differently, a high level of multifactor score implies a higher exposure to low volatility stocks. This result is not true with the ML model and the other benchmark.

Finally, the three t-stats of our models are all significant, the highest being the ML one (2.95) compared with 2.87 and 2.39 respectively for the multifactor and the linear combination.

Due to its more dynamic approach, the ML signal generates a higher level of turnover (189%) compared with the multifactor signal (155%). Still, asset rotation is lower than that of the linear combination of the top 20 features.

Results from this section reveal that portfolios based on the ML signals outperformed both benchmarks on a risk-adjusted basis. The ML signal displayed a better IC for one-year performance forward and a neutral IC for volatility. A long-short strategy based on the ML signal (long the top decile and short the bottom one) outperforms both benchmarks on a dollar-neutral basis.

The non-linear and dynamic approach of the signal based on our ML model proved to be more rewarded and more efficient on all metrics (except turnover). This highlights the added value of the boosted tree algorithm, the regularization and the large dataset of features kept for training the model.

7.6 CONCLUSION

In this chapter, we introduce a boosted tree algorithm applied to systematic equity investing. We demonstrate the efficiency of using feature and label engineering. Applying more conditionality and imposing a more causal structure allows a modern quantitative approach to make accurate long-term predictions. This insightful finding contradicts recent criticisms that ML-based approaches were suitable only when predicting very short-term price movements.

We provide guidance on how to tune, train and test an ML-based model using traditional financial characteristics such as valuation and profitability metrics, but also price momentum, risk estimates, volume and liquidity characteristics. We show that framing the problem is the first priority and we address it by engineering the features and transforming the labels according to the investment objective.

We find that a naïve equally-weighted portfolio using a boosted tree algorithm with 200 features generates an average outperformance of 3.1%, compared with a simple signal blended multifactor portfolio. Our results also suggest that the ML-based signal is complementary to simple multifactor signals. In a context where the risk of commoditization for equity multifactor portfolios is high, suffering from crowding that could lead to arbitrage of the style equity premia, ML-based signal could constitute an effective remedy for the era post *smart beta hangover*. The dynamic nature of the signals could constitute a real advantage even in the simplest weighting scheme and implementation process.

REFERENCES

Ammann, M., Coqueret, G., and Schade, J.P. (2016). Characteristics-based portfolio choice with leverage constraints. *Journal of Banking & Finance* 70: 23–37.

Ang, A. (2014). *Asset Management: A Systematic Approach to Factor Investing*. Oxford University Press.

Arévalo, R., García, J., Guijarro, F., and Peris, A. (2017). A dynamic trading rule based on filtered flag pattern recognition for stock market price forecasting. *Expert Systems with Applications* 81: 177–192.

Ballings, M., Van den Poel, D., Hespeels, N., and Gryp, R. (2015). Evaluating multiple classifiers for stock price direction prediction. *Expert Systems with Applications* 42 (20): 7046–7056.

Banz, R.W. (1981). The relationship between return and market value of common stocks. *Journal of Financial Economics* 9 (1): 3–18.

Bodnar, T., Mazur, S., and Okhrin, Y. (2017). Bayesian estimation of the global minimum variance portfolio. *European Journal of Operational Research* 256 (1): 292–307.

Brandt, M.W., Santa-Clara, P., and Valkanov, R. (2009). Parametric portfolio policies: exploiting characteristics in the cross-section of equity returns. *Review of Financial Studies* 22 (9): 3411–3447.

Chen, T. and Guestrin, C. (2016). XGBoost: A scalable tree boosting system. In: *Proceedings of the 22nd ACM SIGKDD International Conference on Knowledge Discovery and Data Mining*, 785—794. ACM.

Daniel, K. and Titman, S. (1997). Evidence on the characteristics of cross sectional variation in stock returns. *Journal of Finance* 52 (1): 1–33.

Fama, E.F. and French, K.R. (1992). The cross-section of expected stock returns. *Journal of Finance* 47 (2): 427–465.

Fama, E.F. and French, K.R. (1993). Common risk factors in the returns on stocks and bonds. *Journal of Financial Economics* 33 (1): 3–56.

Fischer, T. and Krauss, C. (2018). Deep learning with long short-term memory networks for financial market predictions. *European Journal of Operational Research* 270: 654—669.

Freund, Y. and Schapire, R.E. (1997). A decision-theoretic generalization of on-line learning and an application to boosting. *Journal of Computer and System Sciences* 55 (1): 119–139.

Friedman, J., Hastie, T., and Tibshirani, R. (2000). Additive logistic regression: a statistical view of boosting (with discussion and a rejoinder by the authors). *Annals of Statistics* 28 (2): 337–407.

Friedman, J. (2001). Greedy function approximation: a gradient boosting machine. *Annals of Statistics* 1189–1232.

Friedman, J., Hastie, T., and Tibshirani, R. (2009). *The Elements of Statistical Learning*, 2e. Springer.

Green, J., Hand, J.R., and Zhang, X.F. (2013). The supraview of return predictive signals. *Review of Accounting Studies* 18 (3): 692–730.

Harvey, C.R., Liu, Y., and Zhu, H. (2016). ... and the cross-section of expected returns. *Review of Financial Studies* 29 (1): 5–68.

Ilmanen, A. (2011). *Expected Returns: An Investor's Guide to Harvesting Market Rewards*. Wiley.

Jegadeesh, N. and Titman, S. (1993). Returns to buying winners and selling losers: implications for stock market efficiency. *Journal of Finance* 48 (1): 65–91.

Jegadeesh, N. and Titman, S. (2001). Profitability of momentum strategies: an evaluation of alternative explanations. *Journal of Finance* 56 (2): 699–720.

Kahn, R.N. and Lemmon, M. (2016). The asset manager's dilemma: how smart beta is disrupting the investment management industry. *Financial Analysts Journal* 72 (1): 15–20.

Krauss, C., Do, X.A., and Huck, N. (2017). Deep neural networks, gradient-boosted trees, random forests: statistical arbitrage on the S&P 500. *European Journal of Operational Research* 259 (2): 689–702.

McLean, R.D. and Pontiff, J. (2016). Does academic research destroy stock return predictability? *Journal of Finance* 71 (1): 5–32.

Nair, B.B., Kumar, P.S., Sakthivel, N.R., and Vipin, U. (2017). Clustering stock price time series data to generate stock trading recommendations: an empirical study. *Expert Systems with Applications* 70: 20–36.

Patel, J., Shah, S., Thakkar, P., and Kotecha, K. (2015). Predicting stock and stock price index movement using trend deterministic data preparation and machine learning techniques. *Expert Systems with Applications* 42 (1): 259–268.

Schapire, R.E. (1990). The strength of weak learnability. *Machine Learning* 5 (2): 197–227.

Subrahmanyam, A. (2010). The cross-section of expected stock returns: what have we learnt from the past twenty-five years of research? *European Financial Management* 16 (1): 27–42.

Van Dijk, M.A. (2011). Is size dead? A review of the size effect in equity returns. *Journal of Banking & Finance* 35 (12): 3263–3274.

A Social Media Analysis
of Corporate Culture

Andy Moniz

8.1 INTRODUCTION

In today's globalized, service-based economy, many firms derive substantial value from their intangible assets. Examples include corporate reputation, brand value, innovative efficiency (Chan et al. 2001), human capital (Edmans 2011) and organizational capital. The lack of physical substance associated with intangible assets, their opaque ownership rights and non-existent market prices limit firms from valuing and recording most types of intangible assets in their financial statements. Until accounting standards change, investors seeking to resolve this 'value paradox' and integrate intangible asset valuations into their decision-making processes must seek alternative sources of information beyond a firm's own financial statements. In our view, one alternative source of information is publicly available text published on the web, and in particular, social media.

The term 'social media' describes a variety of 'new and emerging sources of online information that are created, initiated, circulated and used by consumers intent on educating each other about products, brands, services, personalities and issues' (Blackshaw and Nazzaro, 2006; Gaines-Ross 2010). Social media enables individuals to share their opinions, criticisms and suggestions in public. To the best of our knowledge, prior textual analysis studies of social media datasets have mostly captured the perspective of consumers (for example, Amazon product reviews). By contrast, this study seeks to examine a potentially overlooked stakeholder group, namely, a firm's employees. The goal of this study is to describe how mining social media datasets may help investors learn about a firm's corporate culture. This multidimensional concept is typically defined as 'a set of values, beliefs, and norms of behavior shared by members of a firm that influences individual employee preferences and behaviors'.

For the purposes of this study, we retrieve 417 645 posts for 2237 US companies from the career community website Glassdoor.com and employ computational linguistic techniques to analyze employees' discussions about their firms. The website acts as a forum for employees to provide commentary on the 'pros' and 'cons' of their firms' cultures for the benefit of potential job seekers. Employee discussions cover a diverse set of topics ranging from perceptions of canteen food, work/life balance, salaries and benefits to views on company strategy and management.

We offer two important contributions to the academic literature. First, we provide a methodology to infer corporate culture from social media. The intangible nature of corporate culture has generated much controversy regarding the creation of a valid construct (Cooper et al. 2001; Pinder 1998; Ambrose and Kulik 1999; O'Reilly et al. 1991). Prior organizational literature either relies upon measures that lack sufficient depth or contain substantial measurement errors (Waddock and Graves 1997; Daines et al. 2010). In recent years, the development of computational linguistics techniques has enabled researchers to automatically organize, summarize and condense unstructured text data and extract key themes from vast amounts of data. Our approach provides a means to infer employee perceptions at a higher frequency and for a broader cross-section of companies than is possible using traditional survey-based measures. Second, we contribute to the literature on investors' underreaction to intangible information. A growing body of research finds that the stock market fails to fully incorporate information regarding a firm's intangible assets (e.g. Edmans 2011; Chan et al. 2001). Under a mispricing channel, an intangible asset affects the stock price only when it subsequently manifests in tangible outcomes which are valued by the stock market. This finding is attributed to the 'lack-of-information' hypothesis (Edmans 2011). In this study, we provide statistical evidence of a relation between employees' perceptions of performance-orientated cultures (defined as firms where employees frequently discuss the need to meet goals and deadlines) and subsequent earnings surprises. Our findings are consistent with the notion that financial analysts underestimate the tangible benefits of corporate culture.

The remainder of this chapter is organized as follows. Section 8.2 provides an overview of the literature associated with the measurement of corporate culture. Section 8.3 describes the social media dataset. Section 8.4 describes the computational linguistics technique used to infer employees' perceptions of corporate culture. Section 8.5 assesses the relation between corporate cultures and firms' earnings surprises. Section 8.6 concludes.

8.2   LITERATURE REVIEW

Traditionally, investors' abilities to decipher the 'value relevance' of a firm's intangible assets have been hampered by a lack of data. Typically, a firm's human capital management policies may be inferred from corporate social responsibility (CSR) reports (Kolk 2008) or from external surveys such as Fortune's '100 Best Companies to Work for in America' list (Edmans 2011; Levering et al. 1984). These sources suffer from a number of drawbacks. First, CSR disclosures are voluntary in nature and firms' motivations for publishing such disclosures are often unclear. Recent evidence suggests that firms publish CSR reports merely for symbolic purposes to bolster their social image with consumers (Marquis and Toffel 2012; McDonnell and King 2013) rather than to increase transparency and accountability to investors. Second, CSR may be endogenous with respect to a firm's financial performance – companies may publish CSR reports only if they are more profitable or expect their future profitability to be higher. This relation may hinder investors' abilities to disaggregate the value-relevance of non-financial information (Flammer 2013). Third, CSR reports are often seen as a 'relatively low priority for companies' (Gray et al. 1995). Firms typically publish CSR disclosures with substantial delay versus accounting-related information, limiting the relevance of the disclosures for investment decisions. Survey-based measures of corporate culture seek to address some of the limitations associated with companies' own disclosures, yet also suffer from a number of drawbacks. Surveys are typically manually constructed and thus limited in scope by the number of questions they can ask and the number of companies they can cover, and they suffer in their timeliness to collect and process responses. In the case of Fortune's survey, the results are published infrequently (annually), limited to 100 firms, of which only around half are publicly listed, and only composite scores are published, potentially obscuring useful information (see also Daines et al. 2010). Importantly, firms pay to participate in the survey, thereby creating perverse incentives for firms to manipulate survey responses (Popadak 2013).

By contrast, social media describes a variety of 'new and emerging sources of online information that are created, initiated, circulated and used by consumers intent on educating each other about products, brands, services, personalities and issues' (Blackshaw and Nazzaro 2006; Gaines-Ross 2010; Elahi and Monachesi 2012). The textual analysis of social media datasets seeks to overcome many of the drawbacks associated with companies' own disclosures and surveys, offering a significant advancement for timely corporate culture analysis across a vast number of firms (Popadak 2013). Despite these potential benefits, the high costs associated with gathering, processing and structuring text into a standardized format for analysis suggest that intangible information may be overlooked by investors compared with structured datasets associated with traditional accounting information. Thus, even if intangible information is publicly available, it may be ignored by investors if it is not salient (Edmans 2011).

8.3 DATA AND SAMPLE CONSTRUCTION

In this section we describe our social media dataset and discuss the challenges associated with automated cultural analysis.

8.3.1 Description of online career community websites

We retrieve employee reviews posted to Glassdoor.com. While there are a number of career community websites, prior studies suggest that Glassdoor.com attracts the most diverse set of users (see Popadak (2013) for a review). For example, one alternative website provider identifies that its average user is 43 years old with an annual income of $106 000. A second website indicates that its niche market is college students and young professionals. By contrast, Glassdoor.com has an estimated 19 million unique users each month and appears to benefit from the most diverse audience as suggested by web traffic statistics from Quantcast.com. The website specializes in audience measurement and employs tracking software to build a picture of web audiences.

Table 8.1 reports descriptive statistics on the average profile of users of the Glassdoor website. Users' profiles appear to be fairly distributed across different sections of society in terms of age, income, education and ethnicity, suggesting that Glassdoor reviews should be representative of an average employee's perceptions of a firm.

TABLE 8.1　Descriptive statistics on the user profiles of Glassdoor.com

Characteristic	Category	Percentage of web traffic
Gender	Male	50%
	Female	50%
Age	<18	11%
	18–24	18%
	25–34	25%
	35–44	20%
	45–54	17%
	55–64	7%
Household income	65+	2%
	$0–50 k	47%
	$50–100 k	30%
	$100–150 k	13%
	$150 k+	10%
Education level	No College	27%
	College	51%
	Grad School	22%
Ethnicity	Caucasian	65%
	African American	13%
	Asian	10%
	Hispanic	10%
	Other	2%

This table reports descriptive statistics of Glassdoor.com user profiles obtained from the web analytics portal quantcast.com as at June 2015. The website measures audience data and compiles visitor profiles by installing tracking pixels on website pages. User profiles include data on gender, age, household income, education level and ethnicity.

Glassdoor states that its website editors seek to ensure the publication of honest, authentic and balanced reviews. Each review must meet strict community guidelines before it is published. Reviewers are required to provide commentary on both the 'pros' and 'cons' of a company to ensure a balanced profile (illustrated in Figure 8.1). This figure provides an example of a review posted for IBM. Each review includes metadata to identify whether a reviewer is a current or former employee, the employee's job title, location and number of years' service at the company. Each review must meet strict community guidelines before it is published.

Comments are reviewed by website editors to prevent reviewers from posting defamatory attacks, repeat comments or fake reviews, while identities are anonymized to allay employees' concerns of company reprisals in the case of negative comments (Popadak 2013). Approximately 15% of reviews are rejected by the website editors because they do not meet their guidelines. A further advantage of the dataset is a rich set of metadata which includes the publication date stamp of each review, the reviewer's number of years' work experience at the company, job title, employment status (part-time/full-time) and work location. In addition, reviewers summarize their opinions of firms in the form of 'star ratings' (on a scale of 1–5). Firms are rated along six dimensions – Culture and Values, Work/Life Balance, Senior Management, Comp and Benefits, Career Opportunities and an Overall Score. For the purposes of this

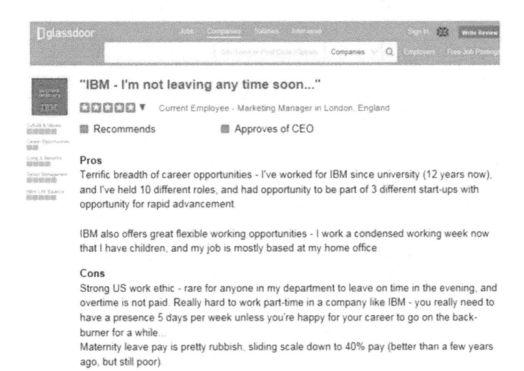

FIGURE 8.1 Illustrative examples of Glassdoor reviews.

study we predominantly rely upon reviewers' texts, which are available from 2008 onwards, compared with the star ratings, which are available on a consistent basis only from 2012.

8.3.2 Adding security identifiers to employee reviews

One of the primary challenges associated with unstructured data retrieval is the need to match reviewers' texts to structured data stored in traditional financial databases (e.g. accounting data). We design an algorithm which matches company names in Glassdoor reviews to the CRSP database. The approach takes into account the 'synonym detection problem' typically encountered when matching company names in text (see Engelberg 2008). For instance, the official company name International Business Machines in the CRSP database is more commonly referred to as IBM in Glassdoor reviews. Our algorithm first detects companies' popular names from company websites and Wikipedia, then uses this list of names to trawl through Glassdoor.com's subdomains to retrieve relevant reviews. In total, we retrieved 417 645 reviews for 2237 US companies for the period 2008–2015.

Table 8.2 displays descriptive statistics for the sample dataset. Panel A shows that the number of reviews has increased steadily over time. The majority of reviews are posted by North American employees. This observation mitigates a potential concern for cross-cultural analysis, namely, that differences in regional locations may account for

TABLE 8.2 Summary statistics of Glassdoor.com dataset

Panel A: Overview of the dataset by employment location[a]

Region	2008	2009	2010	2011	2012	2013	2014	2015	Total	% of total
Asia	189	285	926	1330	6311	6264	7798	2551	25.654	6%
Europe	307	257	796	435	1196	1849	2949	1619	9,40 K	2%
North America	13 139	10 136	15 637	18 068	30 100	45 821	71 444	25.698	230 043	55%
Other	40	53	97	130	632	751	967	429	3099	1%
Anonymous	1537	5001	11 760	13 798	20 931	25 552	46 429	24 433	149.441	36%
Total	15 212	15 732	29 216	33 761	59 170	80 237	129 587	54 730	417 645	
% of Total	3.6%	3.8%	7.0%	8.1%	14.2%	19.2%	31.0%	13.1%	100.0%	100.0%

Panel B: Overview of the dataset by employment status[b]

Region	Full-time employee	Part-time employee	Anonymous	Total	Current employee	Former employee	Total reviews
Asia ex Japan	18 954	224	6276	25 454	17.228	8.226	25.454
EMEA.	1.121	49	388	1558	956	602	1.558
Europe	5787	296	1125	9408	6038	3370	9408
Japan	118	9	73	200	109	91	200
Lath America	1124	18	399	1.541	987	554	1541
North America	119 506	21 290	89 247	230 043	133 114	96 929	230 043
Anonymous	56 464	6798	86 179	149 441	93 480	55 961	149 441
Total	203 074	28 684	185 887	417 645	251 912	165 733	417 645
% of Total	48.6%	6.9%	44.5%	100.0%	60.3%	39.7%	100.0%

Panel C: Overview of dataset by employees' years of service[c]

Region	<1 year experience	1–3 years' experience	5+ years' experience	10+ years' experience	Anonymous	Total	% of total
Asia	3675	12 800	3591	591	4997	25 654	6%
Europe	1254	3422	1348	628	2756	9408	2%
North America	33 242	69 275	30 072	17 326	80 128	230 043	55%
Other	330	1384	616	185	584	3099	1%
Anonymous	7829	24 252	13 282	7.383	96 695	149 441	36%
Total	46 330	111 133	48 909	26 113	185 160	417 645	
% of Total	11.1%	26.6%	11.7%	6.3%	44.3%	100.0%	100.0%

[a]This table provides descriptive statistics for Glassdoor reviews by employee location (region) and the year the review was posted. This information is obtained from reviewers' metadata.

[b]This table provides descriptive statistics for Glassdoor reviews by employee location and employment status (full-time/part-time, current/former employee). The Anonymous category refers to reviews where employment status was not provided.

[c]This table provides descriptive statistics for Glassdoor reviews by location and employees' number of years of service. The Anonymous category refers to posts without the number of years of service.

differences in employees' perceptions (see Hofstede 1980; Triandis et al. 1988). Panel B shows that 60% of the sample consists of reviews posted by individuals stating that they are current rather than former employees. Only a minority (6.9%) of reviewers state that they are part-time employees. Panel C indicates that reviewers have worked in their companies for an average of 1–3 years. Finally, Panel D reports the coverage of reviews by sector using Global Industry Classification Standard (GICS) classifications retrieved from the Compustat database. While the Glassdoor dataset includes reviews from all sectors, just over half of the reviews are from the Information Technology and Consumer Discretionary sectors. We view this coverage as a potential benefit of the dataset as service-based sectors are typically associated with knowledge-based assets such as R&D, human and organizational capital (Lev 2001).

8.3.3 Validating the integrity of employee reviews

One criticism often levied at social media analysis is the potential for sample bias. The bias refers to the potential to select a misrepresentative sample of reviews which may hinder statistical inference. In particular, differences in reviewers' native languages, cultures and human emotional experiences may result in unintended consequences when inferring sentiment (see Hogenboom et al. 2012; Pang and Lee 2004; Wierzbicka 1995). For instance, disgruntled former employees may have greater incentive to post negative comments about their prior companies. To assess the possibility of a sampling bias, we compare the information expressed in employees' star ratings versus their texts (Hogenboom et al. 2012, 2014). This approach is based on the premise that regardless of a reviewer's background, we expect to observe a monotonically increasing relationship between a reviewer's star rating and the expression of sentiment inferred from text. This is because star ratings are universal classifications of a reviewer's intended sentiment, independent of potential language, cultural or emotional differences (Hogenboom et al. 2012, 2014).

We estimate a panel regression where the dependent variable is the overall star rating for a firm and the independent variables are features extracted from reviewers' texts. Company fundamental data is retrieved from standard financial databases. Price-related variables are obtained from CRSP, accounting data is obtained from COMPUSTAT and analyst information from I/B/E/S. For controls, we include the star ratings: COMP is the 'Comp & Benefits' star rating, WORKLIFE is the 'Work/Life Balance' rating, MGT is reviewers' 'Senior Management' rating, CULTURE is the 'Culture & Values' star rating and CAREER is the 'Career Opportunities' rating. We supplement the star ratings with two indicator variables. The variable, Part-time, equals 1 if a reviewer is a part-time worker and zero otherwise. The variable, Former, equals 1 if a reviewer is a former employee and zero otherwise. These features are identified using metadata provided in each review.

We include controls for book-to-market (Log(Book/Market)), analyst revisions (Analyst Revisions), price momentum (Pmom) and one-year historic sales growth (SG). Log(Book/Market)) is the natural log of the book-to-value of equity measured as at the end of the preceding calendar year, following Fama and French (1992). Analyst revisions is the three-month sum of changes in the median analyst's forecast, divided by the firm's stock price in the prior month (Chan et al. 1996). Pmom is the (signed) stock's return measured over the previous 12 months. Finally, we include firm size

TABLE 8.3 Regression of reviewers' overall star ratings

	(1)	(2)
Intercept	0.000	0.040
	(2.320)	(1.657)
Former	−0.058	−0.059
	(−4.863)	(−4.754)
Part-time	0.053	0.053
	(5.296)	(5.875)
Log(Book Market)		0.004
		(1.663)
Log(Market Equity)		0.000
		(2.095)
Analyst revisions		0.632
		(2.312)
SG		0.006
		(0.170)
Pmom		0.009
		(1.417)
R^2	0.734	0.744

This table reports regression results on the relation between reviewers' Overall ratings, employees' metadata and firm characteristics. The dependent variable is Overall star rating score provided by Glassdoor reviewers (scale 1–5). Former is an indicator variable equal to 1 if the reviewer is a former employee of the company and zero otherwise. Part-time is an indicator variable equal to 1 if the reviewer is a part-time worker and zero otherwise. Please refer to the text for a description of the control variables. For presentational reasons, the star ratings 'Comp & Benefits', 'Work/Life Balance', 'Senior Management', 'Culture & Values' and 'Career Opportunities', included as control variables, are hidden from the table. Standard errors are clustered by firm following Petersen (2009). For each variable we report the corresponding robust t-statistic (in parentheses). Sample period: 2008–2015.

(Log(Market Equity)) measured at the end of the preceding calendar year. These controls are designed to account for a potential 'halo' effect caused if reviewers implicitly form their perceptions of companies using publicly available information (Fryxell and Wang 1994; Brown and Perry 1994). Table 8.3 displays the regression results.

The regressions indicate that reviewers' star ratings are, on average, statistically significantly lower than average for former employees and significantly higher than average for part-time employees. To mitigate sampling bias, we choose to exclude reviews posted by former and part-time employees. Although this approach reduces the number of observations in our dataset, we believe that it allows for more meaningful recommendations for corporate culture analysis based upon an analysis of firms' current, full-time employees.

8.4 INFERRING CORPORATE CULTURE

In this section we describe the technique used to infer perceptions of corporate culture. One popular technique for navigating large unannotated document collections is topic modelling. Topic models are useful in obtaining a low dimensional representation of a large dataset and have played an important role in a variety of data mining tasks within computer science (Blei et al. 2003), social and political science and digital humanities for the categorization and summarization of texts. The intuition is that documents are represented as random mixtures of hidden topics, where each topic is characterized by a distribution over words. For each document, we assume that words are generated in a two-stage process:

1. Randomly choose a distribution over topics.
2. For each word in the document:
   a. Randomly choose a topic from the distribution over topics in step #1.
   b. Randomly choose a word from the corresponding distribution over the vocabulary.

Each document exhibits topics in different proportions (step #1); each word in each document is drawn from one of the topics (step #2b), where the selected topic is chosen from the per-document distribution over topics (step #2a). The goal of topic modelling is to automatically discover the topics from a collection of documents. The documents themselves are observed, while the topic structure (the topics, per-document topic distributions and the per-document per-word topic assignments) are hidden structure.

To illustrate this, Figure 8.2 provides an extract of an employee's review posted to a social media site. Words associated with potentially different topics have been manually colour coded within the text. Words that tend to co-occur in the same reviews are more likely to characterize the same topic. Conversely, the words that rarely co-occur are likely to describe different topics. For instance, a discussion about an employee's working environment may include references to 'colleagues', 'co-workers' and 'teams', while a discussion about employee performance may include the terms 'recognition' and 'promotion'.

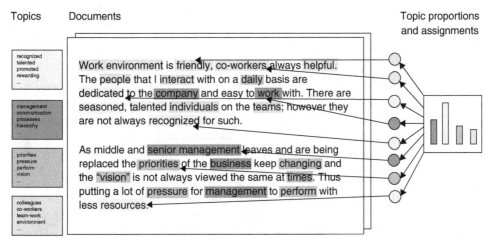

FIGURE 8.2 Illustrative example of topic modelling. A topic model assumes that a number of topics which are distributions over words exist for the whole collection (far left). Each document is assumed to be generated as follows. First choose a distribution over the topics (the histogram at right); then, for each word, choose a topic assignment (the coloured circles) and choose the word from the corresponding topic.

By reversing the generative process, one obtains a predictive model by means of the posterior distribution. The total probability of the topic model is given by:

$$P(W, Z, \theta, \varnothing; \alpha, \beta) = \prod_{k=1}^{K} P(\varnothing_k; \beta) \prod_{j=1}^{M} P(\theta_j; \alpha) \prod_{t=1}^{N_j} P(Z_{j,t} \mid \theta_j) P(W_{j,t} \mid \varnothing_{Z_{j,t}}) \qquad (8.1)$$

where K is the number of topics, M the number of documents and N_j the number of words in document j. The distribution of words in topic k is given by $P(\varnothing_k; \beta)$; a multinomial with Dirichlet prior with uniform parameter β. The topic distribution for document j is given by $P(\theta_j; \alpha)$; a multinomial distribution with Dirichlet prior with uniform parameter α. The standard approach is to set $\alpha = 50/K$ and $\beta = 0$. The assignment of a topic for t^{th} word in document j is represented by $P(Z_{j,t} \mid \theta_j)$. Finally, $P(W_{j,t} \mid \varnothing_{Z_{j,t}})$ represents the probability of word t in document j given topic $Z_{j,t}$ for the tth word in the document. The task of parameter estimation is to learn both what the topics are and which documents employ them in what proportions. The key inferential problem that we need to solve in order to use the model is the posterior distribution of the hidden variables given a document:

$$P(\theta, \varnothing, z \mid w, \alpha, \beta) = \frac{P(\theta, \varnothing, z, w \mid \alpha, \beta)}{P(w \mid \alpha, \beta)} \qquad (8.2)$$

To solve the maximum likelihood estimation, Gibbs sampling is applied to construct a Markov chain that converges to the posterior distributions on topic Z. The results are then used to infer Φ and θ variables indirectly. The model is appealing for noisy data because it requires no annotation and discovers themes in a corpus solely from the learning data without any supervision.

The output of the algorithm is a matrix of dimensions K topics × N documents, where the number of topics is inferred by maximizing the likelihood of fitting the model over the corpus. Table 8.4 presents the resulting six clusters inferred by the model. Each cluster is represented as a distribution of words which form semantically similar concepts. The highest probability document terms for each cluster are reported and ranked in decreasing order of approximately how often they occur in the text in order to aid the reader's interpretation of the inferred clusters.

Given the focus of this study is on the identification of performance-orientated cultures, we limit our analysis to words associated with the 'goal-setting' topic cluster (i.e. employee discussions of 'planning', 'goals' and 'performance'). We label the proportion of words in a Glassdoor review drawn from this cluster as GOAL.

To infer the sentiment expressed in employee reviews we compute TONE, the fraction of positive versus negative terms in each review, using the General Inquirer lexicon (Stone et al. 1966). This approach is commonly adopted in the financial literature (see Tetlock et al. 2008). We employ a slight variant to the traditional 'term counting' approach to account for negation terms which can alter the semantic meaning of text. Negation terms such as 'although', 'but', 'no', 'not', 'yet' are often seen in social media texts due to the more frequent use of colloquialisms (Hu and Liu 2004). Specifically, we reverse the sign of terms listed in the General Inquirer lexicon if there is a negation term within five words of a matched sentiment term within a reviewer's text.

Table 8.5 highlights randomly selected examples of employee reviews for companies within the top quintile of the GOAL score.

TABLE 8.4   Topic clusters inferred by the topic model

'Social value'		'Development value'		'Economic value'	
word	prob.	word	prob.	word	prob.
friends	0.18	opportunity	0.24	work life	0.18
team building	0.14	career opportunities	0.22	conditions	0.07
co-workers	0.12	advancing	0.13	benefits	0.05
team	0.09	professional development	0.07	diversity	0.04
working environment	0.07	initiatives	0.07	location	0.03

'Application value'		'Organizational structure'		'Goal-setting'	
word	prob.	word	prob.	word	prob.
encouragement	0.28	manager	0.27	planning	0.16
responsibilities	0.10	changes	0.17	goals	0.14
talented	0.07	processes	0.12	incentives	0.13
promoted	0.07	senior management	0.10	performance	0.13
rewarding	0.05	communications	0.08	direction	0.01

This table reports the top terms for each topic cluster and their associated probabilities inferred using a topic model.

TABLE 8.5   Illustrative examples of reviewer comments

Panel A: Examples of positive sentiment reviews
Good foundation in place, with a common goal to understand everyone
if your hard working, it's a good place to work, It weeds out the lazy people and the people
    that dont want to work.
Good people that have same goal.
Great place to work if you are not lazy.
Well planned work habits, good company culture.
Panel B: Examples of negative sentiment reviews
The most hardest thing here is hitting your numbers. If you don't reach the desired goal of
    the company, they Mill get rid of you.
Not a very good work life balance and aggressive deadlines.
The fact that the end goal of JPM is always bottom line, the work load and hours are very
    intense but the work is exciting and worth it.
Fast pace and high stress of goal for achievement and success.
Long work hours, stressful sometimes, had to work in weekends to meet deadlines.
This figure provides illustrative examples of employee reviews associated with
    performance-orientated cultures. To aid readers' interpretation, we randomly select five
    comments with positive and negative sentiment. The spelling mistakes and grammatical
    errors are as published in the online reviews.

8.4.1 Data and summary statistics

Panel A of Table 8.6 reports the median fundamental characteristics of firms when sorted into quartiles by their GOAL score. We winsorize firm characteristics at the 1% level to eliminate the impact of outliers. The last column illustrates the statistical significance of a difference of means t-test between top and bottom quartile firms for each fundamental characteristic. Companies with reviews in the highest GOAL quartile exhibit significantly higher growth than firms in the lowest quartile. This finding is consistent across asset, employee and sales growth.

Panel B of Table 8.6 reports the Spearman rank correlations between the average Glassdoor star ratings and GOAL. The correlations between GOAL and the overall composite star rating appear to be relatively low, suggesting that the perceptions inferred from GOAL differ from the information provided by reviewers' star ratings.

8.4.2 Validating the goal measure

We regress firms' GOAL scores on Glassdoor 'star ratings' to examine whether the information inferred from reviewers' texts is incremental to the information provided in star ratings and TONE. We include controls for book-to-market (Log(Book/Market)), analyst revisions (Analyst Revisions), price momentum (Pmom) and one-year historic sales growth (SG). Log(Book/Market)) is the natural log of the book-to-value of equity measured as at the end of the preceding calendar year, following Fama and French (1992). Analyst revisions is the three-month sum of changes in the median analyst's forecast, divided by the firm's stock price in the prior month (Chan et al. 1996). Pmom is the (signed) stock's return measured over the previous 12 months, while firm size (Log(Market Equity)) is measured at the end of the preceding calendar year. We include firms' CSR attributes to account for traditional human capital measures. In line with standard practice, we include an employee relations metric obtained from the KLD social research and analytics database (Waddock and Graves 1997; Hillman and Keim 2001; Statman and Glushkov 2009).We calculate net employee strengths by summing all identified strengths and subtracting all identified weaknesses in a given year (Verwijmeren and Derwall 2010). We label this metric KLD. Finally, we include an employee satisfaction metric to evaluate whether GOAL differs from the information published in Fortune magazine's '100 Best Companies to Work for in America' list (Edmans 2011). We create an indicator variable, BC, equal to 1 if a company is listed in Fortune's list and zero otherwise. Following Petersen (2009), standard errors are clustered by firm to correct for time series dependence in standard errors. Table 8.7 reports the regression results.

Column 2 suggests there is a positive correlation between GOAL and Glassdoor's management quality and opportunities star ratings, and a negative relation between GOAL and firms' compensation star ratings. The latter relation is consistent with the view that performance-orientated firms seek to incentivize individuals by providing a larger proportion of their total compensation in variable rather than fixed pay (Gneezy et al. 2011; Kamenica 2012; Gerhart and Rynes 2003; Adams 1963). Column 2 suggests a positive correlation between GOAL, one-year historic sales growth and Pmom, indicating that performance-orientated firms typically exhibit growth characteristics. Finally, Column 3 controls for traditional CSR metrics and suggests that GOAL is not

TABLE 8.6 Descriptive statistics of firm characteristics

Panel A: Fundamental characteristics[a]					
Characteristic	1st quartile	2nd quartile	3rd quartile	4th quartile	Diff of means T-test (Q1 vs. Q4)
Accruals	−0.044	−0.035	−0.043	−0.042	
Asset growth (yoy)	0.037	0.051	0.086	0.087	***
Employee growth (yoy)	0.021	0.028	0.046	0.052	***
Financial leverage	0.429	0.510	0.318	0.307	
Market capitalisation (US$ m)	13 329	17 178	22 289	28 408	***
Prior price momentum	0.148	0.164	0.150	0.198	*
ROA	0.146	0.149	0.149	0.162	***
Sales growth (yoy)	0.038	0.045	0.057	0.069	***
Tobin's Q	1.329	1.474	1.620	1.837	***
GOAL	0.040	0.072	0.099	0.145	
OVERALL	3.231	3.308	3.505	3.500	***

Panel B: Correlation of Glassdoor.com star rating scores[b]							
	GOAL	OVERALL	COMP	WORKLIFE	MGT	CULTURE	CAREER
GOAL	1.00						
OVERALL	0.04	1.00					
COMP	0.12	0.58	1.00				
WORKLIFE	0.05	0.76	0.56	1.00			
MGT	0.01	0.74	0.44	0.63	1.00		
CULTURE	0.00	0.60	0.41	0.49	0.54	1.00	
CAREER	0.03	0.76	0.54	0.74	065	0.49	1.00

[a]This table reports the median fundamental characteristics of firms when sorted into quartiles by their GOAL score. GOAL is the proportion of reviews that refers to performance-orientated cultures as inferred by the topic model. We winsorize all firm characteristics at the 1% level to eliminate the impact of outliers. OVERALL is the overall star rating score provided by Glassdoor reviewers, averaged between consecutive earnings announcement dates per company. All fundamental data comes from COMPUSTAT Fundamentals Annual Database. The final column of the table indicates the statistical significance of a difference of means t-test between top and bottom quartile firms for each fundamental characteristic where *** indicates statistical significance at the 1% level, ** at the 5% level and * at the 10% level. Sample period: 2008–2015.
[b]This table reports the Spearman rank correlations between the star ratings provided by Glassdoor reviews and GOAL. OVERALL is the overall star rating score provided by Glassdoor reviewers. COMP is the 'Comp & Benefits' star rating provided by Glassdoor reviewers. WORKLIFE is the Glassdoor 'Work/Life Balance' rating. MGT is reviewers' 'Senior Management' rating. CULTURE refers to the 'Culture & Values' star rating and CAREER is the Glassdoor 'Career Opportunities' rating. Sample period: 2008–2015.

TABLE 8.7 Regression of company characteristics for performance-orientated firms

	(1)	(2)	(3)
OVERALL	0.012	0.078	0.011
	(2.867)	(5.663)	(2.63)
TONE	0.023	0.026	0.009
	(0.798)	(0.986)	(0.312)
COUP		−0.047	
		(−3.505)	
WORKLIFE		−0.002	
		(−1.92)	
MOT		0.032	
		(2.581)	
CULTURE		0.001	
		(0.305)	
OPPORTUNITIES		0.022	
		(3.853)	
Log(Book/Market)	−0.003	0.001	−0.002
	(−1.078)	(0.463)	(−0.786)
ROA	0.027	−0.004	0.028
	(1.117)	(−0.175)	(1.19)
SG	0.056	0.030	0.055
	(4.213)	(2.39)	(3.986)
Analyst revisions	0.147	0.070	0.095
	(0.21)	(0.634)	(0.721)
Pmom	0.009	0.009	0.007
	(2.288)	(2.724)	(1.874)
KLD			−0.003
			(−2.754)
BC			−0.018
			(0.885)

This table reports the relation between GOAL and company characteristics. The dependent variable is the GOAL score inferred by the topic model. OVERALL is the Glassdoor Overall star rating provided by Glassdoor reviewers, COMP is the 'Comp & Benefits' star rating. WORKLIFE is the Glassdoor 'Work/Life Balance' rating. MGT is reviewers' 'Senior Management' rating, CULTURE refers to the 'Culture & Values' star rating and CAREER is the Glassdoor 'Career Opportunities' rating. TONE is a measure of document polarity computed by counting the number of positive (P) versus negative (N) terms using the General Inquirer dictionary (Stone et al. 1966). Log (Book/Market) is the natural log of the book-to-value of equity as of the previous year end. Standard errors are clustered by firm following Petersen (2009). For each variable we report corresponding robust t-statistic (in parentheses). Sample period: 2008–2015.

subsumed by KLD's net employee relations metric or Fortune's employee satisfaction indicator. Taken together, our findings suggest that GOAL is a distinct dimension of corporate culture.

8.5 EMPIRICAL RESULTS

This section investigates the relation between performance-orientated cultures, firm value and firms' future earnings. We compute Tobin's Q as a measure of firm value,

TABLE 8.8 Regression of performance-orientated firms and firm value

	(1)	(2)	(3)
GOAL	1.624	1.400	1.720
	(2.691)	(2.023)	(2.823)
TONE	−0.374	−0.034	−0.166
	(−0.701)	(−0.046)	(−0.311)
OVERALL	0.328		0.322
	(4.472)		(4.393)
COMP		−0.211	
		(−1.848)	
WORKLIFE		0.143	
		(1.181)	
MGT		0.261	
		(1.679)	
CULTURE		−0.102	
		(−1.007)	
OPPORTUNITIES		0.300	
		(1.738)	
Log(Book/Market)	−0.762	−0.744	−0.699
	(−2.634)	(−2.488)	(−2.69)
ROA	4.348	4.057	4.725
	(3.364)	(3.282)	(3.192)
SG	2.846	2.635	2.736
	(2.941)	(2.921)	(2.255)
KLD			−0.073
			(−3.727)
BC			1.130
			(2.978)

This table reports the results of running quarterly regressions of firm value on a set of independent variables. The dependent variable is Tobin's Q, defined as the market value of the firm divided by the replacement value of the firm's assets. The definitions for the fundamental variables are described in the text and come from COMPUSTAT Fundamentals Annual Database apart from Standard errors which are clustered by firm following Petersen (2009). For each variable we report corresponding robust t-statistic (in parentheses). Sample period: 2008–2015.

defined as the market value of the firm divided by the replacement value of the firm's assets. The market value of assets is measured as the sum of the book value of assets and the market value of common stock outstanding minus the sum of the book value of common stock and balance sheet deferred taxes. Replacement value is represented by the book value of assets (Kaplan and Zingales 1997). We control for sector, region and year effects and run pooled ordinary least squares (OLS) regressions to estimate models of Tobin's Q. We test for the significance of the coefficients using standard errors that are robust to heteroskedasticity clustered by firm (Petersen 2009). The pooled regression results are reported in Table 8.8.

Column 1 indicates a positive and highly statistically significant coefficient for GOAL, suggesting that performance-orientated firms tend to be more profitable. Column 2 indicates that there is no evidence of a statistical relation between the underlying star ratings and firm value. Column 3 indicates that GOAL is incremental to the employee satisfaction and employee relations metrics.

Next we hypothesize that if financial analysts overlook intangible information, potentially due to the costs associated with gathering, processing and analyzing unstructured data, we would expect that positive benefits of corporate culture are recognized only once they manifest into tangible outcomes post earnings announcements (see Easterwood and Nutt 1999; Edmans 2011). Our main test computes each firm's standardized unexpected earnings (SUEs) using a seasonal random walk with trend model for each firm's earnings (Bernard and Thomas 1989):

$$UE_t = E_t - E_{t-4}$$

$$SUE_t = \frac{UE_t - \mu_{UEt}}{\sigma UE_t}$$
(8.3)

where E_t is the firm's earnings in quarter t, and the trend and volatility of unexpected earnings (UEs) are equal to the mean (μ) and standard deviation (σ) of the firm's previous 20 quarters of unexpected earnings data, respectively. Following Tetlock et al. (2008), we require that each firm has non-missing earnings data for the most recent 10 quarters and assume a zero trend for all firms with fewer than four years of earnings data. We use the median analyst forecast from the most recent statistical period in the I/B/E/S summary file prior to the earnings announcement. We winsorize SUE and all analyst forecast variables at the 1% level to reduce the impact of estimation error and extreme outliers respectively. We create a composite document for each firm to align different frequencies of data by aggregating Glassdoor reviews between consecutive earnings announcement dates. We require a minimum of 30 reviews per company between quarterly earnings announcements to avoid drawing statistical inferences using a limited and potentially unrepresentative set of employee comments. Regressions control for firms' lagged earnings, size, book-to-market ratio, analysts' earnings forecast revisions and analysts' forecast dispersion. We measure firms' lagged earnings using last quarter's SUE. We compute analysts' forecast dispersion (Forecast Dispersion) as the standard deviation of analysts' earnings forecasts in the most recent time period prior to the earnings announcement scaled by earnings volatility (σ). Table 8.9 reports the regression results. Standard errors are clustered by calendar quarter (following Petersen 2009).

Column 2 identifies a positive and highly statistically significant coefficient for GOAL, suggesting that the measure contains incremental information for predicting earnings surprises beyond those of company fundamentals or TONE. Column 3 controls for employee relations and satisfaction and suggests that the information contained in GOAL is not subsumed by these measures.

8.6 CONCLUSION

To date, investors' efforts to 'look inside' a company have been hampered by a lack of data. Traditional survey-based measures are manual and time-consuming to produce, and limited in scope with regards to the number of questions they can ask, the number of companies they can cover and their timeliness to collect and process responses. This study seeks to overcome these limitations by inferring employees' perceptions expressed

TABLE 8.9   Regression of performance-orientated firms and earnings surprises

	(1)	(2)	(3)
Lagged dependent	−0.012	−0.015	−0.012
	(−0.358)	(−0.423)	(−0.351)
Forecast dispersion	−2.700	−2.806	−2.581
	(−3.196)	(−3.318)	(−2.916)
OVERALL	0.067	0.053	0.079
	(0.761)	(0.505)	(0.755)
GOAL		1.770	4.477
		(2.536)	(3.751)
TONE		0.054	1.714
		(2.071)	(1.796)
High_expectations			14.180
			(2.892)
Analyst revisions	15.130	14.730	18.050
	(4.749)	(4.622)	(5.173)
Log(Market Equity)	0.000	0.000	0.000
	(−1.078)	(−1.021)	(−1.552)
Log(Book/Market)	−0.006	−0.018	−0.053
	(−0.096)	(−0.294)	(−0.857)
Pmom	0.716	0.738	0.774
	(7.411)	(7.612)	(8.007)
KLD			0.055
			(1.904)
BC			−0.974
			(−1.699)

This table provides the OLS regression estimates of the relation between GOAL and a firm's one quarter ahead earnings surprise (SUE). The dependent variable, SUE, is a firm's standardized unexpected quarterly earnings. A composite document is computed for each firm by aggregating Glassdoor reviews between consecutive earnings announcement dates for each firm. Earnings announcement dates are sourced for I/B/E/S. A minimum of 30 reviews is required to create a composite document per firm. OVERALL is the Glassdoor Overall star rating averaged across reviews with the composite document. Regressions include control variables for lagged firm earnings, firm size, book-to-market, trading volume, past stock returns, and analysts' quarterly forecast revisions and dispersion (see text for details). Standard errors are clustered by firm following Petersen (2009). For each variable we report corresponding robust t-statistic (in parentheses). Sample period: 2008–2015.

in social media. We demonstrate the merits of computational linguistics techniques to infer the latent dimensions discussed in the text. Our methodology provides an objective framework to infer the topics deemed most relevant to a firm's primary stakeholders (namely its employees). We find evidence of a statistically significant relation between performance-orientated firms and firms' future earnings surprises, suggesting tangible benefits of corporate culture for financial analysis.

REFERENCES

Adams, J.S. (1963). Toward an understanding of inequity. *Journal of Abnormal and Social Psychology* 67: 422–436.

Ambrose, M.L. and Kulik, C.T. (1999). Old friends, new faces: motivation in the 1990s. *Journal of Management* 25: 231–292.

Bernard, V. and Thomas, J. (1989). Post-earnings-announcement drift: delayed price response or risk premium? *Journal of Accounting Research*, 27: 1–36.

Blackshaw, P. and Nazzaro, M. (2006). *Consumer-Generated Media (CGM) 101: Word-Ofmouth in the Age of the Web-Fortified Consumer*. New York: Nielsen BuzzMetrics.

Blei, D.M., Ng, A., and Jordan, M.I. (2003). Latent Dirichlet allocation. *Journal of Machine Learning Research*, 3: 993–1022.

Brown, B. and Perry, S. (1994). Removing the financial performance halo from Fortune's most admired companies. *Academy of Management Journal* 37: 1347–1359.

Chan, L., Jegadeesh, N., and Lakonishok, J. (1996). Momentum strategies. *Journal of Finance*, 51: 1681–1713.

Chan, L., Lakonishok, J., and Sougiannis, T. (2001). The stock market valuation of research and development expenditures. *Journal of Finance*, 56: 2431–2456.

Cooper, C.L., Cartwright, S., Cartright, S., and Earley, C.P. (2001). *The International Handbook of Organizational Culture and Climate*. Wiley.

Daines, R.M., Gow, I.D., and Larcker, D.F. (2010). Rating the ratings: how good are commercial governance ratings? *Journal of Financial Economics*, 98 (3): 439–461.

Easterwood, J. and Nutt, S. (1999). Inefficiency in analysts' earnings forecasts: systematic misreaction or systematic optimism? *Journal of Finance*, 54: 1777–1797.

Edmans, A. (2011). Does the stock market fully value intangibles? Employee satisfaction and equity prices. *JFE*, 101: 621–640.

Elahi, M.F. and Monachesi, P. (2012). An examination of cross-cultural similarities and differences from social media data with respect to language use. Proceedings of the Eight International Conference on Language Resources and Evaluation.

Engelberg, J. (2008). *Costly Information Processing: Evidence from Earnings Announcements*. Working Paper. Northwestern University.

Fama, E.F. and French, K.R. (1992). The cross-section of expected stock returns. *Journal of Finance*, 47: 427–465.

Flammer, C. (2013). *Does Corporate Social Responsibility Lead to Superior Financial Performance? A Regression Discontinuity Approach*. Working Paper. University of Western Ontario.

Fryxell, G.E. and Wang, J. (1994). The fortune corporate reputation index: reputation for what? *Journal of Management* 20: 1–14.

Gaines-Ross, L. (2010). Reputation warfare. *Harvard Business Review* 88 (12): 70–76.

Gerhart, B. and Rynes, S.L. (2003). *Compensation: Theory, Evidence, and Strategic Implications*. Thousand Oaks, CA: Sage.

Gneezy, U., Meier, S., and Rey-Biel, P. (2011). When and why incentives (don't) work to modify behavior. *Journal of Economic Perspectives* 25 (4): 191–210.

Gray, R., Kouhy, R., and Lavers, S. (1995). Corporate social and environmental reporting: a review of the literature and a longitudinal study of UK disclosure, accounting. *Auditing and Accountability* 8 (2): 47–77.

Hillman, A.J. and Keim, G.D. (2001). Shareholder value, stakeholder management, and social issues: What's the bottom line? *Strategic Management Journal*, 22: 125–139.

Hofstede, G. (1980). *Culture's Consequences*. Beverly Hills, CA: Sage.

Hogenboom, A., Bal, M., Frasincar, F., and Bal, D. (2012). Towards cross-language sentiment analysis through universal star ratings. *KMO*, 69–79.

Hogenboom, A., Bal, M., Frasincar, F. et al. (2014). Lexiconbased sentiment analysis by mapping conveyed sentiment to intended sentiment. *Int. J. Web Eng. Technol.*, 9 (2): 125–147.

Hu, M. and Liu, B. (2004). Mining and summarizing customer reviews. in Tenth ACM International Conference on Knowledge Discovery and Data Mining.

Kamenica, E. (2012). Behavioral economics and psychology of incentives. *Annual Review of Economics* 4: 427–452.21.

Kaplan, S.N. and Zingales, L. (1997). Do investment-cash flow sensitivities provide useful measures of financing constraints? *Quarterly Journal of Economics* 112: 169–215.

Levering, R., Moskowitz, M., and Katz, M. (1984). *The 100 Best Companies to Work for in America*. Reading, MA: Addison-Wesley.

Marquis, C. and Toffel, M. (2012). *When Do Firms Greenwash? Corporate Visibility, Civil Society Scrutiny, and Environmental Disclosure*. Harvard Business School Discussion Paper 12–43, 22.

McDonnell, M.H. and King, B. (2013). Keeping up appearances reputational threat and impression management after social movement boycotts. *Administrative Science Quarterly* 58 (3): 387–419.

O'Reilly, C., Chatman, J., and Caldwell, D. (1991). People and organizational culture: a profile comparison approach to assessing person-organization fit. *The Academy of Management Journal*, 34: 487–516.

Pang, B. and Lee, L. (2004). A Sentimental Education: Sentiment Analysis using Subjectivity Summarization based on Minimum Cuts, 42nd Annual Meeting of the Association for Computational Linguistics (ACL 2004), 271–280, Association for Computational Linguistics.

Petersen, M. (2009). Estimating standard errors in finance panel data sets: comparing approaches. *Review of Financial Studies*, 22: 435–480.

Pinder, C.C. (1998). *Work Motivation in Organizational Behavior*. Upper Saddle River, NJ: Prentice-Hall.

Popadak, J. (2013). *A Corporate Culture Channel: How Increased Shareholder Governance Reduces Firm Value*. Duke University Working Paper.

Statman, M. and Glushkov, D. (2009). The wages of social responsibility. *Financial Analysts Journal*, 65: 33–46.

Stone, P., Dumphy, D.C., Smith, M.S., and Ogilvie, D.M. (1966). *The General Inquirer: A Computer Approach to Content Analysis*. The MIT Press.

Tetlock, P.C., Saar-Tsechansky, M., and Macskassy, S. (2008). More than words: quantifying language to measure firms' fundamentals. *Journal of Finance*, 63: 1437–1467.

Triandis, H.C., Bontempo, R., Villareal, M.J. et al. (1988). Individualism and collectivism: cross-cultural perspectives on self-ingroup relationships. *Journal of Personality and Social Psychology* 54: 323–338.

Verwijmeren, P. and Derwall, J. (2010). Employee well-being, firm leverage, and bankruptcy risk. *Journal of Banking and Finance*, 34(5), 956–964.

Waddock, S.A. and Graves, S.B. (1997). The corporate social performance- financial performance link. *Strategic Management Journal* 18 (4): 303–319.

Wierzbicka, A. (1995). Emotion and facial expression: a semantic perspective. *Culture Psychology*, 1 (2): 227–258.

CHAPTER 9

Machine Learning and Event Detection for Trading Energy Futures

Peter Hafez and Francesco Lautizi

9.1 INTRODUCTION

The commodity futures spectrum is an integral part of today's financial markets. Specifically, energy-related ones like crude oil, gasoline and natural gas, among many more, all react to the ebbs and flows of supply and demand. These commodities play a crucial role in everyday life, as they fuel most of the world's transportation systems and they are the input to businesses across all the industrial sectors, hence they are inherently linked to the economic cycle. Economic indicators such as gross domestic product and the unemployment rate to political upheaval and natural disasters, not to mention commodity-specific issues like oil and gas pipeline disruptions or embargos, all contribute to the pricing of commodity futures (Table 9.1).

In previous research, Brandt and Gao (2016) took a novel approach by constructing supply and demand sentiment indices, using RavenPack data, to model the price impact of geopolitical and macroeconomic events and sentiments on crude oil. In particular, they found that news about macroeconomic fundamentals had a predictive ability over a monthly horizon, while geopolitical events sizably affected the price, but without sign predictability in the short term.

Rather than relying on a single commodity strategy, we seek to build predictive models for a group of commodities by means of RPA's event detection capabilities. By utilizing RPA 1.0,[1] investors can benefit from the latest innovations in natural language processing (NLP) technology to identify the information that matters for commodities. With the latest release, the RavenPack event taxonomy has grown to more than 6800 event categories, allowing the swift and precise identification of market-moving events across multiple asset classes and commodities. Events include supply increases, import/export guidance, inventory changes and more.

We select four commodity futures related to energy. We proceed to model the one-day-ahead volatility-adjusted returns for the energy basket using an ensemble of machine learning techniques. Our results indicate that our mix of linear models performs well in terms of risk-adjusted returns. However, including a wider spectrum of non-linear models, e.g. artificial neural networks (ANNs) or gradient boosted trees

---

[1]All references to RavenPack Analytics or RPA hereafter refer to version 1.0.

TABLE 9.1   Performance statistics

Statistics	Out-of-sample		
	Ensemble	High-vol	Low-vol
Annualized return	9.8%	21.3%	−3.0%
Annualized volatility	15.0%	16.9%	15.3%
Information ratio	0.65	1.27	−0.20
Hit ratio	51.1%	53.9%	47.5%
Max drawdown	38.3%	18.0%	62.2%
Per-trade return (bps)	3.88	8.82	−1.97
Number of trades	2740	1929	811

The *high-vol* and *low-vol* strategies trade only during these regimes while the *ensemble* strategy trades irrespective of the regime. The out-of-sample period is January 2015 to December 2017.
Source: RavenPack, January 2018.

regression, provides a way to improve performance and at the same time reduces the risk associated to model selection. Moreover, we demonstrate how return predictability at the basket level can be enhanced by conditioning on volatility regimes.

The study is organized as follows. Section 9.2 discloses the different data sources used, in particular how the input variables from RPA 1.0 are constructed. Section 9.3 describes the modelling framework, which is based on five machine learning algorithms. Section 9.4 compares the performance of the various models introduced in Section 9.3. Section 9.5 presents the general conclusions.

9.2   DATA DESCRIPTION

By using NLP techniques, RavenPack transforms large unstructured datasets, such as traditional news and social media, into structured and machine readable granular data and indicators that can be included in quantitative models, allowing investors to identify entities in the news and to link these to actionable events that are most likely to impact asset prices. Each event is further supported by various analytical measures, including sentiment, novelty (Event Similarity Days[2]), and relevance (Event Relevance[3]).

---

[2]Event Similarity Days: a granular number with up to five decimal places which indicates the number of days since a similar event was detected over the last 365 days. Values range between 0.00 000 and 365 inclusive. A value of 365 means that the most recent similar story may have occurred 365 or more days in the past. The value 0.00 000 means a similar story occurred with the exact same timestamp.
[3]Event Relevance: an integer between 0 and 100 that reflects the relevance of the event in the story. An event relevance score is assigned for records relating to an event, where related records can be identified by having the same EVENT_SIMILARITY_KEY within a story. The score is based on the earliest mention and frequency of the event match. The score is incremented for additional mentions of the event in the same paragraph, up to the maximum score for that paragraph.

To create the strategies, we consider all commodity-related news stories from RPA spanning a period of nearly 13 years, from January 2005 to December 2017.

Some mild restrictions are imposed on the dataset related to event detection and novelty. In particular, it is required that a news story can be matched with an event from the RavenPack event taxonomy. Furthermore, only events with Event Similarity Days (ESD) ≥ 1 are allowed in order to remove duplicated news events on an intraday basis. Contrary to recent in-house research on equities (Hafez and Koefoed 2017a,b; Hafez and Guerrero-Colón 2016; Hafez and Lautizi 2016), we do not condition on event relevance signal (ERS) as the tradeoff between stronger per-event predictability and lower event frequency does not work in our favour herein. Instead, we use it directly in our feature construction, as detailed below in Section 9.3.1.[4]

By imposing these restrictions, we are limited to a subset of all available event categories in RPA. In particular, during our backtest, we find 110 unique event categories[5] with at least one recorded event across our commodities universe. Crude oil is the most prevalent of all our commodities, with 103 unique event categories compared with the average commodity that has 34 categories.

Out of the 89 commodities covered by RavenPack, we select some of the most traded related to energy. The basket contains four commodities, with crude oil and natural gas being the most prominent. Table 9.2 provides an overview of the commodities in our study.

Given the sheer number of event categories available in RPAs, the dimensionality of the matrix of independent variables becomes large – even with the restrictions mentioned above. Put differently, we are facing the well-known curse of dimensionality (Donoho 2000), which renders traditional OLS regression impractical due to overfitting in the absence of feature selection. In previous research (Hafez and Koefoed 2017a,b), we have relied on OLS to model equity returns using RavenPack's *Event Sentiment Score*, but given the dimensionality confronting us, and the fact that there may be nonlinearities at play between the various event categories, we move

TABLE 9.2 Summary statistics for RavenPack Analytics

| Commodity | Events | Days with events | Days with events (%) | Events per day | | | | |
				Mean	25th percentile	Median	75th percentile	Max
Crude oil	316 959	4 721	99.4	67	22	53	94	480
Gasoline	48 838	4 407	92.8	11	3	7	15	147
Heating oil	6 865	3 085	65	2	1	2	3	46
Natural gas	64 932	4 594	96.8	14	6	12	19	99

Summary statistics for four energy commodities from January 2005 to December 2017. The numbers are based on the time-shifted data, see Section 9.2.1.

---

[4]See Hafez and Koefoed (2017a) for a discussion of the benefits of ERS and EDS in the context of US and European equities.
[5]The complete RavenPack event taxonomy covers nearly 6900 event categories.

beyond OLS and instead implement a batch of machine learning techniques as detailed in Section 9.3.

9.2.1   Price data

As part of the study, we use daily *close-to-close* commodity futures returns provided by Stevens Analytics.[6] In addition, to modelling the next-day (logarithmic) return, we use RavenPack data specific to each commodity up until 15 minutes before the settlement price of the given commodity futures. For example, the settlement price for crude oil futures is computed between 2:28 pm ET and 2:30 pm ET on CME Globex,[7] meaning that we use RavenPack data available in the 24 hours up to 2:15 pm ET as input to our models.

Given that we are dealing with a basket of commodity futures with wildly varying volatilities – both across the spectrum and across time – we seek to volatility-adjust the returns by a lagged rolling standard deviation. We do this to avoid over-emphasizing those commodity futures with the highest volatility for each basket when estimating the models.

We define the log-return, standard deviation and volatility-adjusted log-return as follows:

$$r_{t,n} = \ln\left(price_{t,n}/price_{t-1,n}\right) \tag{9.1}$$

$$\sigma_{t,n} = m^{-1}\sum_{j=1}^{m}\left(r_{t-j+1,n} - m^{-1}\sum_{j=1}^{m}r_{t-j+1,n}\right)^2 \tag{9.2}$$

$$y_{t,n} = {r_{t,n}}/{\sigma_{t-1,n}} \times target \tag{9.3}$$

where $n = 1, \ldots, N$ represents the four commodity futures and $t = 1, \ldots, T$ is the time index identifying the day in which the price or return was observed, which can be missing for commodity-specific non-trading workdays. The parameter m defines the length of the window over which the standard deviation is calculated, while *target* defines the target volatility. Throughout this study, we use 21 trading days to calculate the standard deviation ($m = 21$) with an annualized target volatility of 20% ($target = 20/\sqrt{252}$). We have not optimized the parameter m, but we find that it provides a good tradeoff between stability and variability.

9.3   MODEL FRAMEWORK

To evaluate the RPAs suite, we utilize a string of machine learning techniques ranging from a linear model in the shape of elastic net regression to neural network, and tree-based models. In total, we test five different models. To optimize the various

---

[6]The backwards ratio method is used to calculate the contract history.
[7]http://www.cmegroup.com/trading/energy/crude-oil/light-sweet-crude_contract_specifications.html

hyper-parameters of the models, we use ten-fold cross validation (CV) and recalculate the results ten times to account for the inherent randomness in some of the models and the CV process. The five models are:

- elastic net regression (ELNET) (Zou and Hastie 2005)
- k-nearest neighbour regression (KNN) (Altman 1992)
- artificial neural network (ANN) (Hastie et al. 2009)
- random forest (RF) (Breiman 2001)
- gradient boosted trees with Gaussian loss function (GBN) (Friedman et al. 2000).

All five models use an additive error term, e, that is independent across time and commodity, but we do not make any assumptions about its data-generating process:

$$y_{t,n} = f(x_{t-1,n}) + e_{t,n} \qquad (9.4)$$

where the functional form, f, depends on the model and $x_{t,n}$ is a vector of independent variables. Note that the size of $x_{t,n}$ varies over time depending on the number of event categories with enough news stories to be included. We describe the independent variables more thoroughly in Section 9.3.1.

We use a walk-forward method whereby, on the first trading day of the year, we find the best hyper-parameter settings for each of the five models using the previous ten years' worth of data. We then predict the year's daily volatility-adjusted log-returns (Eq. (9.3)) for each of the five models. In other words, we estimate the models for the period 2005–2014 and make daily predictions for 2015. We then step forward one year in time and carry out the estimation and daily prediction steps again.

To overcome the randomness problem, we repeat this procedure ten times – this will result in ten series of predictions per model. In our strategy we will use the average prediction over the ten runs for each of the models.

This procedure starts on 1 January 2015 and ends on 31 December 2017, representing our *out-of-sample period*.

9.3.1 Feature creation

All the models presented herein make use of the same input: as target variable the volatility-scaled log-returns and as features, a matrix of continuous variables. The features are designed to capture the impact of an event category taking place at time t for commodity n as well as its relevance and is constructed as follows:

$$x_{t,n}^j = \begin{cases} \overline{ERS}_{t,n}^j & \text{if event category } j \text{ is recorded at time } t \text{ for commodity } n \\ 0 & \text{else} \end{cases} \qquad (9.5)$$

$$\overline{ERS}_{t,n}^j = I^{-1} \sum_{i=1}^{I} ERS_{t,n,i}^j \qquad (9.6)$$

where $i = 1, \ldots, I$ is the number of events for category j.

In other words, if we detect at least one news story for a given event category for date t and commodity n, the variable switches to $\overline{ERS}$ from 0. This implies that news stories are weighted based on their ERS – thereby giving higher importance to news stories where the event is featured prominently, for example in the headline.

In order for a given event category to be included in the modelling of the commodities basket, we require at least 50 days with one or more events across the in-sample dataset. This requirement is not optimized and is simply introduced to remove very infrequent event categories from consideration. Furthermore, we remove perfectly correlated independent variables as appropriate.

Finally, we perform feature selection based on the *in-sample* data by requiring that there is an absolute correlation of at least 0.5% between each feature and our target variable. This results in a reduction of the number of features of between 37% and 45% depending on the *out-of-sample* year, meaning that we are left with 34–37 predictors. During preliminary research we found that imposing this restriction on the features improved speed and, importantly, in-sample robustness of the five machine learning algorithms.[8]

9.4 PERFORMANCE

All strategies in our study use portfolio weights derived from the predicted returns of the models presented in Section 9.3. The sign of a predicted return determines the direction of the trade, while the relative size of the predicted returns determines the portfolio weight. The vector of predicted returns for a given day is normalized to ensure a gross exposure of 1. The net exposure, meanwhile, can range from −1 to 1. All reported results exclude transaction costs.

9.4.1 Model portfolios

Table 9.3 shows a set of in-sample performance statistics[9] for our five ML models across the commodities basket – resulting in five different portfolios.[10] Overall, we find positive performance, with some rather big discrepancies across the models. In particular, we notice that the linear model is outperformed across all metrics by all the non-linear ones, with the only exception of random forest (RF). In particular, the gradient boosted trees (GBN) and the ANN are the best models in-sample, showing similar IRs of 2.40 and 2.39 respectively.

Having shown the in-sample performance, in Table 9.4 we present the out-of-sample results. We find the RF model to be the best performer as it delivers an IR of 0.85

---

[8]The drawback of this approach is that we use a linear filtering criterion for feature selection before applying both a set of linear and of non-linear models.
[9]All performance statistics refer to the *out-of-sample* period (January 2015 to October 2017) unless otherwise specified.
[10]These statistics are obtained by evaluating the strategies based on the average predictions of each model over the ten runs to account for the randomness in some models and in the CV process.

TABLE 9.3   In-sample performance statistics.

Statistics	ELNET	KNN	ANN	RF	GBN
Ann. return	17.6%	19.9%	34.6%	7.3%	**37.3%**
Ann. volatility	15.6%	**14.3%**	14.5%	15.1%	15.5%
IR	1.13	1.39	2.39	0.48	**2.40**
Hit ratio	53.5%	54.5%	**57.8%**	51.7%	56.0%
Max drawdown	22.4%	17.2%	**16.34%**	35.9%	17.9%

For each statistic, the bolded number is the best among the five models.
Source: RavenPack, January 2018.

TABLE 9.4   Out-of-sample performance statistics

Statistics	ELNET	KNN	ANN	RF	GBN
Ann. return	8.5%	11.7%	4.0%	**13.1%**	12.3%
Ann. volatility	15.8%	**14.1%**	14.7%	15.4%	16.2%
IR	0.54	0.83	0.27	**0.85**	0.76
Hit ratio	51.4%	51.7%	50.6%	**52.6%**	51.3%
Max drawdown	36.2%	**19.1%**	45.1%	30.7%	23.6%

For each statistic, the bolded number is the best among the five models.
Source: RavenPack, January 2018.

on an annualized return of 13.1%. The second-best model is the KNN, which yields an IR of 0.83 and the lowest volatility (14.1%), followed by the GBN, which provides an IR of 0.76 and 12.3% annualized returns. The linear model (ELNET) is the second to last model, suggesting that modelling non-linear relationships between our explanatory variable and commodities returns does indeed provide an edge that allows superior performance to be obtained.

Moreover, it is noteworthy that had we chosen a model based on the in-sample evidence, this would have resulted in suboptimal out-of-sample performance as the best two models in-sample are respectively the third and the last one out-of-sample, an evidence that warns against the risk of model selection.

Considering that there is only a moderate positive correlation between the predicted returns for RF and most of the better-performing models, such as KNN (0.55), we may be able to benefit from combining the predictions of the various models and in this way control for the risk associated with model selection, something that we will explore in Section 9.4.3.

9.4.2   Variable importance

Up until now we have answered only the question of whether our framework can produce alpha, not the question of which variables and in turn which event categories drive that alpha-generating performance. We choose RF to answer this question as it (i) is the best-performing model with an out-of-sample IR of 0.85, and (ii) provides an elegant way of computing and analyzing variable importance.

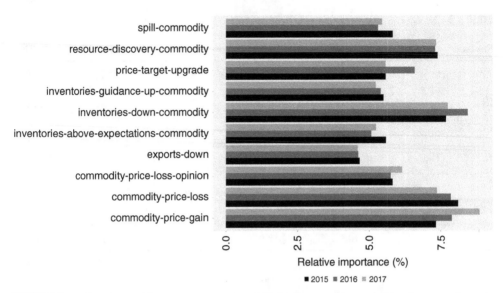

FIGURE 9.1   Relative variable importance using ELNET. Features are scaled by the sum of variable importance over all the variables in each year, thereby providing a relative importance interpretation for each out-of-sample year. For out-of-sample year 2015, the estimation window is 2005–2014, for out-of-sample year 2016, the estimation window is 2006–2015, and for out-of-sample year 2017, the estimation window is 2007–2016.
Source: RavenPack, January 2018.

In order to detect the most important categories, we rely on a measure based on residual sum of squares, i.e. the total decrease in node impurities from splitting on the variable.

In Figure 9.1, we show the top-ten categories. In order to obtain a measure of relative importance by year, we first compute the total decrease in node impurities by year. We then rescale the measure of importance by this amount, in order to provide a measure of the relative importance of each category in each out-of-sample year.

The analysis of the most important variables provides a sensible picture. In particular, we find inventories-related categories among the most important ones, for instance *inventories-down-commodity*. Inventories-related news seems to play a relevant role in driving prices, as three out of the top ten variables belong to this event type.

Moreover, we also find supply-related news to have a relevant role on price dynamics, as news related to resource discoveries, pointing to more supply of a commodity in the future, or spills, pointing to a decrease in the supply, also prove to be among the top predictors for future prices.

9.4.3   Ensemble portfolio

In Section 9.4.1 we demonstrated that the energy basket provides overall positive returns – both in absolute terms and on a risk-adjusted basis. However, with five models to choose from, the question becomes, which one to select? A valid approach is to each year select the model which performed best the previous year. However, we have shown that relying on the in-sample evidence for model selection might result in suboptimal out-of-sample performance: the ANN model had an in-sample

TABLE 9.5   Out-of-sample performance statistics

Statistics	ELNET	KNN	ANN	RF	GBN	Ensemble
Ann. ret.	8.5%	11.7%	4.0%	13.1%	12.3%	9.8%
Ann. vol.	15.8%	14.1%	14.7%	15.4%	16.2%	15.0%
IR	0.54	0.83	0.27	0.85	0.76	0.65
Hit ratio	51.4%	51.7%	50.6%	52.6%	51.3%	51.1%
Max DD	36.2%	19.1%	45.1%	30.7%	23.6%	38.3%

Source: RavenPack, January 2018.

IR comparable to the best model – had we chosen this model, this would have resulted in the worst out-of-sample performance. An alternative approach is to implement an *ensemble* (Breiman 1994; Mendes-Moreira et al. 2012) strategy whereby we combine the predicted returns across all five models via equal weight – thereby taking an agnostic view on which model is best.[11]

In Table 9.5 we repeat the performance statistics for our energy basket with an additional column added for the *ensemble* strategy.

By combining the five models, we generate an IR of 0.65 with an annualized return of 9.8%. Without any prior knowledge about which of the five models perform best, we are able to construct an *ensemble* which is competitive in terms of returns – both in absolute and risk-adjusted terms – and which allows for considerable risk reduction associated with model selection, therefore reducing the risk of potential overfitting. This highlights why *ensemble* methods can be strong performers despite relying on a mixed basket of models; in this particular case, we achieve an IR of 0.65 despite giving 40% weight to models with relatively poor performance (ELNET and ANN).

Since 2015, the *ensemble* basket has yielded a total cumulative return of 29.3%. In comparison, the equivalent long-only daily-rebalanced benchmark portfolio has yielded total returns of −9.0% with an IR of −0.11.

Analyzing the time series of returns, we note the high correlation between our best models (RF and KNN) and the *ensemble*, underlining once again the competitiveness of the model-agnostic *ensemble* approach. Meanwhile, the correlation between the *ensemble* and the long-only basket is negative.[12]

In Figure 9.2 we have plotted the cumulative returns profiles for the *ensemble* strategy against a long-only basket. Overall, the *ensemble* strategy has performed reasonably well out-of-sample, though it is clear that it was more performant in the first half of the period when energy commodities, in general, plummeted across the globe. This indicates that there may have been a regime shift since the middle of 2016 – and commodities have indeed been trading sideways without much volatility since then – which the *ensemble* model struggles to fully capture. In Section 9.4.5, we investigate this in more detail.

---

[11]We did not see any gains from basing the weights on cross-validation error statistics, such as the mean squared error, and we have therefore opted to go with the simple approach of equal-weighting the five models.

[12]The correlation between the realized returns of the ensemble and RF portfolios over the full sample is 0.90 and between the ensemble and the KNN portfolios is 0.80 whereas the correlation between the ensemble and long-only basket is −0.49.

ENSEMBLE   LONG-ONLY

FIGURE 9.2   Cumulative log-returns. The red vertical line marks the beginning of the out-of-sample period.
Source: RavenPack, January 2018.

9.4.4   Ensemble portfolio – marginal contributions

Having determined that our *ensemble* approach offers a simple yet well-performing method for combining our models, in this section we evaluate the performance contribution of each commodity to the overall portfolio. In Figure 9.3 we show the dependency of the portfolio on any single commodity, presenting the IR when systematically leaving out one commodity at a time to capture the marginal contribution of each commodity. The label on the x-axis makes reference to the commodity which is dropped from the basket.

By systematically removing one asset at a time from the basket we achieve IRs of 0.16–0.69 and annualized returns of 2.9–10.9%. Remarkably, the removal of natural gas hurts the portfolio the most, with the IR declining to 0.16, this commodity being the one contributing the most towards the performance of the portfolio.

These results also suggest that there may be additional performance to be had by modelling each commodity individually, but such a step drastically reduces the number of non-zero entries in the explanatory variables, resulting in fewer features and potentially more biased estimates as well. For that reason we have chosen to model all four commodities together, implying that we assume that a news category has the same impact across the basket.

9.4.5   Regime detection in the ensemble portfolio

Up until now, we have traded all signals generated by our models. While such an approach is attractive from a signal diversification point of view, it may still be

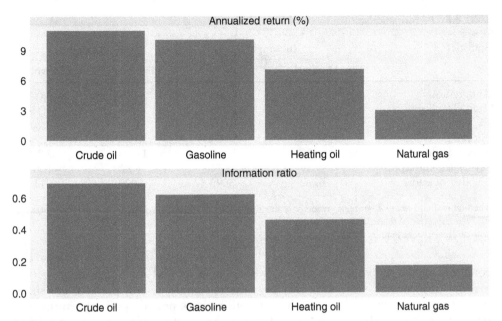

FIGURE 9.3　Out-of-sample information ratios. The names on the x-axes specify which commodity has been left out of the portfolio.
Source: RavenPack, January 2018.

interesting to evaluate whether our signals perform particularly well during certain time periods. For example, volatile market regimes may provide more trading opportunities through stronger signals.[13] Conversely, quiet markets may allow fundamental news to have a more pronounced impact on day-to-day returns without them being clouded by noisy fluctuations. By trading across all regimes, as is the case with the *ensemble* approach in Section 9.4.3, we may fail to take advantage of any regime dependency. In other words, by restricting ourselves to a subset of trades, we may be able to improve the per-trade return, while reducing overall trading and the cost associated with it.

We seek to determine whether there are certain regimes in which the portfolio performance is particularly strong. Concretely, we illustrate this approach by creating various portfolios which only trade the underlying commodities when certain requirements related to the realized volatility are met.

We implement this by testing a volatility filter based on (i) the 1-day lagged 21-day volatility being above its annual average, or (ii) the 1-day lagged 10-day volatility being above its 21-day equivalent. In other words, is volatility high relative to the last 12 months or rising?[14] When at least one of the conditions is fulfilled we are in a *high* volatility environment, otherwise we are in a *low* volatility environment.

In Table 9.6 we present results of conditioning the *ensemble* portfolio from Table 9.5 on the two volatility regimes (*high-vol/low-vol*). As can be observed, by

---

[13]In Hafez and Lautizi (2017) we show this in the context of equity portfolios.
[14]Parameters have not been optimized.

TABLE 9.6 Performance statistics

Statistics	In-sample		Out-of-sample	
	High-vol	Low-vol	High-vol	Low-vol
Ann. return	20.12%	14.05%	21.3%	−3.0%
Ann. volatility	16.3%	15.5%	16.9%	15.3%
IR	1.23	0.91	1.27	−0.20
Hit ratio	55.3%	54.6%	53.9%	47.5%
Max drawdown	35.2%	25.1%	18.0%	62.2%
Per-trade return (bps)	8.59	8.74	8.82	−1.97
Number of trades	6262	3043	1929	811

The *high-vol* and *low-vol* strategies trade only during periods of high/low volatility. The *ensemble* strategy trades irrespective of the volatility regime.
Source: RavenPack, January 2018.

conditioning on the volatility regime, we are able to find discrepancies in performance. In particular, we notice that over the in-sample period, the *high-vol* signal outperformed the *low-vol* one. Although both regimes provide positive returns, this observation, within the training period, raises the question whether we can achieve better out-of-sample performance by avoiding *low-vol* regimes when trading the signal.

Looking at the out-of-sample performance confirms this intuition, as we find that periods of *high* volatility yield considerably higher returns, both in absolute and in risk-adjusted terms. In particular, the out-of-sample period yields an IR of 1.27 with annualized return of 21.3% for the *high-vol* regime compared with an IR of −0.20 and annualized return of −3.0% for the *low-vol* regime. The discrepancy is further supported by Figure 9.4, where we show that the *high-vol* strategy consistently yields superior returns over the full-sample period, and particularly so during the second half of the out-of-sample period, where the *low-vol* strategy yields negative performance.

In Figure 9.5 we compare the profiles of the out-of-sample cumulative returns from the *ensemble* and *high-vol* strategies. In particular, we show that the *high-vol* strategy not only yields higher returns but also has the advantage of being more robust, experiencing a positive trend across most of the out-of-sample period. Specifically, the *high-vol* strategy provides more consistent performance, avoiding most of the negative trend showed by the *ensemble* during 2017, mostly due to the *low-vol* signals. Moreover, even though the *high-vol* strategy is characterized by a lower number of trades compared with the *ensemble* (1929 vs 2740), this is more than compensated by the boost observed in per-trade returns. By only trading the *high-vol* signals, we are able to more than double the per-trade return compared with the *ensemble*, from 3.38 to 8.82 basis points.

The *ensemble* method is a good starting point for developing a trading portfolio, but the results in Table 9.5 and Figures 9.4 and 9.5 underline that it fails to fully take into account potential regime shifts seen in the market. This is not surprising, since our *ensemble* model only includes event relevance-scaled dummy variables based on whether a RavenPack event category was triggered or not – and only for one day. More elaborate models could include information such as lagged category triggers, news volume, sentiment or novelty filters, or even market data such as asset volatility and returns (Hafez and Lautizi 2017).

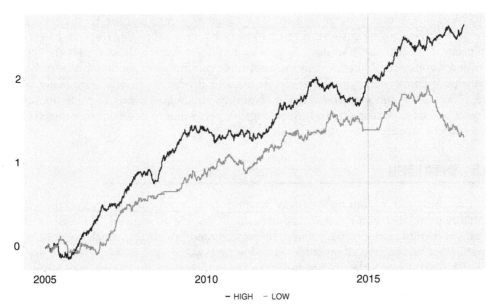

FIGURE 9.4 Cumulative log-returns.
Source: RavenPack, January 2018.

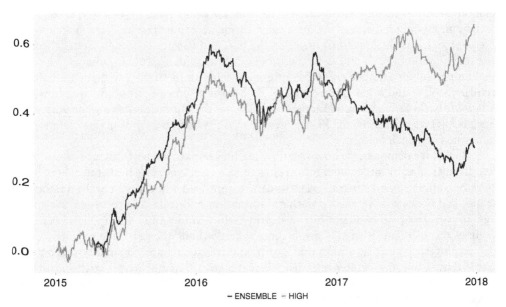

FIGURE 9.5 Out-of-sample performance statistics with Ensemble.
Source: RavenPack, January 2018.

Moreover, looking at the dynamics of cumulative returns over the full sample, we notice that they seem to be affected by seasonality. Preliminary research based on splitting the signals into spring–summer vs autumn–winter[15] showed that the latter produced considerably higher returns, confirming our intuition about seasonality. Such evidence is consistent with the hypothesis that our predictive models work better during spikes in the expected and actual commodity demand occurring in colder months. Trying to exploit seasonality to further improve performance is yet another interesting direction to investigate in future research.

9.5   CONCLUSION

In this study we set out to evaluate the performance of commodity futures using commodity-related news stories captured in RPAs and a suite of five well-known machine learning models. We create an energy commodity basket, which contains four commodity futures, including crude oil and natural gas.

We illustrate how the five machine learning models stack up against each other. An RF model is the top performer with an IR of 0.85, followed the KNN and the GBN. With our linear model (ELNET) among the worst-performing models, our results suggest that the added complexity other models bring to the table – in terms of being able to detect nonlinearities including interaction terms – considerably increases the predictive power for next-day returns.

Nevertheless, by including all these machine learning techniques, we proceed to demonstrate how the implementation of a simple *ensemble* strategy, whereby we equally weight all model predictions for the basket, produces robust results. Taking an *ensemble* approach has the benefit of lowering the bias and variance through aggregation of the individual models – and is furthermore agnostic with regards to what is the optimal individual model. The *ensemble* approach yields an IR of 0.65 with an annualized return of 9.8% and a per-trade return of 3.88 basis points. We also illustrate how the *ensemble* basket changes as a function of the mix of commodities entering the portfolio. Specifically, we show how the IR changes when we systematically drop one commodity at a time from each basket.

Finally, we demonstrate how volatility regimes impact the performance of our basket. In particular, by imposing trading restrictions on our *ensemble* basket, we show how both risk-adjusted and per-trade returns can be improved while lowering the number of trades and hence cost by incorporating information not utilized in the *ensemble* strategy. In particular, we highlight how a strategy which trades only during high volatility regimes results in an IR of 1.27 while more than doubling the per-trade returns.

Exploratory analysis shows that our predictive signals are potentially more profitable during autumn–winter months, which suggests that further research in how to model and take advantage of such seasonality in the predictive models represents an interesting direction to further enhance these strategies.

The event taxonomy in RPAs has capabilities for commodities trading well beyond those investigated in the present study. While we have taken advantage of RPA's capability to detect commodity-related news stories at the event category level, we have

---

[15]Northern hemisphere seasons were used for this quick analysis.

disregarded other types of potentially impactful news, for example about the global economy, as well as metrics such as the Event Sentiment Score, which we used extensively earlier in our research on equities. Lastly, the framework presented herein can be easily modified or extended to include other asset classes which are mainly influenced by the macro economy, such as equity index futures, bond futures and currencies.[16]

REFERENCES

Altman, N.S. (1992). An introduction to Kernel and nearest-neighbor nonparametric regression. *The American Statistician* 46 (3): 175–185.

Brandt, M.W. and Gao, L. (2016). *Macro Fundamentals or Geopolitical Events? A Textual Analysis of News Events for Crude Oil*. Duke University/University of Luxembourg.

Breiman, L. (1994). Stacked regressions. *Machine Learning* 24 (1): 49–64.

Breiman, L. (2001). Random forests. *Machine Learning* 45 (1): 5–32.

Donoho, D.L. (2000). *High-Dimensional Data Analysis: The Curses and Blessings of Dimensionality*. Stanford University, Department of Statistics.

Friedman, J., Hastie, T., and Tibshirani, R. (2000). Additive logistic regression: a statistical view of boosting. *The Annals of Statistics* 28 (2): 337–407.

Hafez, P. and Guerrero-Colón, J.A. (2016). *Earnings Sentiment Consistently Outperforms Consensus*. RavenPack Quantitative Research.

Hafez, P. and Koefoed, M. (2017a). *Introducing RavenPack Analytics for Equities*. RavenPack Quantitative Research.

Hafez, P. and Koefoed, M. (2017b). *A Multi-Topic Approach to Building Quant Models*. RavenPack Quantitative Research.

Hafez, P. and Lautizi, F. (2016). *Achieve High Capacity Strategies Trading Economically-Linked Companies*. RavenPack Quantitative Research.

Hafez, P. and Lautizi, F. (2017). *Abnormal Media Attention Impacts Stock Returns*. RavenPack Quantitative Research.

Hastie, T., Tibshirani, R., and Friedman, J. (2009). *The Elements of Statistical Learning*, 2e. Springer Series in Statistics, chapter 11.

Mendes-Moreira, J., Soares, C., Jorge, A.M., and de Sousa, J.F. (2012). Ensemble approaches for regression: a survey. *ACM Computing Surveys* 45 (1): Article 10.

Zou, H. and Hastie, T. (2005). Regularization and variable selection via the elastic net. *Journal of the Royal Statistical Society, 67(2), 301–320.*

---

[16]This article was originally published by RavenPack as a report to its clients dated 9 October 2017. The views expressed in this article reflect the views of the named authors. Nothing in this article should be considered as an investment recommendation or investment advice. This article is based on information obtained from sources believed to be reliable and no representation or warranty is made that it is accurate, complete or up to date. RavenPack accepts no liability whatsoever for any direct, indirect, consequential or other loss arising from any use of this article.

10

Natural Language Processing of Financial News

M. Berkan Sesen, Yazann Romahi and Victor Li

10.1 INTRODUCTION

News has always been a key factor in investment decisions. It is well established that company-specific, macroeconomic and political news strongly influence the financial markets. As technology advances and the market participants become more connected, the volume and frequency of news are growing rapidly. In fact, more data was created in the past two years than the previous 5000 years of humanity. It is estimated that, in 2017, we created even more data in one year alone (Landro 2016). A significant portion of this comes from news sources, rendering manually processing all news-related information humanly impossible.

This burgeoning abundance of news data, combined with significant developments in machine learning (ML), brought to the fore the application of natural language processing (NLP) in finance. NLP is a subfield of artificial intelligence concerned with programming computers to process natural language corpora in order to gain useful insights. NLP manifests itself in different forms across many disciplines under various aliases, including (but not limited to) textual analysis, text mining, computational linguistics and content analysis (Loughran and McDonald 2016).

The efficient utilization of news data in finance requires identifying relevant news in a timely and efficient manner. Major news can have a significant impact on the market and investor sentiment, resulting in dynamic shifts in the risk characteristics of the investment universe (Mitra and Mitra 2011). In order to make informed and timely decisions, investors increasingly rely on programmatic solutions that help them extract, process and interpret vast volumes of news data in real time.

Effective NLP models that react to news data are highly sought after, not only for asset management and trading but also for risk controls. In finance, NLP is commonly used in monitoring, filtering and sentiment analysis of news articles. In the context of asset management, such technologies can serve as knowledge distillation tools that free the portfolio managers from the burden of reading through all published material and allow them to channel their attention more selectively.

In this chapter, we look at various aspects of financial news data, contemporary academic research on NLP applied to finance and how the industry utilizes these methods to gain a competitive edge. We begin our discussion by introducing different sources of news data in Section 10.2. Following this, in Section 10.3, we review the existing literature and practical applications of NLP applied to solve different problems in finance. In Section 10.4, we provide a brief summary of the common analytical steps involved in NLP analyses, such as preprocessing textual data, feature representation techniques for words, and finally getting the inference required from the model and evaluating its predictive performance. In Section 10.5, we present a real-life NLP solution that is used to filter merger & acquisition (M&A) related news articles from the rest. In Section 10.6, we conclude by summarizing the points raised, and discussing challenges and the future avenues of research in NLP applied to finance.

10.2   SOURCES OF NEWS DATA

The surge in the volume of financial news data in the past decade has been driven largely by the electronification of conventional media outlets, the adoption of web-based dissemination by regulators as well as exchanges, and the rise of web-based social media and content-sharing services. Accordingly, it would be sensible to separate sources of news data into three categories that provide researchers with rich textual datasets to test different financial hypotheses.

10.2.1   Mainstream news

The news articles produced by the mainstream news providers like Thomson Reuters, Bloomberg and Factset are usually accessed via news feeds services provided by the vendors. The news items usually contain a timestamp, a short headline and sometimes tags and other metadata. In the past decade, most data vendors have invested substantially in infrastructure and human resources to process and enrich the articles they publish by providing insights from the textual contents of news. Currently, Bloomberg, Thomson Reuters, RavenPack, among others, provide their own low-latency sentiment analysis and topic classification services.

10.2.2   Primary source news

Primary information sources that journalists research before they write articles include Securities and Exchange Commission (SEC) filings, product prospectuses, court documents and merger deals. In particular, SEC's Electronic Data Gathering, Analysis and Retrieval (EDGAR) system provides free access to more than 21 million company filings in the US, including registration statements, periodic reports and other forms. As such it has been the focus of numerous NLP research projects (Li 2010; Bodnaruk et al. 2015; Hadlock and Pierce 2010; Gerde 2003; Grant and Conlon 2006).

Analysis of most reports in EDGAR is fairly straightforward as they have consistent structure, making section identification and extracting relevant text easy by using HTML parsers. In comparison with EDGAR, the contents and structures of company filings in the UK are less standardized as the firm management has more discretion over which and how much information to publicize on different topics. Without a consistent template, extracting textual data from these filings becomes more difficult for the researchers.

We can further categorize primary source news as scheduled or unscheduled. Examples of scheduled news events include the Monetary Policy Committee announcements or company earnings announcements. Unscheduled, i.e. event-driven, news can be M&A announcements or business reorganizations. An advantage of scheduled news releases is that the market participants are prepared to digest and react to these in a timely manner. Due to consumer demand, scheduled news items are usually made available in structured or semi-structured formats. In contrast, event-driven news is noisy and requires constant monitoring and processing of what is usually unstructured textual data.

10.2.3   Social media

With news from social media services, the barrier for entry and consequentially the signal to noise ratio is low. Social media sources can include tweets, blogs and personal posts. Despite the high level of noise and the lack of verification and editorial, social media can still serve as a valuable information source due to the blisteringly fast speeds that news is made available online. As a matter of fact, the most notable paradigm shift in disseminating information has taken place with the arrival of social media platforms that enable individuals, as well as corporates, to post their reactions to (market) events instantaneously.

There are many arguments in favour of and against the use of social media. One of the arguments in favour is that blog posts or tweets allow one to tap into the 'Wisdom of Crowds', which refers to the phenomenon that the aggregation of information provided by many individuals often results in predictions that are better than those made by any single member of the group (Bartov et al. 2017). However, social media posts may lack credibility as most providers have no mechanism to fact-check the information shared or to incentivize high-quality information. Anecdotal evidence from contemporaneous political elections in developed countries demonstrates that the information in social media posts may be intentionally misleading to serve the posters' own agenda.

The use of social media is also gaining popularity for disseminating company information as an alternative to primary information providers. In April 2013, the SEC approved the use of posts and tweets to communicate corporate announcements such as earnings. Jung et al. (2015) found that, as of 2015, roughly half of the S&P 1500 firms had either a corporate Twitter account or a Facebook page. It has later been reported that firms use social media channels such as Twitter to interact with investors in order to attenuate the negative price reactions to consumer product recalls (Lee et al. 2015).

NLP models that are built to process and pick up patterns from news are all trained using historical data. News data can usually be accessed via subscription to the news stream and/or the database of third-party vendors like Bloomberg, Thomson Reuters or RavenPack. Another common method, which is utilized more by individual investors, is to web-crawl to extract textual as well as metadata regarding historical news, for instance from Rich Site Summary (RSS) feeds, or from the news providers' or regulators' publicly available archives.

Regardless of the categorization, all news items need to be translated into a machine readable format by applying a series of transformations. The news articles are always timestamped, and in most cases, tagged by the publisher with relevant topics, tickers and sometimes even sentiment scores. This sort of metadata assists in processing the information. Before discussing NLP and the common sequential steps applied to raw textual input data, in the next section we focus on the practical applications of NLP in finance.

10.3   PRACTICAL APPLICATIONS

In this section we provide a review of contemporary academic research and industrial applications of NLP in finance. One of the seminal studies in NLP applied to financial news data was carried out by Niederhoffer (1971). The author investigated the broad relations of headlines from *The New York Times* and stock price movements, where headlines were manually extracted from the paper's columns. The study reported that large movements in equity prices were more likely to follow macroeconomic news. However, the particular category of the news item did not add information on the future price movements. Since then, the roles of computers and statistical inference in the field have become gradually more prominent.

Today, NLP research in finance focuses on a broad range of topics, from those that involve trading and investment decisions to market making and risk systems. There a growing number of industrial applications and academic studies that apply NLP in financial news analytics. However, comparatively few industrial reports which describe the proprietary uses of these technologies in financial firms are made publicly available due to obvious intellectual property and trade secrecy concerns.

10.3.1   Trading and investment

One of the most common application areas of NLP in finance is in systematic trading and investment, which have seen dramatic growth in the past decade and continue to grow rapidly in many venues where equities, futures, options and foreign exchange are traded. Market participants turn to NLP as one of the many ways to gain a competitive edge by exploiting predictive patterns through the analysis of news data. The basic rationale is highly analogous to how investors may implicitly apply their knowledge of how markets behaved in the past under similar conditions to predict what is likely to happen next given the current environment.

News is considered to be an 'information event' that influences the market microstructure, impacting price formation, volatility and the liquidity of a particular security or market (Mitra et al. 2015). While the methodologies applied are theoretically domain-agnostic, NLP analysis in trading and investment is most developed in equities.

The sources of information that researchers tap into for this purpose vary by application. Processing SEC filings is quite popular due to the relative ease of extracting data from the EDGAR database, as we have discussed in Section 10.2. In a 2011-dated literature survey, Li (2010) reports that most research on company filings focuses on either the tone or the complexity of disclosures and their implications for earnings or stock prices. In an example study by Bodnaruk et al. (2015), the authors try to predict liquidity events by assessing the tone in 10-K disclosures to communicate their concerns to shareholders. The authors calculate the frequency of a proprietary set of constraining words, e.g. 'obligations', 'impairment', 'imposed', to measure a 10-K filing's tone. They report that 'the percentage of constraining words has a nontrivial economic impact. For example, a one standard deviation increase in constraining words increases the likelihood of a dividend omission by 10.32% and decreases the probability of a dividend increase by 6.46%' (Bodnaruk et al. 2015).

Product prospectuses may serve a similar purpose for predicting returns. Using a large sample of initial public offerings (IPOs) during the period 1996–2005, Hanley and Hoberg (2010) examine how the tone of the IPO prospectuses impact pricing and first-day returns. The authors decompose the text of the prospectus into standard and informative components and find that a prospectus with a low portion of informative content decreases the pricing accuracy since it implies more reliance on investors to price the issue during book-building and results in higher changes in offer prices and higher initial returns. A related strand of research to these is sentiment analysis, which is ever-growing in popularity and therefore deserves its own subsection in our coverage.

10.3.2   Sentiment analysis

Sentiment analysis aims to analyze the opinion that a body of text conveys on a particular subject or entity. In the financial domain, the primary motivation behind most sentiment analysis tasks is to relate these opinions to the directionality of future security returns. This is in contrast with NLP applications that monitor the extent of news coverage to predict trading volume and price volatility, which are arguably simpler tasks. Despite its current popularity in the financial domain, the seminal study in sentiment analysis actually focused on movie reviews to train an algorithm that detects sentiment in text (Lee et al. 2002). Compared with movie reviews, which are self-contained text bodies aimed to clearly express an opinion, extracting sentiment from financial news is a much more difficult task due to the added noise and the uncertainties around the contextual information involved.

In general, sentiment can be modelled as a binary classification of 'positive' versus 'negative' or as an ordinal score that specifies how positive or negative an article is. As a supervised learning exercise, sentiment analysis may involve manually labelling a training dataset with different sentiment categories/scores before feeding these into a classification or regression algorithm. This is a labour-intensive exercise that may be negatively impacted by the subjectivity of the labellers and is prone to inter-labeller inconsistencies in the case of multiple annotators. Indeed, Loughran and McDonald (2016) show that financial news can be easily misclassified.

An alternative to manual labelling is to compile a 'word list' that associates words with distinct sentiments. Using such a list, a researcher can count the number of words associated with a particular sentiment, whereby a higher proportion of pessimistic words in a news article indicates a negative sentiment. While an NLP practitioner may choose to compile and use their proprietary word lists, there also exist publicly available ones, like the Henry Word list (Henry 2008), which was compiled for financial text. With such publicly available word lists, it is more straightforward to replicate the analysis of other researchers.

Finally, a more principled approach that removes researcher subjectivity from sentiment labelling is to associate the news articles with returns over a prediction horizon from the time of the news publication. An example of this is the Reuters NewsScope Event Indices (NEIs) (Lo 2008), which are constructed to have 'predictive' power for asset returns and (realized) volatility. The optimal weights for NEI are determined by regressing the word (topic) frequencies against the intraday asset returns.

One of the most prominent applications of sentiment analysis in finance is the Reuters NewsScope Sentiment Engine (Reuters 2015), which classifies company-specific news according to positive, neutral or negative sentiment. Groß-Klußman and Hautsch (2011) investigated to what extent high-frequency movements in returns, volatility and liquidity can be explained by the intraday unscheduled news arrivals reported by the Reuters NewsScope. The authors concluded that while sentiment labels have some predictability for future price trends, significant spikes in volatility and bid–ask spreads around news arrivals render simple sentiment-based trading strategies unprofitable.

In a separate study, Heston and Sinha (2017) explored the predictability of individual stock returns using sentiment data extracted from the Thomson Reuters NewsScope between 2003 and 2010. They report that news sentiment on a particular trading day is positively correlated with stock returns in the subsequent 1–2 days. They note that the length of this prediction horizon is heavily dependent on the portfolio formation procedure. Similarly, Das and Chen (2007) conclude sentiment analysis provides some explanatory power on the level of the Morgan Stanley High Tech (MSH) index. However, autocorrelation makes it difficult to establish the empirical nature of the relationship.

In addition to the use of mainstream news, there is an increasing body of research focusing on sentiment analysis of social media. An example is Bollen et al. (2011) who investigate whether measurements of collective mood states derived from large-scale Twitter feeds are correlated to the value of the Dow Jones Industrial Average (DJIA) over time. To capture the mood states, they use Opinion Finder and Google-Profile of Mood States (GPOMS), where the former measures positive vs negative mood and the latter categorizes mood in terms of six dimensions (Calm, Alert, Sure, Vital, Kind and Happy). The authors report that some GPOMS mood states match changes in the DJIA values that occur 3–4 days later, while the Opinion Finder mood states seem to carry no predictive information. It is also worthwhile to mention that while some GPOMS mood states have lagged correlations with DJIA values, the authors warn that this offers no guarantees on the causal relationship between the public mood states and DJIA values.

Studies that aim to extract sentiment from primary source news are also common place. Huang et al. (2014) use a Naïve Bayes (NB) approach to predict the sentiment contained in over 350 000 analyst reports issued for the S&P 500 firms during the 1995–2008 period. They categorize more than 27 million sentences from analyst reports into one of positive, negative or neutral sentiment, and aggregate sentence-level opinions to determine an overall report sentiment. They report that investors react more strongly to negative than to positive text, suggesting that analysts are especially important in propagating bad news.

The common challenges associated with sentiment analysis in finance include the difficulty in extracting a consistent sentiment, the need to determine which securities a particular news item refers to (and to what extent), and filtering novel articles from those that have been recycled. It is worth mentioning that sentiment analysis abounds with data availability and bias issues as well. Moniz et al. (2009) report that the volume of news data available for companies depends heavily on their size, to the extent that the top quintile companies by size in the S&P Large-Cap Europe universe accounts for 40% of all news coverage, while the bottom quintile makes up only 5%. In addition to the lack of data for companies with smaller market capitalization, several studies found that there is a larger volume of what is considered to be positive news compared with negative (Das and Chen 2007). In contrast, individual stock prices react more strongly to negative news compared with positive (Tetlock 2007). It is therefore prudent to be aware of the common pitfalls that accompany sentiment analyses.

Another methodological challenge with sentiment analysis is the unintentional over-fitting of the inference algorithm by the NLP practitioner lured by attaining improved results and constantly tweaking model parameterization to this end. This manifests itself in the model being too strongly tailored to the particularities of the training period, in effect generalizing poorly to new data. While it can be argued that this is a more generic pitfall concerning machine learning applied to financial time series, it is accentuated in sentiment analysis, due to the added complexities and degrees of freedom associated with sentiment scoring and labelling.

Finally, as a rule of thumb, following a sentiment analysis exercise the results should be examined to verify that the informational 'edge' captured is indeed due to the news source and not driven by auto-correlation or concurrent information from other market signals. In other words, one should confirm that the predictions based on senti-ment, e.g. price, add information not contained in past values of the predicted market signal itself. We discuss some commonly used evaluation metrics for this purpose in Section 10.4.4.

10.3.3 Market making

Market makers are liquidity providers in financial instruments aiming to make a profit on the spread. In a quote-driven market, market makers provide bid and ask prices. In an order-driven market, limit orders provide liquidity. In the context of market mak-ing, news data can be used to update the broker dealer's estimates of trading volume, market depth and volatility in order to skew prices and adjust bid-ask spreads. Market makers want to be compensated proportionally for exposing themselves at the time of significant market events by widening their bid-ask spreads. As discussed in the previous section, these events can be scheduled monetary policy announcements or unscheduled news releases that may trigger spikes in volatility or trading volumes of the related instruments.

As we have mentioned, unscheduled news items usually require more time to pro-cess the meaning of the announcement and formulate appropriate actions. During such periods of contemplation, market makers are usually more cautious to trade and liq-uidity dries up. Groß-Klußman and Hautsch (2011) report that news releases have a significant impact on bid-ask spreads but do not necessarily affect market depth. Market makers predominantly react to news by revising their quotes and not by order volumes. This is very much in line with the asymmetric information-based market microstructure theory where specialists aim to overcompensate for possible information asymmetries (Mitra et al. 2015).

Von Beschwitz et al. (2013) study how providers of media analytics affect the market microstructure and, in particular, how their existence affects the stock market's reaction to news. They find that providers of media analytics, such as RavenPack, impact the market in a distinct way. The speed of adjustment of stock prices and trading volume to news is faster if an article is consistently covered in RavenPack. The market temporarily reacts to false positives but then reverts quickly. It is therefore important for the market maker to digest this type of information to position themselves accordingly upon financial news releases.

10.3.4   Risk systems

NLP applications in finance are also used in risk management. As markets grow and become more complex, risk management tools evolve to serve more challenging demands. Major news events can have a significant impact on the market environment and investor sentiment, resulting in rapid changes to the risk structure and risk characteristics of traded securities. NLP is used in risk management in various ways, ranging from detecting and managing event risk to enhancing fraud and insider trading detection.

Event risk can be described as the uncertainty posed by unscheduled news that causes major market moves over short time intervals. Often cited but rarely managed, event risk has largely been consigned to qualitative judgement and manager discretion because of the difficulty of quantifying textual news (Healy and Lo 2011). One of the common uses of NLP in financial risk is as a circuit breaker for trade execution algorithms. We have already discussed that major market events commonly result in increased bid-ask spread by the market makers. As the counterparties of the trade, asset managers and proprietary trading shops can react by temporarily halting their current course of action when 'substantive' and 'novel' news is published on the securities being traded. Brown (2011) reports that the use of news analytics as 'circuit breakers' and 'wolf detection' systems in automated trading strategies can help enhance the robustness and reliability of such strategies.

In a similar vein, it may at times be wise to exclude securities that are associated with speculative market news from the investment universe. Such speculative news events are usually followed by price fluctuations and volatility spikes that constitute undiversifiable, i.e. idiosyncratic, risk. In Section 10.5 we provide a real-world NLP application that aims to accurately discriminate news article headlines that are M&A-related from those that are not in order to reduce idiosyncratic risk caused by merger announcements.

Another application field for NLP in financial risk management is outlier detection to identify anomalous activity and fraudulent reports. Purda and Skillicorn (2015) analyze 10-K filings to distinguish between fraudulent and truthful reports based on the language used in the management discussion and analysis sections of the reports. Their methodology relies heavily on identifying the significant deviations of some reports from the one published by the same company, highlighting the efficacy of using the company as its own control. Similar studies in outlier detection can also prove popular in detecting irregular patterns

In addition to the use cases discussed, NLP can be used to improve internal financial reporting and provide timely updates on key matters, particularly compliance. Textual analysis of metadata and 'understanding' of content allows one to efficiently track changes to regulatory requirements and determine compliance-related costs (LaPlanter and Coleman 2017). As such, NLP can significantly reduce the manual processing required to ensure regulatory and legal compliance and can facilitate communications with regulators by aggregating relevant data from different lines of business.

It is important to note that textual analysis of financial news items can also have its unintended consequences. The improved speed that NLP provides us to respond to news also increases the requirement that the response be the right one. Responding rapidly but in the wrong way can prove to be dangerous. For instance, in April 2013, a misleading tweet about an alleged White House explosion caused a mini flash crash, as a result of which some quickly blamed the algorithms. Later in the same year Thomson Reuters was rebuked for selling access to scheduled economic releases a couple of seconds early to high-frequency trading shops (von Beschwitz et al. 2013). In the next section, we will focus on the technical aspects of NLP.

10.4   NATURAL LANGUAGE PROCESSING

As we have already established, NLP is a subfield of artificial intelligence concerned with programming computers to process textual data in order to gain useful insights. It transcends many disciplines in various guises and names, such as textual analysis, text mining, computational linguistics and content analysis. All NLP applications covered in the previous section need to go through some common sequential steps, such as preprocessing of textual data and representing words as predictive features before these are fed into a statistical inference algorithm. In this section we will take a more detailed look at these common steps that are warranted in all NLP tasks.

Naturally, any statistical analysis begins with collecting data. For NLP applications in finance, different methods used to gather data include subscribing to the news feeds of primary information providers like Reuters or Bloomberg, or web-crawling using custom scripts to extract textual as well as metadata regarding historical news, for instance from RSS feeds, or from the news providers' or regulators' publicly available archives.

Once the data is collected, the NLP practitioner will need to first preprocess and clean the data and reduce noise where possible. After preprocessing, it is important to choose a feature representation method suitable for the data and the task at hand. Once the words are translated into predictive features, they can be fed into a statistical inference algorithm to extract useful insights. Figure 10.1 illustrates this common NLP pipeline, which to a large extent overlaps with the steps included in general machine learning analyses as well.

In the next four sections, we will discuss the sequential steps depicted in Figure 10.1 in slightly more detail. We intentionally keep our coverage conceptual and aim to give a flavour of these commonly used steps rather than offering a thorough technical discussion.

10.4.1   Preprocessing textual data

Financial news data is most notably distinguished from quantitative market data by its imprecision. In order to feed news data into the computer, we need to transform a collection of characters into a format that captures the information conveyed in

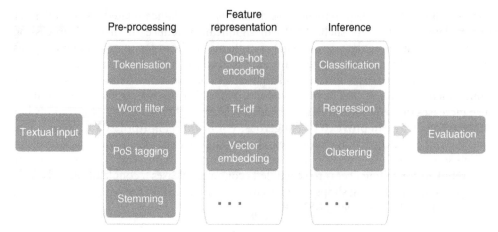

FIGURE 10.1   The NLP pipeline from preprocessing to feature representation and inference.

an unambiguous and precise manner. Below we present some of the most common preprocessing and transformation steps applied to textual data. For a more thorough coverage of the preprocessing steps discussed in this section, the reader is referred to Manning et al. (2009).

10.4.1.1   Tokenization   The first step in most NLP applications is usually to tokenize the raw text data, which breaks it up into units called tokens by locating word boundaries. However, tokens do not have to be just words; they can be numbers or punctuation marks. In fact, tokenization may be bundled with removing punctuation and stop-words, which are extremely common words that may be of little value for the NLP task. Ascertaining these stop-words is clearly a language-specific exercise and may involve different sub-stages depending on the language of the corpus.

10.4.1.2   Vocabulary   While it is certainly possible to model text as a collection of letters, most NLP approaches consider words as the atomic units that serve as the predictive features. Vocabulary in the context of NLP refers to the set of distinct words that appear in the corpus to be processed. A common way to limit the vocabulary is by term frequency, where only the words occurring more frequently are retained. This results in the less frequent words to be bundled into a generic word index and can also be regarded as an application-specific stop-word removal process.

One of the simplest, yet powerful, approaches to NLP is facilitated by targeting a few specific words or phrases among others in a given text. Due to ambiguity, an excessively large vocabulary is usually more prone to error when compared with tests focusing on fewer unambiguous words or phrases. One possible solution is to omit or bundle together tokens such as monetary amounts, numbers and URLs in our vocabulary, since their individual representation greatly expands the size of the vocabulary.

The less frequently encountered words usually include proper nouns, like individual or organization names, and limiting the vocabulary size can potentially help with regularization, where any company or country name is bundled into a generic index, potentially removing biases. Reducing vocabulary size is akin to feature selection in machine learning terminology. This is a very active research in machine learning and there exist more principled techniques than frequency, such as mutual information and gain ratio that are used to score the class-discriminative information captured by distinct features.

10.4.1.3 Part-of-Speech Tagging Part-of-speech (PoS) tagging is the process of assigning a token to its grammatical category, e.g. verb, noun, etc., in order to understand its role within the sentence. PoS taggers are specialized computer programs that take a sequence of words (i.e. a sentence) as input and provide a list of tuples as output, where each word is associated with the related tag. An example utility of PoS tagging is if we want to appoint different weights to words based on their tags, focusing on the segments of text that have high emphasis, e.g. in regions around adjectives and adverbs. For instance as part of their five-classifier ensemble framework for sentiment analysis, Das and Chen (2007) use an adjective–adverb-based classifier that assumes phrases that use adjectives or adverbs contain much of the sentiment and therefore 'deserve' a greater weight in word count-based feature representations.

10.4.1.4 Stemming and Lemmatization Both stemming and lemmatization are used to reduce words from their derived grammatical forms to their base forms. While for most English words stemming and lemmatization generate the same word, the two are not the same thing. Stemming usually operates on a single word without knowledge of the context and uses a crude heuristic process that removes derivational affixes in the hope of reducing the word to its stem. In contrast, lemmatization aims to achieve this in a more principled manner with the use of a vocabulary and morphological analysis of words to return the base or dictionary form of a word, also known as its lemma (Manning et al. 2009). Unlike stemming, lemmatization handles not only basic word variations like singular vs plural but also synonyms like having 'car' match 'automobile'. Also lemmatization usually requires a PoS tagger beforehand to provide the contextual information that it needs to map the words to the appropriate lemmas.

10.4.2 Representation of words as features

The vast majority of news data is created for human consumption and as such is stored in an unstructured format, such as news feed articles, PDF reports, social media posts and audio files, which cannot be readily processed by computers. Following the preprocessing steps discussed in the previous section, in order for the information content to be conveyed to the statistical inference algorithm, the preprocessed tokens need to be translated into predictive features.

The most commonly used feature representation technique in NLP is the bag-of-words model, according to which a document is encoded as an (unordered) set of its words, disregarding grammar and word order but retaining multiplicity. After the text is transformed into a 'bag of words', various measures can be calculated to generate the predictive features. The most common measure generated by a bag-of-words model is term frequency, which we have discussed in the previous section.

In a term frequency representation, all words are assumed to be independent and the text is collapsed down to a term-document matrix consisting of rows that represent individual words and columns that provide the word counts per document.

This approach has various shortcomings. To begin with, it does not retain the order in which words appear and therefore loses context. Consider the Coca-Cola Company's 2017 Q3 earnings report headlined 'Net Revenues Down 15%, Driven by 18-Point Headwind from Refranchising; Organic Revenues (Non-GAAP) Grew 4%, Driven by Price/Mix of 3%' (The Coca-Cola Company 2017). Even in a small body of text like this, a term frequency representation cannot ascertain what is 'down', what 'grew' and driven by which factor.

Representation of a word's meaning based on its neighbouring words is one of the most common extensions beyond the simple bag-of-words approach. N-gram models fall under this category, partially addressing the lack of context by storing sequences of words that occur next to each other. So, for example, a two-word n-gram model, i.e. a bigram model, parses the text into a set of consecutive pairs. This clearly helps with capturing the co-occurrences of words. Theoretically, with larger n, a model can store more contextual information. However, in practice most NLP applications are limited to bigrams or at best trigrams since a comprehensive n-gram approach can be challenging due to computational and time constraints.

Another shortcoming of term frequencies is that common words like pronouns or prepositions are almost always the terms with highest frequency in the text, which does not necessarily mean that the corresponding word is more important. To address this problem, one of the most popular ways to 'normalize' the term frequencies is to weight a term by the inverse of document frequency, namely term frequency-inverse document frequency (tf–idf). Tf-idf is one of the most popular term-weighting schemes in NLP that is intended to reflect how important a word is to a document in a corpus (Aizawa 2003).

An additional dimension across which we should look at feature representation in NLP is how the features are encoded. Much of the earlier NLP work encodes words as discrete atomic symbols, that is if we have a vocabulary that contains both 'buy' and 'acquire' as distinct words, 'acquire' may be represented as Id-102 and 'buy' as Id-052. This numbering is completely arbitrary and provides no useful information to the learning algorithm regarding the relationships that clearly exist between these individual symbols. This means that the model cannot leverage what it has learned about 'buy' when it is processing a news article that contains 'acquire'. In machine learning, this type of feature representation, where categorical features are encoded as unique ids, is referred to as 'one-hot-encoding' and leads to data sparsity. This means we may require more data in order to successfully train a statistical model.

Using distributed representations can overcome some of these obstacles. A distributed representation, also known as a vector space model, or vector embedding, represents words in a continuous vector space where semantically similar words are grouped together. Going back to our example of 'acquire' and 'buy', in a distributed representation setting these two words would be mapped to nearby coordinates in the vector space after training. As a result, the algorithm that encounters these two seemingly distinct predictive features can perceive that they are indeed closely related.

The different approaches that leverage distributed representations can be divided into two categories. The first is coined count-based methods (e.g. latent semantic analysis (LSA)), which quantify the co-occurrence frequencies of words with other words in a large text and map these statistics down to a dense vector for each distinct word. The second category is the so-called predictive methods that are trained by iteratively updating the vector coordinates of words in order to more accurately predict a word from its neighbours. The end result from both models is the same as that of count-based models, a set of dense embedding vectors for each distinct word in the vocabulary (Tensorflow 2017). The distributed representations, computed using such predictive models, are particularly interesting because the vector space explicitly encodes many linguistic regularities and patterns. And, surprisingly, many of these patterns can be represented as linear translations (Mikolov et al. 2013).

Transfer learning is another recently popular topic that goes hand in hand with distributed representations in NLP. The concept has been around for decades and refers to the improvement of learning in a new task through the transfer of knowledge from a related task in a similar domain that has already been learned. In NLP, the transfer of knowledge usually refers to the reuse of distributed representations of words that have been trained on very large corpora to smaller, niche domains. This allows the NLP practitioner to leverage the semantic information and linguistic patterns captured by large-scale studies in their own domain-specific application instead of having to rely on what is usually a more niche and limited dataset to relearn the same information. In Section 10.5, we will provide a real-life NLP application used by one of the leading asset management firms that uses vector embeddings trained on millions of news articles, and apply these to the particular domain of M&A. Among the more commonly used pre-trained vector representations are Google's Word2Vec (Tensorflow 2017) and Stanford University's GloVe (Pennington et al. 2014).

While it is not possible to quantify the entire information content of a collection of words, the overall goal of feature representation is to maximize this amount. Language is inherently complex and relies not only on the letters and symbols that constitute text but also on the human brain's ability to understand connotation and context. Hence, developing NLP tools that capture all of the intricacies of human communication becomes increasingly difficult as we move from syntax-based approaches to those that consider context and semantic associations. It is important to be conscious of how much context is lost by, for instance, methods that assume words are independent units.

10.4.3 Inference

Like all other artificial intelligence tasks, the inference generated by an NLP application usually needs to be translated into a decision in order to be actionable. This natural flow from inference to decision and action is given in Figure 10.2. Inference from an NLP application can be used to aid the decision making by humans, where a utility function is applied to convert the inference into a decision. This utility function can be as simple as a probability threshold, or an implicit weighing down of pros and cons in a domain expert's brain. Alternatively, inference can directly be translated into an action by the computer as part of an automated quantitative strategy.

Inference has always been a central topic in ML, and over the past two decades there has been unprecedented progress in the inferential tools used by NLP practitioners. Inference in ML falls under three broad categories, namely supervised, unsupervised and reinforcement learning. While the type of inference required depends on the business problem and the type of training data, in NLP the most commonly used algorithms are supervised or unsupervised. In a nutshell, supervised learning requires labelled training data that aims to map a set of predictive features to their recorded or desired output.

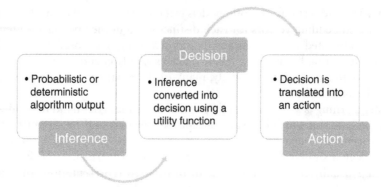

FIGURE 10.2   Flow of inference into decision and action.

In contrast, unsupervised algorithms can learn patterns from unlabelled data. There is also a hybrid category that falls between the two, coined semi-supervised learning. Semi-supervised learning typically uses a small amount of labelled data with a larger portion of unlabelled data to solve supervised problems.

One of the most commonly used supervised methodologies in NLP is the Naïve Bayes model, which assumes that all word features are independent of each other given the class labels. Due to this simplifying but largely false assumption, Naïve Bayes is very compatible with a bag-of-words word representation. Naïve Bayes is commonly described as 'the punching bag' of more complex algorithms in ML. However, despite its simplifying assumptions, it often comes head to head and at times even outperforms more complicated classifiers. Friedman et al. (1997) attribute this paradox to the fact that classification estimation is only a function of the sign (in binary cases) of the function estimation; the function approximation can still be poor while classification accuracy remains high. This refers to poor calibration of a classifier, which we discuss in the next section.

On the opposite end of the complexity spectrum for supervised methodologies lie the modern neural network architectures. In the past five years, neural network architectures, such as recurrent neural networks (RNNs) and convolutional neural networks (CNNs), have dominated NLP-based inference, blowing the previous state of the art out of water. In contrast with the Naïve Bayes model, these architectures are able to learn complex and dependent features that can recognize patterns in the input data and map these to desired outputs. In the domain of NLP, a catalyst in the improved performance of these architectures has been the rise to prominence of distributed representations that we discussed in the previous section.

Most of the existing literature in NLP focuses on supervised learning; as such, unsupervised learning applications constitute a relatively less developed subdomain where measuring document similarity is among the most common tasks. This is usually achieved by calculating the cosine similarity between two news items, where the documents are represented as vectors of term frequencies or term weightings. Recent studies in this area include the analysis by Hoberg and Phillips (2016), focusing on 10-K product descriptions to create text-based industry classifications, and Lang and Stice-Lawrence (2015), who compare annual report similarity.

Another popular unsupervised technique applied in NLP is LSA, also known as latent semantic indexing (LSI). LSA looks at relationships between a set of documents and the words they contain by producing a set of latent concepts related to the documents and terms. Technically, these latent concepts are extracted by applying singular value decomposition (SVD) to reduce the dimensionality of the term-document matrix while preserving the similarity structure within the matrix. In simple terms, we can think of these techniques as essentially factor analysis for words. LSA is commonly used to gauge document similarities and to uncover textual associative patterns across different domains.

The application of LSA to financial news is an underexplored research area. In one of the few studies on the subject, Mazis and Tsekrekos (2017) analyze the impact of the statements that are released by the Federal Open Market Committee (FOMC) on the US treasury market. Using LSA, the authors identify the recurring textual 'themes' used by the Committee that are able to characterize most of the communicated monetary policy in the authors' sample period. The themes are statistically significant in explaining the variation in three-month, two-year, five-year and ten-year treasury yields, even after controlling for monetary policy uncertainty and the concurrent economic outlook.

LSA also has a probabilistic variant named probabilistic latent semantic analysis (pLSA) based on a latent class model (Hofmann 2001). pLSA has paved the way for a more sophisticated approach named latent Dirichlet allocation (LDA) that uses Dirichlet-based priors (Blei et al. 2003). LDA allows the researcher to identify latent thematic structure within a corpus using the term-document matrix. LDA is a generative model, more specifically a hierarchical Bayesian model, under which documents are modelled as a finite mixture of topics and topics in turn are modelled as a finite mixture over words in the vocabulary. Topic modelling is a growing area of research where NLP practitioners build probabilistic generative models for text corpora in order to infer latent statistical structure in groups of documents to reveal likely topic attributions for words

10.4.4 Evaluation

In general, inference in NLP tasks is assessed in a similar way to any other machine learning analysis. For regression models that try to predict a continuous dependent variable, such as return or volatility, evaluation metrics are usually various error terms including, but not limited to, root mean square error (RMSE), mean absolute error (MEA) and mean squared error (MSE). For classification exercises, where the output is categorical, there exist numerous confusion matrix-based metrics, such as accuracy, precision and recall. The confusion matrix is a contingency table that compares predicted class labels from a classifier to the true labels, also referred as the ground truth. As such, for a binary classification task, the confusion matrix is a 2×2 matrix that gives summary statistics comparing the predicted labels to the true labels. The most intuitive confusion matrix-based metric is accuracy, which indicates what portion of the dataset the classifier managed to classify correctly.

It is worthwhile mentioning that for classification tasks, confusion matrix-based metrics give only a partial view of the overall performance. This is due to the fact that in order to form a confusion matrix, the posterior class probabilities, e.g. $P(\text{'Related'}) = 0.78$, output by the classifier need to be converted to a class label by applying a probability cut-off value. For binary classification problems, the most common practice is to pick this probability threshold to be 0.5, whereby any predictions above this value are labelled to be a 'positive' prediction for use in the confusion matrix. As the observant reader may notice, this binarization of the probabilistic output results in information loss, and theoretically one can build myriad confusion matrices using the same classification outputs by simply varying the probability thresholds between 0 and 1.

To combat these shortcomings, there exist methods that evaluate the predictive performance of classifiers across the range of possible thresholds. A common example of such 'systemic' metrics is the Area under the Receiver Operator Characteristic Curve (AUROC). The ROC curve plots recall, i.e. True Positive Rate, versus False Positive Rate for the classifier at varying probability thresholds. Figure 10.3(a) shows an example ROC curve. The value of the AUROC varies between 0.5 and 1, where 1 indicates a perfect classifier and 0.5 represents a totally random one. Another 'systemic' metric that is similar to AUROC but indeed suitable to use when working with highly imbalanced datasets is the Area under the Precision Recall curve (AUPRC). The precision recall curve aims to capture the tradeoff between the classifier precision versus recall (of the positive class) as the probability threshold for the positive class label is varied. Figure 10.3(b) shows a sample precision recall curve. For a thorough coverage on AUROC and AUPRC, the reader is referred to Davis and Goadrich (2006).

Assessing the posterior class probabilities (classifier outputs) rather than the maximum a posteriori (MAP) class labels is useful in giving the NLP practitioner insight into the 'calibration' of the classifiers. Well-calibrated classifiers are probabilistic classifiers for which the posterior probabilities can be directly interpreted as confidence levels. For instance, a well-calibrated (binary) classifier is expected to classify the samples such that among the samples to which it outputs a probability of 0.8 of being a positive observation, approximately 80% actually belong to the positive class. Some models, like Naïve Bayes as we discussed in the previous section, can give acceptable accuracy results while in reality having poor calibration with outputs that may be under- or overconfident.

Mittermayer and Knolmayer (2006) reviewed eight different news-based trading applications, noting that technical performance metrics, like the confusion matrix-based ones, were not reported in most of them. However, with the rise in prominence of

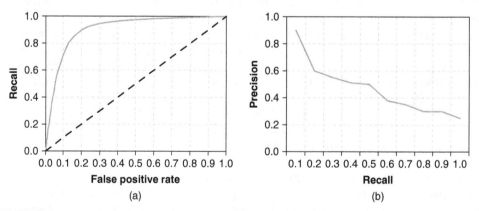

FIGURE 10.3   Example receiver operator characteristics (ROC) and precision-recall curves.

machine learning in the past decade, recent NLP research puts more emphasis on the evaluation of the outcomes with principled performance metrics.

It is also imperative to assess the validity of the outcome along the temporal dimension. Inference from news items is in the form of point-events when modelled as time series. In regression applications, before declaring causal links between such point events and market data (such as price, running volatility, etc.), it is important to verify the Granger causality of the relationship. Granger causality is a hypothesis test used to ascertain whether one time series is useful in predicting another. According to Granger causality, if a signal in time series x_1 'Granger-causes' a signal in time series x_2, then past values of x_1 should contain information that helps predict x_2 above and beyond the information contained in past values of x_2 alone.

For unsupervised learning, the variation in the different algorithms means that each technique warrants a different method of evaluating performance. Even different clustering techniques do not have well-established common performance metrics among themselves. For a k-means clustering task, a within-cluster 'residual sum of squared' score (also known as inertia) would be the metric of choice, whereas for hierarchical clustering a 'silhouette coefficient' is more commonly used. For topic models like LSA and LDA that we discussed in the previous section, various metrics, which evaluate the latent space, like word intrusion and topic intrusion, exist.

10.4.5 Example use case: Filtering merger arbitrage news

In this section we will look at a real-life example of NLP applied to classify financial news, specifically to determine whether a news article is related to M&A activity. Merger arbitrage is a well-established investment strategy. In simple terms it is a risky bet initiated on the merger announcement date by an investor who chooses to bet that the merger will complete. While the profitability of M&A strategies has been decreasing over time, substantial risk premia can still be captured from such strategies even when based only on publicly available information (Jetley and Ji 2010). M&A strategies have traditionally been used by institutional investors such as hedge funds, but they are becoming increasingly accessible to retail investors as well through exchange-traded funds (ETFs) and mutual funds.

We have discussed that the efficient utilization of news data in finance requires identifying relevant news in a timely and efficient manner. In this context, relevance can be with respect to a particular topic, such as mergers, restructurings, tender offers, shareholder buybacks or other capital structure adjustments. The role of the media in M&A deals has been well studied. Media coverage can sway acquirer firms with potential reputational risk to abandon ongoing deals (Liu and McConnell 2013). The media can introduce speculative merger rumours published about firms that interest the newspapers' readers, rumours that may distort prices and may result in return fluctuations (Ahern and Sosyura 2015).

Despite its popularity, the characterization of news flows in merger arbitrage has received relatively limited attention in the literature. Among the NLP studies focused on M&A, several investigate predicting the media-implied completion probability. Buehlmaier and Zechner (2014) use a simple Naïve Bayes methodology to analyze determinants of merger deal completion on a large sample of merger announcements. They find that M&A-related financial news moves slowly, taking several days to be fully priced in. A simple M&A strategy, which is reinforced by financial news content, increases risk-adjusted returns by more than 12 percentage points. More recently, the same authors find that merger arbitrage becomes significantly more profitable if one uses financial news to filter out the deals with low probability of completion (Buehlmaier and Zechner 2017).

As exemplified by existing research, it is in general to the investment manager's advantage to keep abreast of media coverage that concerns not only new but also existing M&A deals. To this end, we investigate the efficacy of a systematic NLP approach that aims to accurately discriminate news article headlines that are related to M&A from those that are not. This is achieved by training a supervised learning algorithm that can pick up the class-discriminative patterns in news articles that were manually labelled as M&A related or unrelated. Our end goal is to utilize this NLP model, namely NewsFilter, to infer whether a previously unseen article falls into the former or the latter category. This is used to act in a timely manner on official M&A announcements to submit arbitrage trades and to filter out stocks that are associated in M&A deals from other equity strategies in order to minimize idiosyncratic risk.

10.5   DATA AND METHODOLOGY

Our dataset consisted of 13 000 news headlines retrieved from formal news sources, such as Bloomberg, between January 2017 and June 2017. These headlines were manually labelled as either 'Related' or 'Unrelated' to merger arbitrage by portfolio managers within one of the leading asset management firms. At the end of the manual labelling, approximately 31% of the dataset were tagged as 'Related' and the rest 'Unrelated' to merger arbitrage.

We have used relevance tags provided by the date vendor to ascertain which tickers a particular news headline concerns. In general, it is quite common for a news article to mention multiple companies with varying degrees of emphasis within its body, and most news providers appoint relevance scores to news items, quantifying to what degree a particular article is about a specific company. Within the M&A domain, there is relatively less ambiguity since the tickers mentioned are predominantly the target and the acquirer.

Our NLP analysis pipeline consisted of the common steps already discussed in Section 10.4. We first preprocessed the manually labelled data to reduce noise and transform the input to be machine readable. To this end, the textual news headlines were first tokenized. Following tokenization, we have removed punctuation and English stop words and have also applied stemming to reduce derivationally related forms of a word to a common base form, such as transforming 'acquiring' to 'acquire'. These steps have helped to consolidate the unique terms in the dataset. Furthermore, we have also reduced our vocabulary by term frequency, including only the most frequent 5000 words as distinct terms and representing the rest under the umbrella category of 'Other'.

For inference, we have used an array of binary classifiers ranging from conventional ones as Sparse Naïve Bayes, Ridge Regression and Random Forest to various neural network architectures. Alongside computer vision, NLP is one of the fields that has benefited greatly from the resurgence of neural networks in the past five years. In our analyses, we have used the following network architectures listed below. For a thorough coverage of the topic, the reader is referred to the *Deep Learning* book by Goodfellow et al. (2016).

1. Feed-forward neural network (FNN): an FNN contains a (possibly large) number of simple neuron-like nodes, organized in layers. Like all neural network architectures, data enters the network at the input layer and, as the name suggests, is fed forward through the network, layer by layer, until it arrives at the output layer. Nodes in a layer alone never have connections and in general two adjacent layers are fully connected (every neuron form one layer to every neuron to another layer). As the information propagates forward, there are no cycles or feedback loops between layers. FNNs were the first and the simplest network structure to be devised.

2. RNN: in contrast with feed-forward architectures, an RNN contains recursive loops that allow it to exhibit dynamic temporal behaviour and capture long-term dependencies in sequential inputs. As a result, RNNs are suitable for NLP since they can evaluate each word/token input in context of the words that appear before it. However, the training of such architectures can be problematic due to the recursive nature of the information and gradient flow. In order to alleviate these, different gating mechanisms have been proposed, resulting in various RNN architectures. In our study we use a popular recursive architecture called long short-term memory (LSTM) (Hochreiter and Schmidhuber 1997).

3. CNN: these consist of a sequence of convolutional blocks in between the input and output layers. For NLP applications, a single convolutional block usually consists of a convolution kernel that convolves the previous layer's input over a single spatial dimension, followed by a max pooling layer for down-sampling the convolutional output to produce a tensor of outputs. The convolution kernels are used to generate position-invariant features that exhibit compositionality. In other words, a CNN can combine basic features, e.g. edges in an image, to form more complex features like silhouettes of objects, etc. As such, CNNs have traditionally been applied in computer vision applications to automatically train position-invariant and compositional features that can detect objects in images, among other applications. Now, it is evident that text inputs have similar properties to images, whereby characters combine to form words; words form n-grams, phrases and sentences. Hence, the use of CNNs for NLP tasks has become gradually more prominent in recent years (Conneau et al. 2016; Yin et al. 2017). In practical implementations like ours, the output from the convolutional block sequence is usually appended with a shallow FNN to further process the convolutional features before producing the output. In our analyses we use a CNN with varying kernel window size with the aim of extracting linguistic features of varying length – we will refer to this as a multi-size CNN.

In terms of feature representation, for the neural network classifiers we have opted to use a distributed representation, using pre-trained GloVe (Pennington et al. 2014) embeddings. We used the version of GloVe that was trained on a 2014-dated snapshot of Wikipedia, and the Gigaword 5 dataset, which is a comprehensive archive of newswire text data containing close to 10 million articles. Applying transfer learning in this manner allowed us to leverage the rich semantic information and linguistic patterns captured by the large-scale news and Wikipedia article corpora that GloVe was trained on.

For all other 'conventional' classifiers, we have used a term frequency–inverse document frequency (tf–idf) representation, which has already been discussed in Section 10.2. All NLP-related preprocessing steps were done by the spaCy package (s. d. team 2017) in Python. For inference, we have used the conventional classifiers as implemented by scikitlearn (Pedregosa et al. 2011) and used tensorflow (Abadi et al. 2016) and keras (Chollet 2015) to build the neural network architecture explained above.

10.5.1   Results

We carried out multiple experiments by partitioning the manually labelled dataset into five equally-sized parts with approximately equal prior outcome probabilities, where probability of 'Relevant' was approximately 0.69. For each experiment, classifiers were trained on four partitions and tested on the remaining one. By iterating this process over all five partitions, we ensured the inclusion of all news headlines in the experiments. The performances of all predictive models were evaluated based on the AUROC, AUPRC values and predictive accuracies of these stratified fivefold cross-validations.

Table 10.1 provides fivefold cross-validated predictive performance results for our binary classification task. To serve as benchmarks, rows i and ii represent predictive results by two rudimentary classifiers. As the name suggests, the Random Predictor randomly assigns half of the news headlines as 'Related' and the rest as 'Unrelated' to merger arbitrage. The Prior Predictor is very similar, apart from the fact that it does the random label allocations in line with the prior class distributions rather than with equal probability. As expected, both the Random and Prior predictors perform poorly in predicting the correct class labels.

Rows iii and iv in Table 10.1 give the results of two instance-based classifiers, namely k-nearest neighbour (k-NN) and nearest centroid. These produce class labels for a new news article based on the class labels of the training samples to which it is the most similar. While substantially outperforming the random classifiers, instance-based classifiers do not perform particularly well. An interesting observation is that while the average accuracies of the instance-based classifiers are almost identical at 0.793, the AUPRC and AUROC metrics indicate that the nearest centroid overall does a better job in classifying articles as 'Related' versus 'Unrelated' to merger arbitrage.

Rows v and vi give the results of two NB variants, namely multinomial and Bernoulli NB. The multinomial NB normally requires integer word counts in the document-term matrix. However, in practice, fractional counts such as tf-idf are also commonly used. In contrast, Bernoulli NB works with binary features, whereby the tf-idf frequencies are reduced to 0 and 1. It is therefore interesting to note that the Multinomial representation, which is richer, only marginally outperforms the Bernoulli NB.

Rows viii to xiv feature other commonly used classifiers ranging from Perceptron to Random Forest and variants of Support Vector Machines with different (L1 and L2) regularization penalties. These can be categorized as conventional but relatively sophisticated classifiers, and as their performance reflects, they do a respectable job in accurately classifying the news items.

Row xv provides the predictive results of an ensemble classifier that takes the majority vote of all conventional classifiers listed between rows iii and xiv for each news article in the test set. As commonly reported in the literature, the ensemble classifier

TABLE 10.1 Fivefold cross validated predictive performance results for the NewsFilter sample dataset

		Accuracy	AUPRC	AUROC
i	Random Predictor	0.498 ± 0.005	0.488 ± 0.006	0.497 ± 0.005
ii	Prior Predictor	0.56 ± 0.01	0.421 ± 0.014	0.493 ± 0.012
iii	k-NN	0.793 ± 0.005	0.707 ± 0.01	0.724 ± 0.003
iv	Nearest Centroid	0.793 ± 0.005	0.74 ± 0.011	0.785 ± 0.007
v	Sparse Bernoulli NB	0.808 ± 0.011	0.733 ± 0.008	0.756 ± 0.012
vi	Sparse Multinomial NB	0.812 ± 0.01	0.746 ± 0.01	0.779 ± 0.012
vii	Passive-Aggressive	0.833 ± 0.009	0.778 ± 0.007	0.812 ± 0.008
viii	Perceptron	0.829 ± 0.009	0.774 ± 0.009	0.81 ± 0.01
ix	Random Forest	0.851 ± 0.005	0.797 ± 0.009	0.812 ± 0.007
x	SVM L1	0.854 ± 0.005	0.803 ± 0.008	0.83 ± 0.004
xi	SVM L2	0.858 ± 0.006	0.808 ± 0.006	0.832 ± 0.006
xii	Linear SVM with L-1 feature selection	0.855 ± 0.006	0.804 ± 0.009	0.829 ± 0.007
xiii	Ridge Classifier	0.858 ± 0.004	0.808 ± 0.005	0.827 ± 0.005
xiv	Elastic Net	0.86 ± 0.003	0.809 ± 0.009	0.827 ± 0.005
xv	Ensemble [iii–xiv]	0.863 ± 0.004	0.814 ± 0.003	0.83 ± 0.003
xvi	Neural Net – FNN	0.849 ± 0.005	0.802 ± 0.007	0.906 ± 0.003
xvii	Neural Net – LSTM	0.869 ± 0.006	0.805 ± 0.006	0.908 ± 0.003
xviii	Neural Net – Multi-size CNN	0.875 ± 0.005	0.817 ± 0.006	0.912 ± 0.004

The columns indicate increased predictive performance. The cells contain the expected values and the standard deviations of the cross-validation results.

unsurprisingly outperforms all its constituents, providing a predictive performance that is marginally better than its best-performing constituent, namely the elastic net in row xiv.

Finally, we can see how the three neural network architectures fared in rows xvi to xviii. The predictive performance of the FNN is better than that of the perceptron. This can be explained by the higher number of hidden layers in the FNN that give it a higher representation power, and also the GloVe vector embeddings that we use for the neural network architectures are likely to give a richer representation of the words. Comparing FNN to the recurrent and convolutional architectures, it is evident that the LSTM and the Multi-size convolutional net significantly outperform the simpler FNN architecture. Comparing the LSTM with the multi-size CNN, we see that the latter outperforms the former, albeit marginally. There is no consensus in the current literature as to whether a recurrent or convolutional architecture is more suitable for NLP tasks (Yin et al. 2017).

10.5.2 Discussion

NewsFilter, as detailed in this section, can be categorized as a risk-orientated NLP application that helps bring securities associated with M&A-related activity to the investment manager's attention in order to exclude idiosyncratic risk from one's portfolio. With every machine learning application, it is important to be conscious of the potential monetary impact of the inaccuracies, such as false positives and false negatives, of the model. Given the application context, the consequences of misclassification by NewsFilter is limited to erroneous exclusion/inclusion of certain securities from the investment universe. This worst-case scenario is arguably lighter compared with the immediate financial consequences of some automated trading or market making applications (covered in Section 10.3) going awry.

More importantly, as opposed to an automated trading application – for instance, based on trade signals derived from sentiment analysis – the inference generated by the model is used to aid the investment manager's decision making, leaving room for expert discretion to pick up and alleviate any potential shortcomings of the model.

Despite the hype around the more complex and powerful neural network methodologies listed herein, it is important to justify the usage of these tools by analyzing the performance edge gained compared with simpler classifiers. This is due to the fact that complex models with larger degrees of freedom are prone to implementation errors and overfitting, and at the hands of the uninformed user the unintended consequences may outweigh the perceived benefits. In addition, as is commonly quoted in machine learning, 'there is no free lunch'. In other words, there is no perfect one-size-fits-all approach in any machine learning problem and as many alternatives as possible should be explored before settling on a final methodology.

While NewsFilter achieves fairly satisfactory predictive performance levels, it relies on news feed metadata for entity extraction, in other words determining which securities/tickers a particular article is referring to. We are currently working on enriching the entity extraction capabilities of the model to complement the tags reported in the metadata. In addition to entity extraction, another active area of research is novelty detection of articles in order to distinguish new information from those that have been recycled. Without this filtering it is possible to be bogged down with duplicate stories, which may result in amplifying the strength/importance of a news-related signal unjustifiably.

10.6　CONCLUSION

Rather than serving as an exhaustive review, this chapter has aimed to provide the uninitiated with a gateway into the increasingly popular application domain of finance in NLP. The application of NLP in finance has become more prominent due to the exponential increase in computing power over the past 30 years and the increased focus on textual methods driven by the requirements to process an ever-growing volume of news data. A 2016 report by MarketsandMarkets estimated the value of the NLP market as $7.6 billion in 2016 and projected it to grow to $16 billion by 2021 (Marketsandmarkets 2016).

The explosion of financial news data in the past decade has been largely driven by the electronification of mainstream media, the adoption of web-based dissemination by regulators as well as exchanges, and the rise of web-based social media. In the financial domain, news is considered as an 'information event' that influences the market microstructure. Using NLP techniques, the vast computing capabilities of modern computers are able to identify and exploit patterns embedded in textual data for financial applications ranging from systematic investing to market making and risk control. In all of these domains, inference from NLP techniques serve as an additional information source that complements the traditional mix of market data and has the potential to uncover patterns not captured by technical or fundamental analyses.

In contrast to conventional market time series data, the vast majority of news data is created for human consumption and as such is stored in an unstructured format. This unstructured format, i.e. human language, is inherently complex and relies not only on the letters and symbols that constitute text but also on the human brain's ability to understand connotation and context. Despite not having reached the point where computers understand all intricacies of language yet, ongoing research in NLP brings us ever closer to this reality. One of the remaining challenges in textual analysis is to move beyond assuming words occur as independent units, a topic we briefly discussed in Section 10.4 in the contexts of feature representation and inference.

In general, unsupervised and semi-supervised learning are less developed research areas in NLP applied to financial news. However, their prominence grows with the unprecedented surge in the pace of data generation, most of which is in unlabelled and also unstructured form. Supervised learning relies on labelled data, and manual labelling of news items is a labour-intensive step. Consistency of labelling, in the case of multiple human labellers, is a vital prerequisite for any inference extracted by the machine to be usable. Particularly in sentiment analysis, discrepancies in the way different market participants are affected by the same events may result in having multiple interpretations of the same events. Even in an application as discussed in Section 10.5, conflicts in labelling may arise as to which news items should be regarded as relevant or irrelevant to M&A activity. These inconsistencies in human labelling naturally become more prominent in cases where multiple experts work on labelling a dataset.

Another potential concern with NLP analyses applied to financial news is the fact that most of these analyses are powered by common sets of data provided by data vendors or accessible publicly, e.g. SEC filings. It has been argued that this may make it more difficult to gain a competitive advantage over other market participants with similar algorithms. While this is a valid concern, the same argument can be made for conventional market data where lack of variability in data sources is just as pervasive. In addition, different applications have variations in the NLP steps we have covered in Section 10.4, the way they label data and some proprietary hand-crafted features to achieve different goals (Mittermayer and Knolmayer 2006). As a result, standing out from the crowd with careful implementation and tailored use cases is not only possible but highly probable.

Although we are still not close to achieving full semantic and contextual understanding of financial news, the field of NLP has made significant progress, allowing for technologies that have and will continue to revolutionize how financial institutions operate. The adoption of NLP in finance leads to the enhancement of performance, yet it can have its unintended consequences. The improved speed that NLP provides us to respond to news also increases the requirement that the response be the right one. Responding rapidly but in the wrong way can lead to increased market instability. Going forward, the challenge for the regulatory authorities is to understand the combined impact of these technologies and postulate regulations which can control volatility, improve the provision for liquidity and generally stabilize the market behaviour.

REFERENCES

M. Abadi, A. Agarwal and P. Barham (2016). 'TensorFlow: Large-Scale Machine Learning on Heterogeneous Distributed Systems,' *arXiv:1603.04467v2*.

Ahern, K.R. and Sosyura, D. (2015). Rumor has it: sensationalism in financial media. *Review of Financial Studies* 28 (7): 2050–2093.

Aizawa, A. (2003). An information-theoretic perspective of tf–idf measures. *Information Processing and Management* 39: 45–65.

E. Bartov, L. Faurel and P. S. Mohanram, 'Can Twitter Help Predict Firm-Level Earnings and Stock Returns?,' Rotman School of Management Working Paper No. 2631421, 2017.

B. von Beschwitz, D. B. Keim and M. Massa, 'Media-Driven High Frequency Trading: Evidence From News Analytics,' Workin Paper, 2013.

Blei, D., Ng, A., and Jordan, M. (2003). Latent Dirichlet allocation. *Journal of Machine Learning Research* 993–1022.

Bodnaruk, A., Loughran, T., and McDonald, B. (2015). Using 10-K text to gauge financial constraints. *Journal of Financial and Quantitative Analysis* 50: 623–646.

J. Bollen, H. Mao and X.-J. Zeng, Twitter Mood Predicts the Stock Market. *Journal of Computational Science*, 2011.

Brown, R. (2011). Incorporating news into algorithmic trading strategies: increasing the signal-to-noise ratio. In: *The Handbook of News Analytics in Finance*, 307–310.

Buehlmaier, M. and Zechner, J. (2014). *Slow-Moving Real Information in Merger Arbitrage*. The European Finance Association.

Buehlmaier, M. and Zechner, J. (2017). Financial media, price discovery, and merger arbitrage. *CFS WP 551*.

Chollet, F. (2015). keras. *GitHub* .

Conneau, A., Schwenk, H., and Cun, Y. L., 'Very Deep Convolutional Networks for Text Classification,' *arXiv:1606.01781*, 2016.

Das, S. and Chen, M. (2007). Yahoo! For Amazon: sentiment extraction from small talk on the web. *Journal of Management Science* 53 (9): 1375–1388.

Davis, J. and Goadrich, M. (2006). The relationship between precision-recall and ROC curves. *Proceedings of Conf. Machine Learning* 233–240.

Friedman, N., Geiger, D., and Goldszmidt, M. (1997). Bayesian network classifiers. *Machine Learning* 29: 131–163.

Gerde, J. (2003). EDGAR-Analyzer: automating the analysis of corporate data contained by the SEC's EDGAR database. *Decision Support Systems* 35 (1): 7–29.

Goodfellow, I., Bengio, Y., and Courville, A. (2016). *Deep Learning*. MIT Press.

Grant, G.H. and Conlon, S.J. (2006). EDGAR extraction system: an approach to analyze employee stock option disclosures. *Journal of Information Systems* 20 (2): 119–142.

Groß-Klußmann, A. and Hautsch, N. (2011). When machines read the news: using automated text analytics to quantify high frequency news-implied market reactions. *Journal of Empirical Finance* 18: 321–340.

Hadlock, C. and Pierce, J. (2010). New evidence on measuring financial constraints: moving beyond the KZ index. *Review of Financial Studies* 23: 1909–1940.

Hanley, K.W. and Hoberg, G. (2010). The information content of IPO prospectuses. *The Review of Financial Studies* 23 (7): 2821–2864.

Healy, A.D. and Lo, A.W. (2011). Managing real-time risks and returns: the Thomson Reuters NewsScope event indices. In: *The Handbook of News Analytics in Finance*, 73–109.

Henry, E. (2008). Are investors influenced by how earnings press releases are written? *Journal of Business Communication* 45: 363–407.

Heston, S.L. and Sinha, N.R. (2017). News vs. sentiment: predicting stock returns from news stories. *Financial Analyst Journal* 73 (3): 67–83.

Hoberg, G. and Phillips, G. (2016). Text-based network industries and endogenous product differentiation. *Journal of Political Economy* 124: 1423–1465.

Hochreiter, S. and Schmidhuber, J. (1997). Long short-term memory. *Neural Computation* 9 (8): 1735–1780.

Hofmann, T. (2001). Unsupervised learning by probabilistic latent semantic analysis. *Machine Learning* 42: 177–196.

Huang, A., Zang, A., and Zheng, R. (2014). Evidence on the information content of text in analyst reports. *The Accounting Review* 89: 2151–2180.

Jetley, G. and Ji, X. (2010). The shrinking merger arbitrage spread: reasons and implications. *Financial Analysts Journal* 66 (2): 54–68.

Jung, M., Naughton, J., Tahoun, A., and Wang, C. (2015). *Corporate Use of Social Media*. New York University.

A. Landro, '5 Web Technology Predictions for 2017,' Sencha, 13 December 2016. [Online]. Available: https://www.sencha.com/blog/5-web-technology-predictions-for-2017. [Accessed 12 December 2017].

Lang, M. and Stice-Lawrence, L. (2015). Textual analysis and international financial reporting: large sample evidence. *Journal of Accounting and Economics* 60: 110–135.

LaPlanter, A. and Coleman, T.F. (2017). *Teaching Computers to Understand Human Language: How NLP is Reshaping the World of Finance*. Global Risk Institute.

L. Lee, B. Pang and S. Vaithyanathan, 'Thumbs up? Sentiment Classification using Machine Learning Techniques,' *Proceedings of the 2002 Conference on Empirical Methods in Natural Language Processing*, 2002.

Lee, F., Hutton, A., and Shu, S. (2015). The role of social media in the capital market: evidence from consumer product recalls. *Journal of Accounting Research* 53 (2): 367–404.

Li, F. (2010). Textual analysis of corporate disclosures: a survey of the literature. *Journal of Accounting Literature* 29: 143–165.

Liu, B. and McConnell, J. (2013). The role of the media in corporate governance: do the media influence managers' capital allocation decisions? *Journal of Financial Economics* 110 (1): 1–17.

Lo, A, 'Reuters NewsScope Event Indices,' AlphaSimplex Research Report, Thomson Reuters, 2008.

Loughran, T. and Mcdonald, B. (2016). Textual analysis in accounting and finance: a survey. *Journal of Accounting Research*.

Manning, C.D., Raghavan, P., and Schütze, H. (2009). *Introduction to Information Retrieval*. Cambridge University Press.

Marketsandmarkets 'Natural Language Processing by Market Type, Technologies, Development, Vertical and Region,' July 2016. [Online]. Available: https://www.marketsandmarkets.com/Market-Reports/natural-language-processing-nlp-825.html. [Accessed 12 December 2017].

Mazis, P. and Tsekrekos, A. (2017). Latent semantic analysis of the FOMC statements. *Review of Accounting and Finance* 16 (2): 179–217.

Mikolov, T., Sutskever, I., Chen, K. et al. (2013). Distributed representations of words and phrases and their compositionality. *Advances in Neural Information Processing Systems* 26.

Mitra, L. and Mitra, G. (2011). Applications of news analytics in finance: a review. In: *The Handbook of News Analytics in Finance*, 1–39. Wiley Finance.

G. Mitra, D. di Bartolomeo, A. Banerjee and X. Yu, '*Automated Analysis of News to Compute Market Sentiment: Its Impact on Liquidity and Trading*,' UK Government Office for Science, 2015.

Mittermayer, M.-A. and Knolmayer, G.F. (2006). *Text Mining Systems for Market Response to News: A Survey*. University of Bern.

Moniz, A., Brar, G., Davies, C., and Strudwick, A. (2009). The impact of news flow on asset returns: an empirical study. In: *The Handbook of News Analytics in Finance*, 211–231.

Niederhoffer, V. (1971). The analysis of world events and stock prices. *Journal of Business* 44: 193–219.

Pedregosa, F., Varoquaux, G., and Gramfort, A. (2011). Scikit-learn: machine learning in python. *Journal of Machine Learning Research* 12: 2825–2830.

Pennington, J., Socher, R., and Manning, C.D. (2014. [Online]. Available: https://nlp.stanford .edu/projects/glove). *GloVe: Global Vectors for Word Representation*. Stanford University [Accessed July 2017].

Purda, L. and Skillicorn, D. (2015). Accounting variables, deception, and a bag of words: assessing the tools of fraud detection. *Contemporary Accounting Research* 32: 1193–1223.

Reuters, T. (2015). *Exploit Signals in News for Quantitative Strategies and Systematic Trading*. Thomson Reuters.

s. d. team, 'Industrial-Strength NLP,' spaCy, 2017. [Online]. Available: https://spacy.io.

Tensorflow, 'Vector Representations of Words,' Google, November 2017. [Online]. Available: https://www.tensorflow.org/tutorials/word2vec. [Accessed December 2017].

Tetlock, P. (2007). Giving content to investor sentiment: the role of media in the stock market. *Journal of Finance* 62: 1139–1168.

The Coca-Cola Company. 'The Coca-Cola Company Reports Solid Operating Results in Third Quarter 2017,' The Coca-Cola Company, Oct 2017. [Online]. Available: http://www .coca-colacompany.com/press-center/press-releases/the-coca-cola-company-reports-third-quarter-2017-results. [Accessed December 2017].

W. Yin, K. Kann, M. Yuz and H. Schutze, 'Comparative Study of CNN and RNN for Natural Language Processing,' *arXiv:1702.01923v1*, 2017.

CHAPTER 11

Support Vector Machine-Based Global Tactical Asset Allocation

Joel Guglietta

11.1 INTRODUCTION

In this chapter we show how machine learning, more specifically support vector machine/regression (SVM/R, can help building global tactical asset allocation (GTAA) portfolio. First, we will present a quick literature review on GTAA, explaining the different families of asset allocation. We will then go through a historical perspective of tactical asset allocation in the last 50 years, introducing the seminal concepts behind it. Section 11.3 will explain the definition of support vector machine (SVM) and support vector relevance (SVR). Section 11.4 will present the machine learning model used for tactical asset allocation and will discuss the results.

11.2 FIFTY YEARS OF GLOBAL TACTICAL ASSET ALLOCATION

Running the risk of stating the obvious, the objective of asset allocation is to obtain the best expected return-to-risk portfolio (Dahlquist and Harvey, 2001). The authors distinguish three families of asset allocation: (i) benchmark asset allocation, (ii) strategic asset allocation, (iii) GTAA (see Figure 11.1). The investment portfolio strategy built in this chapter belongs to the third class of model where predictions models use today's information set in order to forecast asset returns.

Practitioners have been managing GTAA strategies for almost 50 years. GTAA broadly refers to active managed portfolios that seek to enhance portfolio performance by 'opportunistically shifting the asset mix in a portfolio in response to the changing patterns of return and risk' (Martellini and Sfeir, 2003). Ray Dalio, CEO of Bridgewater, made this approach popular in the 1990s with his 'All-Weather' portfolio.

The theory backing such an investment approach is well documented. W. Sharpe showed in 1963 that assets' returns can be decomposed into a systematic and a specific component. Armed with this time-honoured framework, portfolio managers deploy two forms of active strategies: (i) market timing, which aims at exploiting predictability in systematic return, and (ii) stock picking, which aims at exploiting predictability in specific return. The academic literature suggests that there is ample evidence

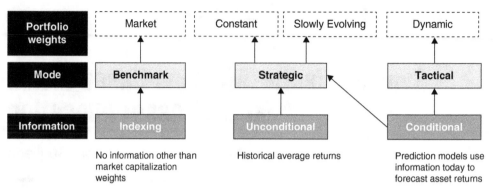

FIGURE 11.1   Three families of asset allocation.
Source: Dahlquist and Harvey (2001).

of predictability in the systematic component (Keim and Stambaugh 1986; Campbell 1987; Campbell and Shiller 1988; Fama and French 1989; Ferson and Harvey 1991; Bekaert and Hodrick 1992; Harasty and Roulet 2000), which is less true for the specific component.

After Samuelson (1969) and Merton (1969, 1971, 1973), who showed that optimal portfolio strategies are significantly affected by the presence of a stochastic opportunity set, optimal portfolio decision rules have been enriched to factor in the presence of predictable returns (Barberis 2000; Campbell and Viceira 1998; Campbell et al. 2000; Brennan et al. 1997; Lynch and Balduzzi 1999, 2000; Ait-Sahalia and Brandt 2001). In a nutshell, all these models suggest that investors should increase their allocation to risky assets in periods of high expected returns (market timing) and decrease their allocation in periods of high volatility (volatility timing). Interestingly enough, Kandel and Stambaugh (1996) argue that even a low level of statistical predictability can generate economic significance and abnormal returns may be attained even if the market is successfully timed only 1 out of 100 times.

In essence, GTAA is a two-step process where first practitioners forecast asset returns by asset classes, then they build portfolios based on this forecast. Close to GTAA but without the forecasting part, risk parity portfolios (Hurst et al. 2010) are now a behemoth in the making, with almost US$3 trillion managed according to this method. Risk parity is often said to be the 'cheap' version of Bridgewater's 'All-Weather' portfolio. We agree. GTAA and risk parity bear some similarities as they both try to exploit the one and only free lunch out there: diversification. However, risk parity is nothing but a mere 'technicality' for portfolio construction (the so-called 'one-to-sigma' approach where the weight of a given instrument is inverse in its realized – sometimes expected – volatility). GTAA tries to condition the asset mix based on the current information set in order to build a portfolio which is 'better' (i.e. hopefully delivering a higher return-to-risk profile) fitted to the current (or expected) economic cycle. For instance, Chong and Phillips (2014) build a GTAA based on 18 economic factors using their 'Eta pricing model'. Whereas one is mean–variance optimized (ECR-MVO), the other is constructed to reduce its economic exposure (MIN). Both are long-only portfolios and are rebalanced semi-annually.

To conclude, the holy grail of GTAA remains to build a portfolio which performs equally well in any kind of economic environment. In order to achieve this, the portfolio manager has to find the optimal asset mix. The asset mix is usually made of fixed income (long-term and intermediary), equity and commodity (others sometimes add real estate). The economic cycle impacting this asset mix can be modelled with different granularity. We follow R. Dalio in trying not to over-complexify things and chose a sparse model of the economic cycle, only using soft data (survey) for real business cycle (RBC) indicators and realized inflation.

11.3   SUPPORT VECTOR MACHINE IN THE ECONOMIC LITERATURE

A thorough introduction to SVM and support vector regression is beyond the scope of this chapter. However, we feel it is appropriate to explain briefly how SVM and support vector regression operate for financial practitioners (and to take time to define some useful mathematical notions) who are not familiar with it and why we chose this method over alternative machine learning algorithms. We address basic technicalities of SVM here.

As Y. Abu-Mostafa (Caltech) puts it, SVM is arguably the most successful classification method in machine learning with a neat solution which has a very intuitive interpretation. Motivated by Statistical Learning Theory, SVM is a 'learning machine' introduced by Boser, Guyon and Vapnik in 1992 that falls into the category of supervised estimation algorithms (a learning algorithm that analyzes the training data and produces an inferred function, which can be used for mapping new data points). It is made up of three steps:

(i) Parameter estimation, i.e. training from a data set.
(ii) Computation of the function value, i.e. testing.
(iii) Generalization accuracy, i.e. performance.

As M. Sewell (2008, 2010) notes, 'the development of Artificial Neural Networks (ANNs) followed a heuristic path, with applications and extensive experimentation preceding theory. In contrast, the development of SVMs involved sound theory first, then implementation and experiments.'

As far as parameter estimation is concerned, 'a significant advantage of SVMs is that whilst ANNs can suffer from multiple local minima, the solution to an SVM is global and unique'. This is due to the fact that training involves optimization of a convex cost function, which explains why there is no local minimum to complicate the learning process. Testing is based on the model evaluation using the most informative patterns in the data, i.e. support vectors (the points upon which the separating hyperplanes lie). Performance is based on error rate determination as test set size grows to infinity.

SVMs have more advantages over ANNs. First, they have a simple geometric interpretation and give a sparse solution. Unlike ANNs, the computational complexity of SVMs does not depend on the dimensionality of the input space. Second, while ANNs use empirical risk minimization (that does not work very well in practice as the bounds are way too loose), SVMs use structural risk minimization (SRM). In their seminal 1974 paper, V. Vapnik and A. Chervonenkis set out the SRM principle which uses the VC (for Vapnik–Chervonenkis) dimension. The VC dimension is a measure of the capacity (complexity) of a space of functions that can be learned by a statistical classification algorithm. The SRM is an inductive principle for model selection used for learning from finite training data sets. It describes a general model of capacity control and provides a tradeoff between hypothesis space complexity and the quality of fitting the training data (empirical error). Sewell (ibid) defines the procedure as below.

 (i) Using a priori knowledge of the domain, choose a class of functions, such as polynomials of degree n, neural networks having n hidden layer neurons, a set of splines with n nodes or fuzzy logic (a form of many-valued logic in which the truth values of variables may be any real number between 0 and 1) models having n rules.
 (ii) Divide the class of functions into a hierarchy of nested subsets in order of increasing complexity. For example, polynomials of increasing degree.
(iii) Perform empirical risk minimization on each subset (this is essentially parameter selection).
(iv) Select the model in the series whose sum of empirical risk and VC confidence is minimal.

SVMs often outperform ANNs in practice because they deal with the biggest problem that ANNs face, i.e. overfitting. As they are less prone to such a cardinal disease, they 'generalize' in a much better way. We should note, however, that while the use of kernel function enables the curse of dimensionality to be addressed, proper kernel function for certain problems is dependent on the specific dataset and as such there is no good method for the choice of kernel function (Chaudhuri 2014). From a practical point of view, the biggest limitation of the support vector approach lies in choice of the kernel (Burges 1998; Horváth 2003).

SVM can be applied to both classification and regression. When an SVM is applied to a regression problem, it is called support vector regression. What is the difference between SVM and SVR? SVR is based on the computation of a linear regression function in a high-dimensional feature space where the input data is mapped via a non-linear function. In order to give an intuition of how SVR works, let's assume we are given a linearly separable set of points of two different classes $y_i \in \{-1, +1\}$. The objective of an SVM is to find a particular hyperplane separating these two classes y_i with minimum error while also making sure that the perpendicular distance between the two closes points from either of these two classes is maximized. In order to determine this hyperplane, we set constraints like this:

$$\vec{w}.\vec{x_i} - b = 1, if\, y_i = 1 \quad \text{and} \quad \vec{w}.\vec{x_i} - b = -1, if\, y_i = -1$$

It is straightforward to transform this classification problem into a regression problem. Let's write: $y_i - w.\, x_i - b \le \varepsilon$ and $-(y_i - w.\, x_i - b) \le \varepsilon$.

The two equations above state that the hyperplane has points on either side of it such that the distance between these points and the hyperplane should not be further than ε. In a two-dimension plane, this comes down to trying to draw a line somewhere in the middle of the set of points such that this line is as close to them as possible. This is precisely what SVR is doing. Instead of minimizing the observed training error, SVR attempts to minimize the generalization error bound so as to achieve generalized performance.

SVM provides a novel approach to the two-category classification problem such as crisis or a non-crisis (Burges 1998). The method has been successfully applied to a number of applications, ranging from particle identification, face identification and text categorization to engine detection, bioinformatics and database marketing. For instance, A. Chaudhuri uses an SVM for currency crisis detection. Lai and Liu (2010) compare the performance in financial market prediction of an ANNs approach and the regression feature of SVM. The historical values used are those of the Hang Sang Index (HSI) from 2002 to 2007 and data for January 2007 and January 2008. SVM performs well in the short-term forecast. Other authors such as Shafiee et al. (2013) get an accuracy rate as high as 92.16% in forecasting Iranian stock returns. Using daily closing prices for 34 technology stocks to calculate price volatility and momentum for individual stocks and for the overall sector, Mage (2015) use an SVM to predict whether a stock price some time in the future will be higher or lower than it is on a given day. Though the author finds little predictive ability in the short run, he finds definite predictive ability in the long run.

Bajari et al. (2015) note that applied econometricians voice scepticism about machine learning models because they do not have a clear interpretation and it is not obvious how to apply them to estimate causal effects. Some recent works suggest, however, that such machine learning methods yield interesting results. For instance, McNelis and McAdam (2004) apply linear and neural network-based 'thick' models for forecasting inflation based on Phillips–curve formulations in the US, Japan and the euro area. Thick models represent 'trimmed mean' forecasts from several neural network models. They outperform the best-performing linear models for 'real-time' and 'bootstrap' forecasts for service indices for the euro are, and do well, sometimes better, for the more general consumer and producer price indices across a variety of countries. Back to the SVM, Bajari and Ali, tackling the problem of demand estimation, focus on three classes of model: (i) linear regression as the baseline model, (ii) logit as the econometric model, (iii) stepwise, forward stage-wise, LASSO, random forest, SVM and bagging as the machine learning models. Interestingly enough, they show that machine learning models consistently give better out-of-sample prediction accuracy while holding in-sample prediction error comparable in order to estimate. SVR has been applied in time series and financial prediction. For example, Zhang and Li (2013) use SVR to model to forecast CPI. Money gap and CPI historical data are utilized to perform forecasts. Furthermore, the grid search method is applied to select the parameters of SVR. In addition, this study examines the feasibility of applying SVR in inflation forecasting by comparing it with back-propagation neural network and linear regression. The result shows that SVR provides a promising alternative to inflation prediction.

11.3.1 Understanding SVM

SVM is essentially an algorithm used to solve a classification problem such as deciding which stocks to buy and to sell. The main notion boils down to maximizing the 'margin' between these two groups of stocks. The so-called 'kernel trick' (defined below) is used to address non-linearities. The main mathematics involved is some college geometry and quadratic optimization (derivative calculus).

We first assume a linearly separable data set, for example a set of four stocks. In order to better visualize our problem, let's assume we measure two attributes x_i

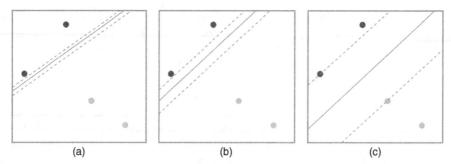

(a)   (b)   (c)

FIGURE 11.2   The kernel trick

on these four stocks (such as earning quality and price momentum for example) in the input space X. These two attributes form a two-dimension space. At a given time, one can plot the four stocks in this plane (scatter plots in Figure 11.2). Let's assume two classes $y_i \in \{-1, +1\}$, with long stocks (+1, the green dots) and short stocks (−1, the red dots). The problem we try to solve is whether there is any advantage to choosing a separating line over other lines. One first should note that such a line is a hyperplane (of dimension 1, a line then) with equation $w'. x = 0$, with w the vector of weights (w' being the transpose).

Let's examine the three examples above and ask ourselves which is the best line to separate the points. In case (a) the margin is lower than the one in case (b), which is lower than the one in case (c). In the three cases, the in-sample error is zero. As far as generalization is concerned, as we deal with four points in a linear separable state, generalization as an estimate will be the same. Intuitively however, one should feel that a fat margin (case c) is better. This brings two questions: (i) Why is a fatter margin better? (ii) How can we solve for the weight w that maximizes this margin?

In all likelihood, the process that generates the data is noisy. Therefore, when the margin is thin, the chance of having a point which is misclassified is higher than in the case of a fatter margin. This gives an intuition as to why a fatter margin is better. The proof is based on the so-called Vapnik-Chervonenkis analysis where one can show that a fatter margin ushers in a lower Vapnik-Chervonenkis dimension (the VC dimension being the cardinality of the largest set of points that the algorithm can shatter). Practically, a fatter margin implies better out-of-sample performance.

Now, let's find the weight w that maximizes the margin. The margin is simply the distance D from a plane to a point, which brings us back to our college geometry. Let's define x_n as the nearest data point to the separating line (hyperplane) $w'. x = 0$. How far is this point from the hyperplane? Before doing this, let's address two technicalities.

First, we normalize w. Let's note that for every point, we have $|w'. x_n| > 0$ for every point. The objective is to relate w to the margin. Note that we can scale w up and down as the hyperplane equation ($w'. x = 0$) is scale-invariant. Without loss of generality, we consider all the representations of the same hyperplane and just pick the one for which we have $|w'. x_n| = 1$ for the minimal point. This will simplify the analysis latter on.

Second, we introduce an artificial coordinate x_0. Think of it as a constant to which we assign a weight w_0. In order to avoid confusion, we rename this weight w_0 as the bias b. We have now a new ('new' compared with the vector w used in w'. $x = 0$) weight vector $w = (w_1, \ldots, w_p)$, with p the number of attributes (such as earning quality, price momentum, Merton's distance to default, liquidity). We will see that this new vector w and b have different roles when we solve for the maximum margin and it is no longer convenient to have both blended in the same vector. The equation for the hyperplane is now: w'. $x + b = 0$ and $w = (w_1, \ldots, w_p)$.

We can now compute the distance D between x_n and the hyperplane of equation w'. $x + b = 0$ where $|w'. x_n + b| = 1$.

First, the vector w is perpendicular to the plane in the input space X. This is straightforward to show. Let's consider any two points x_1 and x_2 on the plane. We have w'. $x_1 + b = 0$ and w'. $x_2 + b = 0$. The difference between these two points is w'. $(x_1 - x_2) = 0$, which shows that w' is orthogonal to every vector $(x_1 - x_2)$ in the plane and therefore is orthogonal to the plane.

Second, we take any point x on the plane. The projection of the vector going from point x to point x_n (i.e. vector $x_n - x$) on the vector w orthogonal to the plane is the distance D to the plane. In order to do so we compute first the unit vector $\hat{w}$, i.e. the vector normalized by its norm $\|w\|$, such that $\hat{w} = w/\|w\|$. The distance is the inner (dot) product such that $D = |\hat{w}'.(x_n - x)|$. Hence, D $= 1/\|w\| * |w'. (x_n - x)| = 1/\|w\| * |w'. x_n + b - w'. x - b| = 1/\|w\|$ as $|w'. x_n + b| = 1$ and $|w'. x - b| = 0$. One sees that the distance between the nearest point to the hyperplane and this hyperplane is nothing but one over the norm $\|w\|$ of w.

We can now formulate our optimization problem. Our objective is to

$$\text{Maximize } 1/\|w\|$$

subject to $min_{n = 1,2,\ldots,N}|w'. x_n + b| = 1$ (meaning minimization over all the points 1, 2, $\ldots$, N of the data set).

This not a friendly optimization problem as the constraint has a minimum (and an absolute value in it, but this one is easy to solve). As a consequence, we try to find an equivalent problem which is easier to solve, i.e. getting rid of the minimization in the constraint mainly.

First, we consider only the points that separate the data set correctly, i.e. the points for which the label y_n (long or short) agrees with the signal $(w'. x_n + b)$, so that we have $|w'. x_n + b| = y_n(w'. x_n + b)$, which allows us to get rid of the absolute value.

Second instead of maximizing $1/\|w\|$, we minimize the following quadratic quantity (objective function) $1/2* w'. w$

subject to $y_n(w'. x_n + b) \geq 1$ for all points $n = 1, 2, \ldots, N$.

Formally speaking, we face a constrained optimization problem where the objective function is to minimize $1/2^* w'. w$. This is usually solved in writing a Lagrangian expression. The minor problem here is that we have an inequality in the constraint. Solving such a Lagrangian under inequality constraint is known as the Karush–Kuhn–Tucker approach (KKT).

The first step is to rewrite the inequality constraint $y_n(w'. x_n + b) \geq 1$ in a zero form, i.e. to write it as a 'slack' $y_n(w'. x_n + b) - 1 \geq 0$ and then multiply it by the Lagrange multiplier α_n so that we get the expression $\alpha_n(y_n(w'. x_n + b) - 1)$ that we add to the objective function.

The Lagrange formulation of our optimization problem becomes:

$$minimise \ L(w, b, \alpha) = 1/2w'w - \sum_{n=1}^{N} \alpha_n(y_n(w'.x_n + b) - 1),$$

w.r.t. w and b with $\alpha_n \geq 0$ (we put a restriction on the domain) being the Lagrange multipliers, each point in the data set having such a Lagrange multiplier.

Writing the gradient $\nabla_w L$ of $L(w, b, \alpha)$ with respect to the vector w, we get the following condition:

$\nabla_w L = w - \sum_{n=1}^{N} \alpha_n y_n x_n = 0$ (we want the gradient to be the vector 0, this is the condition we put to get the minimum).

Writing the partial derivative of $L(w,b,\alpha)$ with respect the scalar b we get another condition:

$$\partial L/\partial b = - \sum_{n=1}^{N} \alpha_n y_n = 0.$$

At this juncture, in order to make the problem easier to solve, we substitute these two conditions in the original Lagrangian and transform this minimization problem into a maximization problem so that maximization over α (which is tricky as α has a range) becomes free from w and b. This refers to the dual formulation of the problem.

From the above condition we get:

$$w = \sum_{n=1}^{N} \alpha_n y_n x_n \quad \text{and} \quad \sum_{n=1}^{N} \alpha_n y_n = 0.$$

If we substitute these expressions in the Lagrangian $L(w,b,\alpha)$, after some manipulation, we get the following minor constrained optimization problem:

$$L(w,b,\alpha) = L(\alpha) = \sum_{n=1}^{N} \alpha_n - 0.5 * \sum_{n=1}^{N} \sum_{m=1}^{N} y_n y_m \alpha_n \alpha_m x'_n x_m$$

one sees that w and b drop from the optimization problem.

We maximize the above expression $L(\alpha)$ w.r.t. α subject to (the annoying constraint) $\alpha_n \geq 0$ for $n = 1,2,\ldots,N$ and $\sum_{n=1}^{N} \alpha_n y_n = 0$.

Solving the above problem requires quadratic programming (quadratic programming package usually uses minimization). We therefore minimize:

$$\min_{\alpha} \left(0.5^* \sum_{n=1}^{N} \sum_{m=1}^{N} y_n y_m \alpha_n \alpha_m x'_n x_m - \sum_{n=1}^{N} \alpha_n \right)$$

The quadratic programming package gives us a vector of $\alpha = \alpha_1, \alpha_2, \ldots, \alpha_n$ from which we infer the w.

$$w = \sum_{n=1}^{N} \alpha_n y_n x_n$$

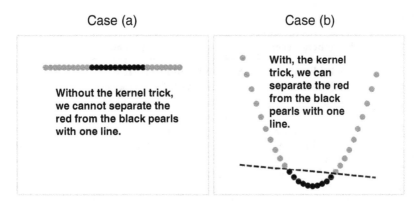

FIGURE 11.3   The kernel trick: a non-separable case

The condition which is key to the final support vector is the KKT condition which is satisfied at the minimum. The zero form of this condition is $\alpha_n (y_n (w' . x_n + b) - 1) = 0$ for $n = 1, 2, \ldots, N$. Which means either the Lagrange multiplier α_n is 0 or the slack $(y_n (w' . x_n + b) - 1)$ is zero. For all the interior points, the slack is strictly positive, which means the Lagrange multiplier α_n is 0.

The most important points in the dataset are those which define the hyperplane and the margin. These points x_n are called support vectors – they support the hyperplane and are the ones for which $\alpha_n > 0$. All the other points are interior points.

Once we have found w we pick any support vector and easily infer b from the equation $y_n (w' . x_n + b) = 1$.

So far, we have talked about the linearly separable case. But what about the non-separable case? We can handle this case in transforming the x into new variables z through a non-linear function. The optimization problem becomes $L(\alpha) = \sum_{n=1}^{N} \alpha_n - 0.5* \sum_{n=1}^{N} \sum_{m=1}^{N} y_n y_m \alpha_n \alpha_m z_n z_m$. This is the 'kernel' trick which make SVM so powerful in dealing with non-linearities. Rather than using a scalar product in the high-dimensional feature space X, we use a kernel function Z such as $z = Z(x)$ in R^k, which plays the role of a scalar product in X. As an example, let's assume we are given a necklace with 30 pearls – 10 black pearls in the middle and then 10 red pearls on both sides. We are asked to draw one line and one line only to separate the black pearls from the red pearls. Let's assume the pearls are first on a one-dimension space (line, case a). Separating the pearls with one line only is not possible. However, in a two-dimension space with the help of a simple kernel $(Z(x) = z = x^a)$, this becomes easy, as Figure 11.3 shows in case (b).

11.4   A SVR-BASED GTAA

Our GTAA is deployed using exchange traded funds (ETFs) covering all the asset classes usually found in such portfolios (14 instruments) (Table 11.1).

TABLE 11.1   Universe traded

Sector	Bloomberg ticker	Instrument name	Expense ratio
	SPY US Equity	SPDR S&P500 ETF Trust	0.09%
	QQQ US Equity	Powershares QQQ Trust Series 1	0.20%
Equity	VGK US Equity	Vanguard FTSE Europe ETF	0.10%
	EWJ US Equity	iShares MSCI Japan ETF	0.48%
	VWO US Equity	Vanguard FTSE Emerging Markets	0.14%
REIT	VNQ US Equity	VANGUARD REIT ETF	0.12%
	AGG US Equity	iShares Core U.S. Aggregate Bo	0.05%
	LQD US Equity	iShares iBoxx $ Investment Gra	0.15%
Fixed income	TIP US Equity	iShares TIPS Bond ETF	0.20%
	MUB US Equity	iShares National Muni Bond ETF	0.25%
	HYG US Equity	iShares iBoxx $ High Yield Cor	0.50%
	EMB US Equity	iShares JP Morgan USD Emerging	0.40%
	GLD US Equity	SPDR Gold Shares	0.40%
	DBC US Equity	PowerShares DB Commodity Index	0.89%

Source: J. Guglietta.

11.4.1   Data

We use ETFs as they have a number of features that make them ideal investments for this purpose. The most attractive feature is diversity as the range of available ETFs includes almost every asset class. The wide range of ETFs allows us to construct a diversified portfolio using fewer investments and therefore less capital. ETFs are now a US$3 trillion global market, are more liquid than mutual funds and can be traded throughout the day. Finally, ETFs are cheaper to run than mutual funds. This lower cost tends to get passed on to investors.

11.4.2   Model description

As explained above, we build a predictions model using today's information in order to forecast asset returns. Each and every week t, for each and any instrument i, we forecast return $\widetilde{R^i_{t+k}}$ one week ahead ($k = 5$ as our data base is daily) using an SVR with a linear kernel (using gaussian, radial basis function or polynomial kernels does not help) and three different categories of factors as 'predictor' variables. Formally speaking we have:

$$\widetilde{R^i_{t+k}} = SVR_T(MacroFactors_t, GreedFearIndex_t, Momenta_t), for\ i = 1, 2, \ldots N$$

and T, the rolling period over which the SVR is calibrated.

The first block is made of macro factors. Following R. Dalio/Bridgewater, we avoid over-complexification and chose a limited number of economics time series in order to model the economic cycle. While Bridgewater uses (quarterly) gross domestic product (GDP) to model the RBC, we use four monthly soft data (survey). We use the same macro-economic factors for all assets. These macro factors do not change from one week to the other. However, our experience suggests that it is wrong to believe financial markets factor in macro-economic information quickly and updating weekly forecast based on monthly data adds value. As this model is still under production, we do not disclose which time series we use. The fifth time series captures inflation.

The second category of factors is a measure of systemic risk. We use our preferred greed and fear index, which is based on the variance risk premium (i.e. distance between the implied and realized volatility) of US equity.

The third and last group of factors are endogenous and have different price momentum, with lookback periods varying from one week to one year.

We chose to rebalance our GTAA on a weekly basis. Note that monthly or quarterly rebalancing yields good results too.

At the end of each and every week, the SVR hands us 14 (number of instruments) forecast returns $\widetilde{R_{t+1}^i}$. We constrain the portfolio to be long only. As it can happen that $\widetilde{R_{t+1}^i} < 0$, we use a transformation (function) ϕ to constrain the forecast returns to be strictly positive such that $\phi(\widetilde{R_{t+1}^i} > 0) > \phi(\widetilde{R_{t+1}^j} < 0)$ and $\phi(\widetilde{R_{t+1}^i}) > 0$ for all i. Finally, we scale these forecast returns by the realized volatility of the instruments' daily returns in order to have a signal-to-noise ratio such as:

$$SN_t^i = \phi(\widetilde{R_{t+1}^i})/\sigma_{t-d,t}^i.$$

The last step boils down to plugging in these signal-to-noise ratios to a portfolio optimization algorithm in order to build the portfolio. Portfolio construction, i.e. finding the optimal weights, is a rich field of research and a detailed discussion is beyond the scope of this chapter.

Many portfolio constructions are possible. Risk-parity (the so-called one-to-sigma) portfolio is the simplest one. Other choices exist, from mean–variance optimization to equal risk contribution or maximum diversified portfolio (that gives interesting results). We believe that portfolio managers are much more worried about left-hand-side risk than they are about volatility per se. This is the reason why our favourite portfolio construction method is a conditional value-at-risk (CVaR) portfolio, a method we use in many of the models currently in production.

CVaR is defined as the expected loss exceeding value-at-risk (VaR). Minimizing CVaR rather than VaR is preferred as VaR is not a coherent measure of risk. However, portfolios with low CVaR necessarily have low VaR as well. We are aware of the limitation of the CVaR portfolio which may give some instable solutions. However, we would want to note that this criticism extends to all portfolio construction methods.

Our GTAA is therefore a two-step process where each and every week we forecast next week returns based on an SVR fed with macro factors, our greed and fear index and instrument price momenta. These expected returns are transformed into signals which are subsequently plugged into a conditional CVaR portfolio. The portfolio weights are given at the end of the week based on close price and executed at the open the next trading day (returns are computed net of expense fees and transaction costs).

11.4.3 Model results

Figure 11.4 shows the relative performance of our process compared with the often-used (Hurst et al. 2010) benchmark strategy invested 60% in bond and 40% in equity.

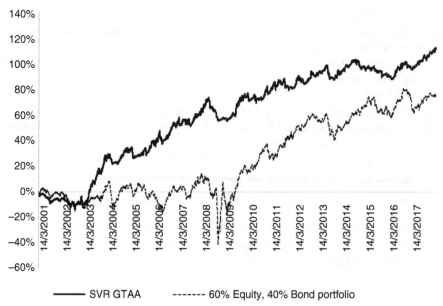

FIGURE 11.4   SVR GTAA compared to 60% bond, 40% equity (non-compounded arithmetic returns).
Source: Bloomberg, J. Guglietta.

The total compounded geometric return over the period (March 2001 to March 2017) is 189% compared with 102% for the benchmark strategy. Our strategy outperforms the benchmarked strategy by 87% and exhibits smaller drawdown, especially during the global financial crisis. The one- and two-year rolling information ratios (units of returns per unit of risk) are (of course) not constant but have been hovering 2 in the recent past. The total-period information ratio is 0.77, i.e. 52.6% higher than that of the benchmark strategy (0.50). The annualized realized volatility of the strategy is 8.9%, i.e. 0.44% lower than the one of the chosen benchmark. The stability of the strategy, measured as the R^2 of a linear fit to the cumulative log returns, has a value of 91.7%, i.e. 40% higher than the one of the benchmark (65.4%) (Figures 11.4 and 11.5).

11.5   CONCLUSION

We have presented a GTAA portfolio resting on a transparent 'quantamental' framework. We believe that diversification remains the only (almost) free lunch, and therefore being able to build robust diversified portfolios should be sought after by all investors. Because of its machine learning characteristics, our SVR-based GTAA portfolio can adapt (modify the asset mix) to different economic environments and provide such investors with a robust solution improving what we described as the main goal of asset allocation: getting the best expected return-to-risk profile.

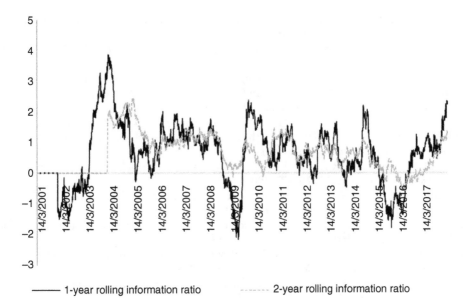

FIGURE 11.5 SVR GTAA compared to 60% bond, 40% equity (non-compounded arithmetic returns).

REFERENCES

Ait-Sahalia, Y. and Brandt, M.W. (2001). Variable selection for portfolio choice. *Journal of Finance* 56: 1297–1351.

Barberis, N. (2000). Investing for the long run when returns are predictable. *Journal of Finance* 55: 225–264.

Bekaert, G. and Hodrick, R.J. (1992). Characterizing predictable components in excess returns on equity and foreign exchange markets. *Journal of Finance* 47 (2): 467–509.

Burges, C.J.C. (1998). A tutorial on support vector machines for patterns recognition. *Data Mining and Knowledge Discovery* 2: 121–167.

Campbell, J.Y. (1987). Stock returns and the term structure. *Journal of Financial Economics* 18: 373–399.

Campbell, J.Y. and Shiller, R.J. (1998). Valuation ratios and the long-run stock market outlook. *Journal of Portfolio Management* 24 (2): 11–26.

Campbell, J.Y. and Viceira, L. (1998). Who should buy long-term bonds? NBER. Working Paper 6801.

Campbell, J., Chan, Y., and Viceira, L. (2000). *A multivariate model of strategic asset allocation.* Working Paper. Harvard University.

Chaudhuri, A. (2014). *Support vector machine model for currency crisis discrimination.* Birla Institute of Technology.

Chong, J. and Phillips, M. (2014). Tactical asset allocation with macroeconomic factors. *The Journal of Wealth Management* 17 (1): 58–69.

Dahlquist, M. and Harvey, C.R. (2001). *Global tactical asset allocation.* Duke University.

Fama, E.F. and French, K.R. (1989). Business conditions and expected returns on stocks and bonds. *Journal of Financial Economics* 25: 2349.

Ferson, W.E. and Harvey, C.R. (1991). The variation of economic risk premiums. *Journal of Political Economy* 99 (2): 385–341.

Harasty, H. and Roulet, J. (2000). Modelling stick market returns. *The Journal of Portfolio Management* 26 (2): 33–46.

Horváth, G. (2003). Advances in learning theory: methods, models and applications. In: *NATO-ASI Series III: Computer and Systems Sciences*, vol. 190 (ed. J.A.K. Suykens, G. Horvath, S. Basu, et al.). Amsterdam: IOS Press.

Hurst, B., Johnson, B.W., and Ooi, Y.H. (2010). *Understanding Risk Parity*. AQR.

Kandel, S. and Stambaugh, R.F. (1996). On the predictability of stock returns: an asset-allocation perspective. *The Journal of Finance* 51 (2): 385–424.

Keim, D.B. and Stambauh, R.F. (1986). Predicting returns in the stock and bond market. *Journal of Financial Economics* 17 (2): 357–390.

Lai, L.K.C. and Liu, J.N.K. (2010). Stock forecasting using Support Vector Machine. International Conference on Machine Learning and Cybernetics (ICMLC).

Lynch, A.W. and Balduzzi, P. (1999). Transaction cost and predictability: some utility cost calculations. *Journal of Financial Economics* 52 (1): 47–78.

Lynch, A.W. and Balduzzi, P. (2000). Predictability and transaction costs: the impact on rebalancing rules and behaviour. *Journal of Finance* 55: 2285–2310.

Madge, S. (2015). Predicting stock price direction using support vector machines. Independent Work Report. Spring 2015.

Martellini, L. and Sfeir, D. (2003). *Tactical Asset Allocation*. EDHEC.

McNelis, P. and McAdam, P. (2004). Forecasting inflation with thick models and neutral networks. European Central Bank, Working Paper Series n352, April.

Merton, R.C. (1969). Lifetime portfolio selection under uncertainty: the continuous-time case. *The Review of Economics and Statistics* 51: 247–257.

Merton, R.C. (1971). Optimal consumption and portfolio rules in a continuous-time model. *Journal of Economic Theory* 3: 373–413.

Merton, R.C. (1973). An intertemporal capital asset pricing model. *Econometrica* 41: 867–888.

Samuelson, P. (1969). Lifetime portfolio selection by dynamic stochastic. *The Review of Economics and Statistics* 51 (3): 239–246.

Sewell, M. (2008). *Structural risk minimization*. Department of Computer Science: University College London.

Sewell, M. (2010). The application of intelligent systems to financial time series analysis. PhD thesis, PhD dissertation, Department of Computer Science, University College London.

Zhang, L. and Li, J. (2013). Inflation forecasting using support vector regression. 2012 Fourth International Symposium on Information Science and Engineering.

CHAPTER 12

Reinforcement Learning in Finance

Gordon Ritter

12.1 INTRODUCTION

We live in a period characterized by rapid advances in artificial intelligence (AI) and machine learning, which are transforming everyday life in amazing ways. AlphaGo Zero (Silver et al. 2017) showed that superhuman performance can be achieved by pure reinforcement learning, with only very minimal domain knowledge and (amazingly!) *no reliance on human data or guidance*. AlphaGo Zero learned to play after merely being told the rules of the game, and playing against a simulator (itself, in that case).

The game of Go has many aspects in common with trading. Good traders often use complex strategy and plan several periods ahead. They sometimes make decisions which are 'long-term greedy' and pay the cost of a short-term temporary loss in order to implement their long-term plan. In each instant, there is a relatively small, discrete set of actions that the agent can take. In games such as Go and chess, the available actions are dictated by the rules of the game.

In trading, there are also rules of the game. Currently the most widely used trading mechanism in financial markets is the 'continuous double auction electronic order book with time priority'. With this mechanism, quote arrival and transactions are continuous in time and execution priority is assigned based on the price of quotes and their arrival order. When a buy (respectively, sell) order x is submitted, the exchange's matching engine checks whether it is possible to match x to some other previously submitted sell (respectively, buy) order. If so, the matching occurs immediately. If not, x becomes *active* and it remains active until either it becomes matched to another incoming sell (respectively, buy) order or it is cancelled. The set of all active orders at a given price level is a FIFO queue. There's much more to say about microstructure theory and we refer to the book by Hasbrouck (2007), but these are, in a nutshell, the 'rules of the game'.

These observations suggest the inception of a new subfield of quantitative finance: reinforcement learning for trading (Ritter 2017). Perhaps the most fundamental question in this burgeoning new field is the following.

FUNDAMENTAL QUESTION 1

Can an artificial intelligence discover an *optimal* dynamic trading strategy (with transaction costs) without being told what kind of strategy to look for?

If it existed, this would be the financial analogue of AlphaGo Zero.

In this note, we treat the various elements of this question:

1. What is an optimal dynamic trading strategy? How do we calculate its costs?
2. Which learning methods have even a chance at attacking such a difficult problem?
3. How can we engineer the reward function so that an AI has the potential to learn to optimize the right thing?

The first of these sub-problems is perhaps the easiest. In finance, *optimal* means that the strategy optimizes expected utility of final wealth (utility is a subtle concept and will be explained below). Final wealth is the sum of initial wealth plus a number of wealth increments over shorter time periods:

$$\text{maximize}:\mathbb{E}[u(w_T)] = \mathbb{E}\left[u\left(w_0 + \sum_{t=1}^{T} \delta w_t\right)\right] \quad (12.1)$$

where $\delta w_t = w_t - w_{t-1}$. Costs include market impact, crossing the bid-offer spread, commissions, borrow costs, etc. These costs generally induce a negative drag on w_T because each δw_t is reduced by the cost paid in that period.

We now discuss the second question: which learning methods have a chance of working? When a child tries to ride a bicycle (without training wheels) for the first time, the child cannot perfectly know the exact sequence of actions (pedal, turn handlebars, lean left or right, etc.) that will result in the bicycle remaining balanced and going forward. There is a trial and error process in which the correct actions are rewarded; incorrect actions incur a penalty. One needs a coherent mathematical framework which promises to mimic or capture this aspect of how sentient beings learn.

Moreover, sophisticated agents/actors/beings are capable of complex strategic planning. This usually involves thinking several periods ahead and perhaps taking a small loss to achieve a greater anticipated gain in subsequent periods. An obvious example is losing a pawn in chess as part of a multi-part strategy to capture the opponent's queen. How do we teach machines to 'think strategically'?

Many intelligent actions are deemed 'intelligent' precisely because they are optimal interactions with an environment. An algorithm plays a computer game intelligently if it can optimize the score. A robot navigates intelligently if it finds a shortest path with no collisions: minimizing a function which entails path length with a large negative penalty for collision.

Learning, in this context, is learning how to choose actions wisely to optimize your interaction with your environment, in such a way as to maximize rewards received over time. Within artificial intelligence, the subfield dedicated to the study of this kind of learning is called *reinforcement learning*. Most of its key developments are summarized in Sutton and Barto (2018).

An oft-quoted adage is that there are essentially three types of machine learning: supervised, unsupervised and reinforcement. As the story goes, *supervised learning* is learning from a labelled set of examples called a 'training set' while *unsupervised learning* is finding structure hidden in collections of unlabelled data, and reinforcement learning is something else entirely. The reality is that these forms of learning are all interconnected. Most production-quality reinforcement learning systems employ elements of supervised and unsupervised learning as part of the representation of the value function. Reinforcement learning is about maximizing cumulative reward over time, not about finding hidden structure, but it is often the case that the best way to maximize the reward signal is by finding hidden structure.

12.2 MARKOV DECISION PROCESSES: A GENERAL FRAMEWORK FOR DECISION MAKING

Sutton and Barto (1998) say:

> The key idea of reinforcement learning generally, is the use of value functions to organize and structure the search for good policies.

The foundational treatise on value functions was written by Bellman (1957), at a time when the phrase 'machine learning' was not in common usage. Nonetheless, reinforcement learning owes its existence, in part, to Richard Bellman.

A *value function* is a mathematical expectation in a certain probability space. The underlying probability measure is the one associated to a system which is very familiar to classically trained statisticians: a Markov process. When the Markov process describes the state of a system, it is sometimes called a *state-space model*. When, on top of a Markov process, you have the possibility of choosing a *decision* (or action) from a menu of available possibilities (the 'action space'), with some reward metric that tells you how good your choices were, then it is called a *Markov decision process* (MDP).

In a Markov decision process, once we observe the current state of the system, we have the information we need to make a decision. In other words (assuming we know the current state), then it would not help us (i.e. we could not make a better decision) to also know the full history of past states which led to the current state. This history-dependence is closely related to Bellman's principle.

Bellman (1957) writes: 'In each process, the functional equation governing the process was obtained by an application of the following intuitive.'

> An optimal policy has the property that whatever the initial state and initial decision are, the remaining decisions must constitute an optimal policy with regard to the state resulting from the first decision.
>
> Bellman (1957)

The 'functional equations' that Bellman is talking about are essentially (12.7) and (12.8), as we explain in the next section. Consider an interacting system: agent interacts with environment. The 'environment' is the part of the system outside of the agent's *direct* control. At each time-step t, the agent observes the current state of the environment $S_t \in S$ and chooses an action $A_t \in A$. This choice influences both the transition to the next state and the reward the agent receives (Figure 12.1).

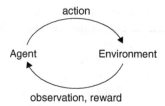

FIGURE 12.1 Interacting system: agent interacts with environment.

Underlying everything, there is assumed to be a distribution

$$p\left(s^0, r \mid s, a\right)$$

for the joint probability of transitioning to state $s^0 \in S$ and receiving reward r, conditional on the previous state being s and the agent taking action a. This distribution is typically not known to the agent, but its existence gives mathematical meaning to notions such as 'expected reward'.

The agent's goal is to maximize the expected cumulative reward, denoted by

$$Gt = R_{t+1} + \gamma R_{t+2} + \gamma^2 R_{t+3} \ldots \tag{12.2}$$

where $0 < \gamma < 1$ is necessary for the infinite sum to be defined.

A *policy* π is, roughly, an algorithm for choosing the next action, based on the state you are in. More formally, a policy is a mapping from states to probability distributions over the action space. If the agent is following policy π, then in state s, the agent will choose action a with probability $\pi(a|s)$.

Reinforcement learning is the search for policies which maximize

$$\mathbb{E}[G_t] = \mathbb{E}\left[R_{t+1} + \gamma R_{t+2} + \gamma^2 R_{t+3} + \ldots\right]$$

Normally, the policy space is too large to allow brute-force search, so the search for policies possessing good properties must proceed by the use of value functions.

The *state-value function* for policy π is defined to be

$$v_\pi(s) = \mathbb{E}_\pi[G_t \mid S_t = s]$$

where Eπ denotes the expectation under the assumption that policy π is followed. For any policy π and any state s, the following consistency condition holds:

$$v_\pi(s) = \mathbb{E}_\pi[G_t \mid S_t = s] \tag{12.3}$$

$$= \mathbb{E}_\pi[R_{t+1} + \gamma G_{t+1}\}S_t = s] \tag{12.4}$$

$$= \sum_a \pi(a \mid s) \sum_{s',r} p(s', r \mid s, a)[r + \gamma E_\pi[G_{t+1} \mid S_{t+1} - s']] \tag{12.5}$$

$$= \sum_a \pi(a \mid s) \sum_{s',r} p(s', r \mid s, a)[r + \gamma v_\pi(s')] \tag{12.6}$$

The end result of the above calculation,

$$v_\pi(s) = \sum_{a,s',r} \pi(a \mid s)p(s',r \mid s,a)[r + \gamma v_\pi(s')]$$

is called the *Bellman equation*. The value function v_π is the unique solution to its Bellman equation. Similarly, the *action-value function* expresses the value of starting in state s, taking action a, and then following policy π thereafter:

$$q_\pi(s,a) := \mathbb{E}\pi[G_t \mid S_t = s, A_t = a]$$

Policy π is defined to be at least as good as π^0 if

$$v_\pi(s) \geq v_\pi 0(s)$$

for all states s.

An *optimal policy* is defined to be one which is at least as good as any other policy. There need not be a unique optimal policy, but all optimal policies share the same optimal state-value function

$$v_*(s) = \max_\pi v_\pi(s)$$

and optimal action-value function

$$q_*(s,a) = \max_\pi q_\pi(s,a).$$

Note that $v_*(s) = \max_a q_*(s,a)$, so the action-value function is more general than the state-value function.

The optimal state-value function and action-value function satisfy the Bellman equations

$$v_*(s) = \max_a \sum_{s',r} p(s',r \mid s,a)[r + \gamma v_*(s')] \tag{12.7}$$

$$q_*(s,a) = \sum_{s',r} p(s',r \mid s,a)[r + \gamma \max_{a'} q_*(s',a)] \tag{12.8}$$

where the sum over s^0,r denotes a sum over all states s^0 and all rewards r.

If we possess a function $q(s,a)$ which is an estimate of $q_*(s,a)$, then the *greedy policy* (associated to the function q) is defined as picking at time t the action a_t^* which maximizes $q(s_t,a)$ over all possible a, where s_t is the state at time t. Given the function q_*, the associated greedy policy is the optimal policy. Hence we can reduce the problem to finding q_*, or producing a sequence of iterates that converges to q_*.

It is worth noting at this point that modern approaches to multi-period portfolio optimization with transaction costs (Gârleanu and Pedersen 2013; Kolm and Ritter 2015; Benveniste and Ritter 2017) are also organized as optimal control problems which, in principle, could be approached by finding solutions to (12.7), although these equations are difficult to solve with constraints and non-differentiable costs.

There is a simple algorithm which produces a sequence of functions converging to q_*, known as Q-learning (Watkins 1989). Many subsequent advancements built upon

Watkins' seminal work, and the original form of Q-learning is perhaps no longer the state of the art. Among its drawbacks include that it can require a large number of time-steps for convergence.

The Watkins algorithm consists of the following steps. One initializes a matrix Q with one row per state and one column per action. This matrix can be initially the zero matrix, or initialized with some prior information if available. Let S denote the current state.

Repeat the following steps until a pre-selected convergence criterion is obtained:

1. Choose action $A \in A$ using a policy derived from Q which combines exploration and exploitation.
2. Take action A, after which the new state of the environment is S^0 and we observe reward R.
3. Update the value of $Q(S,A)$: set.

$$\text{Target} = R + \gamma \max_a Q(S', a)$$

and

$$Q(S, A)+ = \alpha\underbrace{[\text{Target} - Q(S, A)]}_{\text{TD-error}} \tag{12.9}$$

where $\alpha \in (0,1)$ is called the step-size parameter. The step-size parameter does not have to be constant and indeed can vary with each time-step. Convergence proofs usually require this; presumably the MDP generating the rewards has some unavoidable process noise which cannot be removed with better learning, and thus the variance of the TD-error never goes to zero. Hence α_t must go to zero for large time-step t.

Assuming that all state-action pairs continue to be updated, and assuming a variant of the usual stochastic approximation conditions on the sequence of step-size parameters (see (12.10) below), the Q-learning algorithm has been shown to converge with probability 1 to q_*.

In many problems of interest, either the state space, or the action space, or both are most naturally modelled as continuous spaces (i.e. sub-spaces of R^d for some appropriate dimension d). In such a case, one cannot directly use the algorithm above. Moreover, the convergence result stated above does not generalize in any obvious way.

Many recent studies (for example, Mnih et al. (2015)) have proposed replacing the Q-matrix in the above algorithm with a deep neural network. Unlike a lookup table, a neural network has a vector of associated parameters, sometimes called *weights*. We could then write the Q-function as $Q(s,a;\theta)$, emphasizing its parameter dependence. Instead of iteratively updating values in a table, we will iteratively update the parameters, θ, so that the network learns to compute better estimates of state-action values.

Although neural networks are general function approximators, depending on the structure of the truly-optimal Q-function q_*, it may be the case that a neural network learns very slowly, both in terms of the CPU time needed to train and also in terms of efficient sample use (defined as a lower number of samples required to achieve acceptable results). The network topology and the various choices such as activation functions and optimizer (Kingma and Ba 2014) matter quite a bit in terms of training time and efficient sample use.

In some problems, the use of simpler function-approximators (such as ensembles of regression trees) to represent the unknown function $Q(s,a;\theta)$ may lead to much faster training time and much more efficient sample use. This is especially true when q_* can be well approximated by a simple functional form such as a locally linear form.

The observant reader will have noticed the similarity of the Q-learning update procedure to stochastic gradient descent. This fruitful connection was noted and exploited by Baird III and Moore (1999), who reformulate several different learning procedures as special cases of stochastic gradient descent.

The convergence of stochastic gradient descent has been studied extensively in the stochastic approximation literature (Bottou 2012). Convergence results typically require learning rates satisfying the conditions

$$\sum_t \alpha_t^2 < \infty \text{ and } \sum_t \alpha_t = \infty \tag{12.10}$$

The theorem of Robbins and Siegmund (1985) provides a means to establish almost sure convergence of stochastic gradient descent under surprisingly mild conditions, including cases where the loss function is non-smooth.

12.3 RATIONALITY AND DECISION MAKING UNDER UNCERTAINTY

Given some set of mutually exclusive outcomes (each of which presumably affects wealth or consumption somehow), a *lottery* is a probability distribution on these events such that the total probability is 1. Often, but not always, these outcomes involve gain or loss of wealth. For example, 'pay 1000 for a 20% chance to win 10,000' is a lottery.

Nicolas Bernoulli described the St Petersburg lottery/paradox in a letter to Pierre Raymond de Montmort on 9 September 1713. A casino offers a game of chance for a single player in which a fair coin is tossed at each stage. The pot starts at $2 and is doubled every time a head appears. The first time a tail appears, the game ends and the player wins whatever is in the pot. The mathematical expectation value is

$$\frac{1}{2} \cdot 2 + \frac{1}{4} \cdot 4 + \cdots = +\infty$$

This paradox led to a remarkable number of new developments as mathematicians and economists struggled to understand all the ways it could be resolved.

Daniel Bernoulli (cousin of Nicolas) in 1738 published a seminal treatise in the Commentaries of the Imperial Academy of Science of Saint Petersburg; this is, in fact, where the modern name of this paradox originates. Bernoulli's work possesses a modern translation (Bernoulli 1954) and thus may be appreciated by the English-speaking world.

> The determination of the value of an item must not be based on the price, but rather on the utility it yields... There is no doubt that a gain of one thousand ducats is more significant to the pauper than to a rich man though both gain the same amount.
>
> Bernoulli (1954)

Among other things, Bernoulli's paper contains a proposed resolution to the paradox: if investors have a logarithmic utility, then their expected change in utility of wealth by playing the game is finite.

Of course, if our only goal were to study the St Petersburg paradox, then there are other, more practical resolutions. In the St Petersburg lottery only very unlikely events yield the high prizes that lead to an infinite expected value, so the expected value becomes finite if we are willing to, as a practical matter, disregard events which are expected to occur less than once in the entire lifetime of the universe.

Moreover, the expected value of the lottery, even when played against a casino with the largest resources realistically conceivable, is quite modest. If the total resources (or total maximum jackpot) of the casino are W dollars, then $L = b\log_2(W)c$ is the maximum number of times the casino can play before it no longer fully covers the next bet, i.e. $2^L \leq W$ but $2^{L+1} > W$. The mutually exclusive events are that you flip one time, two times, three times, $\ldots$, L times, winning $2^1, 2^2, 2^3, \ldots, 2^L$ or finally, you flip 2^{L+1} times and win W. The expected value of the lottery then becomes:

$$\sum_{k=1}^{L} \frac{1}{2^k} \cdot 2^k + \left(1 - \sum_{k=1}^{L} \frac{1}{2^k}\right) W = L + W2^{-L}$$

If the casino has $W = \$1$ billion, the expected value of the 'realistic St Petersburg lottery' is only about \$30.86.

If lottery M is preferred over lottery L, we write $L \prec M$. If M is either preferred over or viewed with indifference relative to L, we write $L \preceq M$. If the agent is indifferent between L and M, we write $L \sim M$. Von Neumann and Morgenstern (1945) provided the definition of when the preference relation is rational, and proved the key result that any rational preference relation has an expression in terms of a utility function.

Definition 1   (Von Neumann and Morgenstern 1945). A preference relation is said to be *rational* if all of the four axioms hold:

1. For any lotteries L, M, exactly one of the following holds:

$$L \prec M, M \prec L, or L \sim M$$

2. If $L \preceq M$ and $M \preceq N$ then $L \preceq N$
3. If $L \preceq M \preceq N$ then there exists $p \in [0,1]$ such that

$$pL + (1-p)N \sim M$$

4. If $L \prec M$, then for any N and $p \in (0,1]$, one has

$$pL + (1-p)N \prec pM + (1-p)N.$$

The last axiom is called 'independence of irrelevant alternatives'.

An agent whose preferences satisfy the VNM axioms is called 'VNM-rational'. I will leave further discussion of 'what is rationality' to the philosophers, but someone whose preferences don't satisfy these axioms probably shouldn't be allowed near a race track (or the stock market).

Theorem 1 (Von Neumann and Morgenstern 1945). For any VNM-rational agent (i.e. satisfying 1–4), there exists a function u assigning to each outcome A a real number $u(A)$ such that for any two lotteries,

$$L \prec M \text{ iff } E(u(L)) < E(u(M)).$$

Conversely, any agent acting to maximize the expectation of a function u will obey axioms 1–4.

Since

$$Eu(p_1A_1 + \ldots + p_rA_n) = p_1u(A_1) + \cdots + p_nu(A_n).$$

it follows that u is uniquely determined (up to adding a constant and multiplying by a positive scalar) by preferences between *simple lotteries*, i.e. lotteries of the form $pA + (1-p)B$ having only two outcomes.

We now illustrate the intuition behind, and proper use of, utility functions in practical situations requiring decision making under risk. We do this by means of a humorous story of adventure on the high seas. The year is 1776 and you own goods located abroad, worth the equivalent of one standard-size gold bar. These goods cannot increase your wealth until they are shipped back to you via sailing vessels on the high seas, but it's a perilous journey; the probability that a ship is lost at sea is 1/2.

You were planning to have the entire load sent on one ship. Captain Cook advises you that this is unwise and generously offers to split the load in half and send each half on a separate ship at no extra cost. Should you accept Cook's offer?

$$\text{one ship}: \mathbb{E}[w_T] = \frac{1}{2} \times 1 = 0.5 \text{ gold bar}$$

$$\text{two ships}: \mathbb{E}[w_T] = \frac{1}{2} \times \frac{1}{2} + \frac{1}{2} \times \frac{1}{2} = 0.5 \text{ gold bar}$$

You are about to advise Captain Cook that, due to extremely clever use of probability theory, you have proven that it doesn't matter – he can simply use one ship. Just then, Professor Daniel Bernoulli arrives and advises you to instead calculate $\mathbb{E}[u(w_T)]$ where $u(w) = 1 - e^{-w}$, leading to:

$$\text{one ship}: \mathbb{E}[1 - e^{-w_T}] = \frac{1}{2} \times (1 - e^{-1}) \approx 0.32$$

$$\text{two ships}: \mathbb{E}[1 - e^{-w_T}] = \frac{1}{4}(1 - e^{-0}) + \frac{1}{2}(1 - e^{-1/2}) + \frac{1}{4}(1 - e^{-1})$$

$$\approx 0.35$$

Using Bernoulli's method, it seems that two ships are preferred, although the reason for the method's efficacy is perhaps still obscure. Bernoulli asks whether you bothered to consider the *risk* when you compared the two scenarios. You reply angrily that you prefer to act first and consider the risks later. But to make Bernoulli happy, you calculate:

$$\text{one ship} : \mathbb{V}[w_T] = \frac{1}{2}(0 - 0.5)^2 + \frac{1}{2}(1 - 0.5)^2$$

$$= 0.25$$

$$\text{two ships} : \mathbb{V}[w_T] = \frac{1}{4}(0 - 0.5)^2 + \frac{1}{2}(0.5 - 0.5)^2 + \frac{1}{4}(1 - 0.5)^2$$

$$= 0.125$$

Bernoulli says that if

$$u(w) = \frac{1 - \exp(-\kappa w)}{\kappa}$$

where $\kappa > 0$ is any positive scalar, then supposing w_T is normal,

$$\mathbb{E}[u(w_T)] = u\left(\mathbb{E}[w_T] - \frac{\kappa}{2}\mathbb{V}[w_T]\right) \tag{12.11}$$

This implies that maximizing $\mathbb{E}[u(w_T)]$ is equivalent to maximizing

$$\mathbb{E}[w_T] - \frac{\kappa}{2}\mathbb{V}[w_T] \tag{12.12}$$

since u is monotone. It turns out this is true for many fat-tailed distributions as well, as we show in the next section.

12.4   MEAN-VARIANCE EQUIVALENCE

In the previous section we recalled the well-known result that for an exponential utility function and for normally distributed wealth increments, one may dispense with maximizing $E[u(w_T)]$ and equivalently solve the mathematically simpler problem of maximizing $E[w_T] - (\kappa/2)V[w_T]$. Since this is actually the problem our reinforcement learning systems are going to solve, naturally we'd like to know the class of problems to which it applies. It turns out that neither of the conditions of normality or exponential utility is necessary; both can be relaxed very substantially.

Definition 2   A utility function $u : R \rightarrow R$ is called *standard* if it is increasing, concave and continuously differentiable.

The properties which define a 'standard' utility function make economic sense. Even great philanthropists have increasing utility of wealth in their investment portfolio – they would prefer to be able to do more to end hunger, disease, etc. Hence a quadratic function that is not linear can never be a standard utility function. A strictly concave quadratic must go up and come back down, as if after some point, more wealth is somehow worse. In particular (12.12) is *not* a utility function.

Concavity corresponds to risk aversion. Finally, if the utility function is not continuously differentiable, it implies that there is a certain particular level of wealth for which one penny above that is very different than one penny below.

Definition 3 Let 'denote a lottery, and let w' denote the (random) final wealth associated to lottery'. For two scalars $m \in R$ and $s > 0$, let $L(\mu, \omega)$ denote the space of lotteries' under which $E[w'] = \mu$ and $V[w'] = \omega^2$. We say *expected utility is a function of mean and variance* if $E[u(w')]$ is the same for all '$\in L(\mu, \omega)$. This means that the function $\hat{U}$ defined by

$$\hat{U}(\mu, \omega) := \{E[u(w')] : ' \in L(\mu, \omega)\}$$

is single-valued; the right-hand side is always a single number.

Let $r \in R^n$ denote the return over the interval $[t, t+1]$. Hence $r \in R^n$ is an n-dimensional vector whose i-th component is

$$r_i = p_i(t+1)/p_i(t) - 1$$

where $p_i(t)$ is the i-th asset's price at time t (adjusted for splits or capital actions if necessary).

Let $h \in R^n$ denote the portfolio holdings, measured in dollars or an appropriate numeraire currency, at some time t in the future. Let h_0 denote the current portfolio. Hence the (one-period) wealth random variable is

$$\tilde{w} = h'r$$

and the expected-utility maximizer chooses the optimal portfolio h^* defined by

$$h^* := \text{argmax} E[u(w^\sim)] \tag{12.13}$$

Definition 4 The underlying asset return distribution, $p(r)$, is said to be *meanvariance equivalent* if first and second moments of the distribution exist, and for any standard utility function u, there exists some constant $\kappa > 0$ (where κ depends on u) such that

$$h^* = \text{argmax}\{E[\tilde{w}] - (\kappa/2)V[\tilde{w}]\} \tag{12.14}$$

where $h^* = \text{argmax} E[u(\tilde{w})]$ as defined by (12.13).

The multivariate Cauchy distribution is elliptical, but its moments of orders 1 and higher are all infinite/undefined. Therefore, it is not mean-variance equivalent because the requisite means and variances would be undefined.

Which distributions, then, are mean-variance equivalent? We showed previously that the normal distribution is; this is easy. Many distributions, including heavy-tailed distributions such as the multivariate Student-t, are also mean-variance equivalent.

Assuming all lotteries correspond to holding portfolios of risky assets, then Definition 3, like Definition 4, is a property of the asset return distribution $p(r)$; some distributions have this property and some do not.

If Definition 3 does *not* hold for a given distribution, then there isn't much hope for mean-variance equivalence to hold either. Intuitively, if Definition 3 does *not* hold then $E[u(w')]$ must depend on something apart from $E[w']$ and $V[w']$ so it should be easy to construct a counterexample where the right-hand side (12.14) is suboptimal because of this 'extra term'.

Definition 5   An *indifference curve* is a level curve of the surface $\hat{U}$, or equivalently a set of the form $\hat{U}^{-1}(c)$

The intuition behind the terminology of Definition 5 is that the investor is indifferent among the outcomes described by the various points on the curve.

Tobin (1958) assumed that expected utility is a function of mean and variance and showed mean-variance equivalence as a consequence. Unfortunately, Tobin's proof was flawed – it contained a derivation which is valid only for elliptical distributions. The flaw in Tobin's proof, and a counterexample, was pointed out by Feldstein (1969). After presenting a correct proof, we will discuss the flaw.

Recall that for a scalar-valued random variable X, the *characteristic function* is defined by

$$\phi_X(t) = \mathbb{E}[e^{itX}],$$

If the variable has a density, then the characteristic function is the Fourier transform of the density. The characteristic function of a real-valued random variable always exists, since it is the integral of a bounded continuous function over a finite measure space.

Generally speaking, characteristic functions are especially useful when analyzing moments of random variables and linear combinations of random variables. Characteristic functions have been used to provide especially elegant proofs of some of the key results in probability theory, such as the central limit theorem.

If a random variable X has moments up to order k, then the characteristic function ϕ_X is k times continuously differentiable on R. In this case

$$\mathbb{E}[X^k] = (-i)^k \phi_X^{(k)}(0).$$

If φ_X has a k-th derivative at zero, then X has all moments up to k if k is even, but only up to $k-1$ if k is odd, and

$$\phi_X^{(k)}(0) = i^k \mathbb{E}[X^k]$$

If $X_1, \ldots, X_n$ are independent random variables, then

$$\varphi_{X1} + \ldots + X_n(t) = \varphi_{X1}(t) \cdots \phi_{Xn}(t).$$

Definition 6   An R^n-valued random variable **x** is said to be *elliptical* if its characteristic function, defined by $\varphi(\mathbf{t}) = \mathrm{E}[\exp(i\mathbf{t}^0\mathbf{x})]$ takes the form

$$\varphi(\mathbf{t}) = \exp(i\mathbf{t}^0\mu)\psi(\mathbf{t}^0\Omega\mathbf{t}) \tag{12.15}$$

where $\mu \in R^n$ is the vector of medians, and Ω is a matrix, assumed to be positive definite, known as the *dispersion matrix*. The function ψ does not depend on n.

We denote the distribution with characteristic function (12.15) by $\mathrm{E}_\psi(\mu,\Omega)$.

The name 'elliptical' arose because the isoprobability contours are ellipsoidal. If variances exist, then the covariance matrix is proportional to Ω, and if means exist, μ is also the vector of means.

Equation (12.15) does not imply that the random vector **x** has a density, but if it does, then the density must be of the form

$$f_n(\mathbf{x}) = |\Omega|^{-1/2} g_n[(\mathbf{x} - \mu)'\Omega^{-1}(\mathbf{x} - \mu)] \tag{12.16}$$

Equation (12.16) is sometimes used as the definition of elliptical distributions, when existence of a density is assumed. In particular, (12.16) shows that if $n = 1$, then the

$$\sqrt{\ }$$

transformed variable $z = (x - \mu)/\sqrt{\Omega}$ satisfies $z \sim E_\psi(0,1)$.

The multivariate normal is the most well-known elliptical family; for the normal, one has $g_n(s) = c_n \exp(-s/2)$ (where c_n is a normalization constant) and $\psi(T) = \exp(-T/2)$. Note that g_n depends on n while ψ does not. The elliptical class also includes many non-normal distributions, including examples which display heavy tails and are therefore better suited to modelling asset returns. For example, the multivariate Student-*t* distribution with v degrees of freedom has density of the form (12.16) with

$$gn(s) \propto (v + s) - (n + v)/2 \tag{12.17}$$

and for $v = 1$ one recovers the multivariate Cauchy.

One could choose $g_n(s)$ to be identically zero for sufficiently large s, which would make the distribution of asset returns bounded above and below. Thus, one criticism of the CAPM – that it requires assets to have unlimited liability – is not a valid criticism.

Let $\mathbf{v} = \mathbf{Tx}$ denote a fixed (non-stochastic) linear transformation of the random vector **x**. It is of interest to relate the characteristic function of **v** to that of **x**.

$$\phi_\mathbf{v}(t) = \mathbb{E}[e^{it'\mathbf{v}}] = \mathbb{E}[e^{it'\mathbf{Tx}}] = \phi_\mathbf{x}(T't) = e^{it'T\mu}\psi(t'T\Omega T't)$$

$$= e^{it'm}\psi(t'\Delta t) \tag{12.18}$$

where for convenience we define $\mathbf{m} = \mathbf{T}\mu$ and $\Delta = \mathbf{T}\Omega\mathbf{T}^0$.

Even with the same function ψ, the functions f_n, g_n appearing in the density (12.16) can have rather different shapes for different n (=the dimension of $\mathbf{R}^n$), as we see in (12.17). However, the function ψ does not depend on n. For this reason, one sometimes speaks of an elliptical 'family' which is identified with a single function ψ, but possibly different values of μ, Ω and a family of functions g_n determining the densities – one such function for each dimension of Euclidean space. Marginalization of an elliptical family results in a new elliptical of the same family (i.e. the same ψ-function).

Theorem 2 If the distribution of **r** is elliptical, and if u is a standard utility function, then expected utility is a function of mean and variance, and moreover

$$\partial_\mu \widehat{U}(\mu, \omega) \geq 0 \text{ and } \partial_\omega \widehat{U}(\mu, \omega) \leq 0 \tag{12.19}$$

Proof. For the duration of this proof, fix a portfolio with holdings vector $\mathbf{h} \in \mathbf{R}^n$ and let $x = \mathbf{h}^0\mathbf{r}$ denote the wealth increment. Let $\mu = \mathbf{h}^0\mathbb{E}[\mathbf{r}]$ and $\omega^2 = \mathbf{h}^0\Omega\mathbf{h}$ denote moments of x. Applying the marginalization property (12.18) with the $1 \times n$ matrix $\mathbf{T} = \mathbf{h}^0$ yields

$$\varphi_x(t) = e^{it\mu}\psi(t^2\omega^2).$$

The k-th central moment of x will be

$$i^{-k} \frac{d^k}{dt^k} \psi(t^2 \omega^2) \bigg|_{t=0}$$

From this it is clear that all odd moments will be zero and the $2k$-th moment will be proportional to ω^{2k}. Therefore the full distribution of x is completely determined by μ, ω, so expected utility is a function of μ, ω.

We now prove the inequalities (12.19). Write

$$\hat{U}(\mu, \omega) = \mathbb{E}[u(x)] = \int_{-\infty}^{\infty} u(x)f(x)dx. \tag{12.20}$$

Note that the integral is over a one-dimensional variable. Using the special case of Eq. (12.16) with $n = 1$, we have

$$f_1(x) = \omega^{-1} g_1[(x - \mu)^2 / \omega^2]. \tag{12.21}$$

Using (12.21) to update (12.20), we have

$$\hat{U}(\mu, \omega) = \mathbb{E}[u(x)] = \int_{-\infty}^{\infty} (x)\omega^{-1} g_1[(x - \mu)^2 / \omega^2]dx.$$

Now make the change of variables $z = (x - \mu)/\omega$ and $dx = \omega\, dz$, which yields

$$\hat{U}(\mu, \omega) = \int_{-\infty}^{\infty} u(\mu + \omega z)g_1(z^2)dz.$$

The desired property $\partial_\mu \hat{U}(\mu, \omega) \geq 0$ then follows immediately from the condition from Definition 2 that u is increasing.

The case for $\partial_\omega \hat{U}$ goes as follows:

$$\partial_\omega \hat{U}(\mu, \omega) = \int_{-\infty}^{\infty} \tau s'(\mu + \omega z)z g_1(z^2)dz$$

$$= \left[\int_{-\infty}^{0} + \int_{0}^{\infty} \right] u'(\mu + \omega z)z g_1(z^2)dz$$

$$= -\int_{0}^{\infty} u'(\mu - \omega z)z g_1(z^2)dz + \int_{0}^{\infty} u'(\mu + \omega z)z g_1(z^2)dz$$

$$= \int_{0}^{\infty} z g_1(z^2)[u'(\mu + \omega z) - u'(\mu - \omega z)]dz$$

A differentiable function is concave on an interval if and only if its derivative is monotonically decreasing on that interval, hence

$$u^0(\mu + \omega z) - u^0(\mu - \omega z) < 0$$

while $g_1(z^2) > 0$ since it is a probability density function. Hence on the domain of integration, the integrand of $\int_0^\infty zg_1(z^2)[u'(\mu + \omega z) - u'(\mu - \omega z)]dz$ is non-positive and hence $\partial_\omega \hat{U}(\mu, \omega) \le 0$, completing the proof of Theorem 2.

Recall Definition 5 above of indifference curves. Imagine the indifference curves written in the σ, μ plane with σ on the horizontal axis. If there are two branches of the curve, take only the upper one. Under the conditions of Theorem 2, one can make two statements about the indifference curves:

$d\mu/d\sigma > 0$ or an investor is indifferent about two portfolios with different variances only if the portfolio with greater σ also has greater μ,

$d^2\mu/d\sigma^2 > 0$, or the rate at which an individual must be compensated for accepting greater σ (this rate is $d\mu/d\sigma$) increases as σ increases

These two properties say that the indifference curves are convex.

In case you are wondering how one might calculate $d\mu/d\sigma$ along an indifference curve, we may assume that the indifference curve is parameterized by

$$\lambda \rightarrow (\mu(\lambda), \sigma(\lambda))$$

and differentiate both sides of

$$E[u(x)] = u(\mu + \sigma z)g_1[z^2]dz.$$

with respect to λ. By assumption, the left side is constant (has zero derivative) on an indifference curve. Hence

$$0 = \int u'(\mu + \sigma z)(\mu'(\lambda) + z\sigma'(\lambda))g_1(z^2)dz$$

$$\frac{d\mu}{d\sigma} = \frac{\mu'(\lambda)}{\sigma'(\lambda)} = -\frac{\int_{\mathbb{R}} zu'(\mu + \sigma z)g_1(z^2)dz}{\int_{\mathbb{R}} u'(\mu + \sigma z)g_1(z^2)\, dz}$$

If $u^0 > 0$ and $u^{00} < 0$ at all points, then the numerator $^R R z u^0(\mu + \sigma z)g_1(z^2)dz$ is negative, and so $d\mu/d\sigma > 0$.

The proof that $d^2\mu/d\sigma^2 > 0$ is similar (exercise).

What, exactly, fails if the distribution $p(\mathbf{r})$ is not elliptical? The crucial step of this proof assumes that a two-parameter distribution $f(x;\mu,\sigma)$ can be put into 'standard form' $f(z;0,1)$ by a change of variables $z = (x - \mu)/\sigma$. This is not a property of all two-parameter probability distributions; for example, it fails for the lognormal.

One can see by direct calculation that for logarithmic utility, $u(x) = \log x$ and for a log-normal distribution of wealth,

$$f(x; m, s) = \frac{1}{sx\sqrt{2\pi}} \exp(-(\log x - m)^2/2s^2)$$

then the indifference curves are not convex. The moments of x are

$$\mu = em + s^2/2, \quad \text{and} \quad \sigma2 = (em + s^2/2)2(es^2 - 1)$$

and with a little algebra one has

$$\mathbb{E}u = \log \mu - \frac{1}{2} \log(\sigma^2/\mu^2 + 1)$$

One may then calculate $d\mu/d\sigma$ and $d^2\mu/d\sigma^2$ along a parametric curve of the form

$$\mathbb{E}u = \text{constant}$$

and see that $d\mu/d\sigma > 0$ everywhere along the curve, but $d^2\mu/d\sigma^2$ changes sign. Hence this example cannot be mean-variance equivalent.

Theorem 2 implies that for a given level of median return, the right kind of investors always dislike dispersion. We henceforth assume, unless otherwise stated, that the first two moments of the distribution exist. In this case (for elliptical distributions), the median is the mean and the dispersion is the variance, and hence the underlying asset return distribution is mean-variance equivalent in the sense of Definition 4. We emphasize that this holds for any smooth, concave utility.

12.5   REWARDS

In some cases the shape of the reward function is not obvious. It's part of the art of formulating the problem and the model. My advice in formulating the reward function is to think very carefully about what defines 'success' for the problem at hand, and in a very complete way. A reinforcement learning agent can learn to maximize only the rewards it knows about. If some part of what defines success is missing from the reward function, then the agent you are training will most likely fall behind in exactly that aspect of success.

12.5.1   The form of the reward function for trading

In finance, as in certain other fields, the problem of reward function is also subtle, but happily this subtle problem has been solved for us by Bernoulli (1954), Von Neumann and Morgenstern (1945), Arrow (1971) and Pratt (1964). The theory of decision making under uncertainty is sufficiently general to encompass very many, if not all, portfolio selection and optimal-trading problems; should you choose to ignore it, you do so at your own peril.

Consider again maximizing (12.12):

$$\text{maximize:} \left\{ \mathbb{E}[\omega_T] - \frac{k}{2}\mathbb{V}[\omega_T] \right\} \tag{12.22}$$

Suppose we could invent some definition of 'reward' R_t so that

$$\mathbb{E}[\omega_T] - \frac{k}{2}\mathbb{V}[\omega_T] \approx \sum_{t=1}^{T} R_t \tag{12.23}$$

Then (12.22) looks like a 'cumulative reward over time' problem.

Reinforcement learning is the search for policies which maximize

$$E[G_t] = E[R_{t+1} + \gamma R_{t+2} + \gamma^2 R_{t+3} + \dots]$$

which by (12.23) would then maximize expected utility as long as $\gamma \approx 1$.

Consider the reward function

$$R_t := \delta\omega_t - \frac{k}{2}(\delta\omega_t - \widehat{\mu})^2 \tag{12.24}$$

where $\widehat{\mu}$ is an estimate of a parameter representing the mean wealth increment over one period, $\mu = E[\delta w_t]$.

$$\frac{1}{T}\sum_{t=1}^{T} R_t = \underbrace{\frac{1}{T}\sum_{t=1}^{T}\delta\omega_t}_{\rightarrow E[\delta\omega_t]} - \frac{k}{2}\underbrace{\frac{1}{T}\sum_{t=1}^{T}(\delta\omega_t - \widehat{\mu})^2}_{\rightarrow \mathbb{V}[\delta\omega_t]}$$

Then and for large T, the two terms on the right-hand side approach the sample mean and the sample variance, respectively.

Thus, with this one special choice of the reward function (12.24), if the agent learns to maximize cumulative reward, it should also approximately maximize the meanvariance form of utility.

12.5.2 Accounting for profit and loss

Suppose that trading in a market with N assets occurs at discrete times $t = 0,1,2,\dots,T$. Let $n_t \in Z^N$ denote the holdings vector in *shares* at time t, so that

$$h_t := n_t p_t \in R^N$$

denotes the vector of holdings in dollars, where p_t denotes the vector of midpoint prices at time t.

Assume for each t, a quantity δn_t shares are traded in the instant just before t and no further trading occurs until the instant before $t+1$. Let

$$v_t = \text{nav}_t + \text{cash}_t \text{ where } \text{nav}_t = n_t \cdot p_t$$

denote the 'portfolio value', which we define to be net asset value in risky assets, plus cash. The *profit and loss* (PL) before commissions and financing over the interval $[t,t+1)$ is given by the change in portfolio value δv_{t+1}.

For example, suppose we purchase $\delta n_t = 100$ shares of stock just before t at a per-share price of $p_t = 100$ dollars. Then nav_t increases by $10\,000$ while cash_t decreases by $10\,000$, leaving v_t invariant. Suppose that just before $t+1$, no further trades have occurred and $p_{t+1} = 105$; then $\delta v_{t+1} = 500$, although this PL is said to be *unrealized* until we trade again and move the profit into the cash term, at which point it is *realized*.

Now suppose $p_t = 100$ but due to bid-offer spread, temporary impact or other related frictions our effective purchase price was $\widetilde{p}_t = 101$. Suppose further that we continue to use the midpoint price p_t to 'mark to market', or compute net asset value. Then, as a result of the trade, nav_t increases by $(\delta n_t)p_t = 10\,000$ while cash_t decreases by $10\,100$, which means that v_t is decreased by 100 even though the reference price p_t has not changed. This difference is called *slippage*; it shows up as a cost term in the cash part of v_t.

Executing the trade list results in a change in cash balance given by

$$\delta(\text{cash})_t = -\delta n_t \cdot \widetilde{p}_t$$

where $\widetilde{p}_t$ is our effective trade price including slippage. If the components of δn_t were all positive then this would represent payment of a positive amount of cash, whereas if the components of δn_t were negative we receive cash proceeds.

Hence before financing and borrow cost, one has

$$\delta v_t := v_t - v_{t-1} = \delta(\text{nav})_t + \delta(\text{cash})_t$$

$$= n_t \cdot p_t - n_{t-1} \cdot p_{t-1} - \delta n_t \cdot \widetilde{p}_t \tag{12.25}$$

$$= nt \cdot pt - nt - 1 \cdot pt + nt - 1 \cdot pt - nt - 1 \cdot pt - 1 - \delta nt \cdot \widetilde{p}t \tag{12.26}$$

$$= \delta nt \cdot (pt - \widetilde{p}t) + nt - 1 \cdot (pt - pt - 1) \tag{12.27}$$

$$= \delta n_t \cdot (p_t - \widetilde{p}_t) + h_{t-1} \cdot r_t \tag{12.28}$$

where the asset returns are $r_t = p_t/p_{t-1} - 1$. Let us define the *total cost* c_t inclusive of both slippage and borrow/financing cost as follows:

$$c_t := \text{slip}_t + \mathit{fin}_t, \quad \text{where} \tag{12.29}$$

$$\text{slip}_t := \delta n_t \cdot (\widetilde{p}_t - p_t) \tag{12.30}$$

where fin_t denotes the commissions and financing costs incurred over the period, commissions are proportional to δn_t and financing costs are convex functions of the components of n_t. The component slip_t is called the *slippage cost*. Our conventions are such that $\mathit{fin}_t > 0$ always, and $\text{slip}_t > 0$ with high probability due to market impact and bid-offer spreads.

12.6 PORTFOLIO VALUE VERSUS WEALTH

Combining (12.29),(12.30) with (12.28) we have finally

$$\delta v_t = h_{t-1} \cdot r_t - c_t \tag{12.31}$$

If we could liquidate the portfolio at the midpoint price vector p_t, then v_t would represent the total wealth at time t associated to the trading strategy under consideration. Due to slippage it is unreasonable to expect that a portfolio can be liquidated at prices p_t, which gives rise to costs of the form (12.30).

Concretely, $v_t = \text{nav}_t + \text{cash}_t$ has a cash portion and a non-cash portion. The cash portion is already in units of wealth, while the non-cash portion $\text{nav}_t = n_t \cdot p_t$ could be converted to cash if a cost were paid; that cost is known as *liquidation slippage*:

$$\text{liqslip}_t := -n_t \cdot (\widetilde{p}_t - p_t)$$

Hence it is the formula for slippage, but with $\delta n_t = -n_t$. Note that liquidation is relevant at most once per episode, meaning the liquidation slippage should be charged at most once, after the final time T.

To summarize, we may identify v_t with the wealth process w_t as long as we are willing to add a single term of the form

$$E[\text{liqslip}_T] \tag{12.32}$$

to the multi-period objective. If T is large and the strategy is profitable, or if the portfolio is small compared with the typical daily trading volume, then $\text{liqslip}_T \ll v_T$ and (12.32) can be neglected without much influence on the resulting policy. In what follows, for simplicity we identify v_t with total wealth w_t.

12.7 A DETAILED EXAMPLE

Formulating an intelligent behaviour as a reinforcement learning problem begins with identification of the state space S and the action space A. The state variable s_t is a data structure which, simply put, must contain everything the agent needs to make a trading decision, and nothing else. The values of any alpha forecasts or trading signals must be part of the state, because if they aren't, the agent can't use them.

Variables that are good candidates to include in the state:

1. The current position or holding.
2. The values of any signals which are believed to be predictive.
3. The current state of the market microstructure (i.e. the limit order book), so that the agent may decide how best to execute.

In trading problems, the most obvious choice for an action is the number of shares to trade, δn_t, with sell orders corresponding to $\delta n_t < 0$. In some markets there is an advantage to trading round lots, which constrains the possible actions to a coarser lattice. If the agent's interaction with the market microstructure is important, there will typically be more choices to make, and hence a larger action space. For example, the agent could decide which execution algorithm to use, whether to cross the spread or be passive, target participation rate, etc.

We now discuss how the reward is observed during the trading process. Immediately before time t, the agent observes the state p_t and decides an action, which is a trade list δn_t in units of shares. The agent submits this trade list to an execution system and then can do nothing until just before $t+1$.

The agent waits one period and observes the reward

$$R_{t+1} \approx \delta v_{t+1} - \frac{k}{2}(\delta v_{t+1})^2. \tag{12.33}$$

The goal of reinforcement learning in this context is that the agent will learn how to maximize the cumulative reward, i.e. the sum of (12.33) which approximates the mean-variance form $E[\delta v] - (\kappa/2)V[\delta v]$.

For this example, assume that there exists a tradable security with a strictly positive price process $p_t > 0$. (This 'security' could itself be a portfolio of other securities, such as an ETF or a hedged relative-value trade.)

Further suppose that there is some 'equilibrium price' p_e such that $x_t = \log(p_t/p_e)$ has dynamics

$$dx_t = -\lambda x_t + \sigma \, \xi_t \tag{12.34}$$

where $\xi_t \sim N(0,1)$ and ξ_t, ξ_s are independent when $t\,6 = s$. This means that p_t tends to revert to its long-run equilibrium level p_e with mean-reversion rate λ. These assumptions imply something similar to an arbitrage! Positions taken in the appropriate direction while very far from equilibrium have very small probability of loss and extremely asymmetric loss-gain profiles.

For this exercise, the parameters of the dynamics (12.34) were taken to be $\lambda = \log(2)/H$, where $H = 5$ is the half-life, $\sigma = 0.1$ and the equilibrium price is $p_e = 50$.

All realistic trading systems have limits which bound their behaviour. For this example we use a reduced space of actions, in which the trade size δn_t in a single interval is limited to at most K round lots, where a 'round lot' is usually 100 shares (most institutional equity trades are in integer multiples of round lots). Also we assume a maximum position size of M round lots. Consequently, the space of possible trades, and also the action space, is

$$A = \text{LotSize} \cdot \{-K, -K + 1, \ldots, K\}$$

Letting H denote the possible values for the holding n_t, then similarly

$$H = \{-M, -M + 1, \ldots, M\}.$$

For the examples below, we take $K = 5$ and $M = 10$.

Another feature of real markets is the *tick size*, defined as a small price increment (such as US\$0.01) such that all quoted prices (i.e. all bids and offers) are integer multiples of the tick size. Tick sizes exist in order to balance price priority and time priority. This is convenient for us since we want to construct a discrete model anyway. We use TickSize = 0.1 for our example.

We choose boundaries of the (finite) space of possible prices so that sample paths of the process (12.34) exit the space with vanishingly small probability. With the parameters as above, the probability that the price path ever exits the region [0.1, 100] is small enough that no aspect of the problem depends on these bounds.

Concretely, the space of possible prices is:

$$P = \text{TickSize} \cdot \{1, 2, \ldots, 1000\} \subset R+$$

We do not allow the agent, initially, to know anything about the dynamics. Hence, the agent does not know λ, σ, or even that some dynamics of the form (12.34) are valid.

The agent also does not know the trading cost. We charge a spread cost of one tick size for any trade. If the bid-offer spread were equal to two ticks, then this fixed cost would correspond to the slippage incurred by an aggressive fill which crosses the spread to execute. If the spread is only one tick, then our choice is overly conservative. Hence

$$\text{SpreadCost}(\delta n) = \text{TickSize} \cdot |\delta n| \qquad (12.35)$$

We also assume that there is permanent price impact which has a linear functional form: each round lot traded is assumed to move the price one tick, hence leading to a dollar cost $|\delta n_t| \times \text{TickSize}/\text{LotSize}$ per share traded, for a total dollar cost for all shares

$$\text{ImpactCost}(\delta n) = (\delta n)^2 \times \text{TickSize}/\text{LotSize}. \qquad (12.36)$$

The total cost is the sum

$$\text{SpreadCost}(\delta n) + \text{ImpactCost}(\delta n)$$

$$= \text{TickSize} \cdot |\delta n| + (\delta n)^2 \times \text{TickSize}/\text{LotSize}.$$

Our claim is not that these are the exact cost functions for the world we live in, although the functional form does make some sense.

The state of the environment $s_t = (p_t, n_{t-1})$ will contain the security prices p_t, and the agent's position, in shares, coming into the period: n_{t-1}. Therefore the state space is the Cartesian product $S = H \times P$. The agent then chooses an action

$$a_t = \delta n_t \in A$$

which changes the position to $n_t = n_{t-1} + \delta n_t$ and observes a profit/loss equal to

$$\delta vt = nt(pt + 1 - pt) - ct$$

and a reward

$$R_{t+1} = \delta v_{t+1} - \frac{1}{2}k(\delta v_{t+1})^2$$

as in Eq. (12.33).

We train the Q-learner by repeatedly applying the update procedure involving (12.9). The system has various parameters which control the learning rate, discount rate, risk aversion, etc. For completeness, the parameter values used in the following example were: $k = 10^{-4}$, $\gamma = 0.999$, $\alpha = 0.001$, $\varepsilon = 0.1$. We use $n_{train} = 10^7$ training steps (each 'training step' consists of one action-value update as per (12.9)) and then evaluate the system on 5000 new samples of the stochastic process (see Figure 12.2).

The excellent performance out-of-sample should perhaps be expected; the assumption of an Ornstein-Uhlenbeck process implies a near arbitrage in the system. When the price is too far out of equilibrium, a trade betting that it returns to equilibrium has a very small probability of a loss. With our parameter settings, even after costs this is

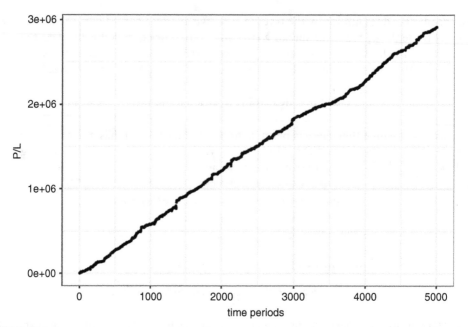

FIGURE 12.2   Cumulative simulated out-of-sample P/L of trained model. Simulated net P/L over 5000 out–of–sample periods.

true. Hence the *existence* of an arbitrage-like trading strategy in this idealized world is not surprising, and perfect mean-reverting processes such as (12.34) need not exist in real markets.

Rather, the surprising point is that the Q-learner does not, at least initially, know that there is mean-reversion in asset prices, nor does it know anything about the cost of trading. At no point does it compute estimates for the parameters λ, σ. It learns to maximize expected utility in a model-free context, i.e. directly from rewards rather than indirectly (using a model).

We have also verified that expected utility maximization achieves a much higher out-of-sample Sharpe ratio than expected-profit maximization. Understanding of this principle dates back at least to 1713 when Bernoulli pointed out that a wealth-maximizing investor behaves nonsensically when faced with gambling based on a martingale (see Bernoulli (1954) for a recent translation).

12.7.1   Simulation-based approaches

A major drawback of the procedure we have presented here is that it requires a large number of training steps (a few million, on the problem we presented). There are, of course, financial datasets with millions of time-steps (e.g. high-frequency data sampled once per second for several years), but in other cases, a different approach is needed. Even in high-frequency examples, one may not wish to use several years' worth of data to train the model.

Fortunately, a simulation-based approach presents an attractive resolution to these issues. We propose a multi-step training procedure:

1. Posit a reasonably parsimonious stochastic process model for asset returns with relatively few parameters.
2. Estimate the parameters of the model from market data, ensuring reasonably small confidence intervals for the parameter estimates.
3. Use the model to simulate a much larger dataset than the real world presents.
4. Train the reinforcement-learning system on the simulated data.

For the model $dx_t = -\lambda x_t + \sigma \, \xi_t$, this amounts to estimating λ, σ from market data, which meets the criteria of a parsimonious model.

The 'holy grail' would be a fully realistic simulator of how the market microstructure will respond to various order-placement strategies. In order to be maximally useful, such a simulator should be able to accurately represent the market impact caused by trading too aggressively.

With these two components – a random-process model of asset returns and a good microstructure simulator – one may generate a training dataset of arbitrarily large size. The learning procedure is then only partially model-free: it requires a model for asset returns but no explicit functional form to model trading costs. The 'trading cost model' in this case would be provided by the market microstructure simulator, which arguably presents a much more detailed picture than trying to distil trading costs down into a single function.

We remark that automatic generation of training data is a key component of AlphaGo Zero (Silver et al. 2017), which was trained primarily by means of self-play – effectively using previous versions of itself as a simulator. Whether or not a simulator is used to train, the search continues for training methods which converge to a desired level of performance in fewer time-steps. In situations where all of the training data is real market data, the number of time-steps is fixed, after all.

12.8 CONCLUSIONS AND FURTHER WORK

In the present chapter, we have seen that reinforcement learning concerns the search for good value functions (and hence, good policies). In almost every subfield of finance, this kind of model of optimal behaviour is fundamental. For examples, most of the classic works on market microstructure theory (Glosten and Milgrom 1985; Copeland and Galai 1983; Kyle 1985) model both the dealer and the informed trader as optimizing their cumulative monetary reward over time. In many cases the cited authors assume the dealer simply trades to maximize expected profit (i.e. is risk-neutral). In reality, no trader is risk-neutral, but if the risk is controlled in some other way (e.g. strict inventory controls) and the risk is very small compared to the premium the dealer earns for their market-making activities, then risk-neutrality may be a good approximation.

Recent approaches to multi-period optimization (Gârleanu and Pedersen 2013; Kolm and Ritter 2015; Benveniste and Ritter 2017; Boyd et al. 2017) all follow value-function approaches based around Bellman optimality.

Option pricing is based on dynamic hedging, which amounts to minimizing variance over the lifetime of the option: variance of a portfolio in which the option is hedged with the replicating portfolio. With transaction costs, one actually needs to solve this multi-period optimization rather than simply looking at the current option Greeks. For some related work, see Halperin (2017).

Therefore, we believe that the search for and use of good value functions is perhaps one of the most fundamental problems in finance, spanning a wide range of fields from microstructure to derivative pricing and hedging. Reinforcement learning, broadly defined, is the study of how to solve these problems on a computer; as such, it is fundamental as well.

An interesting arena for further research takes inspiration from classical physics. Newtonian dynamics represent the greedy policy with respect to an action-value function known as *Hamilton's principal function*. Optimal execution problems for portfolios with large numbers (thousands) of assets are perhaps best treated by viewing them as special cases of Hamiltonian dynamics, as showed by Benveniste and Ritter (2017). The approach in Benveniste and Ritter (2017) can also be viewed as a special case of the framework above; one of the key ideas there is to use a functional method related to gradient descent with regard to the value function. Remarkably, even though it starts with continuous paths, the approach in Benveniste and Ritter (2017) generalizes to treat market microstructure, where the action space is always finite.

Anecdotally, it seems that several of the more sophisticiated algorithmic execution desks at large investment banks are beginning to use reinforcement learning to optimize their decision making on short timescales. This seems very natural; after all, reinforcement learning provides a natural way to deal with the discrete action spaces presented by limit order books which are rich in structure, nuanced and very discrete. The classic work on optimal execution, Almgren and Chriss (1999), does not actually specify how to interact with the order book.

If one considers the science of trading to be split into (1) large-scale portfolio allocation decisions involving thousands of assets and (2) the theory of market microstructure and optimal execution, then both kinds of problems can be unified under the framework of optimal control theory (perhaps stochastic). The main difference is that in problem (2), the discreteness of trading is of primary importance: in a double-auction electronic limit order book, there are only a few price levels at which one would typically transact at any instant (e.g. the bid and the offer, or conceivably nearby quotes) and only a limited number of shares would transact at once. In large-scale portfolio allocation decisions, modelling portfolio holdings as continuous (e.g. vectors in R^n) usually suffices.

Reinforcement learning handles discreteness beautifully. Relatively small, finite action spaces such as those in the games of Go, chess and Atari represent areas where reinforcement learning has achieved superhuman performance. Looking ahead to the next 10 years, we therefore predict that among the two research areas listed above, although reward functions like (12.24) apply equally well in either case, it is in the areas of market microstructure and optimal execution that reinforcement learning will be most useful.

REFERENCES

Almgren, R. and Chriss, N. (1999). Value under liquidation. *Risk* 12 (12): 61–63.

Arrow, K.J. (1971). *Essays in the Theory of Risk-Bearing*. North-Holland, Amsterdam.

Baird, L.C. III and Moore, A.W. (1999). Gradient descent for general reinforcement learning. *Advances in Neural Information Processing Systems* 968–974.

Bellman, R. (1957). *Dynamic Programming*. Princeton University Press.

Benveniste, E.J. and Ritter, G. (2017). Optimal microstructure trading with a long-term utility function. https://ssrn.com/abstract=3057570.

Bernoulli, D. (1954). Exposition of a new theory on the measurement of risk. *Econometrica: Journal of the Econometric Society* 22 (1): 23–36.

Bottou, L. (2012). Stochastic gradient descent tricks. In: *Neural Networks: Tricks of the Trade*, 421–436. Springer.

Boyd, S. et al. (2017). Multi-Period Trading via Convex Optimization. *arXiv preprint arXiv:1705.00109*.

Copeland, T.E. and Galai, D. (1983). Information effects on the bid-ask spread. *The Journal of Finance* 38 (5): 1457–1469.

Feldstein, M.S. (1969). Mean-variance analysis in the theory of liquidity preference and portfolio selection. *The Review of Economic Studies* 36 (1): 5–12.

Gârleanu, N. and Pedersen, L.H. (2013). Dynamic trading with predictable returns and transaction costs. *The Journal of Finance* 68 (6): 2309–2340.

Glosten, L.R. and Milgrom, P.R. (1985). Bid, ask and transaction prices in a specialist market with heterogeneously informed traders. *Journal of Financial Economics* 14 (1): 71–100.

Halperin, I. (2017). QLBS: Q-Learner in the Black-Scholes (–Merton) Worlds. *arXiv preprint arXiv:1712.04609*.

Hasbrouck, J. (2007). *Empirical Market Microstructure*, vol. 250. New York: Oxford University Press.

Kingma, D. and Ba, J. (2014). Adam: A method for stochastic optimization. *arXiv preprint arXiv:1412.6980*.

Kolm, P.N. and Ritter, G. (2015). Multiperiod portfolio selection and bayesian dynamic models. *Risk* 28 (3): 50–54.

Kyle, A.S. (1985). Continuous auctions and insider trading. *Econometrica: Journal of the Econometric Society* 53 (6): 1315–1335.

Mnih, V. et al. (2015). Human-level control through deep reinforcement learning. *Nature* 518 (7540): 529.

Pratt, J.W. (1964). Risk aversion in the small and in the large. *Econometrica: Journal of the Econometric Society* 32 (1–2): 122–136.

Ritter, G. (2017). Machine learning for trading. *Risk* 30 (10): 84–89. https://ssrn.com/abstract=3015609.

Robbins, H. and Siegmund, D. (1985). A convergence theorem for non negative almost supermartingales and some applications. In: *Herbert Robbins Selected Papers*, 111–135. Springer.

Silver, D. et al. (2017). Mastering the game of go without human knowledge. *Nature* 550 (7676): 354–359.

Sutton, R.S. and Barto, A.G. (1998). *Reinforcement Learning: An Introduction*. Cambridge: MIT Press.

Sutton, R.S. and Barto, A.G. (2018). *Reinforcement Learning: An Introduction*. Second edition, in progress. Cambridge: MIT Press http://incompleteideas.net/book/bookdraft2018jan1.pdf.

Tobin, J. (1958). Liquidity preference as behavior towards risk. *The Review of Economic Studies* 25 (2): 65–86.

Von Neumann, J. and Morgenstern, O. (1945). *Theory of Games and Economic Behavior*. Princeton, NJ: Princeton University Press.

Watkins, C.J.C.H. (1989). Q-learning. *PhD Thesis*.

Deep Learning in Finance: Prediction of Stock Returns with Long Short-Term Memory Networks

Miquel N. Alonso, Gilberto Batres-Estrada and Aymeric Moulin

13.1   INTRODUCTION

Recurrent neural networks are models that capture sequential order and therefore are often used for processing sequential data. RNNs are powerful models due to their ability to scale too much longer sequences than would be possible for regular neural networks. They suffer from two serious problems: the first has to do with vanishing gradients and the second with exploding gradients (Graves 2012; Hochreiter and Schmidhuber 1997; Sutskever 2013). Both of these are solved by the LSTM. In recent years LSTMs have solved many problems in speech recognition and machine translation, where the goal is often to match an input series to an output series. The LSTM network can be used to solve both classification and regression problems. There are two important things that distinguish these two domains in machine learning. The first is the type of the output, where in regression it takes values in the real numbers, whereas in classification it takes values in a discrete set. The second is the type of cost function used during training.

The chapter is ordered as follows. Section 13.2 presents related work on the subject of finance and deep learning, Section 13.3 discusses time series analysis in finance. Section 13.4 introduces deep learning in general, Section 13.5 covers RNNs, its building blocks and methods of training. Section 13.6 describes LSTM networks, Section 13.7 covers the financial problem we try to solve with LSTM, the data used and methods. In the same section we present the results. Section 13.8 concludes.

13.2   RELATED WORK

For many years there was little research on finance and neural networks, especially using RNNs. Recently some very interesting papers have been published on the subject, for instance Lee and Yoo (2017) study the construction of portfolios and focus on

10 stocks to trade. They achieve good results constructing portfolios that exhibit a consistent risk-return profile at various threshold levels. Their LSTM has a hidden layer with 100 hidden units. Fischer and Krauss (n.d.) make an exhaustive study comparing many machine learning algorithms and showing that LSTMs outperform the other models in the study. They take a look at the whole S&P 500 list. According to their results, they achieve a return of 0.23% per day, prior to transaction costs.

13.3 TIME SERIES ANALYSIS IN FINANCE

An asset return (e.g. log return of a stock) can be considered as a collection of random variables over time. Then this random variable r_t is a time series. Linear time series analysis provides a natural framework to study the dynamic structure of such a series. The theories of linear time series include stationarity, dynamic dependence, autocorrelation function, modelling and forecasting.

The standard econometric models include autoregressive (AR) models, moving average (MA) models, mixed autoregressive moving average (ARMA) models, seasonal models, unit-root nonstationarity, regression models with time series errors, and fractionally differenced models for long-range dependence.

For an asset return r_t, simple models attempt to capture the linear relationship between r_t and information available prior to time t. The information may contain the historical values of r_t and the random vector Y, which describes the economic environment under which the asset price is determined. As such, correlation plays an important role in understanding these models. In particular, correlations between the variable of interest and its past values become the focus of linear time series analysis. These correlations are referred to as serial correlations or autocorrelations. They are the basic tools for studying a stationary time series. For example, Box–Jenkins ARIMA makes use of underlying information in terms of the lagged variable itself and errors in the past; GARCH can capture the volatility clustering of stock returns. Also, there are many other derivative models like nonlinear GARCH (NGARCH), integrated GARCH (IGARCH), exponential GARCH (EGARCH) which can perform well in situations with different settings (Qian n.d.).

13.3.1 Multivariate time series analysis

One of the most important areas of financial modelling is the modelling of multivariate time series analysis. We have several modelling choices:

- Multivariate distributions.
- Copulas: mainly for risk management and regulatory purposes.
- Factor models: widely used for prediction, interpretation, dimension reduction, estimation, risk and performance attribution.
- Multivariate time series models.

Vector autoregression (VAR) models are one of the most widely used family of multivariate time series statistical approaches. These models have been applied in a wide variety of applications, ranging from describing the behaviour of economic and financial time series to modelling dynamical systems and estimating brain function connectivity.

VAR models show good performance in modelling financial data and detecting various types of anomalies, outperforming the existing state-of-the-art approaches. The basic multivariate time series models based on linear autoregressive, moving average models are:

Vector autoregression VAR(p)

$$y^t = c + \sum_{i=1}^{p} \Phi_i y_{t-i} + \varepsilon_t$$

Vector moving average VMA(q)

$$y^t = c + \sum_{j=1}^{q} \Theta_j \varepsilon_{t-j} + \varepsilon_t$$

Vector autoregression moving average VARMA (p, q)

$$y^t = c + \sum_{i=1}^{p} \Phi_i y_{t-i} + \sum_{j=1}^{q} \Theta_j \varepsilon_{t-j} + \varepsilon_t$$

Vector autoregression moving average with a linear time trend VARMAL(p, q)

$$y^t = c + \delta t + \sum_{i=1}^{p} \Phi_i y_{t-i} + \sum_{j=1}^{q} \Theta_j \varepsilon_{t-j} + \varepsilon_t$$

Vector autoregression moving average with exogenous inputs VARMAX(p, q)

$$y^t = c + \beta x_t + \sum_{i=1}^{p} \Phi_i y_{t-i} + \sum_{j=1}^{q} \Theta_j \varepsilon_{t-j} + \varepsilon_t$$

Structural vector autoregression moving average SVARMA(p, q)

$$\Phi_0 y_t = c + \beta x_t + \sum_{i=1}^{p} \Phi_i y_{t-i} + \sum_{j=1}^{q} \Theta_j \varepsilon_{t-j} + \Theta_0 \varepsilon_t$$

The following variables appear in the equations:

- y_t is the vector of response time series variables at time t. y_t has n elements.
- c is a constant vector of offsets, with n elements.
- Φ_i are n-by-n matrices for each i, where Φ_i are autoregressive matrices. There are p autoregressive matrices and some can be entirely composed of zeros.
- ε_t is a vector of serially uncorrelated innovations, vectors of length n. The $_t$ are multivariate normal random vectors with a covariance matrix Σ.
- Θ_j are n-by-n matrices for each j, where Θ_j are moving average matrices. There are q moving average matrices and some can be entirely composed of zeros.
- δ is a constant vector of linear time trend coefficients, with n elements.

- x_t is an r-by-1 vector representing exogenous terms at each time t and r is the number of exogenous series. Exogenous terms are data (or other unmodelled inputs) in addition to the response time series y_t. Each exogenous series appears in all response equations.
- β is an n-by-r constant matrix of regression coefficients of size r. So the product βx_t is a vector of size n.

LSTMs provide a very interesting non-linear version of these standard models. This paper uses multivariate LSTMs with exogenous variables in a stock picking prediction context in experiment 2.

13.3.2   Machine learning models in finance

Machine learning models have gained momentum in finance applications over the past five years following the tremendous success in areas like image recognition and natural language processing. These models have proven to be very useful to model unstructured data. In addition to that, machine learning models are able to model flexibly non-linearity in classification and regression problems and discover hidden structure in supervised learning. Combinations of weak learners like XGBoost and AdaBoost are especially popular. Unsupervised learning is a branch of machine learning used to draw inferences from datasets consisting of input data without labelled responses – principal component analysis is an example. The challenges of using machine learning in finance are important as, like other models, it needs to deal with estimation risk, potentially non-stationarity, overfitting and in some cases interpretability issues.

13.4   DEEP LEARNING

Deep learning is a popular area of research in machine learning, partly because it has achieved big success in artificial intelligence, in the areas of computer vision, natural language processing, machine translation and speech recognition, and partly because now it is possible to build applications based on deep learning. Everyday applications based on deep learning are recommendation systems, voice assistants and search engine technology based on computer vision, to name just a few. This success has been possible thanks to the amount of data, which today is referred to as big data, now available and the possibility to perform computation much faster than ever before. Today it is possible to port computation from the computer's central processing unit (CPU) to its graphical processing unit (GPU). Another approach is to move computations to clusters of computers in local networks or in the cloud.

The term deep learning is used to describe the activity of training deep neural networks. There are many different types of architectures and different methods for training these models. The most common network is the feed-forward neural network (FNN) used for data that is assumed to be independent and identical distributed (i.i.d.). RNNs, meanwhile, are more suitable for sequential data, such as time series, speech data, natural language data (Bengio et al. n.d.) and other data where the assumption of i.i.d. is not fulfilled. In deep learning, the main task is to learn or approximate some function f that maps inputs x to outputs y. Deep learning tries to solve the following learning problem $\hat{y} = f(\theta;x)$ where x is the input to the neural network, $\hat{y}$ is its output and θ is a set of parameters that gives the best fit of f. In regression, $\hat{y}$ would be represented by real numbers whereas in classification it would be represented by probabilities assigned to each class in a discrete set of values.

13.4.1 Deep learning and time series

Time series models in finance need to deal with autocorrelation, volatility clustering, non-Gaussianity, and possibly cycles and regimes. Deep learning and RNNs in particular can help model these stylized facts. On this account, an RNN is a more flexible model, since it encodes the temporal context in its feedback connections, which are capable of capturing the time varying dynamics of the underlying system (Bianchi et al. n.d.; Schäfer and Zimmermann 2007). RNNs are a special class of neural networks characterized by internal self-connections which in principle can approximate or model any nonlinear dynamical system, up to a given degree of accuracy.

13.5 RECURRENT NEURAL NETWORKS

13.5.1 Introduction

RNNs are suitable for processing sequences, where the input might be a sequence $(x_1, x_2, \ldots, x_T)$ with each datapoint x_t being a real valued vector or a scalar value. The target signal $(y_1, y_2, \ldots, y_T)$ can also be a sequence or a scalar value. The RNN architecture is different from that of a classical neural network. It has a recurrent connection or feedback with a time delay. The recurrent connections represent the internal states that encode the history of the sequence processed by the RNN (Yu and Deng 2015). The feedback can be implemented in many ways. Some common examples of the architecture of RNNs are taking the output from the hidden layer and feeding it back to the hidden layer together with new arriving input. Another form of recurrent feedback is taking the output signal from the network at time step $t-1$ and feeding it as new input together with new input at time step t (Goodfellow et al. 2016).

An RNN has a deep architecture when unfolding it in time (Figure 13.1), where its depth is as long as the temporal input to the network. This type of depth is different from a regular deep neural network, where depth is achieved by stacking layers of hidden units on top of each other. In a sense, RNNs can be considered to have depth in both time and feature space, where depth in feature space is achieved by stacking layers of hidden units on top of each other. There even exist multidimensional RNNs suitable for video processing, medical imaging and other multidimensional sequential data (Graves 2012). RNNs have been successful for modelling variable length sequences, such as language modelling (Graves 2012; Sutskever 2013), learning word embeddings (Mokolov et al. 2013) and speech recognition (Graves 2012).

13.5.2 Elman recurrent neural network

The Elman recurrent neural network (ERNN), also known as simple RNN or vanilla RNN, is considered to be the most basic version of RNN. Most of the more complex

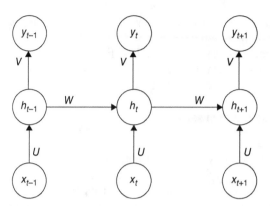

FIGURE 13.1   Recurrent neural network unrolled in time.

RNN architectures, such as LSTM and gated recurrent units (GRUs), can be interpreted as a variation or as an extension of ERNNs. ERNNs have been applied in many different contexts. In natural language processing applications, ERNNs demonstrated to be capable of learning grammar using a training set of unannotated sentences to predict successive words in the sentence (Elman 1995; Ogata et al. 2007). Mori and Ogasawara (1993) studied ERNN performance in short-term load forecasting and proposed a learning method, called 'diffusion learning' (a sort of momentum-based gradient descent), to avoid local minima during the optimization procedure. Cai et al. (2007) trained an ERNN with a hybrid algorithm that combines particle swarm optimization and evolutionary computation to overcome the local minima issues of gradient-based methods.

The layers in an RNN can be divided in an input layer, one or more hidden layers and an output layer. While input and output layers are characterized by feed-forward connections, the hidden layers contain recurrent ones. At each time step t, the input layer process the component $x[t] \in R^{N_i}$ of a serial input x. The time series x has length T and it can contain real values, discrete values, one-hot vectors and so on. In the input layer, each component $x[t]$ is summed with a bias vector $b[i] \in R^{N_h}$, where N_h is the number of nodes in the hidden layer, and then is multiplied with the input weight matrix $W_i^h \in R^{N_h \times N_h}$.

The internal state of the network $h[t-1] \in R^{N_h}$ from the previous time interval is first summed with a bias vector $b \in R^{N_h}$ and then multiplied by the weight matrix $W_h^h \in R^{N_h \times N_h}$ of the recurrent connections. The transformed current input and past network state are then combined and processed by the neurons in the hidden layers, which apply a non-linear transformation. The difference equations for the update of the internal state and the output of the network at a time step t are:

$$h(t) = f(W_i^h(x(t) + b_i) + W_i^h(h(t-1) + b_h)) \qquad (13.1)$$

$$y(t) = g(W_i^o h(t) + b_o) \qquad (13.2)$$

where $f(\cdot)$ is the activation function of the neurons, usually implemented by a sigmoid or by a hyperbolic tangent. The hidden state $h[t]$, which conveys the content of the memory of the network at time step t, is typically initialized with a vector of zeros and it depends on past network states and inputs. The output $y[t] \in R^{N_o}$ is computed through a transformation $g(\cdot)$, usually linear in a regression setting or non-linear for classification problems using the matrix of the output weights $W_h{}^o \in R^{N_T \times N_o}$ applied to the current state $h[t]$ and the bias vector $b_o \in R^{N_o}$. All the weight matrices and biases can be trained through gradient descent, with the back-propagation through time (BPPT) procedure. Unless differently specified, in the following to compact the notation we omit the bias terms by assuming $x = [x;1]$, $h = [h;1]$, $y = [y;1]$ and by augmenting W_i^h, W_h^h, $W_h{}^o$ with an additional column.

13.5.3 Activation function

Activation functions are used in neural networks to transform the input of a neural network, expressed as a linear combination of weights and bias, to an output in feature space

$$h = g(W^T x + b)$$

where T denotes the transpose of the weight matrix. In the forward pass these transformations are propagated forward and eventually reach the last layer of the network and become the output of the whole network. This transformation is what makes neural networks learn nonlinear functions. The rectified linear unit (ReLu) (Figure 13.2) is the most common type of hidden unit used in modern neural networks (Goodfellow et al. 2016). It is defined as $g(z) = \max\{0,z\}$.

Another activation function is the logistic sigmoid, $\sigma(x) = (1 + \exp.(-x))^{-1}$, which is a differentiable squashing function (see Figure 13.2). One of its drawbacks is that

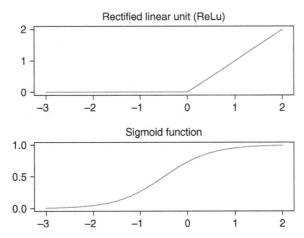

FIGURE 13.2 The rectified linear unit (ReLu) and sigmoid functions.

learning becomes slow due to saturations when its argument either becomes too negative or when it becomes too big. Nowadays its use is discouraged, especially in feed-forward neural networks (Goodfellow et al. 2016). In RNNs the logistic sigmoid can be used as hidden as well as output units. The $\tanh(x)$ is very similar to the sigmoid but with a range in the interval $(-1,1)$. It is employed as an activation function in all types of neural networks: FNN, RNN, LSTM.

13.5.4 Training recurrent neural networks

We start this section with a short introduction to the training procedure of an RNN. In order to train an RNN, we need to compute the cost function in the forward pass. Then we back-propagate the errors committed by the network and use those errors to optimize the parameters of the model, with gradient descent.

The algorithm used to compute the gradients, in the context of RNNs, is called Backpropagation Through Time (BPTT). We introduce the loss and cost functions, then we show how the parameters of the model are updated and finally we present the BPTT algorithm.

13.5.5 Loss function

The loss function measures the discrepancy between the predictions made by the neural network and the target signal in the training data. To assess whether our model is learning we compute the cost (see below) during training and test its generalization power on a test set not seen by the model during training. Depending on the prediction task on which we want to apply our RNN, there are several loss functions to choose from. In what follows we make use of the following definitions. Let y be the target signal and $f(x,\theta)$ the output from the network. Then for a binary classification task the target belongs to the set $y = \{0,1\}$. In this case the loss function is given by (Bishop 2006):

$$L(y, f(x, \theta)) = - \sum_{i=1}^{n} yn \log fn + (1 - yn) \log(1 - fn).$$

Its derivation is as follows. An outcome from a binary classification problem is described by a Bernoulli distribution $p(y \mid x, \theta) = f(x, \theta)^y (1 - f(x, \theta))^{1-y}$. Taking the natural logarithm on the Bernoulli distribution gives a likelihood function, which in this case is equal to the cost function, giving the stated result. In this case the output is given by $f = \sigma(a) = (1 + \exp(-a))^{-1}$ satisfying $0 \le f(x,\theta) \le 1$. For multi-class classification we often use the loss function

$$L(yf(x, \theta)) = \sum_{n=1}^{N} \sum_{k=1}^{K} -ykn \log fk(xn, \theta)$$

where the output of our model is given by the softmax function

$$f_k(x, \theta) = \frac{\exp(a_k(x, \theta))}{\sum_j \exp(a_j(x, \theta))}$$

subject to the conditions $0 \leq f_k \leq 1$ and $P_k\, f_k = 1$. In regression estimation tasks we make use of the mean-squared error as the loss function (Bishop 2006)

$$L(y, f(x, \theta)) = \frac{1}{2} \sum_{n=1}^{N} \| f_n (x_n, \theta) - y_n \|^2$$

where f_n is the output of the network, x_n are input vectors, with $n = 1, \dots, N$, and y_n are the corresponding target vectors. In unsupervised learning, one of the main tasks is that of finding the density $p(x,\theta)$ from a set of densities such that we minimize the loss function (Vapnik 2000)

$$L(p(x, \theta)) = - \log p(x, \theta).$$

13.5.6 Cost function

Learning is achieved by minimizing the empirical risk. The principle of risk minimization can be defined as follows (Vapnik 2000). Define the loss function $L(y,(x,\theta))$ as the discrepancy between the learning machine's output and the target signal y. The risk functional or cost function is then defined as

$$J(\theta) = \int L(y, f(x, \theta)) \mathrm{d}F(x, y)$$

where $F(x,y)$ is a joint probability distribution. The machine learning algorithm then has to find the best function f that minimizes the cost function. In practice, we have to rely on minimizing the empirical risk due to the fact that the joint distribution is unknown for the data generating process (Goodfellow et al. 2016). The empirical cost function is given by

$$\mathbb{E}_{x,y \sim \hat{p}(x,y)}[L(f(x, \theta), y)] = \frac{1}{m} \sum_{i=1}^{m} L(f(x^{(i)}, \theta), y^{(i)})$$

where the expectation, E, is taken over the empirical data distribution $\hat{p}(x,y)$.

13.5.7 Gradient descent

To train RNNs we make use of gradient descent, an algorithm for finding the optimal point of the cost function or objective function, as it is also called. The objective function is a measure of how well the model compares to the real target. For computing gradient descent we need to compute the derivatives of the cost function with respect to the parameters. This can be achieved, for training RNNs, by employing BPTT, shown later in this section. As stated before, we are going to ignore the derivations for the bias terms. Similar identities can be obtained from the ones for the weights.

The name *gradient descent* refers to the fact that the updating rule for the weights chooses to take its next step in the direction of steepest gradient in weight space. To understand what this means, let us think of the loss function $J(w)$ as a surface spanned by the weights w. When we take a small step $w + \delta w$ away from w, the loss function changes as $\delta J \simeq \delta w^T \Delta J(w)$. Then the vector $\Delta J(w)$ points in the direction of greatest rate of change (Bishop 2006). Optimization amounts to finding the optimal point where the following condition holds:

$$\Delta J(w) = 0.$$

If at iteration n we don't find the optimal point, we can continue downhill the surface spanned by w in the direction $-\Delta J(w)$, reducing the loss function until we eventually find the optimal point. In the context of deep learning, it is very difficult to find a unique global optimal point. The reason is that the deep neural networks used in deep learning are compositions of functions of the input, the weights and the biases. This function composition spanning many layers of hidden units makes the cost function to be a nonlinear function of the weights and biases, thus leaving us with a non-convex optimization problem. Gradient descent is given by

$$w(t + 1) = w(t) - \eta \Delta J(w(t))$$

where η is the learning rate. In this form, gradient descent processes all the data at once to do an update of the weights. This form of learning is called *batch learning* and refers to the fact that the whole training set is used at each iteration for updating the parameters (Bishop 2006; Haykin 2009). Batch learning is discouraged (Bishop 2006, p. 240) for gradient descent as there are better batch optimization methods, such as conjugate gradients or quasi-Newton methods (Bishop 2006). It is more appropriate to use gradient descent in its *online learning* version (Bishop 2006; Haykin 2009). This means simply that the parameters are updated using some portion of the data or a single point at a time after each iteration. The cost function takes the form

$$J(w) = \sum_{n=1}^{N} J_n(w)$$

where the sum runs over each data point. This leads to the *online* or *stochastic gradient descent* algorithm

$$w(t + 1) = w(t) - \eta \Delta J_n(w(t)).$$

Its name, stochastic gradient descent, derives from the fact that the update of parameters happens either one training example at a time or by choosing points at random with replacement (Bishop 2006).

13.5.7.1 Back-Propagation Through Time   The algorithm to compute the gradients used in gradient descent, in the case of the RNN, is called BPTT. It is similar to the regular back-propagation algorithm used to train regular FNNs. By unfolding the RNN in time we can compute the gradients by propagating the errors backward in time. Let us define the cost function as the sum of squared errors (Yu and Deng 2015):

$$J = \frac{1}{2} \sum_{t=1}^{T} \| \tau_t - y_t \|^2 = \frac{1}{2} \sum_{t=1}^{T} \sum_{j=1}^{L} (\tau_t(j) - y_t(j))^2$$

where τ_t represents the target signal and y_t the output from the RNN. The sum over the t variable runs over time steps $t = 1, t, \ldots, T$ and the sum over j runs over the j units. To further simplify notation let us redefine the equations of the RNN as:

$$h_t = f(W^T h_{t-1} + U^T x_t + b) \tag{13.3}$$

$$y_t = g(V^T h_t). \tag{13.4}$$

Employing the local potentials or activation potentials $u_t = W^T h_{t-1} + U^T x_t$ and $v_t = V^T h_t$, by way of Eqs. (13.3) and (13.4) and using $\theta = \{W, U, V\}$, we can define the errors (Yu and Deng 2015)

$$\delta_t^y(j) = -\frac{\partial J(\theta)}{\partial v_t(j)} \tag{13.5}$$

$$\delta_t^h(j) = -\frac{\partial J(\theta)}{\partial u_t(j)} \tag{13.6}$$

as the gradient of the cost function with respect to the units' potentials. The BPTT proceeds iteratively to compute the gradients over the time steps, $t = T$ down to $t = 1$. For the final time step we compute

$$\delta_T^y(j) = \frac{\partial J(\theta)}{\partial y_T(j)} \frac{\partial y_T(j)}{\partial v_T(j)} = (\tau_T(j) - y_T(j)) g_0'(v_T(j))$$

for the set of units $j = 1, 2, \ldots, L$. This error term can be expressed in vector notation as follows:

$$\delta_T^y = (\tau_T - y_T) \odot g_0'(v_T),$$

where is the element-wise Hadamard product between matrices. For the hidden layers we have:

$$\delta_T^h = -\sum_{i=1}^{L} \frac{\partial J}{\partial v_T(i)} \frac{\partial v_T(i)}{\partial h_T(i)} \frac{\partial h_T(j)}{\partial u_T(j)} = \sum_{i=1}^{L} \delta_T^y(i) v_{hy}(i, j) f'(u_T(j))$$

for $j = 1, 2, \ldots, N$. This expression can also be written in vector form as

$$\delta_T^h = V^T \delta_T^y \odot f'(u_T).$$

Iterating for all other time steps $t = T - 1, T - 2, \ldots, 1$ we can summarize the error for the output as:

$$\delta_t^y = (\tau_t - y_t) \odot g'(v_t),$$

for all units $j = 1, 2, \ldots, L$. Similarly, for the hidden units we can summarize the result as

$$\delta_t^h = (W^T \delta_{t+1}^h + V^T \delta_t^y) \odot f'(u_t)$$

where δ_t^y is propagated from the output layer at time t and δ_{t+1}^h is propagated back from the hidden layer at time step $t + 1$.

13.5.7.2 Regularization Theory Regularization theory for ill-posed problems tries to address the question of whether we can prevent our machine learning model from overfitting and therefore plays a big role in deep learning.

In the early 1900s it was discovered that solutions to linear operator equations of the form (Vapnik 2000)

$$Af = F$$

for a linear operator A and a set of functions $f \in \Gamma$, in an arbitrary function space Γ were ill-posed. That the above equation is ill-posed means that a small deviation like changing F by F_δ satisfying $kF - F_\delta k < \delta$ for δ arbitrary small leads $kf_\delta - fk$ to become large. In the expression for the functional $R(f) = kAf - F_\delta k^2$, if the functions f_δ minimize the functional $R(f)$, there is no guarantee that we find a good approximation to the right solution even if $\delta \to 0$.

Many problems in real life are ill-posed, e.g. when trying to reverse the cause-effect relations, a good example being to find unknown causes from known consequences. This problem is ill-posed even though it is a one-to-one mapping (Vapnik 2000). Another example is that of estimating the density function from data (Vapnik 2000). In the 1960s it was recognized that if one instead minimizes the regularized functional (Vapnik 2000)

$$R^*(f) = \|Af - F_\delta\|^2 + \gamma(\delta)\Omega(f),$$

where $\Omega(f)$ is a functional and $\gamma(\delta)$ is a constant, then we obtain a sequence of solutions that converges to the correct solution as $\delta \to 0$. In deep learning, the first term in the functional, $R^*(f)$, will be replaced by the cost function, whereas the regularization term depends on the set of parameters θ to be optimized. For L_1 regularization $\gamma(\delta)\Omega(f) = \lambda \sum_i^n |Wi|$ whereas for L_2 regularization, this term equals $\frac{\lambda}{2}\|W\|^2$ (see Bishop 2006; Friedman et al. n.d.).

13.5.7.3 Dropout Dropout is a type of regularization which prevents neural networks from overfitting (Srivastava et al. 2014). This type of regularization is also inexpensive (Goodfellow et al. 2016), especially when it comes to training neural networks. During training, dropout samples from an exponentially number of different thinned networks (Srivastava et al. 2014). At test time the model is an approximation of the average of all the predictions of all thinned networks only that it is a much smaller model with less weights than the networks used during training. If we have a network with L hidden layers, then $l \in \{1,\ldots,L\}$ is the index of each layer. If $z^{(l)}$ is the input to layer l, then $y^{(l)}$ is the output from that layer, with $y^{(0)} = x$ denoting the input to the network. Let $W^{(l)}$ denote the weights and $b^{(l)}$ denote the bias, then the network equations are given by:

$$z_i^{(l+1)} = w_i^{(i+1)}y^l + b_i^{(l+1)} \tag{13.7}$$

$$y_i^{(l+1)} = f(z_i^{(l+1)}), \tag{13.8}$$

where f is an activation function. Dropout is then a factor that randomly gets rid of some of the outputs from each layer by doing the following operation (Srivastava et al. 2014):

$$r_j^{(l)} \sim \text{Bernoulli(p)},$$

$$\widetilde{y} = r^{(l)} * y^{(l)},$$

$$z_i^{(l+1)} = w_i^{(l+1)}\widetilde{y} + b_i^{(l+1)},$$

$$y_i^{(l+1)} = f(z_i^{(l+1)})$$

where * denotes element-wise multiplication.

13.6 LONG SHORT-TERM MEMORY NETWORKS

The LSTM architecture was originally proposed by Hochreiter and Schmidhuber (1997) and is widely used nowadays due to its superior performance in accurately modelling both short- and long-term dependencies in data. For these reasons we choose the LSTM architecture over the vanilla RNN network.

When computing the gradients with BPTT, the error flows backwards in time. Because the same weights are used at each time step in an RNN, its gradients depend on the same set of weights, which causes the gradients to either grow without bound or vanish (Goodfellow et al. 2016; Hochreiter and Schmidhuber 1997; Pascanu et al. 2013). In the first case the weights oscillate; in the second, learning long time lags takes a prohibitive amount of time (Hochreiter and Schmidhuber 1997). In the case of exploding gradients there is a solution referred to as clipping the gradients (Pascanu et al. 2013), given by the procedure below, where $^\wedge g$ is the gradient, δ is a threshold and L is the loss function. But the vanishing gradient problem did not seem to have a solution. To solve this problem, Hochreiter and Schmidhuber (1997) introduced the LSTM network, similar to the RNN but where the hidden units are replaced by memory cells. The LSTM is an elegant solution to the vanishing and exploding gradients encountered in RNNs. The hidden cell in the LSTM (Figure 13.3) is a structure that holds an internal state with a recurrent connection of constant weight which allows the gradients to pass many times without exploding or vanishing (Lipton et al. n.d.).

Algorithm 1 Gradient clipping

$$\widehat{g} \leftarrow \frac{\partial L}{\partial \theta}$$

$$\text{if } \| \widehat{g} \| \geq \delta \text{ then}$$

$$\widehat{g} \leftarrow \frac{\delta}{\| \widehat{g} \|}\widehat{g}$$

$$\text{end if}$$

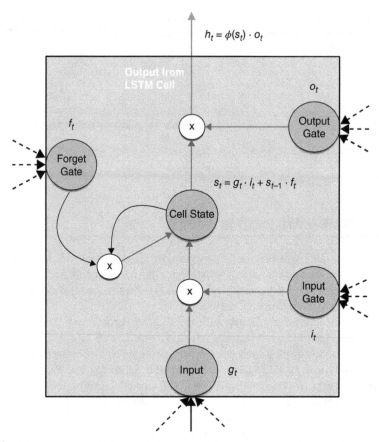

$$h_t = \phi(s_t) \cdot o_t$$

Output from
LSTM Cell

f_t

o_t

x

Output
Gate

Forget
Gate

$$s_t = g_t \cdot i_t + s_{t-1} \cdot f_t$$

Cell State

x

x

Input
Gate

i_t

Input　　g_t

FIGURE 13.3　Memory cell or hidden unit in an LSTM recurrent neural network.

The LSTM network is a set of subnets with recurrent connections, known as memory blocks. Each block contains one or more self-connected memory cells and three multiplicative units known as the input, output and forget gates, which respectively support read, write and reset operations for the cells (Graves 2012). The gating units control the gradient flow through the memory cell and when closing them allows the gradient to pass without alteration for an indefinite amount of time, making the LSTM suitable for learning long time dependencies, thus overcoming the vanishing gradient problem that RNNs suffer from. We describe in more detail the inner workings of an LSTM cell. The memory cell is composed of an input node, an input gate, an internal state, a forget gate and an output gate. The components in a memory cell are as follows:

- The input node takes the activation from both the input layer, x_t, and the hidden state h_{t-1} at time $t-1$. The input is then fed to an activation function, either a tanh or a sigmoid.
- The input gate uses a sigmoidal unit that get its input from the current data x_t and the hidden units at time step $t-1$. The input gate multiplies the value of the

input node and because it is a sigmoid unit with range between zero and one, it can control the flow of the signal it multiplies.

■ The internal state has a self-recurrent connection with unit weight, also called the constant error carousel in Hochreiter and Schmidhuber (1997), and is given by $s\,t = g_t \odot i_t + f_t \odot s_{t-1}$. The Hadamard product denotes element-wise product and f_t is the forget gate (see below).

■ The forget gate, f_t, was not part of the original model for the LSTM but was introduced by Gers et al. (2000). The forget gate multiplies the internal state at time step $t-1$ and in that way can get rid of all the contents in the past, as demonstrated by the equation in the list item above.

■ The resulting output from a memory cell is produced by multiplying the value of the internal state s_c by the output gate o_c. Often the internal state is run through a tanh activation function.

The equations for the LSTM network can be summarized as follows. As before, let g stand for the input to the memory cell, i for the input gate, f for the forget gate, o for the output gate and (Figure 13.4)

$$g_t = \varphi(W^{gX}x_t + W^{gh}h_{t-1} + b_g) \tag{13.13}$$

$$i_t = \sigma(W^{iX}x_t + W^{ih}h_{t-1} + b_i) \tag{13.14}$$

$$f_t = \sigma(W^{fX}x_t + W^{fh}h_{t-1} + b_f) \tag{13.15}$$

$$o_t = \sigma(W^{oX}x_t + W^{oh}h_{t-1} + b_o) \tag{13.16}$$

$$s_t = g_t \odot i_t + s_{t-1} \odot f_t \tag{13.17}$$

$$h_t = \phi(s_t) \odot o_t. \tag{13.18}$$

where the Hadamard product denotes element-wise multiplication. In the equations, h_t is the value of the hidden layer at time t, while h_{t-1} is the output by each memory cell in the hidden layer at time $t-1$. The weights $\{W^{gX}, W^{iX}, W^{fX}, W^{oX}\}$ are the connections between the inputs x_t with the input node, the input gate, the forget gate and the output gate respectively. In the same manner, $\{W^{gh}, W^{ih}, W^{fh}, W^{oh}\}$ represent the connections between the hidden layer with the input node, the input gate, the forget gate and the output gate respectively. The bias terms for each of the cell's components is given by $\{b_g, b_i, b_f, b_o\}$.

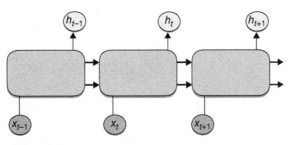

FIGURE 13.4   LSTM recurrent neural network unrolled in time. s for the cell state (Lipton et al. n.d.).

13.7   FINANCIAL MODEL

The goal with this work is to predict the stock returns for 50 stocks from the S&P 500. As input to the model we used the stock returns up to time t and the prediction from the model, an LSTM, is the stock returns at time $t+1$. The predictions from the model help us decide at time t which stocks to buy, hold or sell. This way we have an automated trading policy. For stock i we predict the return at time $t+1$ using historical returns up to time t.

13.7.1   Return series construction

The returns are computed as:

$$R_{t+1}^i = \frac{P_{t+1}^i}{P_t^i} - 1$$

where P_t^i is the price at time t for stock or commodity i and R_{t+1}^i is its return at time $t+1$. Our deep learning model then tries to learn a function $G_\theta(\cdot)$ for predicting the return at time $t+1$ for a parameter set θ:

$$R_{ti+1} = G_\theta(R_t, R_{t-1}, \ldots, R_{t-k})$$

where k is the number of time steps backward in time for the historical returns. We used a rolling window of 30 daily returns to predict the return for day 31 on a rolling basis. This process generated sequences of 30 consecutive one-day returns $\{R_{t-29}^i, R_{t-28}^i, \ldots, R_t^i\}$, where $t \geq 30$ for all of stocks i.

13.7.2   Evaluation of the model

One solution to machine learning-driven investing with the use of deep learning would be to build a classifier with class 0 denoting negative returns and class 1 denoting positive returns. However, in our experiments we observed that solving the problem with regression gave better results than using pure classification. When learning our models, we used the mean squared error (MSE) loss as objective function. First, after the models were trained and validated with a validation set, we made predictions on an independent test set, or as we call it here, live dataset. These predictions were tested with respect to the target series of our stock returns (see experiments 1 and 2) on the independent set, with a measure for correctness called the hit ratio. In line with Lee and Yoo (2017), we chose the HR as a measure of how correct the model predicts the outcome of the stock returns compared to the real outcome. The HR is defined as:

$$HR = \frac{1}{N} \sum_{t=1}^{N} U_t$$

where N is the total number of trading days and U_t is defined as:

$$U_t = \begin{cases} 1 \text{ if } R_t \widehat{R_t} \\ 0 \text{ otherwise} \end{cases}$$

where R_t in the realized stock returns and $\widehat{R_t}$ is the predicted stock returns at trading day t. Thus, HR is the rate of correct predictions measured against the real target series. By using the HR as a measure of discrepancy we could conclude that the predictions either moved in the same direction as the live target returns or moved in the opposite direction. If HR equals one, it indicates perfect correlation and a value of zero indicates that the prediction and the real series moved in opposite directions. A value of $HR > 0.50$ indicates that the model is right more than 50% of the time while a value of $HR \leq 0.50$ indicates that the model guesses the outcome.

For the computations we used Python, as well as Keras and PyTorch deep learning libraries. Keras and PyTorch use tensors with strong GPU acceleration. The GPU computations were performed both on an NVIDIA GeForce GTX 1080 Ti and an NVIDIA GeForce GTX 1070 GDDR5 card on two separate machines.

13.7.3   Data and results

We conducted two types of experiments. The first was intended to demonstrate the predictive power of the LSTM using one stock at a time as input up to time t and as target the same stock's returns at time $t+1$. From now on we refer to it as experiment 1. The second experiment was intended to predict the returns for all stocks simultaneously. This means that all of our 50 stock returns up to time t were fed as input to an LSTM which was trained to predict the 50 stock returns at time $t+1$. Additionally, to the 50 stocks we fed to the model the returns from crude oil futures, silver and gold returns. We refer to this as experiment 2. All the stocks used in this chapter are from the S&P 500, while the commodity prices were from data provider Quandl (Quandl n.d.).

13.7.3.1   Experiment 1

13.7.3.1.1   Main Experiments   For experiment 1, our model used the stock returns as input up to time t, one at a time, to predict the same returns at time $t+1$ – see the discussion above on return series construction. A new model was trained for each stock. Most of the parameters where kept constant during training for every stock. The learning rate was set to 0.001 and we used a dropout rate of 0.01, the only exception being the number of hidden units. The number of hidden units is different for different stocks. For every stock we started with an LSTM with 100 hidden units and increased that number until the condition $HR > 0.70$ was met, increasing the number of units with 50 units per iteration up to 200 hidden units.

Note that the condition $HR > 0.70$ was never met, but this value was chosen merely to keep the computations running until an optimum was found. At most we ran the experiments for 400 epochs but stopped if there was no improvement in the test error or if the test error increased. This technique is called early stopping. For early stopping we used a maximum number of 50 epochs before stopping the training. The training was performed in batches of 512.

Because we trained different LSTMs for different stocks, we ended up with different amounts of data for training, testing and validating the models. Sometimes we refer to the test data as live data. The data was divided first in 90% to 10%, where the 10% portion was for testing (live data) and corresponded to the most recent stock prices. The 90% portion was then divided once again in 85% to 15% for training and validation respectively. The number of data points and periods for the datasets are given in the appendix in Table 13.A.1. For optimization we tested both the RMSProp and Adam algorithms, but found that the best results were achieved with stochastic gradient descent and momentum. This is true only when processing one time series at a time. For experiment 2 we used the Adam optimization algorithm. The results from experiment 1 are shown in Table 13.1.

13.7.3.1.2 Baseline Experiments The LSTM model was compared to two other models. The baseline models were a support vector machine (SVM) (Friedman et al. n.d.) and a neural network (NN). The NN consisted of one hidden layer, where the number of hidden units were chosen with the same procedure as that for the LSTM, the only difference being that the range for choosing hidden units lies in the range 50–150. Additionally, we used the same learning rate, number of epochs, batch size and drop rate as those used for the LSTM. For the NNs we trained the models in a regression setting using the MSE. For the predictions produced by the NN we computed the HR on the live dataset. The results are presented together with those for the LSTM in Table 13.1.

By inspecting Table 13.1 we can get the following figures. The LSTM achieved a value $HR > 0.50$ for 43 stocks out of 50 and did not better than chance ($HR \leq 0.50$) for the remaining 7 stocks. The SVM got it 'right' ($HR > 0.50$) for 21 stocks, while the NN did just a little better with 27 stocks moving in the same direction as the true series. If we imagine that $HR = 0.51$ can be achieved by rounding the results, those values can be questioned as also being achieved by chance. The LSTM had a value of $HR = 0.51$ for 10 stocks, the SVM for 3 stocks while the NN for 8 stocks. Even if the LSTM seems superior to the other models, the difference in performance is not that big, except for some cases. On some stocks both the SVM and the NN can be as good as the LSTM or better. But what this experiment shows is that the LSTM is consistent in predicting the direction in which its predictions move with respect to the real series.

13.7.3.2 Experiment 2 In this experiment we used the returns of all the 50 stocks. Additionally, we used oil, gold and S&P 500 return series of the 30 previous days as input. The output from our model is the prediction of the 50 stock returns. To test the robustness of the LSTM we also performed experiments against a baseline model, which in this case consisted of an SVM (Friedman et al. n.d.), suited for regression. To test the profitability of the LSTM, we ran experiments on a smaller portfolio consisting of 40 of our initial stocks (see Table 13.4) and the return series from the S&P 500, oil and gold. This part of the experiment is intended to show that the LSTM is consistent in its predictions independent of the time periods. Especially we were interested to see whether the model was robust to the subprime financial crisis. These results are shown in Table 13.5.

Because this section consists of many experiments, we present the experiment performed on the 50 stocks plus commodities in the main experiment subsection. The baseline experiment is presented in the subsection above and the last experiment for time periods in the 'Results in different market regimes' subsection below.

13.7.3.2.1 Main Experiment All the features in this experiment were scaled with the min-max formula:

$$x^0 = \Delta x \cdot (b - a) + a,$$

TABLE 13.1 Experiment 1: comparison of performance measured as the HR for LSTM, SVM and NN

Stock	Hidden units	HR LSTM	HR SVM	HR NN
AAPL	150	0.53	0.52	0.52 (130)
MSFT	100	0.51	0.49	0.49 (150)
FB	100	0.58	0.58	0.56 (90)
AMZN	100	0.55	0.56	0.53 (90)
JNJ	100	0.52	0.47	0.50 (50)
BRK/B	150	0.51	0.51	0.51 (50)
JPM	100	0.52	0.51	0.50 (90)
XOM	100	0.52	0.52	0.49 (50)
GOOGL	100	0.54	0.53	0.53 (70)
GOOG	100	0.55	0.55	0.55 (50)
BAC	100	0.47	0.50	0.59 (50)
PG	100	0.50	0.50	0.50 (110)
T	150	0.52	0.48	0.50 (70)
WFC	150	0.51	0.47	0.50 (70)
GE	100	0.51	0.50	0.50 (110)
CVX	150	0.50	0.53	0.50 (70)
PFE	100	0.49	0.49	0.49 (50)
VZ	150	0.51	0.53	0.50 (50)
CMCSA	150	0.54	0.49	0.50 (110)
UNH	100	0.52	0.48	0.52 (130)
V	100	0.59	0.51	0.55 (70)
C	150	0.52	0.50	0.51 (50)
PM	100	0.56	0.56	0.52 (110)
HD	100	0.53	0.50	0.53 (70)
KO	150	0.51	0.48	0.50 (70)
MRK	200	0.54	0.49	0.50 (110)
PEP	100	0.55	0.52	0.51 (50)
INTC	150	0.53	0.45	0.51 (110)
CSCO	100	0.51	0.48	0.50 (90)
ORCL	150	0.52	0.48	0.50 (130)
DWDP	150	0.51	0.48	0.50 (90)
DIS	150	0.53	0.49	0.52 (130)
BA	100	0.54	0.53	0.51 (50)
AMGN	100	0.51	0.52	0.53 (90)
MCD	150	0.55	0.48	0.52 (130)
MA	100	0.57	0.57	0.55 (130)
IBM	100	0.49	0.49	0.50 (50)
MO	150	0.55	0.47	0.52 (50)
MMM	100	0.53	0.46	0.52 (90)
ABBV	100	0.60	0.38	0.41 (110)
WMT	100	0.52	0.50	0.51 (50)
MDT	150	0.52	0.49	0.50 (50)
GILD	100	0.50	0.52	0.51 (70)
CELG	100	0.51	0.52	0.50 (90)
HON	150	0.55	0.46	0.52 (130)
NVDA	100	0.56	0.55	0.54 (90)
AVGO	100	0.57	0.57	0.51 (130)
BMY	200	0.52	0.49	0.50 (50)
PCLN	200	0.54	0.54	0.53 (70)
ABT	150	0.50	0.47	0.50 (70)

The results are computed for the independent live dataset. The numbers in parentheses in the NN column stand for the number of hidden units.

where $\Delta x = \dfrac{x - \min(x)}{\max(x) - \min(x)}$, and a, b is the range (a,b) of the features. It is common to set $a = 0$ and $b = 1$. The training data consisted of 560 days from the period 2014-05-13 to 2016-08-01. We used a validation set consisting of 83 days for choosing the meta parameters, from the period 2016-08-02 to 2016-11-25 and a test set of 83 days from the period 2016-11-28 to 2017-03-28. Finally, we used a live dataset of 111 days for the period 2017-03-29 to 2017-09-05.

We used an LSTM with one hidden layer LSTM and 50 hidden units. As activation function we used the ReLu; we also used a dropout rate of 0.01 and a batch size of 32. The model was trained for 400 epochs. The parameters of the Adam optimizer were a learning rate of 0.001, $\beta_1 = 0.9$, $\beta_2 = 0.999$, $\varepsilon = 10^{-9}$ and the decay parameter was set to 0.0 As loss function we used the MSE.

To assess the quality of our model and to try to determine whether it has value for investment purposes, we looked at the 'live dataset', which is the most recent dataset. This dataset is not used during training and can be considered to be an independent dataset. We computed the HR on the predictions made with the live data to assess how often our model was right compared to the true target returns. The hit ratio gives us information if the predictions of the model move in the same direction as the true returns. To evaluate the profitability of the model we built daily updated portfolios using the predictions from the model and computed their average daily return. A typical scenario would be that we get predictions from our LSTM model just before market opening for all 50 daily stock returns. According to the direction predicted, positive or negative, we open a long position in stock i if $R_t^i > 0$. If $R_t^i < 0$ we can either decide to open a short position (in that case we call it a long-short portfolio) for stock i or do nothing and if we own the stocks we can choose to keep them (we call it a long portfolio). At market closing we close all positions. Thus, the daily returns of the portfolio on day t for a long-short portfolio is $\sum_{i=1}^{50} \mathrm{sign}(\widehat{R}_t) \cdot R_t$.

Regarding the absolute value of the weights for the portfolio we tried two kinds of similar, equally-weighted portfolios. Portfolio 1: at the beginning we allocate the same proportion of capital to invest in each stock, then the returns on each stock are independently compounded, thus the portfolio return on a period is the average of the returns on each stock on the period. Portfolio 2: the portfolio is rebalanced each day, i.e. each day we allocate the same proportion of capital to invest in each stock, thus the portfolio daily return is the average of the daily returns on each stock. Each of the portfolios has a long and a long-short version. We are aware that not optimizing the weights might result in very conservative return profiles in our strategy. The results from experiment 2 are presented in Table 13.2.

13.7.3.2.2 Baseline Experiments This experiment was designed first to compare the LSTM to a baseline, in this case an SVM, and second to test the generalization power between the models with respect to the look-back period used as input to the LSTM and the SVM. We noticed that using a longer historic return series as input, the LSTM remains robust and we don't see overfitting, as is the case for the SVM. The SVM had very good performance on the training set but performed worse on the validation and test sets. Both the LSTM and the SVM were tested with a rolling window of days in the set: {1,2,5,10}.

TABLE 13.2   Experiment 2 (main experiment)

Stock	HR	Avg Ret %(L)	Avg Ret %(L/S)
Portfolio 1	0.63	0.18	0.27
Portfolio 2	0.63	0.18	0.27
AAPL	0.63	0.24	0.32
MSFT	0.71	0.29	0.45
FB	0.71	0.31	0.42
AMZN	0.69	0.27	0.41
JNJ	0.65	0.12	0.19
BRK/B	0.70	0.19	0.31
JPM	0.62	0.22	0.38
XOM	0.70	0.11	0.25
GOOGL	0.72	0.31	0.50
GOOG	0.75	0.32	0.52
BAC	0.70	0.30	0.55
PG	0.60	0.60	0.90
T	0.61	0.80	0.22
WFC	0.67	0.16	0.38
GE	0.64	0.50	0.24
CVX	0.71	0.18	0.31
PFE	0.66	0.70	0.14
VZ	0.50	0.10	0.10
CMCSA	0.63	0.23	0.36
UNH	0.59	0.20	0.22
V	0.65	0.23	0.31
C	0.69	0.28	0.39
PM	0.64	0.17	0.28
HD	0.61	0.10	0.17
KO	0.61	0.80	0.90
MRK	0.61	0.90	0.16
PEP	0.60	0.80	0.11
INTC	0.63	0.16	0.31
CSCO	0.68	0.14	0.31
ORCL	0.52	0.80	0.40
DWDP	0.60	0.21	0.35
DIS	0.59	0	0.90
BA	0.57	0.23	0.16
AMGN	0.65	0.21	0.36
MCD	0.58	0.16	0.12
MA	0.66	0.25	0.34
IBM	0.54	−0.40	0.60
MO	0.59	0.10	0.13
MMM	0.63	0.16	0.24
ABBV	0.61	0.18	0.22
WMT	0.50	0.14	0.16
MDT	0.59	0.90	0.17
GILD	0.50	0.16	0.11
CELG	0.64	0.28	0.45
HON	0.66	0.15	0.20
NVDA	0.68	0.54	0.68
AVGO	0.65	0.37	0.59
BMY	0.57	0.13	0.19
PCLN	0.61	0.14	0.24
ABT	0.63	0.21	0.28

HR, average daily returns for long portfolio (L) and long-short portfolio (L/S) in percent. The results are computed for the independent live dataset.

TABLE 13.3 Experiment 2 (baseline experiment)

Model	HR	Avg Ret %(L)	Avg Ret %(L/S)
LSTM (1)	0.59	0.14	0.21
LSTM (2)	0.61	0.17	0.26
LSTM (5)	0.62	0.17	0.26
LSTM (10)	0.62	0.17	0.26
SVM (1)	0.59	0.14	0.21
SVM (2)	0.58	0.13	0.18
SVM (5)	0.57	0.12	0.16
SVM (10)	0.55	0.11	0.14

The table shows the HR and the daily average returns for each model; all computations are performed on the out-of-sample live dataset. The number in parentheses in the model name indicates the look-back length of the return series, i.e. trading days.

The results of the baseline experiment are shown in Table 13.3. We can see from the results that the LSTM improves its performance in the HR and the average daily returns in both the long and long-short portfolios. For the SVM, the opposite is true, i.e. the SVM is comparable to the LSTM only when taking into account the most recent history. The more historic data we use, the more the SVM deteriorates in all measures, HR, and average daily returns for the long and long-short portfolios. This is an indication that the SVM overfits to the training data the longer backward in time our look-back window goes, whereas the LSTM remains robust.

13.7.3.2.3 Results in Different Market Regimes To validate our results for this experiment, we performed another experiment on portfolio 1. This time, instead of using all 50 stocks as input and output for the model, we picked 40 stocks. As before, we added the return series for the S&P 500, oil and gold in this portfolio. The data was divided as training set 66%, validation (1) 11%, validation (2) 11%, live dataset 11%. The stocks used for this portfolio are presented in Table 13.4 and the results are shown in Table 13.5. Notice that the performance of the portfolio (Sharpe ratio) reaches a peak in the pre-financial crisis era (2005–2008) just to decline during the crisis but still with

TABLE 13.4 Experiment 2 (stocks used for this portfolio)

AAPL	MSFT US	AMZN US Equity	JNJ US
BRK/B	JPM	XOM	BAC
PG	T	WFC	GE
CVX	PFE	VZ	CMCSA
UNH	C	HD	KO
MRK	PEP	INTC	CSCO
ORCL	DWDP	DIS	BA
AMGN	MCD	IBM	MO
MMM	WMT	MDT	GILD
CELG	HON	BMY	ABT

The 40 stocks used for the second part of experiment 2.

TABLE 13.5 Experiment 2 (results in different market regimes)

Training period	HR %	Avg. Ret % (L)	Avg. Ret % (L/S)	Sharpe ratio (L)	Sharpe ratio (L/S)
2000–2003	49.7	−0.05	−0.12	−0.84	−1.60
2001–2004	48.1	0.05	−0.02	2.06	−0.73
2002–2005	52.5	0.11	0.10	6.05	3.21
2003–2006	55.9	0.10	0.16	5.01	5.85
2004–2007	54.0	0.14	0.12	9.07	5.11
2005–2008	61.7	0.26	0.45	7.00	9.14
2006–2009	59.7	0.44	1.06	3.10	6.22
2007–2010	53.8	0.12	0.12	5.25	2.70
2008–2011	56.5	0.20	0.26	6.12	6.81
2009–2012	62.8	0.40	0.68	6.31	9.18
2010–2013	55.4	0.09	0.14	3.57	3.73
2011–2014	58.1	0.16	0.21	5.59	6.22
2012–2015	56.0	0.15	0.21	5.61	5.84

This table shows HR, average daily return for a long (L) portfolio, average daily return for a long-short (L/S) and their respective Sharpe ratios (L) and (L/S). The results are computed for the independent live dataset. Each three-year period is divided into 66% training, 11% validation (1), 11% validation (2) and 11% live set.

a performance quite high. These experiments are performed with no transaction costs and we still assume that we can buy and sell without any market frictions, which in reality might not be possible during a financial crisis.

The LSTM network was trained for periods of three years and the test on live data was performed on data following the training and validation period. What this experiment intends to show is that the LSTM network can help us pick portfolios with very high Sharpe ratio independent of the time period chosen in the backtest. This means that the good performance of the LSTM is not merely a stroke of luck in the good times that stock markets are experiencing these times.

13.8 CONCLUSIONS

Deep learning has proven be one of the most successful machine learning families of models in modelling unstructured data in several fields like computer vision and natural language processing. Deep learning solves this central problem in representation learning by introducing representations that are expressed in terms of other, simpler representations. Deep learning allows the computer to build complex concepts out of simpler concepts. A deep learning system can represent the concept of an image of a person by combining simpler concepts, such as corners and contours, which are in turn defined in terms of edges.

The idea of learning the right representation for the data provides one perspective on deep learning. You can think about it as the first layers 'discovering' features that allow an efficient dimensionality reduction phase and perform non-linear modelling.

Another perspective on deep learning is that depth allows computers to learn a multi-step computer program. Each layer of the representation can be thought of as the state of the computer's memory after executing another set of instructions in parallel. Networks with greater depth can execute more instructions in sequence. Sequential instructions offer great power because later instructions can refer back to the results of earlier instructions.

Convolutional neural networks for image processing and RNNs for natural language processing are being used more and more in finance as well as in other sciences. The price to pay for these deep models is a large number of parameters to be learned, the need to perform non-convex optimizations and the interpretability. Researchers have found in different contexts the right models to perform tasks with great accuracy, reaching stability, avoiding overfitting and improving the interpretability of these models.

Finance is a field in which these benefits can be exploited given the huge amount of structured and unstructured data available to financial practitioners and researchers. In this chapter we explore an application on time series. Given the fact that autocorrelations, cycles and non-linearities are present in time series, LSTM networks are a suitable candidate to model time series in finance. Elman neural networks are also a good candidate for this task, but LSTMs have proven to be better in other non-financial applications. Time series also exhibit other challenging features such as estimation and non-stationarity.

We have tested the LSTM in a univariate context. The LSTM network performs better than both SVMs and NNs – see experiment 1. Even though the difference in performance is not very important, the LSTM shows consistency in its predictions.

Our multivariate LSTM network experiments with exogeneous variables show good performance consistent with what happens when using VAR models compared with AR models, their 'linear' counterpart. In our experiments, LSTMs show better accuracy ratios, hit ratios and high Sharpe ratios in our equally-weighted long-only and unconstrained portfolios in different market environments.

These ratios show good behaviour in-sample and out-of-sample. Sharpe ratios of our portfolio experiments are 8 for the long-only portfolio and 10 for the long-short version, an equally-weighted portfolio would have provided a 2.7 Sharpe ratio using the model from 2014 to 2017. Results show consistency when using the same modelling approach in different market regimes. No trading costs have been considered.

We can conclude that LSTM networks are a promising modelling tool in financial time series, especially in the multivariate LSTM networks with exogeneous variables. These networks can enable financial engineers to model time dependencies, non-linearity, feature discovery with a very flexible model that might be able to offset the challenging estimation and non-stationarity in finance and the potential of overfitting. These issues can never be underestimated in finance, even more so in models with a high number of parameters, non-linearity and difficulty to interpret like LSTM networks.

We think financial engineers should then incorporate deep learning to model not only unstructured but also structured data. We have interesting modelling times ahead of us.

APPENDIX A

TABLE 13.A.1   Periods for training set, test set and live dataset in experiment 1

Stock	Training period	Test period	Live period
AAPL	1982-11-15 2009-07-08 (6692)	2009-07-09 2014-03-18 (1181)	2014-03-19 2017-09-05 (875)
MSFT	1986-03-17 2010-04-21 (6047)	2010-04-22 2014-07-17 (1067)	2014-07-18 2017-09-05 (791)
FB	2012-05-21 2016-06-20 (996)	2016-06-21 2017-03-02 (176)	2017-03-03 2017-09-05 (130)
AMZN	1997-05-16 2012-12-07 (3887)	2012-12-10 2015-08-31 (686)	2015-09-01 2017-09-05 (508)
JNJ	1977-01-05 2008-02-20 (7824)	2008-02-21 2013-08-14 (1381)	2013-08-15 2017-09-05 (1023)
BRK/B	1996-05-13 2012-09-11 (4082)	2012-09-12 2015-07-24 (720)	2015-07-27 2017-09-05 (534)
JPM	1980-07-30 2008-12-19 (7135)	2008-12-22 2013-12-20 (1259)	2013-12-23 2017-09-05 (933)
XOM	1980-07-30 2008-12-19 (7136)	2008-12-22 2013-12-20 (1259)	2013-12-23 2017-09-05 (933)
GOOGL	2004-08-20 2014-08-25 (2490)	2014-08-26 2016-05-23 (439)	2016-05-24 2017-09-05 (325)
GOOG	2014-03-31 2016-11-22 (639)	2016-11-23 2017-05-08 (113)	2017-05-09 2017-09-05 (84)
BAC	1980-07-30 2008-12-19 (7134)	2008-12-22 2013-12-20 (1259)	2013-12-23 2017-09-05 (933)
PG	1980-07-30 2008-12-19 (7136)	2008-12-22 2013-12-20 (1259)	2013-12-23 2017-09-05 (933)
T	1983-11-23 2009-10-02 (6492)	2009-10-05 2014-04-24 (1146)	2014-04-25 2017-09-05 (849)
WFC	1980-07-30 2008-12-19 (7135)	2008-12-22 2013-12-20 (1259)	2013-12-23 2017-09-05 (933)
GE	1971-07-08 2006-11-06 (8873)	2006-11-07 2013-01-29 (1566)	2013-01-30 2017-09-05 (1160)
CVX	1980-07-30 2008-12-19 (7136)	2008-12-22 2013-12-20 (1259)	2013-12-23 2017-09-05 (933)
PFE	1980-07-30 2008-12-19 (7135)	2008-12-22 2013-12-20 (1259)	2013-12-23 2017-09-05 (933)
VZ	1983-11-23 2009-10-02 (6492)	2009-10-05 2014-04-24 (1146)	2014-04-25 2017-09-05 (849)
CMCSA	1983-08-10 2009-09-09 (6549)	2009-09-10 2014-04-14 (1156)	2014-04-15 2017-09-05 (856)
UNH	1985-09-04 2010-03-08 (6150)	2010-03-09 2014-06-27 (1085)	2014-06-30 2017-09-05 (804)
V	2008-03-20 2015-06-26 (1800)	2015-06-29 2016-09-29 (318)	2016-09-30 2017-09-05 (235)
C	1986-10-31 2010-06-14 (5924)	2010-06-15 2014-08-08 (1046)	2014-08-11 2017-09-05 (775)
PM	2008-03-19 2015-06-26 (1801)	2015-06-29 2016-09-29 (318)	2016-09-30 2017-09-05 (235)
HD	1981-09-24 2009-03-31 (6913)	2009-04-01 2014-02-04 (1220)	2014-02-05 2017-09-05 (904)
KO	1968-01-04 2006-01-13 (9542)	2006-01-17 2012-09-20 (1684)	2012-09-21 2017-09-05 (1247)
MRK	1980-07-30 2008-12-19 (7135)	2008-12-22 2013-12-20 (1259)	2013-12-23 2017-09-05 (933)
PEP	1980-07-30 2008-12-19 (7135)	2008-12-22 2013-12-20 (1259)	2013-12-23 2017-09-05 (933)
INTC	1982-11-15 2009-07-08 (6692)	2009-07-09 2014-03-18 (1181)	2014-03-19 2017-09-05 (875)
CSCO	1990-02-20 2011-03-24 (5287)	2011-03-25 2014-12-08 (933)	2014-12-09 2017-09-05 (691)
ORCL	1986-04-16 2010-04-29 (6032)	2010-04-30 2014-07-22 (1064)	2014-07-23 2017-09-05 (788)
DWDP	1980-07-30 2008-12-19 (7135)	2008-12-22 2013-12-20 (1259)	2013-12-23 2017-09-05 (933)
DIS	1974-01-07 2007-06-06 (8404)	2007-06-07 2013-04-26 (1483)	2013-04-29 2017-09-05 (1099)
BA	1980-07-30 2008-12-19 (7136)	2008-12-22 2013-12-20 (1259)	2013-12-23 2017-09-05 (933)
AMGN	1984-01-04 2009-10-13 (6473)	2009-10-14 2014-04-29 (1142)	2014-04-30 2017-09-05 (846)
MCD	1980-07-30 2008-12-19 (7135)	2008-12-22 2013-12-20 (1259)	2013-12-23 2017-09-05 (933)
MA	2006-05-26 2015-01-23 (2149)	2015-01-26 2016-07-26 (379)	2016-07-27 2017-09-05 (281)
IBM	1968-01-04 2006-01-13 (9541)	2006-01-17 2012-09-20 (1684)	2012-09-21 2017-09-05 (1247)
MO	1980-07-30 2008-12-19 (7134)	2008-12-22 2013-12-20 (1259)	2013-12-23 2017-09-05 (933)
MMM	1980-07-30 2008-12-19 (7135)	2008-12-22 2013-12-20 (1259)	2013-12-23 2017-09-05 (933)
ABBV	2012-12-12 2016-08-05 (888)	2016-08-08 2017-03-22 (157)	2017-03-23 2017-09-05 (116)
WMT	1972-08-29 2007-02-09 (8664)	2007-02-12 2013-03-08 (1529)	2013-03-11 2017-09-05 (1133)
MDT	1980-07-30 2008-12-19 (7135)	2008-12-22 2013-12-20 (1259)	2013-12-23 2017-09-05 (933)
GILD	1992-01-24 2011-09-07 (4912)	2011-09-08 2015-02-19 (867)	2015-02-20 2017-09-05 (642)
CELG	1987-09-02 2010-08-27 (5755)	2010-08-30 2014-09-11 (1016)	2014-09-12 2017-09-05 (752)
HON	1985-09-23 2010-03-11 (6139)	2010-03-122014-06-30 (1083)	2014-07-01 2017-09-05 (803)
NVDA	1999-01-25 2013-05-03 (3562)	2013-05-06 2015-10-29 0(466)	2015-10-30 2017-09-05 (466)
AVGO	2009-08-07 2015-10-22 (1533)	2015-10-23 2016-11-17 (271)	2016-11-18 2017-09-05 (200)
BMY	1980-07-30 2008-12-18 (7135)	2008-12-19 2013-12-19 (1259)	2013-12-20 2017-09-01 (933)
PCLN	1999-03-31 2013-05-20 (3527)	2013-05-21 2015-11-05 (622)	015-11-06 2017-09-05 (461)
ABT	1980-07-30 2008-12-19 (7135)	2008-12-22 2013-12-20 (1259)	2013-12-23 2017-09-05 (933)

In parentheses we show the number of trading days in each dataset.

REFERENCES

Bengio, S., Vinyals, O., Jaitly, N., Shazeer, N. n.d. *Scheduled Sampling for Sequence Prediction with Recurrent Neural Networks.* Google Research, Mountain View, CA, USA bengio,vinyals,ndjaitly,noam@google.com.

Bianchi, F. M., Kampffmeyer, M., Maiorino, E., Jenssen, R. (n.d.). *Temporal Overdrive Recurrent Neural Network, arXiv preprint arXiv:1701.05159.*

Bishop, C.M. (2006). *Pattern Recognition and Machine Learning.* Springer Science, Business Media, LLC. ISBN: 10: 0-387-31073-8, 13: 978-0387-31073-2.

Cai, X., Zhang, N., Venayagamoorthy, G.K., and Wunsch, D.C. (2007). Time series prediction with recurrent neural networks trained by a hybrid PSO-EA algorithm. *Neurocomputing* 70 (13–15): 2342–2353. ISSN 09252312. https://doi.org/10.1016/j.neucom.2005.12.138.

Elman, J.L. (1995). Language as a dynamical system. In: *Mind as motion: Explorations in the dynamics of cognition* (ed. T. van Gelder and R. Port), 195–223. MIT Press.

Fischer, T. and Krauss, C. *Deep Learning with Long Short-term Memory Networks for Financial Market Predictions.* Friedrich-Alexander-Universität Erlangen-Nürnberg, Institute for economics. ISSN: 1867-6767. www.iwf.rw.fau.de/research/iwf-discussion-paper-series/.

Friedman, J.; Hastie, T.; Tibshirani, R.. *The elements of statistical learning, Data Mining, Inference and Prediction.* September 30, 2008.

Gers, F.A., Schmidhuber, J., and Cummins, F. (2000). Learning to forget: continual predictions with LSTM. *Neural computation* 12 (10): 2451–2471.

Goodfellow, I., Bengio, Y., and Courville, A. (2016). *Deep Learning.* MIT Press, www.deep learningbook.org,.

Graves, A. (2012). *Supervised Sequence Labelling with Recurrent Neural Networks.* Springer-Verlag Berlin Heidelberg. ISBN: 978-3642-24797-2.

Haykin, S. (2009). *Neural Networks and Learning Machines*, 3e. Pearson, Prentice Hall. ISBN: 13 : 978-0-13-147139-9, 10 : 0-13-147139-2.

Hochreiter, S. and Schmidhuber, J. (1997). Long short-term memory. *Neural Computation* 9: 1735–1780. ©1997 Massachusetts Institute of Technology.

Lee, S.I. and Yoo, S.J. (2017). A deep efficient frontier method for optimal investments. *Expert Systems with Applications* .

Lipton, Z.C., Berkowitz, J.; Elkan, C.. *A critical review of recurrent neural networks for sequence learning.* arXiv:1506.00019v4 [cs.LG] 17 Oct 2015.

Mokolov, T., Sutskever, I., Chen, K., Corrado, G., Dean, J.. Google Inc. Mountain View. *Distributed Representations of Words and Phrases and their Compositionality* ArXiv;1310.4546v1 [cs.CL] 16 Oct 2013.

Mori, H.M.H. and Ogasawara, T.O.T. (1993). A recurrent neural network for short-term load forecasting. In: *1993 Proceedings of the Second International Forum on Applications of Neural Networks to Power Systems*, vol. 31, 276–281. https://doi.org/10.1109/ANN.1993 .264315.

Ogata, T., Murase, M., Tani, J. et al. (2007). Two-way translation of compound sentences and arm motions by recurrent neural networks. In: *IROS 2007. IEEE/RSJ International Conference on Intelligent Robots and Systems*, 1858–1863. IEEE.

Pascanu, R., Mikolov, T.; Bengio, Y.. *On the difficulty of training recurrent neural networks.* Proceedings of the 30*th* international conference on machine learning, Atlanta, Georgia, USA, 2013. JMLR WandCP volume 28. Copyright by the author(s) 2013.

Qian, X.. *Financial Series Prediction: Comparison between precision of time series models and machine learning methods.* ArXiv:1706.00948v4 [cs.LG] 25 Dec 2017.

Quandl (n.d.). https://www.quandl.com

Schäfer, A.M. and Zimmermann, H.-G. (2007). Recurrent neural networks are universal approximators. *International Journal of Neural Systems* 17 (4): 253–263. https://doi.org/10.1142/S0129065707001111.

Srivastava, N., Hinton, G., Krizhevsky, A. et al. (2014). Dropout: a simple way to prevent neural networks from overfitting. *Journal of Machine Learning Research* 15: 1929–1958.

Sutskever, I.. *Training recurrent neural networks: Data mining, inference and prediction*. PhD thesis, department of computer science, University of Toronto, 2013.

Vapnik, V.N. (2000). *The Nature of Statistical Learning Theory*, 2e. Springer Science, Business Media New York, inc. ISBN: 978-1-4419-3160-3.

Yu, D. and Deng, L. (2015). *Automatic Speech Recognition, a Deep Learning Approach*. London: Springer-Verlag. ISBN: 978-1-4471-5778-6. ISSN 1860-4862. https://doi.org/10.1007/978-1-4471-5779-3.

Biography

CHAPTER 1

Michael Kollo is Deputy Global Head of Research at Rosenberg Equities and is focused on applications of machine learning and big data, factor research and quantitative strategy for equity portfolios. Prior to joining Rosenberg Equities, Michael was Head of Risk for Renaissance Asset Management, in charge of dedicated emerging market equity strategies. Before Renaissance, Michael held senior research and portfolio management positions at Fidelity and BlackRock. Michael's experience spans factor investing from risk modelling to signal generation, portfolio management and product design. Michael obtained his PhD in Finance from the London School of Economics and holds bachelor's and master's degrees from the University of New South Wales in Australia. He lectures at Imperial College and is an active mentor for FinTech firms in London.

CHAPTER 2

Rado Lipuš, CFA, is the founder and CEO of Neudata, an alternative data intelligence provider. Prior to founding Neudata, Rado's professional experience spanned 20 years of FinTech leadership, sales management and data innovation for the buy side. He spent several years in quantitative portfolio construction and risk management at MSCI (Barra) and S&P Capital IQ and raised funds for CITE Investments. Rado worked latterly as Managing Director at PerTrac in London, a leading FinTech and data analytics solutions provider to hedge fund allocators and institutional investors in EMEA and Asia. He also has experience with financial data firms such as eVestment, 2iQ Research, I/B/E/S and TIM Group. An acknowledged expert on alternative data, Rado is regularly invited to speak at conferences and industry events. Rado received his Master of Business Administration from the University of Graz, Austria, and is a CFA charter holder.

Daryl Smith, CFA, is Head of Research at Neudata. He and his team are responsible for researching and discovering alternative datasets for a wide range of asset managers worldwide. Prior to Neudata, Daryl worked as an equity research analyst at boutique investment firm Liberum Capital across a number of sectors, including agriculture, chemicals and diversified financials. Prior to Liberum, he worked at Goldman Sachs as an equity derivatives analyst and regulatory reporting strategist. Daryl holds a master's degree in mechanical engineering from the University of Bath and is a CFA charter holder.

CHAPTER 3

Ekaterina Sirotyuk is a Portfolio Manager, Investment Solutions and Products at Credit Suisse and the lead author of 'Technology enabled investing', a department piece on applications of AI/big data in investment management. Prior to joining Credit Suisse in 2014, Ekaterina was a manager at a German investment company, responsible for sourcing and evaluating energy-related investments as well as deal structuring. Before that she was an associate at Bank of America Merrill Lynch in London in the Fixed Income, Currencies and Commodities department, doing cross-asset class structuring for European pensions and insurers. Ekaterina started her career as an investment analyst at UBS Alternative and Quantitative Investments, based in New York and Zurich. She received her BSc in Economics and Management (first-class honours) from the University of London (lead college – London School of Economics) and her MBA from INSEAD, where she also did her doctorate coursework in finance. In addition, Ekaterina has been a leader at the Swiss Finance + Technology Association.

CHAPTER 4

Vinesh Jha is CEO and founder of ExtractAlpha, established in 2013 in Hong Kong with the mission of bringing analytical rigour to the analysis and marketing of new datasets for the capital markets. From 1999 to 2005, Vinesh was Director of Quantitative Research at StarMine in San Francisco, where he developed industry-leading metrics of sell-side analyst performance as well as successful commercial alpha signals and products based on analyst, fundamental and other data sources. Subsequently he developed systematic trading strategies for proprietary trading desks at Merrill Lynch and Morgan Stanley in New York. Most recently he was Executive Director at PDT Partners, a spinoff of Morgan Stanley's premiere quant prop trading group, where in addition to research he applied his experience in the communication of complex quantitative concepts to investor relations. Vinesh holds an undergraduate degree from the University of Chicago and a graduate degree from the University of Cambridge, both in mathematics.

CHAPTER 5

Saeed Amen is the founder of Cuemacro. Over the past decade, Saeed has developed systematic trading strategies at major investment banks including Lehman Brothers and Nomura. Independently, he is also a systematic FX trader, running a proprietary trading book trading liquid G10 FX since 2013. He is the author of *Trading Thalesians: What the Ancient World Can Teach Us About Trading Today* (Palgrave Macmillan, 2014). Through Cuemacro, he now consults and publishes research for clients in the area of systematic trading. Saeed's clients have included major quant funds and data companies such as RavenPack and TIM Group. He is also a co-founder of the Thalesians. Saeed holds an MSc in Mathematics and Computer Science from Imperial College London.

Iain J. Clark is managing director and founder of Efficient Frontier Consulting Ltd, an independent quant consultancy that provides consultancy and training services to banks, hedge funds, exchanges and other participants in the financial services sector. He specializes in FX, FX/IR and commodities, and is an industry expert in volatility modelling and the application of numerical methods to finance. Iain has 14 years' finance experience, including being Head of FX and Commodities Quantitative

Analysis at Standard Bank and Head of FX Quantitative Analysis at UniCredit and Dresdner Kleinwort; he has also worked at Lehman Brothers, BNP Paribas and JP Morgan. He is the author of *Foreign Exchange Option Pricing: A Practitioner's Guide* (Wiley, 2011) and *Commodity Option Pricing: A Practitioner's Guide* (Wiley, 2014). Iain is a hands-on quant technologist as well as an expert quant modeller and strategy consultant, having considerable practical expertise in languages such as C++ (multithreading, Boost, STL), C#, Java, Matlab, Python and R.

CHAPTER 6

Giuliano De Rossi heads the European Quantitative Research team at Macquarie, based in London. He joined from PIMCO where he was an analyst in the Credit and Equity Analytics and Asset Allocation teams. Prior to that he worked for six years in the quant research team at UBS. He has a PhD in economics from Cambridge University and worked for three years as a college lecturer in economics at Cambridge before joining the finance industry on a full-time basis. Giuliano's master's degree is from the London School of Economics; his first degree is from Bocconi University in Milan. He has worked on a wide range of topics, including pairs trading, low volatility, the tracking error of global ETFs, cross-asset strategies, downside risk and text mining. His academic research has been published in the *Journal of Econometrics* and the *Journal of Empirical Finance*.

Jakub Kolodziej joined the European Quantitative Research team in London in 2014, prior to which he worked as an investment analyst at a quantitative hedge fund. He holds a master's degree in Finance and Private Equity from the London School of Economics and a bachelor's degree in Finance and Accounting from Warsaw School of Economics.

Gurvinder Brar is Global Head of Quantitative Research group at Macquarie. The Global Quantitative Research group comprises 13 analysts, with teams operating in all the major equity market regions. They aim to produce cutting-edge, topical and actionable research focusing on alpha, risk and portfolio construction issues and are keen to form deep partnerships with clients. The regional teams work closely, aiming to build a common global knowledge base of techniques, backed up with specific local expertise where required. In addition, the group undertakes custom projects for clients which assist with all aspects of the investment processes.

CHAPTER 7

Tony Guida is a senior quantitative portfolio manager, managing multi-factor equity portfolios for the asset manager of a UK pension fund in London. Prior to that Tony was Senior Research Consultant for smart beta and risk allocation at EDHEC RISK Scientific Beta, advising asset owners on how to construct and allocate to risk premia. Before joining EDHEC Tony worked for eight years at UNIGESTION as a senior research analyst. Tony was a member of the Research and Investment Committee for Minimum Variance Strategies and he was leading the factor investing research group for institutional clients. Tony is the editor and co-author of *Big Data and Machine*

Learning In Quantitative Investment (Wiley, 2018). He holds bachelor's and master's degrees in econometry and finance from the University of Savoy in France. Tony is a speaker on modern approaches for quantitative investment and has held several workshops on 'Machine learning applied for quants'.

Guillaume Coqueret has been an Assistant Professor of Finance at the Montpellier Business School since 2015. He holds a PhD in Business Administration from ESSEC Business School. Prior to his professorship at MBS, he was a senior quantitative research analyst at the EDHEC Risk Institute from 2013 to 2015. He holds two master's degrees in the field of quantitative finance. His work has been published in such journals as *Journal of Banking and Finance*, *Journal of Portfolio Management* and *Expert Systems with Applications*.

CHAPTER 8

Andy Moniz is the Global Markets Chief Data Scientist at Deutsche Bank. Andy is an expert in natural language processing and was previously a quantitative portfolio manager at UBS, responsible for long-short stock selection and macro strategies at UBS O'Connor and systematic environmental social and governance (ESG) strategies at UBS Asset Management using accounting signals with unstructured data. Prior to UBS, Andy was a senior quantitative portfolio manager at APG Asset Management, where he was responsible for factor premia, text mining and ESG stock selection strategies. Andy began his career in 2000 as a macroeconomist at the Bank of England. Between 2003 and 2011 he worked in quantitative equities for various investment banks. Andy holds a BA and MA in Economics from the University of Cambridge, an MSc in Statistics from the University of London, and a PhD in Information Retrieval and Natural Language Processing from Erasmus University, The Netherlands.

CHAPTER 9

Peter Hafez is the head of data science at RavenPack. Since joining RavenPack in 2008, he's been a pioneer in the field of applied news analytics, bringing alternative data insights to the world's top banks and hedge funds. Peter has more than 15 years of experience in quantitative finance with companies such as Standard & Poor's, Credit Suisse First Boston and Saxo Bank. He holds a master's degree in Quantitative Finance from Sir John Cass Business School along with an undergraduate degree in Economics from Copenhagen University. Peter is a recognized speaker at quant finance conferences on alternative data and AI, and has given lectures at some of the world's top academic institutions, including London Business School, Courant Institute of Mathematics at NYU and Imperial College London.

Francesco Lautizi is Senior Data Scientist at RavenPack, where he researches how big data and news analytics are reshaping financial markets and provides insights on how these new sources of information can be used by financial institutions for portfolio and risk management purposes. He holds a PhD in Economics and Finance from University of Rome Tor Vergata, where he studied how estimation error impacts the performance on large-scale portfolios. He has been a visiting student at EIEF and has a Master of Science in Finance from University of Rome Tor Vergata.

CHAPTER 10

M. Berkan Sesen, PhD, vice president, is a quantitative researcher and portfolio manager in a major US asset manager. Prior to this, he worked as a quantitative analyst at Citigroup, supervising a small team with the mandate to build/maintain statistical models to assist algorithmic trading and electronic market making. He also co-led the global data analytics working group within the quantitative analysis department in Citigroup. Berkan holds a doctorate in artificial intelligence from the University of Oxford and specializes in machine learning and statistics. He also holds an MSc with Distinction in Biomedical Engineering from the University of Oxford.

Yazann Romahi, PhD, CFA, managing director, is CIO at a major US asset manager focused on developing the firm's factor-based franchise across both alternative beta and strategic beta. Prior to that he was Head of Research and Quantitative Strategies, responsible for the quantitative models that help establish the broad asset allocation reflected across multi-asset solutions portfolios globally. Yazann has worked as a research analyst at the Centre for Financial Research at the University of Cambridge and has undertaken consulting assignments for a number of financial institutions, including Pioneer Asset Management, PricewaterhouseCoopers and HSBC. Yazann holds a PhD in Computational Finance/Artificial Intelligence from the University of Cambridge and is a CFA charter holder.

Victor Li, PhD, CFA, executive director, is Head of Equity and Alternative Beta Research and a portfolio manager at a major US asset manager. Victor's primary focus includes management of the research agenda, as well as model development and portfolio management for the quantitative beta suite of products. Victor holds a PhD in Communications and Signal Processing from Imperial College London, where he was also employed as a full-time research assistant. Victor obtained an MSc with Distinction in Communications Engineering from the University of Manchester and is a CFA charter holder.

CHAPTER 11

Joel Guglietta is Macro Quantitative Portfolio Manager of Graticule Asset Management in Hong Kong, managing a multi-assets hedge funds using machine learning algorithms. Prior to that Joel was a macro quantitative strategist and portfolio manager for hedge funds and investment banks in Asia and Australia (Brevan Howard, BTIM, HSBC) for more than 12 years. His expertise is in quantitative models for asset allocation, portfolio construction and management using a wide range of techniques, including machine learning techniques and genetic algorithms. Joel is currently a PhD candidate at GREQAM (research unit jointly managed by CNRS, EHESS and Ecole Centrale). He has been a speaker at many deep learning and machine learning events in Asia.

CHAPTER 12

Gordon Ritter completed his PhD in Mathematical Physics at Harvard University in 2007, where his published work ranged across the fields of quantum computation, quantum field theory, differential geometry and abstract algebra. Prior to Harvard he earned his bachelor's degree with honours in mathematics from the University of Chicago. Gordon is a senior portfolio manager at GSA Capital and leader of a team trading a range of systematic absolute return strategies across geographies and asset classes. GSA Capital has won the Equity Market Neutral & Quantitative Strategies category at the EuroHedge Awards four times, with numerous other awards including in the long-term performance category. Prior to joining GSA, Gordon was a vice president of Highbridge Capital and a core member of the firm's statistical arbitrage group, which although operating with fewer than 20 people, was responsible for billions in profit and trillions of dollars of trades across equities, futures and options with low correlation to traditional asset classes. Concurrently with his positions in industry, Gordon teaches courses including portfolio management, econometrics, continuous-time finance and market microstructure in the Department of Statistics at Rutgers University, and also in the MFE programmes at Baruch College (CUNY) and New York University (both ranked in the top five MFE programmes). Gordon has published original work in top practitioner journals including *Risk* and academic journals including *European Journal of Operational Research*. He is a sought-after speaker at major industry conferences.

CHAPTER 13

Miquel Noguer Alonso is a financial markets practitioner with more than 20 years of experience in asset management. He is currently Head of Development at Global AI (big data artificial intelligence in finance company) and Head of Innovation and Technology at IEF. He worked for UBS AG (Switzerland) as Executive Director. He has been a member of the European Investment Committee for the past 10 years. He worked as a chief investment officer and CIO for Andbank from 2000 to 2006. He started his career at KPMG. Miquel is Adjunct Professor at Columbia University, teaching asset allocation, big data in finance and FinTech. He is also Professor at ESADE, teaching hedge funds, big data in finance and FinTech. He taught the first FinTech and big data course at London Business School in 2017. Miquel received an MBA and a degree in Business Administration and Economics at ESADE in 1993. In 2010 he earned a PhD in Quantitative Finance with a Summa Cum Laude distinction (UNED – Madrid, Spain). He completed a postdoc at Columbia Business School in 2012. He collaborated with the mathematics department of Fribourg University, Switzerland, during his PhD. He also holds the Certified European Financial Analyst (CEFA) 2000 distinction. His academic collaborations include a visiting scholarship in the Finance and Economics Department at Columbia University in 2013, in the mathematics department at Fribourg University in 2010, and presentations at Indiana University, ESADE and CAIA, plus several industry seminars including the Quant Summit USA 2017 and 2010.

　　Gilberto Batres-Estrada is a senior data scientist at Webstep in Stockholm, Sweden, where he works as a consultant developing machine learning and deep learning algorithms for Webstep's clients. He develops algorithms in the areas of computer vision, object detection, natural language processing and finance, serving clients in the financial industry, telecoms, transportation and more. Prior to this Gilberto worked developing trading algorithms for Assa Bay Capital in Gothenburg, Sweden. He has more than nine years of experience in IT working for a semi-government organization in Sweden. Gilberto holds both an MSc in Theoretical Physics from Stockholm university and an MSc in Engineering from KTH Royal Institute of Technology in Stockholm, with a specialization in applied mathematics and statistics.

Aymeric Moulin is a graduate student at Columbia University in the IEOR department where he is majoring in Operations Research. He studied theoretical mathematics and physics in classes préparatoires in France and completed a Bachelor of Science at CentraleSupélec engineering school, from which he will soon receive a master's degree. He has spent the past few years focusing on deep learning and reinforcement learning applications to financial markets. He is currently an intern at JP Morgan in Global Equities.